ICE GHOSTS

ICE GHOSTS

The Epic Hunt for the Lost Franklin Expedition

PAUL WATSON

W. W. NORTON & COMPANY

Independent Publishers Since 1923

New York   London

Excerpts from *John Rae's Arctic Correspondence 1844–1855, with a Foreword by Ken McGoogan* reprinted with permission of TouchWood Editions.

Excerpt from Captain James Fitzjames's letter to his wife quoted in James P. Delgado's *Across the Top of the World: The Quest for the Northwest Passage* reprinted with permission of Harbour Publishing.

Excerpt from "Longfellow and Dickens: The Story of a Transatlantic Friendship" courtesy of the Cambridge Historical Society, The Proceedings, Volume 28. Cambridge, MA.

For information about permission to reproduce selections from this book, write to Permissions, W. W. Norton & Company, Inc., 500 Fifth Avenue, New York, NY 10110

For information about special discounts for bulk purchases, please contact W. W. Norton Special Sales at specialsales@wwnorton.com or 800-233-4830

Manufacturing by LSC Communications, Harrisonburg, VA
Book design by Helene Berinsky
Maps by Adrian Kitzinger
Production manager: Anna Oler

Library of Congress Cataloging-in-Publication Data

Names: Watson, Paul, 1959– author.
Title: Ice ghosts : the epic hunt for the lost Franklin Expedition / Paul Watson.
Description: First edition. | New York : W.W. Norton & Company, 2017. | Includes bibliographical references and index.
Identifiers: LCCN 2016054683 | ISBN 9780393249385 (hardcover)
Subjects: LCSH: John Franklin Arctic Expedition (1845–1851) | Northwest Passage—Discovery and exploration—British. | Arctic regions—Discovery and exploration—British. | Shipwrecks—Canada, Northern. | Erebus (Ship) | Terror (Ship) | Franklin, John, 1786–1847.
Classification: LCC G660 .W37 2017 | DDC 917.1904/1—dc23
LC record available at https://lccn.loc.gov/2016054683

ISBN 978-0-393-35586-4 pbk.

W. W. Norton & Company, Inc.
500 Fifth Avenue, New York, N.Y. 10110
www.wwnorton.com

W. W. Norton & Company Ltd.
15 Carlisle Street, London W1D 3BS

1 2 3 4 5 6 7 8 9 0

The first time a young shaman experiences this light,
while sitting up on the bench invoking his helping spirits,
it is as if the house in which he is suddenly rises;
he sees far ahead of him, through mountains,
exactly as if the earth were one great plain,
and his eyes could reach to the end of the earth.
Nothing is hidden from him any longer;
not only can he see things far, far away,
but he can also discover souls, stolen souls,
which are either kept concealed in far, strange lands
or have been taken up or down to the Land of the Dead.

—KNUD RASMUSSEN, Danish polar explorer, anthropologist, and first European to cross the Northwest Passage by dogsled, reporting on his research into Inuit origins in the early 1920s

For all the souls
lost at sea

CONTENTS

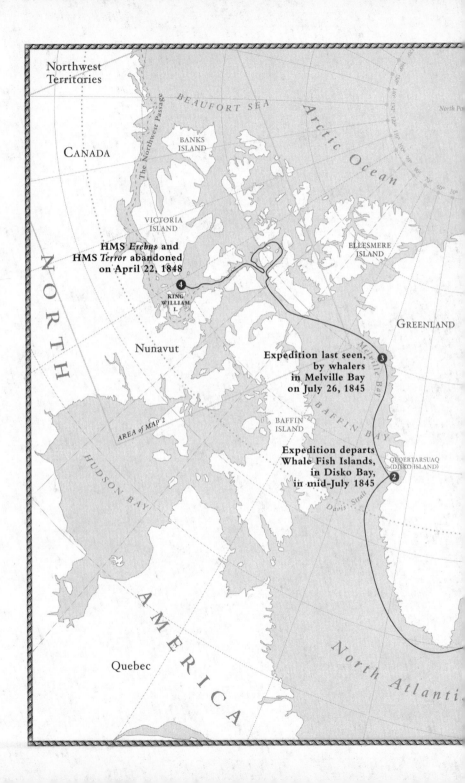

Northwest
Territories

CANADA

BANKS
ISLAND

BEAUFORT SEA

Arctic Ocean

VICTORIA
ISLAND

ELLESMERE
ISLAND

**HMS *Erebus* and
HMS *Terror* abandoned
on April 22, 1848**

④

KING
WILLIAM
I.

GREENLAND

Nunavut

**Expedition last seen,
by whalers
in Melville Bay
on July 26, 1845**

③

Melville Bay

BAFFIN
BAY

NORTH

AREA of MAP 2

BAFFIN
ISLAND

**Expedition departs
Whale Fish Islands,
in Disko Bay,
in mid-July 1845**

QEQERTARSUAQ
(DISKO ISLAND)

②

HUDSON
BAY

Davis Strait

AMERICA

Quebec

North Atlanti

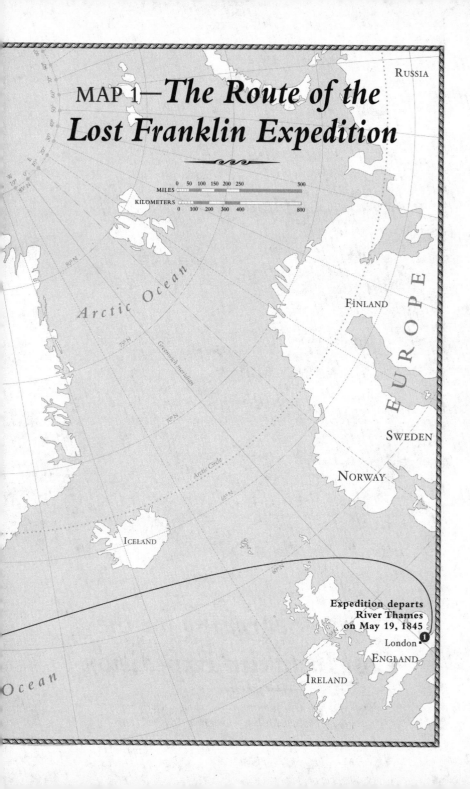

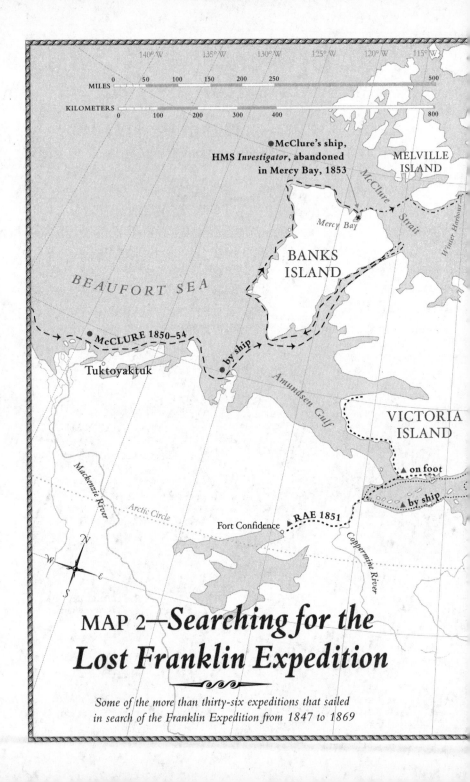

MAP 2—*Searching for the Lost Franklin Expedition*

Some of the more than thirty-six expeditions that sailed in search of the Franklin Expedition from 1847 to 1869

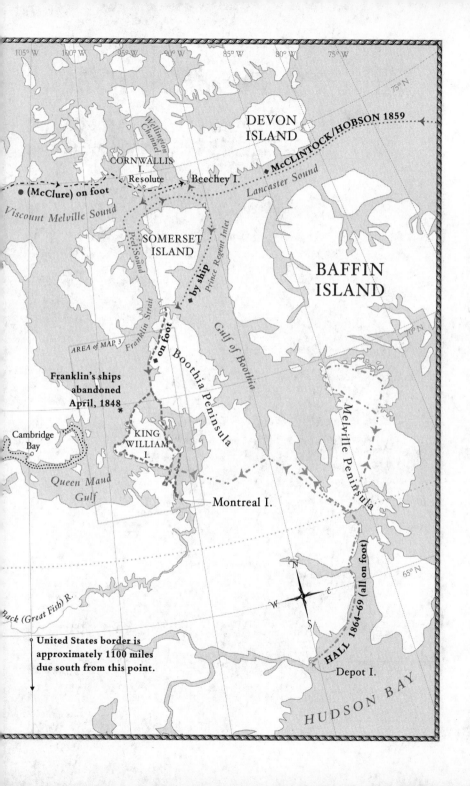

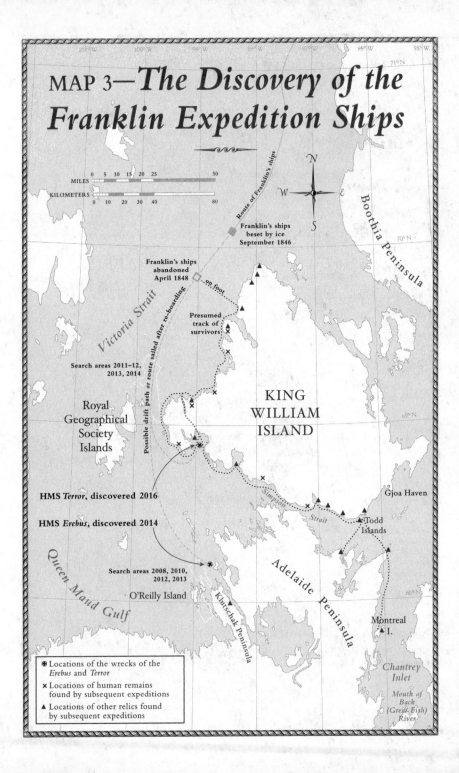

MAP 3—*The Discovery of the Franklin Expedition Ships*

MILES
0 5 10 15 20 25   50

KILOMETERS
0   10   20   30   40   80

Route of Franklin's ships

Franklin's ships
beset by ice
September 1846

Franklin's ships
abandoned
April 1848

on foot

Presumed
track of
survivors

Search areas 2011–12,
2013, 2014

Victoria Strait

Royal
Geographical
Society
Islands

Possible drift path or route sailed after re-boarding

KING
WILLIAM
ISLAND

Boothia Peninsula

71° N

70° N

69° N

HMS *Terror*, discovered 2016

HMS *Erebus*, discovered 2014

Simpson Strait

Gjoa Haven

Todd
Islands

Queen Maud Gulf

Search areas 2008, 2010,
2012, 2013

O'Reilly Island

Kirtschak Peninsula

Adelaide Peninsula

Montreal
I.

68° N

Chantrey Inlet

Mouth of
Back
(Great Fish)
River

Locations of the wrecks of the
Erebus and *Terror*

× Locations of human remains
found by subsequent expeditions

▲ Locations of other relics found
by subsequent expeditions

CHRONOLOGY

1576–1578—English explorer Martin Frobisher makes three voyages in search of the Northwest Passage, instead discovering Labrador, Baffin Island, and Frobisher Bay (present-day Iqaluit).

1771—English explorer Samuel Hearne is the first European to reach the Arctic coast of North America, where he witnesses a native massacre of Inuit while surveying the Coppermine River.

1805—British warships defeat the French and Spanish in the Battle of Trafalgar, leading to decisive victory in the Napoleonic Wars a decade later.

1814—Almost a decade after narrowly surviving the Battle of Trafalgar, Lieutenant John Franklin is wounded in a British naval assault on New Orleans.

1818—Amid massive Royal Navy layoffs, Sir John Barrow persuasively argues the case for a return to Arctic exploration and a renewed search for the Northwest Passage as a peacetime mission. John Ross commands an expedition to the Arctic Archipelago but mistakenly concludes that Lancaster Sound is blocked by mountains. John Franklin serves on a second, failed expedition seeking a polar passage northwest of Spitsbergen, off Norway.

1819–1822—English explorer John Franklin leads an overland expedition instructed to map the Arctic coastline east of the Coppermine River. Eleven of twenty men die. Franklin is heralded as a hero, despite rumors of murder and cannibalism on the trek south.

1823—Romantic poet Eleanor Anne Porden marries John Franklin.

1825–1827—John Franklin leads his second overland expedition, leaving his ill wife, Eleanor, with her blessing. She dies six days after he departs for the Arctic. Franklin and surgeon John Richardson map more than 1,000 miles of Arctic coastline.

1828—Sir John Franklin weds Jane Griffin, a friend of his late wife.

1831—James Clark Ross discovers the North Magnetic Pole, on the Boothia Peninsula, while serving under his uncle John Ross in an expedition funded by gin magnate Felix Booth.

1836–1843—Sir John Franklin is governor of Van Diemen's Land, a penal colony that becomes Tasmania. Political opponents force his humiliating recall to England.

1839–1843—The Royal Navy sends James Clark Ross in search of the South Magnetic Pole with HMS *Erebus* and HMS *Terror*. The ships collide, but stay afloat, in stormy Antarctic seas.

1845—Eager to rebound from the Van Diemen's Land fiasco, Sir John Franklin persuades the Royal Navy command to let him lead another expedition with HMS *Erebus* and HMS *Terror* to find the final missing link in the Northwest Passage.

1846—HMS *Erebus* and HMS *Terror* are beset by heavy sea ice on September 12, off the northwest coast of King William Island.

1847—His ships still trapped in the ice, Sir John Franklin dies in the High Arctic on June 11. The cause of death and the whereabouts of his body remain unknown.

1850—Britain's Royal Navy launches the first full-scale search for the Franklin Expedition. An American expedition joins the massive search on land and sea.

1853—HMS *Breadalbane*, bearing fresh supplies for Franklin Expedition searchers, is nipped by sea ice and sinks off Beechey Island. HMS *Investigator* is abandoned to the ice.

1854—Scottish fur trader and explorer John Rae has a chance encounter with Inuk hunter In-nook-poo-zhee-jook, who provides the first account describing dozens of white men dying at what is later named Starvation Cove.

1859—On Irish explorer Francis Leopold McClintock's expedition, financed by Lady Jane Franklin, Irish Lieutenant William Hobson discovers the notes and remains left by Franklin's men at Victory Point, providing the first written evidence in the disappearance of the Franklin Expedition.

1869—American explorer Charles Francis Hall's expedition to King William Island includes the discovery of skeletal remains of Franklin Expedition members.

1964—Walter Zacharchuk, a former child laborer under the Nazis who went on to build his own diving equipment, becomes Canada's first professional underwater archaeologist.

1966—Louie Kamookak, an Inuk boy caring for his dying great-grandmother Hummahuk on the tundra, hears the stories that set him on a lifelong search for Sir John Franklin's grave.

1967—In honor of Canada's centenary, its military launches an air, land, and sea search for Sir John Franklin's Arctic grave, and any documents it might contain, but finds nothing significant.

1980—Canadian inventor and explorer Joseph MacInnis discovers the submerged wreck of HMS *Breadalbane* after a three-year search.

2008—The Conservative government of Prime Minister Stephen Harper announces a renewed search for the wrecks of *Erebus* and *Terror*, committing to a three-year effort.

2010—A team of Parks Canada underwater archaeologists discovers the wreck of HMS *Investigator* in Mercy Bay.

2014—Helicopter pilot Captain Andrew Stirling finds an iron davit piece on an island shore in eastern Queen Maud Gulf on September 1. Following up on that lead the next day, Parks Canada marine archaeologists find the wreck of Sir John Franklin's flagship, HMS *Erebus*.

2016—Acting on a mysterious tip from Inuk guide Sammy Kogvik, Adrian Schimnowski's Arctic Research Foundation team discovers the almost perfectly preserved wreck of HMS *Terror*.

INTRODUCTION

At sea in the High Arctic, it's easy to lose sight of where you are.

We've been steaming for days on the Canadian Coast Guard ice-breaker CCGS *Sir Wilfrid Laurier* without seeing much more than ocean and sky, the gray threads of distant island shorelines, and vast stretches of fractured, drifting ice. It's late summer, in the few weeks between the final melt and the next full freeze. Like clouds parting after a storm, the sea ice is cracking and drifting. The Northwest Passage is opening.

By the thousands, pans of ice weighing many tons, carved by wind and sea into a floating gallery of blue, green, and aquamarine sculptures, slowly glide past. Any that get in our way crash against the icebreaker's thick steel hull with a slushy *smush* that rises above the rumble of the *Laurier*'s powerful diesel engines. As she ploddingly shoves aside the blocks of sea ice, they dive and pop up like corks, stirring the ocean to a frothy roil.

After months of meticulous planning, and years of frustrated searching, everyone in this latest expedition is on edge. More than a hundred people are making the renewed push to find Sir John Franklin's sunken ships. Second-guessers are sniping from afar, politicians with an eye to reelection pressing for results. The searchers urgently need to know how much leeway the Arctic will grant before the sea ice closes again, and more than 165 years of hunting pauses once more until the Arctic deigns to let the big ships back in.

That's if the money doesn't dry up first.

Year to year, it's anyone's guess what the mercurial North, and fickle taxpayers, will allow. So it was in the mid-nineteenth century, when the British Admiralty sent the Franklin Expedition to search for the passage's elusive western exit. So it is now. An ice-free channel one August can be clogged with hull-crushing floes the next. There's never much time to fathom the Arctic's moods. They swing wildly from sunny, with warm rays glinting off seas so calm they look like metallic mirrors, to stormy, when wicked gales send waves crashing over an icebreaker's massive bow for days.

More than a century and a half after Franklin and his men were lost, the 2014 Victoria Strait Expedition is only days old and the Arctic is already closing the search window. For years, as the global climate grew steadily warmer, the climb in average temperatures way up here has been increasing faster than anyplace else on Earth. But northerly winds howling down from the North Pole can still blow a vengeful cold. Darkness is starting to eat into the twenty-four-hour daylight, devouring a larger slice of the midnight sun with each passing day. Another hard season of winter darkness is descending fast.

It's the sixth year of a government-led quest for the wrecks of Franklin's storied ships, HMS *Terror* and HMS *Erebus*. The expedition's objective is a search box on coldly vengeful seas, where some of the depth soundings on navigation charts are almost as old as the hunt for the lost Franklin Expedition itself. Roughly 10 percent of Canada's Arctic waters, and some 40 percent of the Northwest Passage, have been charted to modern standards. That's one reason the long effort to find *Erebus* and *Terror* has been so difficult in what ought to be the most promising place: off the northern tip of King William Island. Franklin's crew, their commander dead from unknown causes, abandoned *Erebus* and *Terror* to the ice there in 1848. As they fought scurvy, possible lead poisoning, botulism, hunger, bone-chilling cold, and a creeping madness, the shrinking group of survivors struggled desperately to save themselves from the Arctic, praying for salvation farther south.

IN THEIR DAY, they were like voyagers to Mars would be now, sailing into the unknown, knowing they might never make it home but drawn forward by the fierce need to discover that defines our species. If that meant death, then that was the sacrifice empire and discovery demanded. Get back alive, though, and the gratitude of a great nation was theirs to enjoy as the bravest of conquering heroes. The Vikings are thought to have been the first to try, and fail, to find a Northwest Passage well over a thousand years ago. The idea of a sea trading route from the Atlantic to the markets of Asia had tantalized European minds since at least the early sixteenth century. But there were also skeptics. As William Scoresby Jr., son of a whaler and an accomplished pioneer of Arctic science wrote in 1820, "There have been only three or four intervals of more than fifteen years, in which no expedition was sent out in search of one or other of the supposed passages, from the year 1500." Since nearly a hundred voyages had tried and failed to find the passage up to that point, "it is not a little surprising that . . . Britain should again revive and attempt the solution of this interesting problem."

A Northwest Passage was, and still is, pitched more as a promise than a practical way to boost trade and commerce by sharply cutting the distance between Europe and Asia. That makes more sense when looking at a map than it does surrounded by ice floes, in a part of the world constantly hammered by storms, where even in the early twenty-first century countless shoals and other hazards lie uncharted and hidden, waiting to ground a ship or rip a hole in its hull. Scoresby thought his country was embarking on an expensive, dangerous, and pointless venture. His was a dissident voice in a growing public debate, with the Admiralty eyeing the Arctic as the next conquest for a Royal Navy that had just won the Napoleonic Wars. At the core of the chief proponent's case was the notion that warmer, open water awaited beyond the pack-ice barrier well known to whalers and other Arctic mariners. Find a way through to that polar sailors' paradise, the leading theory went, and it would be clear sailing over the North Pole to the riches of the East. Scoresby wasn't buying it.

"It has been advanced as a maxim, that *what we wish to be true, we readily believe*;—a maxim which, however doubtful in general, has met with a full illustration in the northern voyages of discovery," he wrote. "A single trial is often sufficient for satisfying us as to the truth of a disputed point; but, in this instance, though nearly an hundred trials have been made, the problem is still considered as unresolved."

As strange as it sounds today, when anyone with an Internet connection can get a clear view of Earth's polar ice caps, leading nineteenth-century experts were convinced explorers would find open water at the top of the world. That may have been a miscalculation based on long experience in Spitsbergen, where the North Atlantic Drift funnels warmer water up from the Gulf of Mexico to moderate Norway's Arctic shores. If explorers could just find a way through the ice in what is now Canada's Arctic Archipelago, proponents of the Open Polar Sea insisted, the other side of the world was theirs to behold. Problem was, temperate currents didn't reach there. It was going to take a lot of time, hardship, and death to figure that out.

Among Arctic experts in the early nineteenth century, empiricists had the upper hand. Make enough observations based on direct experience, they insisted, and truth would reveal itself. If centuries of trying hadn't found a path through the pack ice to a temperate Open Polar Sea, that wasn't proof one didn't exist. It simply meant navigators hadn't found the right lead through the ice that would deliver their ships to the awaiting route north. The Royal Navy hadn't won its dominance over the world's seas by turning for home when things got rough. Just one more expedition could mean victory. Run into another wall of ice? Well, maybe the triumphant breakthrough awaited farther to the northwest. Still more ice? Perhaps history would be made by an earlier departure, in spring instead of summer.

Even Scoresby acknowledged intriguing hints of an undiscovered passage in the observable evidence, such as the unexplained travel of whales over the high latitudes. That seemed impossible if the northern polar region was solid pack ice. How would they surface to breathe? The evidence, however dubious to some, included "whales with stone lances sticking in their fat, (a kind of weapon used by no nation now known,) having been caught both in the sea of Spitzbergen, and in Davis' Strait." Fischal Zeeman of India had reported a whale killed in the Strait of Tartary, linking the Sea of Japan and Russia's Sea of Okhotsk, "in the back of which was sticking a Dutch harpoon, marked with the letters W. B." The harpoon was traced back to William Bastiaanz, admiral of the Dutch Greenland fleet. It "had been struck into the whale in the Spitzbergen Sea," off Norway's northern coast. Intelligent people of the day cited it as proof of open water. More experienced observers like Scoresby knew that ice cover was variable.

Franklin sided with him in doubting the theory of the Open Polar Sea. Captain James Fitzjames reported from *Erebus*, the expedition flagship christened in the name of the lowest, darkest region of Hell, in a letter home before turning in on the night of June 6, 1845: "At dinner to-day Sir John gave us a pleasant account of being able to get through the ice on the coast of America, and his disbelief in the idea that there is an open polar sea to the northward." But the expedition commander's orders came from Sir John Barrow, the Admiralty's top civil servant and chief architect of the revived search for the Northwest Passage. He was a believer.

To a public hungry for stories from the Far North—just as the world was mesmerized by the Apollo missions to the moon in the

1960s—picturing their heroes voyaging through the forbidding Arctic was irresistible. British seamen had been searching for it since the sixteenth century. Robert Thorne, an English merchant, proposed a passage to India by way of the North Pole as early as 1527. Martin Frobisher led three voyages to the Arctic in the latter decades of that century. He made it as far as Baffin Island, in what is now the eastern Canadian Arctic. Queen Elizabeth I imagined that a colony could exploit minerals in the icy wilderness, which she named *Meta Incognita*. On Frobisher's third and final expedition in 1578, he sailed with fifteen vessels and ended up in Frobisher Bay, where the city of Iqaluit, capital of the autonomous Inuit territory of Nunavut, now stands. But Frobisher's settlement failed.

More than 260 years had passed when the Admiralty chose Franklin, a celebrated Arctic explorer seemingly past his prime, to search for the last several hundred miles that would complete the passage to the Pacific. His two vessels were converted bomb ships that had been to Antarctica with James Clark Ross from 1839 to 1843. They had also won glory in battle. In one of the last clashes in the War of 1812, mortars mounted near *Terror*'s bow fired bombs at Baltimore's Fort McHenry. After watching some of those bombs bursting in air, American lawyer Francis Scott Key wrote the poem that became the lyrics to the US national anthem, "The Star-Spangled Banner."

THE ROYAL NAVY outfitted Franklin's men with woolen mitts and coats that became damp with their own sweat and froze as stiff as wet socks on a winter clothesline. The commander's mitts, presumably of a quality suiting a knight of the realm on the best-equipped polar expedition, were hand sewn from coarse pieces of white wool blanket from the Hudson's Bay Company, with a black baize cuff and red silk edging. They look painful next to the elbow-high wolfskin mitts that keep an Inuit traveler's hands toasty on long journeys. Snow goggles, possibly made aboard ship, put a strip of stiff leather and wire-mesh gauze between a Franklin sailor's eyes and the relentless winds that tormented them, striking like millions of tiny needles. The gear couldn't have offered much hope to men who had to survive two vicious winters before the survivors tried to walk out, some dragging heavy sledges or boats over the snow and ice. There were too many easy breaches for the wind to break through and ravage poorly protected skin: Trouser buttons broke and fell off, holes in the cloth were patched with thick flannel, which became frayed and rank in the endless cycle of freeze and thaw. It was only after the Franklin Expedition was lost that the Admiralty made a greater effort to develop clothing specifically for the Arctic.

After abandoning their best shelter, *Erebus* and *Terror*, in 1848, the mariners had to trek for months, through snow and ice in winter and sucking mud if the weather warmed enough those summers. Their feet were shielded by relatively thin boots insulated with whatever the wearer could scrounge. Royal Navy seamen's boots were long, square-toed, and rounded at the top to fit a man's calf. They wouldn't be much against a January storm on a southern city's streets today, let alone in an especially cold few years in the Arctic. Brass screws bored through the soles might have improved the traction slightly, and straw or cloth shoved into the empty toe space might have preserved a hint of heat. Compared with the skins of seal, caribou, or polar bear, among the excellent natural insulators in multilayered Inuit *kamiik*, a blue cloth legging attached to the ankles of the British sailors' seaboots was useless adornment. Severe frostbite was more likely to occur the longer a man survived, only to die a slow, excruciating death. For men hauling the bulky sledges, sweating and freezing as they leaned into hammering winds, gangrene eating through their toes, the boots would have squeezed and scraped like painful shackles.

In the Age of Discovery, it seemed science and technology could solve any problem given enough time and determined thought. But just as Mary Shelley had warned in *Frankenstein; or, The Modern Prometheus*, published the same year Barrow was making his case for Arctic exploration, humans had to be cautious about just how far they wanted to test the limits of nature. Franklin may well have gone too far, expecting *Erebus* and *Terror* to take him the final, unknown distance. He had seen for himself part of the western exit from the passage on his earlier overland expeditions. He only had to find a way through the archipelago's uncharted middle. Late in the summer of 1846, when gales strike suddenly from the north and sea ice can close hard and fast like a vise, faith in steam power might have tempted Franklin to go deeper into Peel Sound than was wise. At that time of year, the Arctic likely gave him fair warning to stop. Instead, a hero past his prime, struggling to regain lost glory, pressed southward along the eastern shores of Prince of Wales Island toward an ice trap waiting to spring shut at the top of Victoria Strait.

Other expeditions had recovered from disaster, with inevitable losses, and made it home after more than one winter stuck in the Arctic. But that was hardly a sure thing. Getting out of trouble in the High Arctic depends largely on where, and how, you got into it, and whether you can think clearly enough to make lifesaving decisions. Recovering from a stupid choice, or sheer bad luck, was especially difficult where Franklin and his men got stranded: off the northern tip of King William Island, where the easiest big game to hunt—caribou and musk ox—were hard to find in those years. Without good nutrition, the cold wears a man down faster, and the sound judgment of long experience can vanish like a waking dream. That's how it looked to Sir John Richardson, a surgeon and Franklin friend who had served alongside him in the grueling overland journeys and certified the commander's fitness for his final attempt at the transit by sea. Based on the scattered clues that searchers had gathered by 1861, which included suspicions the sailors may have been poisoned by improperly canned food and threw much of the rest away, Richardson concluded the survivors were wasting away on short rations.

"Even on the ordinary full allowance of the navy, scurvy has almost invariably assailed the crews of ships after a second winter within the Arctic circle, the expeditions that have escaped that scourge having had either a large supply of preserved meats and pemican to resort to, and plenty of dried vegetables and vegetable acids, or been successful in adding deer, musk-oxen, and bears, to their stock of provisions."

The winters that finished off Franklin and his 128 men were so severe that they became part of Inuit legend. They would long lay blame on the *qalunaaq*, the white men, for unleashing malevolent spirits upon the island. When American Charles Francis Hall gave up small-town newspapering to go north and hunt for the Franklin Expedition in the 1860s, an Inuit mother told him two shamans, or *angakkuit*, had cast a spell on the area where the ships were abandoned: "The Innuits wished to live near that place (where the ships were) but could not kill anything for their food. They (the Innuits) really believed that the presence of Koblunas (whites) in that part of the country was the cause of all their (the Innuits') trouble."

You don't have to walk far beyond the edge of Nunavut's Gjoa Haven today to be at the mercy of the same wilderness that trapped and killed Franklin and his men, with a vengeance that the Royal Navy had never seen in its long and glorious history of Arctic exploration. A person feels very small, and frail, standing alone in the dead of winter, when the rolling sea is frozen hard and thick, the birds have flown far south, and the air is still. The only sound is your own breathing. Hold that for a moment, out of fear or awe, and you hear nothing but silence, complete and true. Life isn't so certain anymore.

As Canadian geographer and author W. Gillies Ross wrote, quoting yet another Franklin buff, Alfred Friendly: "The Franklin search—grandiose yet hugely ineffective—has been called 'the most extensive, expensive, perverse, ill-starred and abundantly written-about manhunt in history.'" Based on information from salvors, who plumb the depths for wrecks with the zeal of prospectors digging for the next motherlode, UNESCO estimates that more than three million shipwrecks lie on the bottom of the Earth's rivers, lakes, and oceans. Some are more than a thousand years old. None have spawned so many search expeditions, spanning so many generations, or fueled as much historical debate and political intrigue, as *Erebus* and *Terror*.

Sir John Franklin and his brave sailors have sustained a puzzling hold on the minds of many people for more than 170 years. From 1847 to 1859, no fewer than thirty-six expeditions sailed in search of the men or their remains or to resupply those who were searching. Three others tried but had to abort before reaching the Far North. The Admiralty offered a reward of £20,000, equivalent to more than $1.8 million today, for rescuing the Franklin Expedition, or half that amount for determining its fate. That helped sweeten the prospect of solving a mystery that had become a public obsession in Britain. Lady Franklin spent most of her own fortune to bankroll efforts when the Admiralty tried to move on. In more recent decades, countless others have gone looking—from obsessed adventurers trekking across the tundra to billionaires seeking the kind of legacy mere money can't buy. Add in the cost of professional searches and the total bill easily runs into tens of millions of today's dollars.

Like Shakespeare, it seems, the Franklin tale never grows old because people of each generation can read into it what they want, or need, to see. When science and pushing the boundaries fall out of favor, Sir John Franklin is regarded as a fool. When cynical politics is the problem with the world, Franklin is seen as a wise man pushing the limits of the wilderness while cloistered Lords of the Admiralty, and their backstabbing friends, are to blame for the catastrophe. One truth is eternal: Royal Navy prejudice toward indigenous people helped doom the Franklin Expedition, and the arrogant disregard for Inuit knowledge prolonged efforts to find out what happened to Sir John Franklin and the men he led to their deaths. Today, as the Arctic loses the ice cover that helps cool the planet, it would be wise to heed the cost of ignoring the people who best know that fragile, wrathful place.

The long hunt for *Erebus* and *Terror* was never purely about finding lost sailors or solving the riddles of a naval disaster that rattled British faith in their power over the sea. Like any epic, this one is rich with the timeless contradictions of the human condition. There is courage and folly, hubris and blind ambition, ingenuity and synchronicity. As those meaningful coincidences unfold, and lines of fate converge, they seem to defy mere chance. Perhaps there is more to those metaphysical moments than archaeologists, historians, and others investigating the tangible can concede. The people who have lived in the High Arctic the longest—the Inuit who have understood a capricious place for centuries—are certain of this: If you must see to know, you will miss many things that are real.

After generations of political and bureaucratic maneuvering, the building of careers and the burnishing of legacies, it's easy to forget that this is a long, costly hunt for two sunken ships with no cargo of gold or jewels or any other treasure beyond the relics of history. Finding the commander's body, perhaps mummified by the permafrost, would be an even bigger breakthrough, worthy of a hero's funeral in England. Still, at the heart of the Franklin mystery is why people would spend so much time, money, and effort, for so many generations, searching one of the most unforgiving places on Earth to discover what seems obvious: Franklin and his men challenged the Arctic and the Arctic won. Many have tried the Arctic's patience since then and paid dearly. It's one of the last places left on our planet that holds out, as long as it can, refusing to bow to human will. Which, of course, only tempts more conquerors to try.

The bigger questions, burning like distant lanterns in an endless Arctic night, are about the nature of the people who went looking for Franklin and his lost sailors, why they did it, and what that tells us about ourselves.

After all, one way or another, we're each searching for something.

PART I

THE EXPEDITION

1

Franklin's Last Mission

K nowing when to bow out can be a hero's saving grace. Sir John missed his cue. Franklin thought he needed one last try at the Northwest Passage to salvage a legacy badly damaged by colonial politics. The woman he loved, his wife Jane, convinced him to go for broke in the very place that had made him a hero. He overplayed a bad hand and it killed him, along with the 128 men who followed Franklin to the High Arctic. For a time, history has been relatively kind to him anyway. Doubters have questioned whether the Admiralty was wise to put a man of his advanced age and fading abilities as an Arctic explorer in charge of the 1845 expedition. Some have been more blunt and called him incompetent. Others point to factors out of his control, such as lead poisoning or botulism in shoddily tinned food, as the real culprits behind the worst disaster in the Royal Navy's long history of polar exploration. A more likely explanation lies in the volatile moods of the Arctic itself, a land that still resists conquest. As Inuit have long understood, survival at the top of the world is impossible without due respect and cooperation. Like many Royal Navy men before them, Franklin and his crew assumed they could beat the Arctic on their own, eschewing Inuit as irrelevant, godless savages. Until it was too late.

Sir John had practically begged for the mission. He was only able to talk the Royal Navy high command into letting him go because their preferred commanders wouldn't. A month shy of his fifty-ninth birthday, when the Franklin Expedition set sail from Greenhithe on the River Thames, he went to sea for the last time as a hard-worn, elderly man. War, polar exploration, and ugly bureaucratic fights had knocked him around many times, but he always found a way to get back on his feet and keep going. A fourth journey in search of the Northwest Passage, the third as commander, seemed Franklin's last, best chance to reclaim a good name that colonials had tried to steal in Van Diemen's Land, which would become Tasmania. He had already done more than enough to earn a quiet, comfortable retirement. But that was not the Franklin way. Win or lose, he would make his stand where he belonged: in the ice-choked passage that was a mammoth maritime puzzle waiting to be solved.

FRANKLIN'S LEGACY should have been strong enough to survive the failure of good intentions in a minor colony built with convict labor and the blood of dispossessed aboriginal people. A veteran of Britain's most revered victory at sea, Franklin was a signal midshipman in Admiral Viscount Lord Nelson's fleet in 1805 when the Royal Navy defeated French and Spanish forces in the epic Battle of Trafalgar. HMS *Bellerophon* closed on the *L'Aigle*, their masts entangled, and French troops tried to board the British ship. From her clear side, a French man-of-war let loose with a cannon barrage twice, killing some three hundred British sailors. All but seven of the forty-seven British seamen on the *Bellerophon*'s quarterdeck died. Nearly deaf from the relentless cannonade, Franklin barely made it. A French sniper in a cocked hat overlooked him from the *L'Aigle*'s foretop, a wooden platform roughly two-thirds of the way up the foremast. He took aim and dropped Franklin's friend dead on the deck. When Franklin turned to help a Marine sergeant carry a black sailor below to have his wounds wrapped, a sniper shot the injured man through the chest.

"He'll have you next," Franklin told the sergeant, who quickly ducked down into the lower deck, still looking for a good line of sight on the sniper. Seeing the French shooter raise his rifle for another try, Franklin took cover behind a mast, dodging a lead ball that struck a few feet away. Franklin got a good look at the man who wanted to kill him and vowed to remember the French sniper's face as long as he lived. With the seventh shot, the sergeant finally dispatched the sniper and Franklin watched him plunge headfirst into the sea.

Almost a decade after Trafalgar, Franklin was a lieutenant on HMS *Bedford* when she joined an attack on New Orleans, in the third and final year of the War of 1812. The *Bedford* was tasked to help move some eight thousand British troops ashore for what they expected would be a rout of General (and future president) Andrew Jackson's outnumbered defenders. He had around 4,500 fighters, a mishmash of army regulars, Choctaw Indians, freed slaves, and frontiersmen, backed up by French pirate Jean Lafitte. One of Jackson's men, likely among his famed Tennessee sharpshooters, winged Franklin in the shoulder, wounding him slightly.

Before seeking command of *Erebus* and *Terror*, Franklin had been on three Arctic expeditions, two of them as commander. He was best known for exploring North America's Arctic coast overland. The first, poorly planned mission nearly killed him. The British press heralded Franklin as the man who ate his leather boots to avoid starvation in 1821, at the end of a three-year expedition that left eleven of twenty men dead, and a whiff of murder, even cannibalism. After such a glorious career in the navy Franklin had served since he was fourteen, petty political backstabbing was his undoing. Sir John took a posting as governor of the island colony of Van Diemen's Land in 1836. The penal colony's entrenched family compact, which did whatever was necessary to protect the wealth and privileges that came with access to cheap convict labor, had it in for Sir John and Lady Franklin from the start.

They wanted to reform the system, not abolish it, but even tinkering was enough to make very determined enemies. Free settlers running a penal colony—mere masters of a brutal backwater—were nothing next to a man who had accomplished, and survived, as much as Sir John. But on their turf, in a bureaucratic knife fight, he was vulnerable. Franklin's top official conspired against him. The local press maligned him and took special glee in running down Lady Franklin. On a grueling cross-country expedition with her husband and a few friends in 1842, Jane hiked through brush, waded through marshes and swamps, climbed mountains and forded raging rivers, often getting drenched and pelted by rain, hail, sleet, and snow. She was carried part of the way in a palanquin, a spartan wooden armchair with a narrow footrest and four metal rings to hold the bearers' poles. Four prisoners conveyed her in half-hour shifts.

The colony was scandalized. The *Van Diemen's Land Chronicle* accused the governor of paying "thrice-convicted felons" to join a journey portrayed as a self-indulgent lark. Then came the kicker. The *Chronicle* claimed the governor rewarded the prisoners with tickets of leave, or a form of parole that could lead to a full pardon. Lord Stanley, the colonial secretary in London, sided with Franklin's political enemies and recalled him. Humiliated, he lobbied hard with Jane's help to get back to the place that had made him a hero—the High Arctic. An unshakable sense of betrayal by small men drove Franklin to his death. He took 128 men with him. Jane's gnawing guilt for urging him to go, as much as her love for a man she had admired since long before they married, compelled her to topple any obstacle in a ceaseless struggle to find him, or at least figure out why he died, lost and forsaken in the ice.

Portly and bald but for an imperial fringe of unruly hair, Franklin was not the Admiralty's first choice for the 1845 expedition. He struck Sir John Barrow, and others in the naval establishment, as too old for the job. Franklin complained to his wife that the Earl of Haddington, the top political appointee overseeing the Royal Navy as

First Lord of the Admiralty, had confided in Sir James Clark Ross that advancing age wasn't all that worried him about Franklin. The earl also spoke "of my suffering greatly from cold," Franklin wrote to his wife.

With cabinet rank, Lord Haddington was the man through whom politicians expressed their will and, in return, the conduit for the navy to air its complaints to Parliament. If the Admiralty screwed up, the First Lord could expect to feel the heat. Already severely weakened by his political clashes with the Colonial Office, Franklin wasn't exactly in a strong position to take on someone of Lord Haddington's clout. Yet he did, with two of the toughest allies he could muster: his wife and Sir John Ross, a polar explorer who couldn't imagine age or cold hampering Franklin. In his indignant letter to Lady Franklin, Sir John said, "Ross expressed his astonishment at the latter reason, for he had never heard it even hinted at before, which, if it had been the case, must have been spoken of by someone or other of the officers and men who served under him." Franklin, it seems, scented enemies all around.

At the top of the Admiralty's short list for the 1845 expedition commander was Sir Edward William Parry. But the explorer who pioneered survival on ice in the High Arctic was tired of the place. He turned down the high command. The Royal Navy then tried Sir James Clark Ross, whose discovery of the North Magnetic Pole made him ideal for the expedition's twin goals of science and exploration. One potential problem: His uncle John had written that nasty pamphlet excoriating Barrow as a fraud. But there was a much bigger hurdle: Sir James had promised his newlywed wife that he too had put the Arctic behind him. Barrow thought the younger James Fitzjames, who made captain the year of the voyage, would do well. But the Admiralty ruled him out as too green at age thirty-two and put him in charge of the magnetic observations instead. As the Admiralty's leaders worked their way farther down the list of prospects, both Franklin and his wife were lobbying hard. Sir John knew Jane feared what would happen if he sat idle in retirement. In 1830, during a hiatus before he took the governor's job in Van Diemen's Land, Lady Franklin had warned of "the shame and remorse" of being idle and vain again. She wanted him back in the Arctic and insisted the wives of two other polar veterans wanted the same for their husbands. Jane was hardly subtle, writing:

"When all the latent energies of your nature are elicited, not only I, but all the world (most proudly do I say even literally that *all the world*) knows what you can do, and England has acknowledged with shouts which almost drowned the declaration that:—

> *'In the proud memorials of her fame,*
> *Stands, linked with deathless glory, Franklin's name.'"*

Lady Franklin stepped up the pressure after Sir John's disgraced callback from the colony. In a letter to Sir James Clark Ross, who had already told Franklin he would turn down the Arctic expedition command if offered, Jane stressed that support from "his own department," the Royal Navy, would help him overcome the Colonial Office's opposition. She confided "the most conflicted feelings" about her aging husband going back to the Arctic. But if Sir James, whom she called "the right person," wasn't going, "I should wish Sir John to have it in his power to go and not be put aside for his age. I do not think he would wish to go unless he felt himself equal to it." She was worried about the impact of Lord Stanley's "injustice and tyranny" on Franklin's spirit if the great explorer ended up jobless. Death in the cold, northern desert seemed a better fate than that.

"I dread exceedingly the effect on his mind of being without honourable and immediate employment," she said, "and it is this which enables me to support the idea of parting with him on a service of difficulty and danger better than I otherwise should."

Before settling on a final choice for commander, the Admiralty sought Franklin's views on the proposed expedition, which he summarized in a letter in early 1844. This was his chance to impress the decision-makers and secure his spot on the bridge for what could well be the discovery of the Northwest Passage. Steam engines would give ships a good chance of making the final, uncharted distance between the already explored entrance and exit from the archipelago, he suggested in a reply to Lord Haddington. Even if that failed, the overriding benefit of continued exploration justified another attempt, Franklin maintained, leaving no doubt he was eager to go north under any circumstances. Age, and the pain of colonial politics, hadn't sapped his passion for discovery. He wanted to finish the job. With the best-equipped ships ever to sail for the Arctic ready to search for the passage's relatively short missing link, it seemed the next to try for the biggest prize left in navigation was destined to grab it.

"Should there be any who say of these Arctic expeditions, To what purpose have they been? I would desire them to compare our present map of that region and of the northern coast of America with that of 1818, when these expeditions commenced," Franklin argued against the growing number of doubters. "They will find in the latter only three points marked on the northern coast of America, and nothing to the northward of it. Surely it cannot be denied that so large an addition to the geography of the northern parts of America and the Arctic regions is, in itself, an object worthy of all the efforts that have been made in the course of former expeditions."

On a winter's day in February 1845, Lord Haddington summoned Franklin to his London office. Franklin thought his legacy was riding on the outcome. In fact, Sir John's very life was on the line as he made his way to the Admiralty buildings on the west side of Whitehall, which housed important government offices, including the Treasury. The seat of Royal Navy power was across the cobblestone street from Great Scotland Yard, home of the Metropolitan Police. The Admiralty was an imposing eighteenth-century brick building with three stories. It was easy to spot from a distance because of its towering rooftop semaphore, a city landmark in its day. A Victorian-era travel guide, which included thirty-five thousand fares for horse-drawn cabs, described the tower as "one of the minor sights of London." Operators of the device, similar to mechanical arms on railway tracks, sent coded messages through relay stations, where men watching through telescopes passed them along to seaports on the horizon. Urgent communications, like the warning of a looming invasion from the continent, once took days to convey via messengers on horseback. The semaphore network could transmit them within hours.

The front entrance to the Admiralty's main building took Franklin past sentries and panels of dolphins in relief, through a triumphal arch in a broad stone screen. That was built in the eighteenth century to ward off troublemakers after sailors rioted. Franklin walked beneath sculptures of winged sea horses, flanked by colonnades of Tuscan columns, shadowed by three-bay domed pavilions. This was the majesty to which he was accustomed, a far cry from the humiliation of Van Diemen's Land. This place, the exalted fulcrum of the Royal Navy that had made him a man to be reckoned with, emanated the might of a navy that raised Britain to the pinnacle of her imperial power. The Admiralty, it seemed, could accomplish anything the Admiralty wanted. Why not Sir John Franklin too?

Upstairs, the six Lords Commissioners and the civil servants who advised them met in a high-ceilinged boardroom with tall windows along one side and a fireplace on the other. There they decided weighty matters of a military force overseeing a far-flung empire, such as whether even to bother trying for the Northwest Passage again, with all the cost and risk that entailed. Seated around a long mahogany table, surrounded by pull-down charts and a big, mounted wind vane, they decided the fates of many men and, at times, the course of naval history. Sir John's meeting didn't start well. Lord Haddington promptly told the explorer that time might have passed him by. He suggested Franklin take heart from the fame he had already earned and stay comfortable at home. In a question that must have hurt, the man who held the key to Franklin's destiny asked whether his body could withstand another run at the Arctic.

"Have you really thought seriously of the nature of the undertaking at your age, for, you know, I know your age: you are 59," Lord Haddington said.

"Not quite," Sir John interjected, eager not to be unfairly aged a couple of months short of his birthday.

The cabinet minister responsible for the Royal Navy was still worried he'd be to blame if Franklin "broke down" on what would be his fourth polar expedition, his third as commander. Franklin, either thinking Lord Haddington was being kind in his concern or simply desperate to please, repeatedly offered to undergo a physical examination.

"I know all your services," Lord Haddington continued. "They have been very various, and latterly you have been on a civil service which must have caused you great care and anxiety."

That one, bringing the ugliness of Van Diemen's Land into the room, certainly stung. Franklin insisted again that the Arctic, brutal as nature could be, wasn't too much for him. If he weren't sure of it, he wouldn't ask to go. After all, this one wouldn't be a walking expedition, like his first two. Admitting the obvious, he was too fat for that now.

Franklin pressed one last, simple argument, the humble words of a fallen man grasping for lost honor by denying the almost pathetically obvious: "I have nothing to gain by it."

Silent for a moment, Lord Haddington said: "We'll consider the conversation as not having passed. It requires a little consideration. In a day or two you will hear from me."

To deal with questions of his age, strength, and ability to withstand the cold, Franklin decided to get a note from a doctor. He contacted his friend and surgeon Sir John Richardson, who knew a few things about being cold in the Arctic. On Franklin's disastrous, first overland expedition to the mouth of the Coppermine River, a storm destroyed their canoes, forcing Richardson to swim for his life. He suffered severe hypothermia. During six Arctic winters with Franklin, including two overland expeditions that covered thousands of miles, Richardson wrote, he had never seen his friend and leader suffer frostbite. The surgeon certified Franklin fit for duty.

Lord Haddington was true to his word. In two days, February 7, 1845, a letter arrived at Franklin's door bearing the Admiralty's seal. He had received his command. Once again, he would be facing his preferred opponent, the Arctic. Franklin liked his chances.

FRANKLIN'S OFFICIAL instructions followed three months later, dated May 5, 1845, deeming it "expedient that further attempt should be made for the accomplishment of a north-west passage by sea from the Atlantic to the Pacific Ocean, of which passage a small portion only remains to be completed." That principal objective was set out in the first of twenty-three clauses, eight of which covered scientific observations, using equipment on board to study magnetism. That responsibility, along with recording observations of the atmosphere and weather, would fall to Fitzjames. He would also be captain of *Erebus*, Franklin's flagship. The commander was further told "to make use of every means in your power to collect and preserve specimens of animal, mineral and vegetable kingdoms." At sea, Franklin reminded Fitzjames that meant "observing everything from a flea to a whale in the unknown regions we are to visit."

The bulk of the Admiralty's orders—which would become the focus of a lively debate among experts as months, and then years, passed without word from the expedition—spelled out the route Franklin was to take. The steam engines and propellers were only to be used to push through any leads that opened in the ice pack, or to beat unfavorable winds or complete calm, and always with an eye on the small supply of coal *Erebus* and *Terror* carried. Sir John was ordered to follow a well-known course through Barrow Strait to Melville Island. From there, "it is hoped that the remaining portion of the passage, about 900 miles, to the Bhering's Strait [between Alaska and Russia] may also be found equally free from obstruction," the Admiralty's instructions read. On this point, the orders were very clear: Franklin was not to stop to examine any routes northward or southward until he reached Cape Walker, at the northeast tip of Russell Island, which sits just north of Prince of Wales Island.

The Admiralty was concerned about the "unusual magnitude and apparently fixed state of the barrier ice" that Sir William Parry reported when he and his crew were beset a quarter century earlier in HMS *Hecla* and HMS *Griper*, off Cape Dundas, on the southern shores of Melville Island. They named the spot Winter Harbor and spent ten months there, showing that sailors could survive a winter on the ice. It was the farthest point west that Royal Navy explorers had reached in the Arctic Archipelago, and Parry proved to be the ideal leader in a horrible situation. He knew that discipline, routine, innovation, and entertainment were essential to surviving not just the cold and gloom but also the interminable boredom. The commander and his men learned the hard way to deal with basic problems that came with hunkering down in a Royal Navy ship for an Arctic winter, lessons that were passed down to the Franklin Expedition.

In dank quarters below deck, where condensation from stoves, a makeshift brewery, and sailors' breath showered the men with a steady drip, they published a weekly newspaper, the *North Georgia Gazette and Winter Chronicle*. Someone had accidentally brought along a book of plays, so Parry ordered his officers to perform for the crewmen. For Christmas, they wrote a musical about being stuck in the Arctic Archipelago, and surviving into the dead of winter. Gathered in the candlelit fog on the *Hecla*, the air they breathed below freezing, the men laughed and sang and forgot, for the moment, that they might never escape. Parry kept morale high, his men working together, until the Arctic let him take them home.

Writing instructions to Franklin almost twenty-six years later, the Admiralty heeded the ordeal of Parry and his men. They provided some intriguing leeway once Sir John was sailing west for Melville Island: If permanent ice blocked his way farther to the east, and an alternate route north between Devon and Cornwallis Islands appeared to be open—and if the quick shift from summer to winter allowed him enough time—he should head up there. In apparent contradiction to the earlier clause ordering Franklin to follow Parry's well-known route, the instruction allowed him the option to see if he could find "a more ready access to the open sea, where there would be neither islands nor banks to arrest and fix the floating masses of ice." That crucial alternative may have come from Franklin himself as an amendment to a first draft, because the section is written in the margin of the original document. The added option may very well have set him and his sailors on course to their doom.

Other clauses seemed unnecessary for an explorer of Franklin's experience, but the Admiralty preferred to nail things down wherever possible. If the expedition had to winter over, the commander should try to find safe harbor and attend to his men's health. If Franklin happened to meet "either Eskimaux or Indians, near the place where you winter, you are to endeavor by every means in your power to cultivate a friendship with them, by making them presents of such articles as you may be supplied with, and which may be useful or agreeable to them; you will, however, take care not to suffer yourself to be surprised by them but use every precaution, and be constantly on your guard against any hostility."

Science was just as important to the mission as completing the Northwest Passage. The empire stood to gain a lot from observations recorded with the expedition's magnetometers because of the potential improvements to the humble compass. Declination had troubled navigators since Yi Xing, a Chinese Buddhist monk who was an astronomer, mathematician, and engineer in the Tang Dynasty, first described the gap between magnetic north and true north around 720 AD. That was long before Chinese navigators pioneered the use of compasses at sea near the end of the eleventh century. The compass reached European hands the following century. Understanding the gap between the two norths, and potentially cutting hundreds of wasted miles off a navigator's course, was critical to the world's greatest naval power. But the expedition's magnetic readings were also meant to feed a radically new phenomenon: the unprecedented international scientific effort to understand Earth's magnetic field.

A Prussian nobleman's chance encounter with a magnetic rock led to a global effort to gather data to unlock the secrets of Earth's magnetic field, one of the most ambitious international undertakings the scientific world had ever seen. The accomplishment is even more remarkable because it began in a Europe rebuilding after a long, deeply divisive, and costly war. Its roots run back to the Fichtel Mountains of northeastern Bavaria, where, in 1796, a mining inspector and Prussian nobleman named Alexander von Humboldt was measuring a large block of serpentine rock. His compass went haywire, completely reversing direction. That began a lifelong crusade to crack the secrets of Earth's geomagnetic field. Humboldt became especially interested in geomagnetic storms, which erupt when solar winds roil the magnetosphere. The disturbances amp up the aurora borealis, or northern lights, and give a fresh jolt to the Arctic's magic. He wondered whether magnetic storms occurred simultaneously around the planet.

Humboldt built his first observatory in Berlin in the fall of 1828. Over the next two years, he persuaded colleagues to set up a chain of them to take measurements at the same time, in precisely the same way, in several places. They included Paris and sites across the Russian Empire, including what was then the czarist possession of Alaska. In Beijing, a Greek Orthodox monastery housed one of the new observatories. The British joined the effort when Humboldt wrote, in a long letter that blended history, theory, engineering, and discovery, to the president of the Royal Society, the Duke of Sussex.

Humboldt's pitch in April 1836, and the needs of a vast scientific endeavor that demanded synchronized observations in key parts of the world, played perfectly to the Victorian sense that the British Empire was an essential engine of human progress. He asked that the Royal Society "exert its powerful influence" to extend the chain of stations measuring the Earth's magnetic field, with equipment matching precise specifications, either in the tropics or in the high latitudes of the Southern Hemisphere and in Canada. Soon the list of geomagnetic observatories in British colonies included Toronto, Singapore, and Madras. The global total eventually reached around 150. Like the international space station orbiting Earth at the end of the Cold War, Humboldt's plan gave nations a compelling scientific reason to work together.

To help improve the understanding of Arctic Ocean currents, and to increase the possibility of tracking the expedition, the Royal Navy's high command instructed Franklin, once past latitude 65 degrees north, to record the ships' position each day on a printed form. Each one was to be sealed in a bottle or copper cylinder and tossed overboard to ride the ocean currents. *Erebus* and *Terror* each carried two hundred of the cylinders. The preprinted forms had instructions for anyone who might find one in six languages, including French, Spanish, German, and Danish. They asked that the retrieved document be forwarded to the Secretary of the Admiralty in London, or the closest British consul, with a note of the time and place where it was discovered. Only one of the cylinders was ever reported found. In July 1849, it was recovered from the rocks on Greenland's coast. That raised hopes, but only briefly because the smudged relic wasn't much of a clue in what had become the growing Franklin mystery. The report gave the expedition's position on June 30, 1845, when *Erebus* and *Terror* were still traveling with their coal-laden supply ship *Barretto Junior*, and about to cross the Arctic Circle on their way to Disko.

In every detail of the expedition's preparation, the Royal Navy expressed confidence that Sir John and his men would sail through the Arctic in historic triumph. They had great faith in technology. The ships were fitted with cutting-edge screw propellers, powered by a converted train engine. Fitzjames, who had been sailing in the Royal Navy since he was a twelve-year-old cabin boy, described *Erebus*'s upgrade in a letter to his wife after watching a locomotive engine from the London–Greenwich Railway, minus the wheels, arrive dockside. "It came drawn by ten coal black horses and weighs fifteen tons," he wrote. Cranes lowered the used engines, rated to provide Franklin's ships up to thirty horsepower, into each vessel. It was a quick, clever way to transform aging bomb vessels into more modern steamers with, designers hoped, just enough power on call to propel them through narrow leads in sea ice.

Bricks of coal dust and coal tar formed under hydraulic pressure, called "patent fuel," were stacked up in the ships' stores, to be used sparingly when the commander ordered power from their new retractable screw propellers. The boilers were to be fired up only when wind conditions weren't right, or the leads were closing too fast, for *Erebus* and *Terror* to make progress on their own. But this early version of steam power was no panacea in the High Arctic. Even under the best conditions, the train engines could provide a top speed of four knots, or just a little faster than an easy jog in the park. Not much good against stiff head currents, which are common in the maze of channels through the Arctic Archipelago, but completely useless in a thirty-five-knot gale. Those are as regular as snowfall when winter blows away summer and things get really rough.

Deploying more high-tech gear of the day, the navy installed newly engineered propellers in wells that Franklin's crewmen could uncouple and lift, along with the rudders. That reduced drag or kept them from being crushed if leads through the sea ice closed on their vulnerable hulls. Of course, as any early adopter knows, the latest gadget can go badly wrong when severely tested in real-world conditions, especially the Arctic's. No one can say whether *Erebus* and *Terror*'s storable propellers and keels worked in an Arctic emergency or got stuck. To defend against powerful pack ice, the navy reinforced their hulls with iron plating and buttressed their frames with ten-inch beams.

Desalinators turned seawater into freshwater, for both the crew and the steam engines, which sucked up more than a ton of water each hour. High levels of lead found in the soft tissues and bones of recovered corpses from the Franklin Expedition point to the freshwater pipes, and not the men's tinned food, as the likely reason the sailors were slowly poisoned. By one popular theory, that may have impaired the dying men's judgment as they grew weaker. The most recent science, though, casts strong doubt on whether lead played any role at all in the expedition's demise. A heating system, probably one that drew hot air off the ships' galley stoves and piped it along wooden walls, reduced the cold and damp that could foster disease and make it harder for men living in close quarters to survive a winter trapped in ice.

The Admiralty sent along another piece of Victorian-era experimental equipment that was of more dubious value. Fitzjames called it an "India-rubber boat" in his journal. The patent office knew it as the recently invented Halkett Boat, an inflatable dinghy just big enough to carry three men precariously. *Erebus* and *Terror* each carried one into the Arctic for the first time. Inuit descriptions of the strange craft to early searchers helped establish the credibility of their stories. Who could concoct a story of Royal Navy sailors deploying foldable boats, pumped full of air, and bobbing about in seas cold enough to kill a man in minutes?

Lieutenant Peter Halkett came up with the dinghy design after Franklin's canoes were lost in his first Arctic expedition, when eleven of the twenty men died. That got inventive minds thinking. Halkett's idea was to take the waterproof cloth used to make the Mackintosh raincoat, the venerable British mac, infuse it with India rubber, and sew an inflatable, oval-shaped bladder inside. In the prototype, which Halkett tested on the River Thames, a man's cloak contained the airtight bladder. It was a cloak boat. In the pockets of what was officially called the Inflated Cloak, the wearer conveniently carried a small paddle blade that could be attached to a gentleman's walking stick. There was also a handy bellows to inflate the thing. An umbrella served as a sail.

For the Arctic, Halkett modified the cloak boat into a boat-in-a-knapsack. On the test run, he paddled several miles from Kew to the Westminster Bridge, dodging numerous Metropolitan steamers that almost ran him over. Franklin endorsed the portable airboat. He gave up the one assigned to him to an overland expedition led by the Hudson's Bay Company's Dr. John Rae, but he got a replacement just in time for *Erebus* and *Terror*'s May 19, 1845, departure from England. Eleven days before Franklin's expedition set sail, the Secretary of the Admiralty wrote to Halkett to offer qualified support.

"My Lords are of the opinion that your invention is extremely clever and ingenious, and that it might be useful in Exploring and Surveying Expeditions, but they do not consider that it would be applicable for general purposes in the Naval Service."

In the end, the best-laid plans didn't amount to much. The Arctic would decide the fate of Franklin and his crewmen. The sailors took comfort from knowing *Erebus* and *Terror* had already been through Hell and back.

Terror had probably proven her Arctic mettle best. In 1836, when Sir George Back tried to sail her to Repulse Bay, on the northwest shore of Hudson Bay, he got trapped in a moving minefield of ice floes, some massive with pressure ridges towering above the ship's deck. When a September gale struck, with the sea ice closing in,

Back's sailors and officers hacked away with axes, ice chisels, hand-spikes, and long poles, trying to break open a lead. An early winter soon trapped them, about four miles from land, in powerful shore ice that squeezed hard. The violent force created several ice peaks, up to twenty feet high, which pushed *Terror* hard to starboard and threat-ened to keel her over. Back and his men could only pray that their ship wouldn't be torn apart and sink.

"None but those who have experienced it can judge of the wea-riness of heart, the blank of feeling, the feverish sickliness of taste which gets the better of the whole man under circumstances like these," he wrote.

Six years later, *Erebus* and *Terror* nearly went down together in stormy Antarctic seas under Sir James Clark Ross's command. With a huge iceberg bearing down through a howling blizzard and ice floes, *Erebus* tacked hard to port. *Terror* couldn't avoid both the iceberg and her sister ship. She hit *Erebus* so hard that the shock threw almost every man off his feet and embedded an anchor close to eight inches into solid wood.

"Our bowsprit, fore-topmast and other smaller spars, were car-ried away," Ross wrote, "and the ships hanging together, entangled by their rigging, and dashing against each other with fearful violence, were falling down upon the weather face of the lofty berg under our lee, against which the waves were breaking and foaming to near the summit of its perpendicular cliffs. Sometimes she rose high above us, almost exposing her keel to view, and again descended as we in our turn rose to the top of the wave, threatening to bury her beneath us, whilst the crashing of the breaking upperworks and boats increased the horror of the scene."

The storm raged through the night. At first light of daybreak, the ships' "all's well" signals hoisted high, Ross saw an almost continuous line of icebergs to windward. The collision had probably saved the mariners' lives by pushing *Erebus* and *Terror* through a small opening that was their only escape.

"It seems, therefore, not at all improbable that the collision with the *Terror* was the means of our preservation, by forcing us backwards to the only practicable channel, instead of permitting us, as we were endeavouring, to run to the eastward, and become entangled in a labyrinth of heavy bergs, from which escape might have been impracticable, or perhaps impossible."

Surely ships that had beaten both polar seas could do it again. *Erebus* was the larger of the two at 372 tons, and more than 104 feet long. *Terror* was slightly smaller at 325 tons, and close to 102 feet long. Each had three masts that rose several stories into the air. The tallest pierced more than 100 feet into the sky. Under full sail in the High Arctic, the ships seemed like spirits to the Inuit. Newly armored against the ice, with train engines to propel them, Franklin's ships were a force unto themselves. They had been through war, Antarctic gales, and pack ice, yet they had stayed afloat to do it all again.

2

HMS *Erebus* and *Terror*

On the eve of Franklin's 1845 voyage into the Arctic Archipelago, *Erebus* and *Terror* were packed to the gunwales. It took the expedition's sailors and officers longer than expected, from four in the morning until six at night, to transfer all the supplies from the transport ship *Barretto Junior* at their last stop together in Greenland's Whale Fish Islands. Even after all Captain Fitzjames had seen in his relatively young naval career, two of her majesty's finest ships getting set to sail into such a forbidding, yet stunningly beautiful new world was a sight to behold. Intoxicating enchantment left no room for fear.

"The deck is covered with coals and casks, leaving a small passage fore and aft, and we are very deep in the water," he wrote in his journal on a July night in Greenland. "We sail, if possible, to-morrow night, and hope to get to *Lancaster Sound* by the 1st of August, which, however, is a lottery. It is now eleven o'clock, and the sun shines brightly above the snowy peaks of *Disco*. From the top of one of the islands, the other day, I counted 280 icebergs, and beautiful objects they are."

Brimming with the optimism of a fresh voyage, Fitzjames told his adoptive family that a long silence would likely mean he had made it safely through the Northwest Passage all the way to Russia.

"Should you hear nothing till next June, send a letter, *vià Petersburg*, to *Petro Paulowski*, in *Kamschatka*, where Osmar was in the BLOS-

SOM, and had letters from England in three months. And now God bless you, and everything belonging to you."

The bomb ships' hulls strained under the burden of provisions, locomotive engines, heating systems, iron plate, and the men who had to coax the overtaxed vessels through tight leads in sea ice. They were so stuffed that some supplies had to be returned on the *Barretto* to England. Sir John also sent home five of his original contingent of 134 men, declared unfit for service. They turned out to be the lucky ones. Essentials loaded onto Franklin's vessels included custom-made wolfskin blankets and clothing that the Royal Navy thought sufficient for the cold. That was an improvement over earlier polar expeditions, which were kitted out mainly with standard naval uniforms better suited to the South. But the clothes, coats, and boots supplied to Franklin and his men still couldn't match the thick, layered furs that kept Inuit alive through tough winters, even during long hours of sledding and hunting.

If that bothered Sir John, he didn't leave any record of a complaint. Judging from what the commander requisitioned, his focus was on making the ships comfortable homes for winter, well stocked with food, drink, and entertainment, on the assumption the Arctic would beckon him forward each summer with a parting of the sea ice. Franklin knew from hard-earned experience, and from his physician friend Sir John Richardson, that healthy food was the essential of all essentials. Even heavy clothing couldn't keep an Arctic traveler warm if he were starving. When Franklin's disastrous 1819–1822 overland expedition to the western exit of the Northwest Passage lost eleven men, the nine survivors ate what they could scrounge. They choked down pieces of year-old caribou skins and scarfed the plump white larvae of warble flies, also known as "bomb flies," which better describes the big, aggressive bugs that feed off the blood of deer, caribou, and musk ox. Fortunately, they taste much better than they look. Squeezed between molars, the squirming larva explodes with a burst of salty, milky fluid. More of a snack than a meal, however, the bugs don't pack nearly enough energy for a starving man to save himself.

Richardson learned firsthand about the link between good nutrition and staying warm when he and the other slowly starving men of the first Franklin Expedition tried to ford a raging river in late September. The plan was to run a line across so the men could pull themselves to the other side on a raft made from nearby willow trees. But the wood was too green to float very well. When two hardy French Canadian voyageurs couldn't make it across by wading through bone-chilling, waist-deep water, Richardson tied a rope around his waist and accidentally stepped on a dagger that cut his foot to the bone. He jumped in anyway and tried to swim across. Richardson's arms immediately numbed and he couldn't move them. The physician turned onto his back and kicked closer to the opposite bank, but his legs froze up and he started to sink. The others hauled Richardson in, wrapped him in blankets, and sat their hypothermic doctor in front of a fire of burning willow. It was several hours before he could speak again. The feeling on his left side didn't return until the following summer. In his journal, when he recalled the brush with death, he blamed it not on a risky move but on weeks of hunger.

"It may be worthy of remark that I should have had little hesitation in any former period of my life, at plunging into water even below 38 degrees Fahrenheit, but at this time I was reduced almost to skin and bone and, like the rest of the party, suffered from degrees of cold that would have been disregarded in health and vigor. During the whole of our march we experienced that no quantity of clothing would keep us warm whilst we fasted, but on those occasions on which we were enabled to go to bed with full stomachs, we passed the night in a warm and comfortable manner."

Franklin, a known stickler for detail in both his planning and his observations as an explorer, kept in mind the importance of full stomachs when making his request to the Royal Navy's Victualling

Department. It sent so much food that he estimated it would keep the expedition well fed for at least three years—even longer if the men were forced to get by on emergency rations. The long menu included 32,224 pounds of beef, almost as much pork, and more than 33,000 pounds of tinned meat, including boiled and roast beef and mutton, veal and ox-cheek. The ships' holds also carried canned vegetables, including potatoes, carrots, and parsnips. Each man got about a pint of soup a day. To make the crews' rations more palatable, cooks could dip into 200 pounds of pepper, 580 gallons of pickled cabbage, onions, and walnuts, 170 pounds of cranberries, and half a ton of mustard. With 23,576 pounds of sugar, and a tenth as much tea, there was an abundance of warm, sweetened beverages to get stranded mariners through a bleak winter's day.

Then there was the hard stuff, the grog that had kept Royal Navy sailors in good spirits since the mid-eighteenth century, usually in a concoction of weak beer, rum, and lime or lemon juice loaded with Vitamin C to combat scurvy. The Franklin Expedition carried 3,684 gallons of alcohol, likely rum, along with 9,300 pounds of lemon juice and 200 gallons of wine for the sick. Officers packed private caches of more refined wine for their own dining pleasure. They also brought along cigars. Energy boosts came from 9,450 pounds of chocolate. Stores of biscuits, pemmican, suet, raisins, peas, vinegar, Scotch barley, and oatmeal made up the bulk of the remaining stores.

Anyone too ill to be fixed up with a tot or two of wine didn't have much more to hope for on a Royal Navy ship in the Arctic. An expedition medicine chest, made of mahogany with a lock and strap, and measuring fourteen inches by thirteen inches and some five inches deep, contained twenty-three medicine bottles. They were clear glass, with glass stoppers and leather caps attached with brown thread. Their contents included some of the leading remedies of the day. One was camphorated tincture of opium, spooned out to subdue coughs or to still bowels erupting with diarrhea. There was also perchloride of mercury, a heavy, white crystalline powder used as an escharotic or corrosive salve, often to burn off sores or growths.

Sir John also was prepared to care for his men's mental health. That lesson was well learned from the Parry Expedition's long, tedious winter stuck in sea ice. Franklin made sure there was space for an abundant supply of diversions in case he and his men had a lot of time to kill. *Terror* had a library of 1,200 books, and the one aboard the *Erebus* was even bigger by a few hundred more. After cataloguing all the volumes at sea, Fitzjames praised them as a "most splendid collection." At the practical end were manuals on keeping steam engines running and earlier Arctic explorers' journals for quick reference. There was also the sentimental read, such as Oliver Goldsmith's popular *The Vicar of Wakefield*, as well as the comedy and drama of William Shakespeare's plays and Charles Dickens's novels *Nicholas Nickleby* and *The Pickwick Papers*. For laughs at the establishment's expense, the library shelves offered issues of the satirical weekly magazine *Punch*. Not long before the ships sailed, Franklin asked the Admiralty to provide 100 Christian books, including Bibles and prayer books, which he planned to sell on board at cost. But he canceled that order after friends and religious groups donated the books the commander wanted.

If the expedition had to winter over, Franklin was ready to make good use of the delay by teaching his largely illiterate sailors how to read and write. Supplies included seventy slates and pencils, along with 200 pens, ink, paper, and *Common Arithmetic* books. Officers had the pleasure of privacy in cramped cabins where they could work, or settle into a book, at mahogany desks. In the long winter darkness, when crewmen weren't out on the ice hauling sledges or keeping busy with odd jobs, they would live and toil below deck by the flickering light of candles or oil lamps. The expedition carried 2,700 pounds of candles made from beeswax, the wax of carnauba palms, or from spermaceti, a waxy substance drawn from the head of a sperm whale. The ships also had Argand lamps, which burned whale or vegetable oil. Glass prisms bolted into the outer deck, called Preston's Patent Ventillating Illuminators, funneled sunlight and fresh air into cabins and mess areas.

For musical distraction, or spiritual inspiration, each ship had its own hand organ capable of playing fifty tunes, ten of which were psalms or hymns. Franklin also asked for a daguerreotype camera, which French inventor Louis Daguerre had made available to the world just six years earlier. Sir John hoped to use it to document an arduous voyage, perhaps even a historic breakthrough, but that would take a lot of effort in itself. The world's first widely used photographic process was a time-consuming prospect when far from any city and its workshops. First, the photographer had to buff silvered copper sheets to a mirror polish. Clamped to a table, that was then scoured with powdered rottenstone, a finely ground limestone, using a square of flannel moistened with alcohol. Then it was buffed again to get the photographic plate as smooth, and as clean, as possible. In a darkroom, iodine and bromine created a surface ready to capture images with exposure to light.

Lady Franklin sent along some animal companionship. *Erebus* already had two four-legged passengers: a Newfoundland dog called Neptune and a cat that didn't seem to have a name. Likely a working feline; mousers don't need to be known by anything but their skill. The commander's wife made a gift of a third pet, a female monkey the sailors named Jacko, which Lady Franklin got from eminent zoologist John Gould. The Franklins knew Gould from their time in Van Diemen's Land, when he was working on the seven-volume ornithological study *The Birds of Australia.* Jacko was playful, at times mischievous. She knew how to take bored or miserable seamen's minds off their troubles, as she did on June 23, 1845, when the expedition's ships passed through the highest seas Fitzjames had ever seen. Waves pounded *Erebus* so hard that seawater spilled down on the commander's table, where his officers had trouble holding on and eating at the same time. The gale was one sign, the increasing cold another. The Arctic Archipelago was getting closer.

"The air is still 41°, but to-day it felt delightfully cold," Fitzjames wrote in his journal. "The monkey has, however, just put on a blanket, frock, and trowsers, which the sailors have made him (or rather her), so I suppose it is getting cold."

Reviewing the meticulous preparations, checking presumptions against long experience, Sir John thought he was ready for what was to come. But he couldn't shake every doubt. He kept probing, testing for any flaws he had overlooked. Several times in the weeks before setting sail, the commander spoke with his friend Sir John Ross to learn as much as possible from the ordeals he had endured to survive several Arctic winters beset by ice. Ross also understood what motivated a great man wronged by lesser critics.

What once looked like Ross's own sure course to a national pedestal as a hero of war and polar exploration suddenly went south on August 31, 1818, when Ross was leading Britain's high-risk return to Arctic exploration aboard the flagship HMS *Isabella*, a chartered whaler. After a night of clear sailing, under a yellow sky, the weather was thick, the temperature dropping, and the water near freezing. Banks of fog blotted out parts of the horizon. Men crowded the masthead and the crow's nest, craning to see any sign of an opening. At half past two, Ross gave orders that he be called if anyone spotted land or ice ahead. Then he went below for dinner. Half an hour later, Benjamin Lewis, the ship's master and a Greenland pilot, entered Ross's cabin with news that the fog seemed to be clearing.

"I immediately, therefore, went on deck, and soon after it completely cleared for about ten minutes, and I distinctly saw the land, round the bottom of the bay, forming a connected chain of mountains with those which extended along the north and south sides."

Ross named them the Croker Mountains, confident he was doing a great honor to the Admiralty's first secretary, John W. Croker, an

Irish politician and writer. Instead, Ross ruined his own career. A later expedition proved he had mapped a mirage, a common problem in the Arctic, where airborne ice crystals, too tiny to see without a microscope, mingle with layers of cold, dense air at the surface to bend light and sound waves. Sir John Barrow was livid. His Arctic gambit had opened with a Royal Navy explorer seeing obstacles that weren't there. He made sure Ross never got a polar command again, even when the life of his friend, Sir John Franklin, hung in the balance.

Determined to reclaim his good name, Ross turned to a private sponsor: Sir Felix Booth, who had made a fortune distilling the country's best-selling dry gin. Booth put up £20,000, worth roughly $1.8 million today, to buy and outfit an eighty-five-ton paddle-wheel steamer out of Liverpool. She was called the *Victory*, a name that would loom large decades later as the Franklin Expedition mystery unfolded. Ross, his nephew James Clark Ross, and their crew of twenty-one officers and men sailed her to the Arctic from Scotland in June 1829, towing a small launch named the *Krusenstern*. The expedition, funded by liquor profits, explored roughly 620 miles of unmapped coastline and pinpointed the North Magnetic Pole. It has been called one of the most remarkable Arctic voyages of the nineteenth century. Sea ice trapped the *Victory* in Lord Mayor Bay, on the Boothia Peninsula's east coast, in September 30, 1829.

Inuit oral history tells of a seal hunter named Aviluktoq spotting Ross's ship in a small bay. Seeing the tall masts, he thought it was a great spirit and ran back to his camp, where the men, fearing the strange giant of the sea might destroy them, spent the night discussing what to do. They decided to attack first with harpoons and bows. Hiding behind a block of ice, they realized human figures were walking around the vessel on the sea ice. The sailors spotted the Inuit and approached with their rifles, but both sides laid down their weapons on the sea ice. The sailors invited the Inuit to the ship, where they received gifts of nails, knives, and sewing needles.

With countless bodies of fresh water, including Lake Netsilik, there was no shortage of fish, along with a bounty of caribou and seals. As thanks for the food that the Inuit brought the British sailors, the ship's carpenter carved a prosthetic leg for one of the hunters who had lost his to a polar bear. For his kindness, the Inuit named Ross "Toolooark," or Raven. It was a high compliment, likely an attempt to bond with Tulluhiu, the man who now walked on the wooden leg. With a borrowed pencil, two Inuit dressed in furs by a crackling fire drew a chart in the stranded steamer's cabin to show Ross he had sailed into a dead end.

By the summer of 1833, in their fourth year in the Arctic, Ross and his men were so wretched that felt patches barely held together the clothes that Inuit had provided. The commander guessed "no beggar that wanders in Ireland could have outdone us in exciting the repugnance of those who have known what poverty can be. Unshaven since I know not when, (we were) dirty, dressed in rags of wild beasts instead of the tatters of civilization, and starved to the very bones. . . ." Ross and his crewmen had another stroke of incredibly good luck on August 26. Spotting a sail in the distance, his sailors launched boats and, after chasing the ship for a morning, they finally got close to two vessels. One suddenly turned and came to their rescue.

"She was soon alongside, when the mate in command addressed us, by presuming that we had met with some misfortune and lost our ship," Ross recalled. "This being answered in the affirmative, I requested to know the name of his vessel, and expressed our wish to be taken on board. I was answered that it was 'the *Isabella* of Hull, once commanded by Captain Ross' on which I stated that I was the identical man in question, and my people the crew of the *Victory*."

With "the usual blunderheadedness of men of such occasions, he assured me that I had been dead two years."

IN HIS FINAL HOURS with Franklin, Ross urged him to take practical steps as insurance in case *Erebus* and *Terror* were ever frozen in. He should leave a depot of provisions and, if possible, a boat or two en route to give survivors a chance at escape, Ross recommended. Franklin replied that he wouldn't have enough boats to spare. Two days before the expedition departed, Ross spoke to his friend again and heard Franklin's orders from the Admiralty. Ross told him the ships would surely get stuck in ice near Cornwallis Island and asked whether anyone, including Ross's nephew James, would serve as backup.

"Has anyone volunteered to follow you?" Ross asked.

"No, none," Franklin replied.

"Has not my nephew volunteered?"

"No, he has promised his wife's relations that he will not go to sea anymore—Back is unwell—and Parry has a good appointment."

"Then," Ross assured him, "I shall volunteer to look for you, if you are not heard of in February, 1847; but pray put a notice in the cairn where you winter, *if you do not proceed*, which of the routes you take."

The last time they spoke, at Franklin's lodgings in London, Ross repeated the request, shook hands, and heard the final words from his friend: "Ross, you are the only one who has volunteered to look for me: God bless you." Ross made his sacred promise one last time. As two old friends, both disgraced by smaller men, they shared a visceral understanding of just how unfair life can be. With a final handshake, they bade each other farewell. Friends thought Franklin looked haggard and nervous in those last sobering days before he departed. He was, after all, recovering from a bout of flu. But he was also touchy about bad omens. When Franklin lay down on the sofa in the lodgings that he had taken with Jane in Lower Brook Street, she was sitting beside him, sewing a flag that he would take to the Arctic. Lest he get cold feet, she draped it over them, startling Franklin awake.

"Why, there's a flag thrown over me," he protested. "Don't you know that they lay the Union Jack over a corpse!"

SIR JOHN FRANKLIN spent his final days before the expedition sailed in a tempest of writing. Franklin, hero that he was, hungered for vindication. With Jane's help, he produced an impassioned pamphlet that laid out his defense against his colonial attackers, who had already won the political contest. It's the sort of priority a man has when, in a much darker corner of his mind, he wonders how long he will live, and wants history to treat him well when he is gone. For Sir John, political scores in this world had to be settled. If he made it home alive, as the first to complete the Northwest Passage, who would remember the petty dustup in Van Diemen's Land? Yet he was determined to finish his account of the colonial ambush and wrote the last word on May 15, 1845, just four days before he departed on *Erebus* for the Arctic. It hurt that he had to leave before his defense was published. But as the clock ticked down, Sir John conceded that more pressing matters demanded his attention.

"And thus it has happened that, to my extreme vexation and regret, I find the day of my departure at hand without the satisfaction of seeing my pamphlet out of the press." Wary that whispers of nasty rumors would follow him to sea, Franklin took a copy of the pamphlet aboard *Erebus* as ammunition.

The sloop HMS *Rattler*, the first Royal Navy warship converted to steam power, towed *Erebus* and *Terror* down the Thames from the Woolwich dockyard to the village of Greenhithe. Sir John's daughter Eleanor made the trip with her father aboard *Erebus*. To her, the aging explorer had seemed in much better shape after giving up snuff. As *Erebus* glided down the river, ever closer to the sea, she watched a dove settle on one of his flagship's three masts and rest there for a while.

"Every one was pleased with the good omen," Eleanor told her aunt, "and if it be an omen of peace and harmony, I think there is every reason of it being true."

Franklin waved his white handkerchief as Jane, Eleanor, and his niece Sophia (Sophy) Cracroft watched the expedition pull away from the pier at 10:30 on the morning of May 19, 1845, to begin their voyage to the North. If Francis Crozier, Franklin's second-in-command, had had the strength to turn and watch the well-wishers recede from *Terror*, it would have been with a broken heart and a sense of foreboding. Crozier had fallen madly in love with Sophy when *Erebus* and *Terror* stopped at Hobart Town, the once-swampy capital of Van Diemen's Land, while serving with James Ross's Antarctic expeditions. But Sophy seemed infatuated with Ross, who was already betrothed to another woman. Crozier did not depart in an optimistic mood.

"What I fear is that from our being so late we shall have no time to look round and judge for ourselves, but blunder into the Ice and make a 1824 of it," he wrote to Ross, referring to the ill-timed Parry Expedition, when sea ice forced HMS *Fury* aground and the explorers had to abandon ship. "James, I wish you were here, I would then have no doubt as to our pursuing the proper course. . . ."

When the ships reached the Orkneys, Franklin received a final letter from his wife. She sent him almost nothing but news from that vexing place, Van Diemen's Land, except for one parting, impossible desire: "I wish we could see you in a glass as they do in the fairy-tales." That wouldn't be the last time Jane longed for a vision of her husband, even if it came second-hand through the eyes of a clairvoyant or from the voice of a ghost.

3

Frozen In

The man at the helm of Franklin's flagship was new to polar exploration. Born in Rio de Janeiro just five years before Ross's first, failed Arctic expedition, Captain James Fitzjames was a bright veteran with hooded eyes, a large, hooked nose, and cumulus curls fronting wisps of thinning hair. In his early thirties, he would have the added responsibility for the all-important magnetic observations. Fitzjames was a good choice for a job that required meticulous observations. He reveled in the detail of the world around him, especially the people with whom he shared *Erebus*.

They were immortalized as colorful characters in a journal the captain kept. Those accounts of expedition life before all contact was lost are portholes on what, by his description, was a fine group of mariners who got along well, no matter how bad the weather or how rough the waves. He especially enjoyed Franklin's anecdotes during evenings at the captain's table over dinner and drinks, even when storm-thrashed seas poured over *Erebus*'s deck. Spirits were so high heading into the mission that even a raging storm couldn't dampen them.

"I dined at our mess to-day, Sir John finding his guests could not hold on and eat too. We are packed close, and can't move very far. But the good humour of everyone is perfect; and we do dance before it so finely—I mean before the wind."

Erebus and *Terror* were well on their way, nearing Iceland, when Fitzjames reveled in the sight of porpoises, bounding out of the waves at the ships' bows, and a sea bird similar to a petrel. That signaled the Arctic was drawing closer. June 10, 1845, with more than a month to go before the expedition would reach the Arctic Archipelago, was a clear day with little wind when the northern sun set at a quarter to ten. Franklin invited Dr. Harry Goodsir, *Erebus*'s assistant surgeon and naturalist, to use a table in the commander's cabin, at the ship's stern, for his study of crustaceae. As soon as more molluscs, fish, or tiny, butterfly-shaped creatures were dredged up from the sea, the doctor hurried to Franklin's cabin to draw and describe them. A Scot, he struck Fitzjames as canny, with a low, hesitant, monotonous tone of voice that wasn't always easy to understand.

"He is long and straight, and walks upright on his toes," Fitzjames observed, "with his hands tucked up in each jacket pocket."

In his late twenties, Goodsir was conservator at the Museum of the Royal College of Surgeons of Edinburgh and "draws the insides of microscopic animals with an imaginary-pointed pencil, catches phenomena in a bucket, looks at the thermometer and every other meter." Fitzjames also liked the man's laugh. The surgeon's large lower lip, protruding above a deep groove in his receding chin, would later prove important to forensic archaeologists. Franklin thought the doctor diffident and said so in a letter he sent from Greenland to Richardson, Sir John's friend and physician.

At the commander's urging, Fitzjames decided to pass the day with a slow read, which Franklin kindly provided in galleys. It was Sir John's rushed, unpublished pamphlet about how he got roughed up in Van Diemen's Land. It wasn't the best material in *Erebus*'s extensive library, but likely the most politic under the circumstances. Goodsir, by the captain's description, was having a decidedly more interesting time "examining 'mollusca,' in a *meecroscope*." He was "in ecstacies about a bag full of blubber-like stuff, which he has just hauled up in a net, and which turns out to be whales' food and other animals," Fitzjames wrote playfully in his journal. "I have been reading Sir John Franklin's vindication of his government of Van Diemen's Land, which was to come out a week or two after we sailed. He had ready all the sheets, and cuts up Lord Stanley *a few*, and says he is haughty and imperious."

Franklin entrusted Lieutenant-Colonel Edward Sabine, on the rise to become head of the Royal Society, to offer a strong, experienced shoulder to Jane and Eleanor if Sir John took longer than expected to return. An Irish veteran of the War of 1812 who, six years later, served as the astronomer in the renewed search for the Northwest Passage, Sabine was also a leading expert on magnetism, an ornithologist, and an explorer. He had the knowledge, wisdom, and respect to offer rational assurances, even in the vacuum of rumor, speculation, and occult murmuring, that one would need to calm someone as strong willed as the woman Franklin loved.

"I hope my dear wife and daughter will not be over anxious if we should not return by the time they have fixed upon," Franklin wrote to Sabine on July 12, 1845, just before heading northwest from the Whale Fish Islands into Baffin Bay. "And I must beg of you to give them the benefit of your advice and experience when that time arrives, for you know well that, without success in our object, even after the *second winter*, we should wish to try some other channel if the state of our provisions and the health of the crews justify it."

Thomas Blanky, ice master aboard *Terror*, was a veteran of the Ross Expedition's four arduous years in the Arctic aboard the steam-powered paddle wheeler *Victory*. Making it through that agony apparently made him an incurable optimist. In his last letter home, Blanky tried to prepare his loved ones for a long wait, telling them they should never give up hope of seeing him again, no matter how long and troubling the delay.

"We are all in good spirits, one and all appearing to be of the same determination, that is, to persevere in making a passage to the northwest. Should we not be at home in the fall of 1848, or early in the spring of 1849, you may anticipate that we have made the passage, or are likely to do so; and if so, it may be from five to six years—it might be into the seventh—ere we return; and should it be so, *do not allow any person to dishearten* you on the length of our absence, but look forward with hope, that Providence will at length of time restore us safely to you."

Erebus sailed steadily closer to the Arctic, putting Franklin back in his element. It was getting colder, but her crew warmed to their commander. The bracing sea-tang drifting on Arctic air was doing him good.

"Sir John is in much better health than when we left England, and really looks ten years younger," Lieutenant J. W. Fairholme, a junior officer, wrote home from Greenland. "He takes an active part in everything that goes on, and his long experience in such services as this makes him a most valuable adviser." Like the lieutenant, Captain Fitzjames thought everyone was pleased with Sir John's steady hand under intense pressure. He was, it seemed, at peace with himself, in a fight he knew well, with everything riding on the outcome.

"We are very happy, and very fond of Sir John Franklin, who improves very much as we come to know more of him," Fitzjames told his journal. "He is anything but nervous or fidgety; in fact I should say remarkable for energetic decision in sudden emergencies; but I should think he might be easily persuaded where he has not already formed a strong opinion."

Franklin could also deliver a rousing sermon, which must have helped when the ice closed in and frightened men with much less experience could only wonder, and worry, what came next. On a Sabbath at sea, when *Erebus*'s deck was rolling in heavy swells and the commander had to raise his voice against a stiff breeze, he led his crew in solemn prayer. Franklin, who knew his Bible well, felt God at his side and wanted his men to share the comfort and confidence.

He "read the church service to-day and a sermon so very beautifully, that I defy any man not to feel the force of what he would convey," Fitzjames reported home. "The first Sunday he read was a day or two before we sailed, when Lady Franklin, his daughter, and niece attended. Everyone was struck with his extreme earnestness of manner, evidently proceeding from his real conviction."

Fitzjames described his shipmates as "fine, hearty fellows, mostly north-countrymen, with a few man-of-war's men," by which he meant a small contingent of armed troops. There were fourteen Royal Marines assigned to the expedition, in equal units posted to each ship, made up of a sergeant, a corporal, and five privates. The armed forces were aboard more to keep sailors in line, ready to deal harshly with any mutiny attempts, than to fight foreign enemies. Franklin's orders from the Admiralty included a clause that instructed, in the event that war broke out while they were at sea, that he and his men must remain neutral. A captain on Parry's second Arctic voyage reported Inuit actually found the Marines entertaining: "The gay appearance of the marines, such, even in this climate, is the attractive influence of a red coat, so delighted the ladies, that they all danced and shouted in an ecstasy of pleasure as each soldier passed before them on church parade."

Fitzjames called in the Marines early in the mission, to handle booze control in a crackdown that followed his decision to grant shore leave when the ships docked at Stromness, in Orkney, Scotland. Two sailors headed off for Kirkwall, fourteen miles away: one, "a little old man" to be with the wife he hadn't seen in four years, the other to visit his mother, after seventeen years apart. Fitzjames also sent one man from each ship's mess ashore for fresh provisions. Somewhat to his surprise, they all came back. But when the men discovered the ships weren't sailing until the next morning, several took a small boat without permission, including the old sailor, now drunk on whiskey. He pined for his wife. They were all rounded up and brought back aboard *Erebus* by 3 a.m.

Possible punishments for going AWOL included losing their pay to the constables who apprehended the sailors. Fitzjames thought that would be unnecessarily cruel, especially since the crew wouldn't have any chance to jump ship again until *Erebus* and *Terror* were through the Arctic and in port at Valparaiso, Chile, or the Sandwich Islands, now Hawaii, far off in the Pacific. It must have occurred to the young captain as he emerged, bleary-eyed, from his small cabin that night: The errant sailors would soon be in the High Arctic with no escape. Surely that would be punishment enough for everyone's sins.

"So I got up at 4 o'clock, had everybody on deck, sent Gore and the Sergeant of marines below, and searched the whole deck for spirits, which were thrown overboard. This took two good hours; soon after which we up anchor, and made sail out. I said nothing to any of them. They evidently expected a rowing, and the old man with the wife looked very sheepish, and would not look me in the face; but nothing more was said, and the men have behaved not a bit the worse ever since."

Fitzjames seemed to get the biggest charge out of another Scottish seaman named James Reid, a whaler from Aberdeen with a sailor's salty wit. *Erebus*'s ice master, Reid manned the crow's nest when sea ice was in sight. Apparently wary of Reid's skills, his captain qualified the description, adding "so-called" in parentheses after "ice master." Reid's job was to perch high up *Erebus*'s main-top-gallant masthead, watching for channels through the shifting floes or pack ice. A crow's nest could be as basic as a cask lined with canvas, but Reid called his "a very expensive one," which consisted of a hooped canvas cylinder. It couldn't have been comfortable in an Arctic wind, with ice all around, and the lives of 128 men, as well as his own, riding on Reid's judgment of any risks. Unlike the scorned Scoresby, Reid knew ice only from hard experience, not scientific study. So his call on whether to stop at the pack edge, try to go around, or sail forward, was based more on what his gut rather than his mind told him.

To Fitzjames, Reid was "the most original character of all—rough, intelligent unpolished, with a broad north-country accent, but not vulgar, good humoured, and honest hearted." When *Erebus*'s crew had all sails set and well trimmed in a following sea, she was a beautiful thing. The taut canvas and network of lines running to scores of wooden belaying pins pegged along the bulwarks hummed and whistled and twanged, like the wind's vocal chords. If a mariner kept a close ear, he could hear the Arctic speak. When she and *Terror* were approaching Cape Farewell, on Greenland's coast, Fitzjames asked Reid whether he expected a gale. The ice master's reply sounds like buccaneer dialogue that Robert Louis Stevenson might have written, but with more sea air blowing through it.

"Ah! now, Mister Jems, we'll be having the weather fine, sir! fine! No ice at arl about it, sir, unless it be the bergs—arl, the ice'll be gone, sir, only the bergs, which I like to see. Let it come on to blow, look out for a big 'un. Get under his lee, and hold on to him fast, sir, fast. If he drifts near the land, why, he grounds afore you do."

Reid had learned the mercurial ways of sea ice during his years harpooning whales. He knew as well as any man on the expedition that he might not come home. But Reid assured his wife in a letter he wrote during a stop in Greenland that he was glad to be going to the Arctic, even if it took four years to see her again. The promised payoff was too good to turn down, even though, Reid griped to his wife days before the expedition departed, he had to spend £100 on life insurance and, as an officer must, buy his own silver fork and spoon for the voyage.

"Sir John told me that if I went the voyage with him, and landed safely in England again, I would be looked after all my life."

"A number of people think it strange of me going," he conceded in the letter dated May 13, 1845, "but they would go if they knew as much about ice as I know."

And then Reid wrote this portentous postscript: "No doubt there will be a great talk about me going this voyage. It will show that I am not frightened for my life like some men. It is for you and the family. Why should a man stop at home?"

The Arctic, as well as the ice that flowed through her veins, was harder to fathom than even Reid knew. Franklin and his men were sailing for the Arctic near the end of the Little Ice Age, which lasted until about 1850. For some five hundred years, following a warmer Middle Ages in Europe, glaciers were growing and mean annual temperatures across the Northern Hemisphere dropped by more than one degree Fahrenheit. But some years were warmer than others, and in any given one, extremes of regional weather could vary. Two relatively ice-free years that Scoresby noted before the Admiralty launched the mission to find the Northwest Passage quickly gave way to much colder, more severe Arctic winters. Reid couldn't have known it, but he was about to face one of the worst winters Inuit could recall. It's anyone's guess what the ice master advised Franklin before he gave the order for *Erebus* and *Terror* to make a run through the floes that bore down and finally trapped them.

Neither could have been so popular anymore as the sea ice gripped tight and shipmates slowly began to die.

Erebus GROANED and creaked as Fitzjames wrote each night in flickering light at a mahogany desk. He called it a drawer table, "three feet long, or from the bed to the door," a tight squeeze in a cabin about six feet wide. With several years of food and supplies loaded, and the weather favorable, the expedition was finally just hours away from sailing for Baffin Bay, where Franklin would prepare for a push into the archipelago and whatever awaited. The hard nib of his pen scratching across brittle paper, Fitzjames imagined great things to come. The captain could barely contain his excitement. It seemed the Arctic was ready to cooperate and, after centuries of trying, the Northwest Passage would soon be conquered. A Dane, married to an Inuit woman, had come aboard *Erebus* from the *Lively* at Greenland, "and they believe it to be one of the mildest seasons and earliest summers ever known, and that the ice is clear away from this to *Lancaster Sound*."

"Keep this to yourself," Fitzjames instructed the Coninghams, his adoptive family, "for Sir John is naturally very anxious that people in England should not be too sanguine about the season. Besides, the papers would have all sorts of stories, not true. I do believe we have a good chance of getting through this year, if it is to be done at all; but I hope we shall not, as I want to have a winter for magnetic observations."

In the Arctic, it's wise to be especially careful what you wish for. Fitzjames was tempting fate. A brave, adventurous seaman who had fought in battle and survived, he was now a little high on a whiff of maritime history in the making. In a hurry to taste it, he also hoped to savor the experience as long as possible. Maybe he would make the papers, perhaps even bow to be knighted by the queen. To explain what sounded impulsive, even devil-may-care in the face of unknown dangers, the giddy captain invoked the American spirit.

"Don't care is the order of the day. I mean, don't care for difficulties or stoppages—go a-head is the wish. We hear this is a remarkable clear season, but clear or not clear we must go a-head, as the Yankees have it; and if we don't get through, it won't be our fault."

By then, Fitzjames was very familiar with his commander's sailing habits and knew Sir John wasn't timid. The old sea dog liked his ships moving fast, under full sail, and wasn't quick to order sailors to reef them in when the wind was blowing hard.

"I can scarcely manage to get Sir John to shorten sail at all," Fitzjames remarked.

Erebus and *Terror* reached Baffin Bay in July 1845, just in time for the approach of winter. Franklin paused there to wait for the weather to improve before sailing into Lancaster Sound, by now the well-charted eastern entrance to the Northwest Passage. From three miles off, whalers spotted the Royal Navy vessels moored to an iceberg on the northern part of the vast bay. Franklin was waiting for an opening to make a run either around or through the "middle ice" due west in the sound. Fitzjames and six other officers from the discovery ships boarded the *Prince of Wales*. Like the whaler that had rescued Ross and his men fourteen years earlier, she sailed out of Hull. In high spirits, Franklin's men invited the ship's commander, Captain Dannett, to join Franklin for dinner the next night on *Erebus*. He never made it. A favorable breeze picked up, and Dannett sailed off toward the south. A chance for the explorers to send their last letters home disappeared with him. The whaling captain later reported that three weeks of fine weather followed his departure.

The 349-ton whaling barque *Enterprise* came alongside the larger *Erebus* so that Captain Robert Martin, a respected veteran of Arctic navigation, could join Franklin for dinner. Martin chatted with Franklin and his ice master Reid and asked if the commander had a good supply of provisions. Franklin told him they had enough to last for five years and said he could "make them spin out seven years" if necessary, Martin later testified in a deposition. They had plenty of gunpowder and lead shot to shoot birds, or anything else edible, along the way. Two hunting parties, one from each ship, had already bagged enough birds to fill several casks with their salted carcasses. Sailors called them "rotges," claiming they were as tasty as young pigeons and therefore served a fair substitute for squab. Better still, they were easy prey. A single rifle blast could bring down several at a time.

At their dinner on July 26 or 28, Franklin and his officers said they expected their voyage to last four or five, maybe even six years, leaving them with ample supplies. A few days after the captains dined and chatted, as *Erebus* and *Terror* still lay tethered to the iceberg and the *Enterprise* gradually drifted off, the Franklin Expedition disappeared from sight. The Admiralty's planners didn't expect the men to be gone as long as Franklin and his officers seemed ready to stay at sea. Already, Sir John's overland expeditions had helped show the way out of the Northwest Passage, by following a fairly easy route along the North American mainland. That leg of the passage was mapped more thoroughly by Peter Dease and Thomas Simpson, both of the Hudson's Bay Company. Parry had charted the way in, along the 74th parallel to Melville Island, for which he collected Parliament's £5,000 prize, or close to half a million dollars today. All that remained for Franklin and his men to do was close the gap between the two routes, a distance of roughly three hundred miles.

Most anywhere else, that would be a jaunt. In the High Arctic, it was an eternity.

Soon after the whalers left *Erebus* and *Terror* in Baffin Bay, Franklin set a course due west through Lancaster Sound and into Barrow Strait. His ships were making good progress, but it was now August, and the gales of early September would soon be upon them. Vicious storms at summer's end were, and still are, one of the Arctic's most predictable, and lethal, traits. Franklin must have seen open water to the north, because he followed that option in the Admiralty's instructions, the alternative that Franklin may have pushed to be added in the margins of the original. *Erebus* and *Terror* ascended Wellington Channel, following the east coast of Cornwallis Island. By autumn, they made it 150 miles north to latitude 77 degrees north. There, either sea ice or the sense that he had gone far enough in pursuit of the elusive Open Polar Sea persuaded Franklin to turn back.

Others who followed in search of the missing expedition wouldn't be nearly so bold. For Franklin and his crewmen to get that far north so quickly, things were going extraordinarily well. They went past Cornwallis's northern tip, under a thousand miles from the North Pole, before turning south along the west coast of Cornwallis to complete a circumnavigation of the island. By then, Franklin had no choice but to find safe harbor. The explorers could be proud of their first months in the Arctic Archipelago. They had, as ordered, gone as far north as it was sensible to do in search of a passage to the Pacific. On their way up, they explored a new strait, Queen's Channel, between Bathurst and Cornwallis Islands. Then they made it safely south to an ideal spot for wintering over, near the cathedral cliffs of Beechey Island, all before the worst months of winter. Sir John had every reason to break out the hand organs and let the men celebrate as they settled in for the long darkness. He would have known Beechey well as a recommended High Arctic waypoint. His friend and confidant Parry had visited there in August 1819 and had a burst of speed that summer, feeling the rush of breaking free from the eastern archipelago's tighter, ice-choked channels. But it came with a warning to any who came after him.

"It is impossible to conceive any thing more animating than the quick and unobstructed run with which we were favored, from Beechey Island across to Cape Hotham," Parry recalled. "Most men have, probably, at one time or another, experienced the elevation of spirits which is usually produced by rapid motion of any kind; and it will readily be conceived how much this feeling was heightened in us, in the few instances in which it occurred, by the slow and tedious manner in which the greater part of our navigation had been performed in these seas. Our disappointment may therefore be imagined, when, in the midst of these favorable appearances, and of the hope with which they had induced us to flatter ourselves, it was suddenly and unexpectedly reported from the crow's nest, that a body of ice lay directly across the passage between Cornwallis Island and the land to the southward."

If only Beechey Island had been so gracious to Franklin and his men. During their first winter, three died and were buried in shallow graves scraped out of the island's rocky permafrost. John Torrington, a twenty-year-old leading stoker who shoveled coal for *Terror*'s steam engine, passed on January 1, 1846. Torrington's lungs, stained by the black dust and smoke he had inhaled for hours each day, were scarred by a disease that had infected him long before he boarded the *Terror*. He was suffering from tuberculosis. At first, the bacteria spread through his body without symptoms. Then the disease ravaged him— draining the stoker's strength, forcing him to cough up bloody sputum, slowly wasting him away. Emphysema made breathing all the more difficult. Pneumonia then set in, which probably killed him. Below deck, surgeons cleaned his corpse, dressed him in trousers and a striped shirt with mother-of-pearl buttons, and used a strip of cotton cloth to bind the dead man's arms tightly to his body at the elbows. They tied it off with a bow at the front before Torrington was lifted into a brass-handled mahogany coffin, carefully built by the ship's carpenters. A heart-shaped plaque nailed to the lid declared, in white hand-painted script, his name, date of death, and age. Interred in the permafrost, the sailor was mummified by ice, his eyes half open, lips drawn back, to expose rows of straight white teeth in a ghoulish rictus grin.

Three days after Torrington succumbed, death struck again. The expedition lost John Hartnell, a twenty-five-year-old able seaman aboard *Erebus*. His death was so sudden that it called for an autopsy aboard *Erebus*. The surgeon made a long, Y-shaped incision in Hartnell's chest and abdomen to remove the sailor's heart and part of his windpipe and also examined the lungs. There was evidence of tuberculosis and pneumonia. He had been injured at some point, suffering what appeared to be a compression fracture in his lower neck. A small bone in his left foot showed signs of infection. Wrapped in a shroud, Hartnell was buried dressed only from the waist up, with a wool cap and a pullover shirt woven with blue-and-white stripes, tied shut where buttons had fallen off. Underneath, he wore a wool jumper and a cotton undershirt. Carved in his wooden headboard was the biblical admonition: "Thus saith the Lord of Hosts, consider your ways."

Then, on April 3, William Braine, thirty-two, a Royal Marine private serving aboard *Erebus*, passed away. Years earlier, a sharp blow had left a scar across his forehead. He was developing arthritis in his hands and feet. Sores on the front of his shoulders, right where thick ropes would cut into the skin as a man hauled something heavy, suggested in an autopsy decades later that Braine died on a sledge trip. He also had signs of pneumonia. As Braine lay in the chill darkness below deck, perhaps because a storm delayed his funeral, rats gnawed at his bone-thin corpse, leaving tiny bite marks on his groin, chest, and shoulders. Before he was finally laid to rest, with his undershirt on backward and other hints of a hurried burial, someone placed a bright red kerchief over Braine's decomposing face.

"Choose ye this day whom ye will serve," the inscription on his headboard read, quoting Joshua.

All three of the men had suffered more than one illness, but without any records showing cause of death, modern experts were left to wonder exactly what killed them. Generations after the Franklin Expedition vanished, it is still a virtual blank slate for theorists to argue all sorts of possibilities. Some point to botulism, perhaps a strain endemic in the Arctic or one that bred in improperly tinned food. Other research suggested that pneumonia, possibly made worse by tuberculosis and lead poisoning, likely killed the men and others who succumbed to the Arctic. But like many of the explanations

offered for the loss of every man, monkey, dog, and cat that sailed with
Franklin on *Erebus* and *Terror*, lead poisoning hasn't held up under scientific scrutiny. The corpses exhumed from Beechey Island 138 years
after the men died did show elevated lead levels. The solder used to
seal the expedition's canned food may have contributed some of the
neurotoxin in the mariners' bodies. But lead from many sources con-
taminated Europeans in the nineteenth century. In the twenty-first
century, scientists ruled out the suggestion that any of the metal
ingested during the sailors' Arctic voyage had a significant impact.
That means it is very unlikely Franklin and his crews suddenly
became addled by lead poisoning just when they needed to think their
way clearly out of a lethal bind.

That winter of 1845–46, while he waited for the Arctic to free
his ships, Sir John had a lot of time to think, reread the Admiralty's
instructions, and chart his next course. The lengthy orders told him
"it will be a matter of your mature deliberation whether in the ensuing
season" to proceed westward, as Parry had, or "persevere to the south-
westward." Franklin apparently headed south through Peel Sound.
Some historians believe he got farther west and made the turn into
McClintock Channel. No physical evidence was found to prove either
route. But the ultimate end isn't in dispute: Sea ice, likely driven by
one or more storms that always mark the High Arctic's sudden turn
from summer to winter, trapped *Erebus* and *Terror* again on September
12, 1846. Like a noose cinched tight, pack ice quickly closed around
Erebus and *Terror* at the northern end of Victoria Strait, some twelve
miles off the northwest shore of King William Island.

WHILE THE ROYAL NAVY expedition waited for the sun to return and
begin melting the ice, change was marching steadily ahead in the rest
of the world. British East India Company troops advanced in their
brutal war to crush Sikh opposition. In the US, Mormons started

their trek to the west. Then the Mexican-American War broke out on the southern border. Kerosene was invented. The planet Neptune was discovered. Far from any headlines, Franklin continued to send out parties to explore uncharted territory in anticipation of the next season's breakup.

Lieutenant Graham Gore and ship's mate Charles F. Des Voeux left the Franklin Expedition vessels with six men on a mission in May 1847. Whatever else they accomplished on that trip across the sea ice, fraught with untold dangers, they would be remembered for five fragmented, handwritten sentences. Following Royal Navy procedure, they wrote a note in ink on a printed form before concealing it in a stone cairn. A prayer would have been appropriate, in hopes that a divine hand might lead anyone looking for the expedition to find guidance in this piece of paper. The first note, very brief and hopeful, said the expedition had wintered at Beechey Island after sailing up Wellington Channel to latitude 77 degrees north and then heading back south along the west coast of Cornwallis Island.

"Sir John Franklin commanding the expedition," read the note, signed by Gore and Des Voeux on May 28, 1847. "All well."

Those sparse words masked a dire truth. It didn't mention three men had died. One of the few sentence fragments also contained an intriguing error: It said the expedition wintered over at Beechey in 1846–47, but the correct years were 1845–46. Some would later seize on that as evidence Franklin's men were losing their minds early in their ordeal. Des Voeux's party also seemed slightly lost, making another mistake that might easily be explained by the endless torment of Arctic survival. But, it seems, they were also trying to follow a sensible emergency plan that Franklin had discussed before his departure.

The men first placed the note in a soldered canister beneath what they mistakenly thought was a cairn of stacked stones that John Ross's nephew James had built seventeen years earlier. That is when he named nearby Cape Felix after the gin maker who funded his uncle's expedition aboard the steam-powered paddle wheeler *Victory*. Just as John Ross had advised Franklin in the final days before *Erebus* and *Terror* sailed, it appeared the commander's men were now leaving a trail his friend might follow to find them.

I shall volunteer to look for you, if you are not heard of in February, 1847; but pray put a notice in the cairn where you winter, if you do not proceed, which of the routes you take.

The expedition commander may have known his own days were numbered and ordered his men to place the note where Ross would be most likely to look for it. Franklin died, also of unknown causes, soon after the report was deposited and his men returned to the ships. That fact was recorded in a scrawl of ink around the margins of the first record. Lieutenant John Irving went to the trouble of retrieving it from the mistaken cairn so that it could be moved four miles to the south at Victory Point, to what they decided was a real Ross cairn. Ross's nephew James had named the point after their ship in 1830 and left, in a stone cairn, a brief account of his voyage to date. Around midnight on May 29, looking out on "the vast extent of ocean then before our eyes," he thought his exhausted sled-dog team had brought him to the top of that stretch of the continent. The sea ice was stunning.

"The pack of ice which had, in the autumn of the last year, been pressed against that shore, consisted of the heaviest masses that I had ever seen in such a situation."

Ross couldn't believe his eyes. Like a seaborne bulldozer, the thick, multiyear ice had shoved lighter floes up the shoreline, "turning up large quantities of the shingle before them, and, in some places, having travelled as much as half a mile beyond the limits of the highest tide mark." The floes had poured down from the northwest, through McClintock Channel, just as the sea ice had now clamped shut on *Erebus* and *Terror*. Ross named a cape to the southwest after Franklin and piled limestone slabs to make a six-foot cairn. That's where Captain Fitzjames had now come to leave the note reporting Franklin's death and his expedition's demise. He covered the remaining edges of the Admiralty form that Des Voeux had filled out almost a year before him. The captain's hand obviously was trembling, his handwriting a shaky scrawl.

> *April 25th, 1848.—H.M. ships Erebus and Terror were deserted on the 22nd of April, five leagues N.N.W. of this; having been beset since 12th Sept., 1846.*

Then, after describing the transfer of the original note, the worst news:

> *Sir John Franklin died on 11 June, 1847, and the total loss by death in the Expedition has been, to this date, nine officers and fifteen men.*

Fitzjames and Crozier, Franklin's second-in-command, signed. Then Crozier wrote a final line, as if it were an afterthought from a drained mind. The desperate expression of a high-risk decision, to give up their shelter and try to walk out of the Arctic, was without a hint of explanation. It had to be curt. There was too little space left to say anything more. Squeezed into the upper right corner of the document, scrawled upside down, the terse conclusion said:

> *And start on tomorrow 26th for Back's Fish River.*

Strict Royal Navy protocol had required the sailors to follow prescribed steps in those final hours aboard *Erebus* and *Terror*. Anything loose, like boats, booms, and sails, had to be lashed down or stowed. As the final moment of abandonment approached, the commander ordered codebooks to be burned. Carpenters used tarry oakum to caulk shut any entryways to the ship that hadn't already been sealed against the long winter cold. Crewmen were allowed to pack some personal things, the necessary clothes and gear, any family mementos, with limitations on weight. Officers could take more, ordinary seamen less. As they worked, spirits lifted with the hope of getting home after the long, painful months trapped in the High Arctic wilderness. Counting down the hours until it was time to start walking, the crewman on watch struck the clapper against *Erebus*'s bronze bell at least once at the top of each hour, tolling a solemn clang that resonated across the vacant sea ice. Carpenters sealed entryways, leaving one open for their commander to make his final inspection, climb out on deck, and order the final hatchway secured.

If Crozier and his closest officers were still well enough, the commander would have led them in a toast, maybe even a prayer. The expedition was not over. Honor was due to the men—those already lost and the others still fighting for their lives—and to the great vessels they were now abandoning to fend against the Arctic on their own. The requisite flags were raised, to ensure their Royal Navy colors were flying if *Erebus* and *Terror* went down, and the bell was tied off to prevent its sounding on an empty ship, trembling in the wind. Much more than a device to mark time, or sound the alarm, the bell was symbolic of a ship's very heart. Crewmen even had their newborns christened in their ship's upturned bell. The new baby's name could be engraved in its metal to welcome the child into the navy fold. If the sea eventually took their ship, sailors believed, the bell would ring once more as she slipped beneath the waves into her watery grave.

When all the required steps were complete, and it was time to cede *Erebus* and *Terror* to the Arctic, the last man aboard climbed down to the sea ice.

For weeks before the day of abandonment, crewmen had gathered a massive amount of equipment, supplies, and unusual extras to be cached ashore. They collected utilitarian items, like heavy iron stoves to cook for more than a hundred camped men, plus canned food, blankets, and medicine. But the weary men also carried more puzzling things, like novels, brass curtain rods, button polish, silk handkerchiefs, and a mahogany writing desk. In stages, they packed as much as ten tons of stuff into thirty-foot whaleboats, which the sailors dragged on ropes across some twenty-five miles of sea ice that separated the ships from shore. It took them up to five days, slipping and falling on the ice, fighting off the searing pain of frostbite, maneuvering around pressure ridges as tall as small buildings, to make one delivery ashore. When that exhausting work was done, there was no way survivors could carry most of what they had moved as they continued south toward the continent. So they abandoned most of their cache, just as they had their ships.

The Franklin Expedition's survivors, now down to 105 haggard men, would try to reach safety in the same place that starving remnants of Ukjulingmiut Inuit had sought salvation decades earlier, only to suffer mass death. They quickly split into groups. Inuit watched some men break away, never to return, while those who remained died of starvation. At a place Inuit call Teekeenu, roughly halfway down the west coast of King William Island at present-day Washington Bay, hunters were sealing when they spotted what they thought was a polar bear on smooth ice in the distance. It was likely the sail flapping above a boat the escaping sailors hauled on a sledge full of supplies. As they rose from the horizon, the Inuit realized they were looking at men not a bear. The group made a turn with the bay. Now the hunters feared they might become the prey. Two Inuit men, Ow-wer and Too-shoo-art-thar-u, walked out on the ice to meet the *qalunaaq*. Two of the white men, one carrying a gun, approached and stopped at a large crack in the ice, the armed one staying slightly back, weapon in his arms.

"C'hi-mo," the unarmed one shouted in greeting. The other laid down his gun and joined him.

The Inuit called the man who appeared to be a leader Aglooka, meaning "He Who Takes Long Strides." The man knelt down by the crack that separated them from the Inuit and scraped the ice with an *ulu*, a knife with a blade shaped like a half moon, normally used by women. At the same time, he raised his other hand to his mouth and motioned down his neck to his stomach, which the Inuit took to mean he was hungry and needed food. The white men walked along the crack until they found a place to cross. This time Aglooka pantomimed his hunger again, repeating "Man-nik-too-me" over and over. The officer then got across that two ships were behind them to the north. He made the sound of whirring and buzzing, and blowing wind, apparently acting out ice crushing the vessels. The other Inuit, less afraid now, came forward to join the group. Aglooka asked the Inuit men and women to open all their packs, which they did, so he could take seal meat from each one. After paying two women with large beads, he piled the food on a dog's back and four Inuit went with him to the other *qalunaaq* and their boat. Some were putting up a tent. They all raised their arms, hands open above their heads, to show they had no weapons. Aglooka spoke to one of them, a short man with a narrow face and big nose, who may have been Dr. Alexander McDonald, *Terror*'s assistant surgeon. He could speak some Inuktitut, learned on previous voyages with whalers.

Another witness described Aglooka's eyes as sunken in, his face so drawn that the Inuk's cousin was too afraid to look. A searcher later concluded the dying man was Crozier, who gave the order to abandon *Erebus* and *Terror* and try to walk out. At some point, several of the men returned to the expedition's flagship. Suddenly freed from the solid pack as the breaking ice shrieked, moaned, and cracked with the terrifying cries of a dying beast, *Erebus* and *Terror* stirred to life again to make a final, mysterious voyage southward.

PART II

THE HUNT

4

The Hunt Begins

Back home, many people were getting more anxious with each day that passed without any word from *Erebus* or *Terror*. The Admiralty had raised expectations high with the publicity leading up to Sir John's send-off, and the public's attention span was long in an age when experiments with carrier pigeons were cutting-edge communications technology. The best hope the Franklin Expedition had of communicating beyond the Arctic was if the currents carried one of their message canisters to a far-off beach, someone found it, and the finder took the trouble to send the report it contained to British authorities. So the British public was left to wonder, and speculate, about what was going on with the best-equipped expedition ever sent in search of the Northwest Passage. Some even appealed to the paranormal, hoping for at least a hint of good news or bad.

In the corridors of power, an argument was slowly building over what should be done to find out where the expedition was, and whether Sir John and his men were still in good shape. In the autumn of 1846, when the sea ice first stranded Franklin's ships, Sir John Ross was due for retirement. He refused to take it. Ross thought Franklin should have been clear of the Arctic by then. To his ear, continued silence from the expedition was a bad sign. Ross saw another fight ahead and wasn't going to do anything that would prevent him from leading a rescue mission. He had been certain one would be necessary since the day he last saw Franklin.

Just as Scoresby had warned decades earlier, Ross thought it was wrong to send such large ships into the Arctic Archipelago. Adding steam engines only compounded the dangers for a bomb vessel like *Erebus* or *Terror* because the engines "took up too much of her stowage, and brought the ships deeper in their draught of water." Worst of all, Ross insisted in a scathing postmortem, canned meat in the ships' provisions proved to be "putrid and unfit for human food." Tinned meat was a relatively new luxury for sailors. For centuries, sailors at sea had subsisted on salted meat, hardtack, and pickles. In Napoleon's France, Nicolas Appert had revolutionized the feeding of a military on the move. He developed an early sterilization process by which food was heated in sealed glass jars and bottles, which were then boiled in water to make them ready for packing. The British improved Appert's method by using tin-plated cans, which were lighter and less likely to explode.

When the Admiralty's Victualling Department was provisioning the Franklin Expedition, its main contractor for canned meat was Stephen Goldner, a Hungarian immigrant who ran a canning factory in Moldavia, now part of Romania. The cheaper labor, and lower-cost supplies of cattle and pork, allowed him to turn a profit as the navy's demand for more tinned meat grew. That was despite the great distance between his factory and Britain's dockyards. His process was far from perfect, and it exposed Royal Navy crews to lethal toxins, such as botulism. Making matters worse, Goldner's employees were constantly bickering about the low wages, and frequent beatings from the boss, which didn't improve the poor quality control. After separating meat from fat, they scalded or boiled the meat in vats, packed as much as possible into each can, and filled in the spaces with soup from the vats. Then they soldered on lids, punctured with small holes to let steam escape as the cans were dipped in calcium chloride heated to around 260 degrees Fahrenheit. After the steam hole was patted with a wet sponge, a drop of solder sealed it. The finished cans were then stored for three weeks at 80 degrees Fahrenheit. Any that burst were removed. The rest went to the Royal Navy. Dockworkers loaded many cases of Goldner's canned meat, 33,289 pounds of it, deep into the holds of *Erebus* and *Terror*.

Goldner won the Royal Navy supply contract in 1844. Franklin's expedition was among the first to get his cans of meat, but others had eaten it before his crews did, without catastrophic consequences. It was long after he sailed for the Arctic that politicians and the press took serious notice of waves of complaints rolling in from Royal Navy seamen who found bits of bone, offal, and other nonmeat items in their tins. Worse, the cans were often bent out of shape by pressure from gassy microbes breeding inside. A Parliamentary Select Committee investigated and concluded, among other things, that Goldner's workers were probably stealing meat and substituting bits banned under a strict contract, either out of revenge or to make up for the terrible pay.

It also found that Goldner was more focused on producing tallow and hides, which provided a better profit and in turn subsidized his canning operation, allowing him to undercut other bidders for the Royal Navy contract. Investigators discovered cans that were supposed to contain only meat actually had such things as putrefying "pieces of heart, roots of tongues, pieces of palates, pieces of tongues, coagulated blood, pieces of liver, ligaments of the throat, pieces of intestines." The Admiralty's comptroller reported that improper substances appeared very infrequently in checked cans, but rotting meat was a widespread problem. Blame fell on Goldner's shoddy canning and the navy's poor handling of the tins in its warehouses and aboard ships.

Sir John Ross's accusation that bad food helped doom Franklin and his men was at best a guess, based on the broader Goldner scandal. But the explorer's charge that the Admiralty didn't pay careful attention to weather warnings has survived closer scrutiny. After studying forty years of weather records from Archangel, Copenhagen, Stockholm, and St. Petersburg, Ross believed that severe winter in northern Europe predicted the same in Baffin Bay. He warned Franklin that he wouldn't get past Cornwallis Island in his first season in the Arctic Archipelago. Among the evidence Ross offered was personal experience during the winter before Franklin left for the Arctic. Ross had traveled in a carriage drawn by four horses from Helsingborg, Sweden, where he was British consul, to Elsinore in Denmark, and "when I passed Hamburg they were roasting an ox on the Elbe." That winter was so extreme that he had to detour and make his way home via Rotterdam.

Wisdom and instinct honed during four years trapped in sea ice made Ross's concerns about the timing of the Franklin Expedition all the more grave. But other naval officers, the overwhelming majority of polar experts, disagreed. Franklin chose to believe them. He had too much on the line to listen to a doubter, no matter how close a friend he was. Ross later claimed "that neither the Government nor those consulted ever took into consideration the mildness or the severity of the preceding winters, which is absolutely necessary in order to judge of the navigation and state of the sea and ice during the succeeding summer." Certain he was right, Ross had several conversations with Franklin about how he should plan to minimize the risk and what Ross would do to back him up if things went as badly as that voice in the wilderness predicted.

The men had known each other since Sir John Barrow and the Royal Navy launched Britain's return to polar exploration in 1818. Ross was a captain and Franklin a young lieutenant on a failed, four-vessel attempt to sail to the North Pole. As members of the tight brotherhood of polar explorers, they grew close over the years. Ross was sixty-eight by the time he promised Franklin to personally come looking for him in the High Arctic. More than a year later, he wasn't about to let advancing age scuttle a solemn commitment. Ross watched the weather closely after Sir John headed out to sea. Friends in Sweden, Denmark, and Russia, as well as returning whalers, told Ross that the following winter of 1845–46 was particularly bad. In Baffin Bay, the "'land-ice' extended from the west coast further than they had seen it," he reported.

"I had a fair prospect," Ross thought, "of being able to complete the relief or rescue (in the case of accident) of my gallant friend, to whom I had pledged my word, especially as it was now evident that he had not found or accomplished the north-west passage."

Ross wrote his first, brief letter to the Admiralty offering to lead a relief mission in 1847 "to proceed to certain positions we had agreed upon in search of him and his brave companions." The letter was dated September 28, 1846, just over two weeks after *Erebus* and *Terror* were beset. Of course, Ross and the rest of the world didn't know that yet. Still, the discredited explorer thought the Admiralty would jump at his offer. After all, he was the only volunteer to step forward. But the naval command insisted there was no cause for alarm because the expedition had only been in the Arctic roughly a year, which meant they would have used up, at most, only two-thirds of their provisions. That assumed at least some of the canned meat was still edible, and nothing else had gone wrong with the crews' health and supplies.

Ross's anger with the Admiralty's stubborn refusal to back him went from simmer to boil as he watched the next northern winter arrive. It was milder, offering the perfect opportunity to go looking for Franklin's ships. Other vessels had left Stockholm at the start of January 1847 and made it through the sea ice in midmonth, which got Ross studying charts to figure out the best places to search around Cornwallis Island. His argument still had a gaping hole. Without hard evidence to prove the Admiralty and other polar experts wrong, Ross was trying to persuade one of the world's most powerful military institutions to trust his gut feeling that Franklin and his men were in trouble. He continued to press for permission to act on it. The predictable reply came from the second secretary, Captain William A. B. Hamilton, who assured Ross "that although your gallant and humane intentions are fully appreciated by their Lordships, yet no such service is at present contemplated by my Lords. . . ."

Ross, as he often did, took the anodyne reply personally. He was sure the Admiralty was being evasive and, by his description, puerile, "doubtless in order to induce me to accept the retirement and thereby throw me on the shelf." As anyone who knew Ross would have expected, he only dug his heels in deeper. He rewrote his pitch to the Admiralty, this time appealing to the establishment's obsession with the North Pole. Ross proposed he lead an expedition to the top of the world by sledge, which he said Scoresby supported. After returning from the pole, Ross suggested, he could go looking for Franklin and his men if they still hadn't been heard from. The Admiralty still wasn't interested.

So A WHALER made the first, feeble attempt to hunt for *Erebus* and *Terror*. In the mid-nineteenth century, killing whales was a very lucrative business. Fleets from Britain and America regularly lost ships and men in a relentless push deeper into Arctic waters in search of the animals whose blubber was a chief source of light and lubrication. By the 1840s, whalers had harvested so many whales from the easiest fishing grounds that supply was getting tighter as demand steadily rose for the oil their hulking corpses provided. That sparked research into alternatives. In 1853, Canadian physician and geologist Abraham Gesner patented the process of distilling lamp oil from crude, which he had discovered in experiments the same year that sea ice had stranded *Erebus* and *Terror*. He named the new fuel "kerosene," which gave birth to a global petroleum industry and a violent new era of geopolitics that followed. As kerosene caught on, research developed other ways of refining crude into fuel, spurring more technological change and even higher demand for a resource once shunned as dirty and virtually worthless. The first internal combustion engines made automobiles possible, and world demand for still more crude oil exploded. Whaling slid ever deeper into decline.

One of the boldest of the Arctic whalers, who bravely fought to stave off the inevitable, was William Penny. He tried to save the shrinking whaling fleet, and get around worsening ice conditions, by exploring for new breeding grounds farther south. The son of a veteran whaler, he was twelve years old when he made his first voyage from the Scottish whaling hub of Peterhead into the Greenland Sea on his father's ship. Thirty years later, with the help of an Inuk hunter and trader named Eenoolooapik, he explored the entrance to Cumberland Sound, which Europeans hadn't visited for more than 250 years. To campaign for a government-backed expedition to the area, Penny brought his new friend Eenoolooapik, then around nineteen years old, to Aberdeen aboard the *Neptune*. The first Inuk seen there in seventy years, the man they called Bobbie was an immediate sensation. During the five-month visit, he was celebrated as bright and witty, with a knack for mimicry. He received gilded invitations to fine dinner parties, attended the theater, and was even a guest at two balls honoring the wedding of Queen Victoria and Prince Albert.

A portrait shows him dressed like a gentleman, hair greased flat and neatly parted, wearing a white shirt with a neck-pinching high collar, beneath a tartan waistcoat and a wide-collared jacket. Local crowds really wanted to see him as something more exotic. They wanted an Eskimo, one of what a Victorian writer called the "fur-clad savages." Reluctantly, Eenoolooapik obliged his hosts. Just a few days after arriving in Aberdeen, he agreed to give a kayak demonstration on the Dee River, fully wrapped in traditional furs on an especially warm November day. He would only give the performance on condition that he not be asked again to dress as if he were in the Arctic. Under the strain of it all, Eenoolooapik overheated and became so sick with a lung ailment that he had to be nursed through a lengthy illness that nearly killed him.

And it was all for naught. Despite lots of excited press coverage, and the warm welcomes in the salons and ballrooms of Britain, Eenoolooapik and William Penny failed to persuade the Admiralty to support the whalers by launching an expedition to explore the Cumberland Sound area. Instead, they gave Penny precisely £20 to buy the hunter any equipment he might want before leaving. So the two men went off to search for whales on their own and reported promising new hunting grounds to the Admiralty that had snubbed them. But they were too late to save British whaling, Penny's own business, or his friend Eenoolooapik. Seven years after returning to his Arctic home, Penny's friend died from tuberculosis.

Penny was knocked out of the whaling business for three years, but he hadn't given up. When he returned to the helm, this time on a new owner's ship, he went straight back to Cumberland Sound and returned to Aberdeen after killing nineteen whales in a single season, briefly boosting the industry's prospects. By the summer of 1846, just as Ross described from his sources, whaling captains working the Eastern Arctic were reporting unusually severe cold weather and extensive sea ice. The temperature rose above freezing for only twenty days and the normal breakup didn't come that year, leaving the pack so solid that whalers couldn't enter Lancaster Sound. In July of the following year, Penny took a shot at the eastern entrance to the Northwest Passage. The first try at finding Franklin and his men accomplished nothing. Penny couldn't have known it, but some five hundred miles southwest as the crow flies, *Erebus* and *Terror* were still stuck in summer ice, Franklin had been dead a matter of weeks, and his men were still months away from abandoning their ships. A carefully planned overland expedition might have had a better chance. The Arctic refused to let Penny through by sea.

"The whales having disappeared, I determined to proceed to Lancaster Sound, both with a view to the capture of whales and in search of her majesty's ships," Penny reported to the Admiralty. "I contended for a week against an adverse wind and a strong swell down the sound."

Still, the whaler kept trying.

"Being a little acquainted with the Esquimaux language, I made every enquiry of the various tribes I met at Pond's Bay, but could procure no information respecting Sir John Franklin, who, I think, must have attained a very high longitude."

Several years later, the Inuit of Cumberland Sound would tell Penny of white men who starved to death while heading for Great Fish River—a story too vague, of a place too distant, for him to know if there was anything to it. For a time, he kept the gruesome possibility to himself.

By MID-OCTOBER, Penny pulled up anchor off Baffin Island and sailed for home in Scotland. He would return to the archipelago in an onslaught of search expeditions, summoned by a force rivaling an Arctic that had stopped others before them: Lady Jane Franklin, Sir John's second wife. His first wife, Romantic poet Eleanor Anne Porden, died aged twenty-one, when Sir John was en route to the Arctic in 1825. Her friend Jane, who had admired Sir John from afar for years, was a woman who refused to be ignored or, worse, patronized. A powerful queen sat on the United Kingdom's throne, but Victorian social mores required other women to mind their words. Jane was supposed to occupy her troubled mind with prayer or domestic diversions, such as parlor games, drawing, or embroidering, while men handled weighty matters outside the cloistered world of the home. The male was, after all, intellectually superior; women's minds were clouded by emotion. That was the conventional view, but Lady Franklin would have none of it. If rules had to be broken, and important people's sensibilities offended, so be it. Her husband was missing, good men were lost with him, and she was going to do whatever it took to find them or find out what went wrong. Her relentless pressure, from any platform she could hold, with any means available, forced the longest, broadest, and most expensive search for two lost ships in maritime history.

Probably her most potent weapon was the pen, sharpened during a lifetime of obsessive journal writing. In letters to Benjamin Disraeli, a family friend and rising political star, as well as US President Zachary Taylor, she cajoled and sweet-talked two of the era's most powerful men to back her demands for costly and dangerous expeditions. Sometimes writing anonymously, she mobilized public opinion by deftly using newspapers, and literary allies including Charles Dickens, to stir popular outrage. Knowing that sympathy alone wouldn't get her far, Lady Franklin studied maps, consulted experienced polar explorers, and became a compelling Arctic expert herself. When that wasn't enough to get the quick results she wanted, Jane appealed to the paranormal for guidance. She spent most of her fortune, and made enemies of her own family members, to keep the search going. *The Athenaeum*, the establishment's favorite journal of literature, science, and fine arts, was so impressed by what she pulled off that it gave "Thanks to a feminine courage which no disaster could dismay, which arose above difficulties as a bird arises above the earth—which neither dulled nor wearied even when strong men grew faint and dubious."

The men blocking her way, throwing up walls of false reassurances and weak excuses, almost drove her mad. At first, when Sir John was still in the early stages of his expedition, Lady Franklin dealt with her husband's absence the same way she had done many times before: She went traveling. Starting out, Jane crossed the channel to France and then sailed the Atlantic with Eleanor to the West Indies and America, where they landed in the summer of 1846. Lady Franklin found Americans lacking in levity, telling a bishop she thought "the term 'Merry England' more appropriate than ever," because she "had never seen any social hilarity here, they had not time to get sociable at table—

their hurry however had one good aspect, that of self-denial of appetite." On her tour of factories, hospitals, and institutions for people unable to see, speak, or hear, she was often mistaken for the widow of founding father Alexander Hamilton. The fate of her husband's Arctic expedition was never far from mind, but conversations often turned to American preoccupations: the war with Mexico, which started that April; the Oregon Treaty reached in June with the British, setting the western border at the 49th parallel, except for Vancouver Island; and the debate over whether the United States should seize California, which rebelled against the Mexican government that summer and joined the Union in 1850.

In Boston, Lady Franklin bent the ear of Mayor Josiah Quincy Jr. for the rough reception that Dickens received from a fire-and-brimstone preacher. During the novelist's first visit to the United States in 1842, poet Henry Wadsworth Longfellow showed him around town. Their long Sunday-morning walk took them along the wharves where John Adams and the Sons of Liberty had dumped British tea chests into the sea during the Boston Tea Party. Dickens had a sharp eye, and ear, for the eccentric, so Longfellow took him to a service at the Seamen's Bethel church in North Square, where the Reverend E. T. Taylor ministered to his flock of grizzled sailors. He bellowed from the pulpit beneath theater curtains painted to show a shipwreck, with a small angel lowering a much bigger golden anchor, apparently to warn the sailors to beware moral shoals ready to ground them without warning in life. Spotting the strangers in their midst, the preacher clasped the Bible in his left hand and leveled a finger on his right at the novelist and poet. "Who are these—Who are they—who are these fellows?" he demanded to know. "Where do they come from? Where are they going to? Come from! What's the answer? . . . From below! From below, my brethren. From under the hatches of sin, battened down above you by the evil one. That's where you come from!"

Thumping his Bible, shouting to the heavens, the former mariner the sailors called Father Taylor declared: "And where are you going? Where are you going? Aloft! Aloft! Aloft! That's where you are going—with the fair wind—all taut and trim, steering direct for heaven in its glory, where there are no storms or foul weather, and where the wicked cease from troubling, and the weary are at rest. That's where you are going too, my friends. That's it. That's the place. That's the port. That's the haven. It's a blessed harbor. . . . Peace—Peace—Peace—all peace!"

When it was time for Lady Franklin to leave in August, Mayor Quincy was more comforting. He encouraged her with this wry thought: If her husband had made it through the Bering Strait, "it might be said he was the first man who ever got around Americans."

She craved any news, no matter how sketchy, of the expedition's progress. Back in London, a cryptic paragraph in the *Morning Herald* in early November caught Eleanor's eye. It claimed Eskimos had heard gunfire in the autumn of 1845. If it was in celebration of *Erebus* and *Terror* completing the passage, Eleanor wondered in a letter to her aunt, then "they all ought to have been home long ago. . . . We have now given up all expectation of hearing from Papa this year; in October or November next I trust we shall either see or hear from him."

As time ran out on 1846, the expedition was about to finish its first full year in the Arctic. There still was no word on its whereabouts, and Lady Franklin was bracing for bad news. She began to plan for the worst and asked Sir James Clark Ross if he was prepared to go searching for her husband and crewmen as he once had for lost Arctic whalers, in a heroic voyage aboard HMS *Cove* a decade earlier. She was just thinking that he might help if called on. The thought alone was sometimes comforting, she told him. "In your energy and friendship I have at all times the most unbounded reliance."

For the moment, she had stopped wishing for a vision.

"I sometimes think it is better perhaps that we should thus be in happy ignorance of any disaster that may have happened to them, or of any dreadful difficulty they may have yet to overcome than to be viewing as in a magic mirror in a fairy tale, their daily vicissitudes."

FOR MUCH OF 1847, when most of Franklin's officers and crew were still alive, there was little the men could do but try to stay warm and dry in the damp, cramped confines of *Erebus* and *Terror*. Franklin knew the lessons of wintering over, beset in sea ice, that Parry and Ross had passed on. So he likely kept his sailors busy cleaning, fixing, and attending the literacy classes he was so eager to hold. Small groups went out exploring and making magnetic observations that were an essential part of the mission. As long as Sir John's health held up in the weeks before he died that summer, he could have encouraged Fitzjames to dig into the library to find plays for the officers and crewmen to perform. And on Sundays, the most frightened among them might have found strength, even hope, in the commander's stirring sermons. Against the winter wind beating at the ships' heavy hulls, whistling through any cracks, they could sing hymns as a mate cranked the handle on one of the hand organs.

While the stranded mariners waited for the Arctic to release them, veteran polar explorers back in England quibbled over what, if anything, should be done to help. Ross was still pestering the Admiralty for permission to go searching for his friend. He took the silence from Franklin by mid-January of that year as proof that he hadn't made it through the Western Arctic and the Bering Strait. And, "in the second place, the probability is, that his ships have been carried by drift ice into a place from which they cannot be extricated," Ross told the Admiralty's Lords Commissioners. He was still bucking the institution that had humiliated him for his Croker Mountains mistake. The establishment was still dismissing his views. Ross turned to an influential intermediary.

"I have been induced to renew my application to my Lords Commissioners of the Admiralty mainly from the fact of my having promised to Sir John Franklin that I would volunteer to rescue him and his brave companions if not heard of in the spring of 1847," he protested to the Marquis of Northampton, head of the powerful Royal Society, on February 15.

The whalers were all back from Baffin Bay, without any sign of the Franklin Expedition. To Ross, that was yet another bad sign. It was likely "that the ships are either frozen up or that some misfortune has befallen them," Ross insisted. He wanted to start preparations immediately so that if nothing were heard by July 1, his expedition could set sail for Lancaster Sound. The marquis agreed to meet Ross and hear him out, only to dismiss him as he had earlier.

"It will be of no use sending you by sea to search for Franklin; you will be frozen in as he is, and we should have to send after you, and then perhaps for them that went to look for you!"

"Surely your Lordship does not mean to say that no steps should be taken to rescue Franklin?" Ross demanded.

No one wanted to be accused of abandoning a knighted hero and all of his men. Imagine the rabid press attacks. So the marquis relented and agreed to put Ross's letter in front of the Admiralty board. It had now been a year and a half since *Erebus* and *Terror* were last seen preparing to sail into the eastern entrance to the Northwest Passage. But when their chances of hearing good news were shrinking, the Lords were patient men. They also knew the wisdom of cutting one's losses. If Franklin and his men were trapped deep in the archipelago, there was little to gain with a rushed effort to try to find them, and much to lose if another costly mission failed. They were happy to wait on the diminishing prospect that Sir John would soon emerge from the Western Arctic to announce to an astonished world that he had made history.

Extrapolating from the Admiralty's original instructions to Franklin, and his understanding of Arctic weather and sea currents, Ross insisted that sea ice must have driven *Erebus* and *Terror* southward until their crews were forced to abandon them. He turned out to be correct, albeit early, on that prediction. Franklin's crews wouldn't give up their ships for another fifteen months. Ross also guessed, based on Parry's failed route more than a quarter century earlier, that Sir John had sailed farther west than he did. Survivors, Ross insisted, would therefore head for safety on Melville Island, so that is where he demanded to be sent. Which would have been another major mistake. Still, however impertinent, Ross's basic point—the urgent need for a rescue mission—was sound. The Admiralty, backed by most of the polar brotherhood, continued to ignore him.

Ross called the Admiralty's preferred option of offering rewards to induce whalers and the Hudson's Bay Company to search "utterly inefficient." He cited his own escape across "300 miles of much smoother ice" as proof that Franklin and his men could not possibly travel twice that distance from the High Arctic to the mainland.

"Unless I reach Melville Island next summer, they will have nothing," he warned.

Ross offered the Royal Navy a fair shot at averting catastrophe and the brass blew it. Once in the Arctic, where Ross could get a clearer sense of conditions, perhaps an opportunity to listen to Inuit witnesses, he might well have realized the errors in his assumptions. The Franklin Expedition status report written on the Admiralty form, which would have given a rescue mission a solid lead, was waiting on the same windswept coast where Ross's nephew James had erected a stone cairn. It would have been a logical place to check, since John Ross and Franklin had talked about doing precisely that. Blocked at every turn, certain that each day wasted only pushed lost men closer to death, Ross's promise to come looking for his friend reverberated in his vexed mind.

The Admiralty listened instead to the advice of Sir William Parry,

who had pioneered the route Franklin was ordered to follow, as long
as sea ice, and weather, permitted. It was too early to worry, Parry
assured the Lords. His own experience proved an expedition could
survive at least two winters. In a separate letter, Ross's nephew James
sided with Parry, repeating the officers' assurances, before departing
Greenland, "that they had taken on board provisions for three years
on full allowance, which they could extend to four years without any
inconvenience." He also recommended that two rescue ships should
be specially prepared, as *Erebus* and *Terror* had been for his Antarctic voyage, and if none were available, two should be purpose-built for
the mission. Parry disagreed and argued strongly against mounting
another major attempt at the Northwest Passage by sea. He made the
case for traveling overland, with expert guides, to try to pick up the
Franklin Expedition's trail.

"I do not think that anything further can be done by ships, except
at a heavy expense, and virtually involving the exposure of a second expedition to the risks inseparable from such an enterprise," he
advised the Admiralty. "The only plan which appears to me to hold
out a reasonable prospect of success, is by making an effort to push
supplies to the northern coast of the American Continent, and the
islands adjacent thereto, with the assistance of the Hudson's Bay
Company, and by the modes of travelling in ordinary use among their
servants."

Parry's plan had a hidden advantage: Launched at the right time,
with enough support to survive for more than a few months, it might
well have followed fresh clues from Inuit and found Franklin survivors moving south as searchers headed north. Instead, the protracted
debate led in the wrong direction. The longer the explorers were gone,
without any hard facts, the more people speculated. That opened
the dam on a torrent of unwelcome advice and criticism. The mighty
Royal Navy had little patience for second-guessing, especially when it
seemed to come from crackpots. Some of the best unsolicited advice

came from a brilliant eccentric easily disregarded. Dr. Richard King was the Arctic Cassandra in Victorian times.

He had a knack for annoying people who disagreed with him, which made enemies across the exploration establishment—in the Royal Geographical Society, the Hudson's Bay Company, as well as the Royal Navy. Trouble is, King also had an uncanny ability to read the Arctic, which could have helped the lost Franklin Expedition if decision-makers hadn't loathed the messenger so deeply. Early on, for instance, King predicted accurately that Boothia was a peninsula. He had a deep interest in indigenous culture and believed, as he heard from Inuit while exploring with Sir George Back, that the best route for a Northwest Passage was along the North American coast—not the phantom Open Polar Sea that the navy sought. The physician also had an innate sense of the Arctic's layout. He accurately pre-dicted the rough locations of some undiscovered landmasses without seeing them.

Dr. King's medical specialty was obstetrics, but he was also an accomplished explorer, ethnologist, and geographer. When the Rosses and their crew were in their fourth year stranded with *Victory*, the doctor served as naturalist and surgeon on the Back overland expedi-tion that ended up surveying the northern coast after whalers reached the men first and rescued them. King, like Scoresby, thought it was smarter to travel light in the Arctic, which pitted him not only against the Admiralty but also against the expedition commander. When speculation was rife about the fate of *Erebus* and *Terror*, the doctor drew a map that foresaw Victoria Island blocking the route that the Admiralty insisted the ships should take. Before they sailed, King warned Barrow that he was sending Franklin "to form the nucleus of an iceberg." Once he was certain they were stuck, King was no more diplomatic.

"My Lord, one hundred and thirty-eight men at this moment are in danger of perishing from famine," the pesky doctor told Colonial

Secretary Earl Grey in a letter dated June 10, 1847, the day before
Franklin died.

The doctor was off on the number of men at risk but closer than
most in suggesting where they could be found and "saved from the
death of starvation."

"The position, then, that I should assign to the lost expedition
is . . . midway between the Hudson Bay Company settlements on the
Mackenzie (River) and the fishing grounds of the whalers in Barrow
Strait."

More specifically, by a lucky guess or some mysterious revelation,
he placed *Erebus* and *Terror* west of Somerset Island, which Parry had
visited almost three decades earlier. Franklin had in fact sailed south
along the western coast of Somerset, through Peel Sound, but by the
time King was writing, the expedition commander was farther south,
close to death off the tip of King William Island. The colonial secretary passed the obstetrician on to the Admiralty, which wasn't interested. Had it listened, lives might well have been saved. King wanted
to lead a rescue team overland to the Great Fish River, where he'd been
with Back, carrying food and other supplies to cache for any Franklin
Expedition survivors who might make it that far. Ten months later,
they would set off for exactly where King wanted to go to help them.

THINGS WERE ONLY getting worse in the High Arctic. As summer
gave way to another winter in 1847, the captain of the 313-ton *Lady Jane*,
one of the British whaling fleet's most successful vessels, reported that
sea ice in the approach to the Northwest Passage was unusually thick
and heavy.

"In places where it has been generally found six feet thick, this year
it was ten feet; and this the natives accounted for by the wind having
prevailed so much from the south-east all the winter, which pressed
the ice upon the west land."

Those best placed to act had more to talk about. The debate among experts competing for the Admiralty's ear droned on. They couldn't even agree on where to look, let alone when to start and how best to do it. What remained of Lady Franklin's forbearance finally ran out. Frustrated by the male dithering, she did her best to embarrass them with her own courage. She volunteered to make the voyage to the Arctic herself. Her idea was to join a search by land from a Hudson's Bay Company outpost, and be ready to care for her husband if anyone managed to find him. Coming from another woman, that might have sounded like the unhinged ramblings of a distraught mind. But Lady Franklin knew what hard travel was all about.

Years earlier, she had earned considerable respect, while raising a lot of troubled moralists' eyebrows, with some courageous exploring of her own. Sailing the Aegean Sea on a *goletta* schooner, she slept atop the stores in the hold next to thirty-two sheep and goats. She joined an expedition up the Nile, dined at a harem, and, after a drenching rain, slept with rats "who, in spite of mosquito [nets] laid their claws on my head repeatedly, jumping on till beat off—the havoc and sound they were making was dreadful." A German missionary taught her some Arabic and verses of the Koran. She rode with him on a raft of date-tree trunks, crawled into a mummy pit, and suffered through a hurricane in his arms. Three camels carried her on a litter to Mount Sinai. She even crossed the Levant to Damascus when communal tensions were running high. A married Christian woman traveling without her husband was not only rare but risky.

Heading from Alexandria to the Holy Land, Jane carried letters of approval from Muhammad Ali Pasha, the Ottoman ruler of Egypt, to his officials in Syria. Good fortune got her through alive and unharmed. At Haifa, she came "within the sight & sound of actual war" for the first time. She mounted a donkey and headed to Nazareth, her head covered by a cotton cambric handkerchief folded over a *tarboosh*, or fez. Her retinue consisted of a guide, an Egyptian servant, five Janissaries (elite Ottoman Turkish soldiers), and a dozen Bedouin. Between Jaffa and Jerusalem, Jane's host was Abou-Gosh, whom she called the "Prince of Robbers." Patting her on the back, he assured his guest the whole country was hers. She kept a close eye on her belongings just the same. When she reached Jericho, on the West Bank of the Jordan River, Jane wished she could share the experience with her sister Mary—until an especially trying night that she "will not wish on my cruelest enemy."

"It was not, therefore, in order to herd with us under a filthy shed, with our horses and Bedouins, obliged to cling close under the dwarf-walls of the most wretched of villages in order to be safe from robbers, devoured by mosquitos, so entirely lame in one inflamed leg in consequence that I was obliged to be carried whenever I moved or got up, and suffering much in head and stomach besides from having been eight hours on horseback under a hot and unshaded sun."

After a night's sleep with a poultice on her leg, Jane's spirit was back. Her heart raced from the adrenaline rush of the mounted guards "exciting one another by wild screams; letting off their muskets and pistols, balancing and thrusting their lances at full gallop, wheeling, pursuing, receding, sweeping across our path. . . ."

Lady Franklin knew how to travel rough and get the best out of it. She could only imagine how brutal the cold and deprivation of the High Arctic could be. Still, she longed to go where her husband was. Maybe, in her darkest thoughts, she knew he wasn't coming home and hoped the Arctic would take her too. Experienced polar explorers talked Lady Franklin into staying home, for a time at least. So she poured all of her strength, and considerable powers of persuasion, into lobbying. In her first moves, she made an end run around her government, defying its staid protocols and the Royal Navy's plodding bureaucracy. Jane appealed to a potential American donor, confiding that she had lost hope in bureaucrats and their political bosses, "for Governments are not so tenderhearted as you and I are." Wary of closing any door, she assured him that "there is no trial I am not prepared to go through if it become necessary."

King kept up his battle of wills with the Royal Navy well into 1848. He pleaded for permission to proceed by March 18, the deadline he calculated for leaving in time to reach the search area he mapped out before the next winter set in. He got the same cold shoulder that John Ross repeatedly ran into.

"I am commanded by my Lords Commissioners of the Admiralty, to acquaint you that they have no intention of altering their present arrangements, or of making any others that will require your assistance or force you to make the sacrifices which you appear to contemplate," came the aloof reply from an aide on March 3, 1848.

They weren't alone in dismissing King's advice. Lady Franklin didn't support his plan. Neither did John Ross. Only Frederick Beechey, Franklin's former companion in exploration, backed the physician, who was mostly barking at a brick wall. But the dissent was opening Jane's ears to other views, some more unorthodox than others, and stiffening the resolve to get things done her way, in search areas she decided were most promising.

"I do not desire that he should be the person employed," she wrote to James Ross, "but I cannot but wish that the Hudson's Bay Company might receive instructions or a request from Govt. to explore those parts which you & Sir J. Richardson cannot immediately do, & which if done by you at all, can only be when other explorations have been made in vain—And then, does he *not* say truly, it will be *too late*?"

Most experts believed any hunt should focus on Wellington Channel between Devon and Cornwallis Islands. But early in the debate, Lady Franklin switched and sided with the minority view that searchers must instead concentrate their efforts farther south and east. She, like John Ross and King, was closer to the mark. Long before anyone discovered the expedition's curt note at Victory Point, Jane suggested to supporters in the United States, in an analysis copied to the Admiralty, that the North American Arctic coastline was the best place to go. The area she mapped out included the stretch between the Coppermine and Great Fish Rivers, the latter being precisely where Captain Fitzjames, with a shaky hand, wrote that he and other survivors were heading. For Lady Franklin, some of the most persuasive voices spoke from the spirit world.

With nothing but ominous silence from *Erebus* or *Terror*, another winter came, along with prayers that the men might have found a way to survive the cold. There was still reason to hope. This winter seemed relatively warmer. To John Ross, that meant an Arctic opening, maybe a final chance, "especially as it is on record that a mild is always succeeded by a severe winter (which unfortunately took place in 1847–8)." It made no difference whether he was right or wrong about that. The Admiralty didn't seem to care what he thought. It wasn't until Ross's nephew James broke his promise to his wife to stay away from the Arctic, and volunteered to go looking for the lost expedition, that the government finally decided to act. He made his offer in writing on November 8, 1847. The Admiralty accepted three weeks later, notifying Sir James that it intended to name him commander of an expedition to Baffin Bay, as part of a three-pronged rescue effort. But the expedition couldn't be launched until the following year, and an early winter could push the search back several months more while ships waited for the sea ice to open.

"How can anyone speak of 1849?" Lady Franklin asked in despair.

The Admiralty bungled its grudging start to the hunt so badly that Jane would suffer the anguish of not knowing where her husband was, or whether he was even alive, for much longer than that. The first of three search missions headed for the Western Arctic. Commander Thomas Moore, aboard the 213-ton storeship HMS *Plover*, left Plymouth at the end of January 1848. He had experience in polar navigation, serving first as a mate on Ross's Antarctic expedition, then commanding a follow-up voyage and also doing a magnetic survey in northern Canada. But the *Plover* was not built for speed. She made such slow headway that Moore took eight months to reach the Sandwich Islands in the Pacific. That was too late for him to attempt a voyage above the Arctic Circle that year. Along with relief supplies for the Franklin Expedition, Moore was carrying letters from Jane to her husband, and she asked others who sent messages "to say nothing whatever that can distress his mind—who can tell whether they will be in a state of body or mind to bear it."

Moore couldn't deliver the letters, or the supplies, and missed his assigned rendezvous with HMS *Herald*, commanded by Captain Henry Kellett. Another Opium War veteran, he was doing survey work in the Pacific when the order came to go looking for Franklin and his men. Neither his ship nor the crew was prepared for winter or exploring in ice. In several years of searching, Moore and Kellett got no closer to the missing sailors than chasing down false sightings reported by Inuit.

Physicians Sir John Richardson and John Rae, then a chief factor at the Hudson's Bay Company, headed the search's second division. They made their hazardous journey north across wild land—first through the western Barren Lands to Great Slave Lake, then north via the Mackenzie River, Canada's largest and longest river system. Second only in the continental stakes to the more languorous Mississippi, the Mackenzie experiences northern storms that can whip it up into a mania. It can capsize a canoe as easily as a child flipping a coin. Rae and Richardson journeyed in two canoes, with eight voyageurs as paddlers and guides. The group finally reached the Arctic coast in September, right on time for winter.

Far to the northeast of them, Franklin Expedition survivors were in their fifth month trudging south across King William Island's snow and ice, which in late summer normally gave way to gray, sharp-edged limestone and sucking mud. When winter lingered long, snow and ice remained. Sailors who had spent lifetimes on the water, some of them starting as child cabin boys, could scurry up rigging in a storm like spiders up a wet wall or keep their balance on a tossing deck, in the foaming wash of pounding waves, as deftly as if they had tentacles on their feet. Franklin's toughest men, the ones with the best chance of getting home, were sea creatures with limbs made for survival in oceans. Now their lives depended on walking, cursing the land for as long as they could keep going against the searing pain of frostbite, hunger, and whatever else the Arctic threw at them.

The searchers tried to reach the southwestern tip of Victoria Island (then known as Wollaston Land) in small boats, but they couldn't penetrate the ice. A huge barrier to mariners, Victoria Island stands like a big stop sign in the middle of the Arctic Archipelago. The world's eighth largest island, its east coast is just across Victoria Strait from King William Island, where Franklin Expedition survivors tried to make their escape. But the stretch of southern coast that Rae and Richardson had hoped to explore, near the mouth of the Coppermine River, was far from where *Erebus* and *Terror* were beset. The two explorers were able to speak with hundreds of Inuit, from several groups, but to no avail. The doctors found not a trace. Rae eventually met up with Moore, only to be disgusted by the Royal Navy officer's ill-disciplined diversions when he had been sent to look for dying men. The Hudson's Bay Company factor dressed the captain down for keeping an Inuit girl in his cabin, "for purposes which were all too evident," and for "selling spirits to the natives, and cheating them as much or more than the most rascally fur trader ever heard of."

FRUSTRATED BY the long wait for action, Lady Franklin didn't let up when the first, tentative hunt for her husband and his men began. The government had started paying her Sir John's "vacant good service pension." She didn't like it, but she accepted the gesture as an honor. She would soon need every penny she could get her hands on to fund the search the Admiralty was so reluctant to order, only to lose interest as one search expedition after another failed to find anyone alive. She tapped the family fortune to offer a substantial reward of £3,000, or more than $270,000 today, to any whalers who either found the expedition or gave it an extraordinary try. But Jane also put her faith in the third component of the navy's plan, the most expensive and risky. Sir James Ross sailed for the Eastern Arctic with two ships, HMS *Enterprise* and HMS *Investigator*. His orders were to follow the same route that the Admiralty told Franklin to navigate, as far west as Wellington Channel. Ross and his men wintered over in Somerset Island's Leopold Harbour and searched tirelessly, with teams of men dragging their food and supplies on heavy sledges in countless directions. They even tied notes around foxes' necks, hoping the missing seamen would find one and follow the directions to the rescue mission's base camp. In the end, all Ross found were the provisions he had left at Fury Beach sixteen years earlier, when ice had its hold on his uncle's ship, *Victory*. The younger Ross now tried sailing farther west. He was eager to deliver some important mail: a letter from Lady Franklin, written in a hurry, to her lost husband.

"My dearest love," it read, "May it be the will of God if you are not restored to us earlier that you should open this letter & that it may give you comfort in all your trials. . . . May you have found your refuge & strength in Him whose mercies you have so often experienced when every human aid was gone. . . I try to prepare myself for every trial which may be in store for me, but dearest, if you ever open this, it will be I trust because I have been spared the greatest of all. . . ."

Expecting Sir John to be miserable, or worse, after unimaginable tribulations, Jane sent along some copies of the *Illustrated London News* to lighten his mind. She offered a summary to get him caught up on the wider world, mostly about upheaval in Europe as decrepit monarchies tottered. She must have thought a good shot of British pride would be a powerful elixir, writing that "almost all the kingdoms of

Europe (are) in commotion, England alone steady & erect amidst the crash of thrones and dynasties." She talked about a trip to the country, prayers from the bishop of Tasmania and his flock, and why she couldn't be in the Arctic to help get him home. Jane sounded haunted by guilt for being so far away from the man she had urged to challenge the Arctic once more.

"It would have been a less trial to me to come after you, as I was at one time tempted to do, but I thought it my duty & my interest to remain, for might I not have missed you, & wd it have been right to leave Eleanor—yet if I had thought you to be ill, nothing should have stopped me.

"God bless you again," she closed. "You will be welcomed back with joy & honor by your friends & family & country—*most* of all by your affect & devoted wife."

Eleanor, who would soon be married without a father at her side, assured Sir John in a separate note, carried by another relief expedition: "Mama has been very active in stirring up people to consider the necessity of searching every where at once."

Sir James Ross never found anyone to receive Lady Franklin's letter. He didn't even get close. His ships couldn't get through a barrier of sea ice. Rather than risk more good men's lives, he gave up and headed back to London, where he returned the letter to Jane. Wherever her husband was, entombed in the permafrost, refrigerated in the dark cold of his cabin-cum-morgue at *Erebus*'s stern, or buried at sea, he could only communicate now if the dead could talk. Jane believed they very well might and would try hard to reach him on the other side.

THE EXPEDITIONS' dwindling survivors were still fighting the Arctic winter when they set out on their final journey in April 1848. In the first leg, they hauled boats, at least one a lifeboat twenty-eight feet long, modified for shallow water and lashed to a heavy sledge. Crewmen dragged it, loaded down with supplies and equipment, some fifteen miles across the ice-covered Victoria Strait. Then they left it near the site of the sailors' first landfall, just above the high-tide mark, on King William Island. When it was discovered more than a decade later, two partial skeletons lay inside the boat, which was pointing toward the spot where *Erebus* and *Terror* were surrendered to the sea ice. Eight pairs of boots were left behind, along with numerous abandoned items that included soap, towels, tobacco, and silk handkerchiefs. Near them were two double-barreled rifles, a barrel in each weapon loaded and cocked, standing muzzle-up against the side of the lifeboat.

Slipping and sliding on ice and hard snow in thin-soled leather seaboots, the survivors had lowered their shoulders against howling, whirling winds and blizzards. Or, if the sky was clear, they squinted against the blinding, disorienting sunlight that reflected off the never-ending white stretched out all around them. Climbing up and over pressure ridges that might as well have been mountains, they limped deeper into the unknown, praying for a way home. Sometimes they sang for strength against the pain. Among the boatloads of things the seamen had brought from *Erebus* and *Terror* were pocket-size Christian books, including a Holy Bible, the New Testament in French, a prayer book with a black leather cover and a gold-tooled spine, the Book of Common Prayer, and hymnbooks.

Along with those comforts for the soul, the men carried countless personal necessities, such as pocket watches, a toothbrush, a clay pipe, an ivory-handled table knife, and other silverware engraved with family crests, including a silver fiddle-patterned tablespoon bearing the Franklin family crest. The sailors also packed seaboots, seventy kilos of chocolate, a lacquered tea canister, a clothes brush with an ivory veneer wooden handle, a cobbler's awl, several packets of F. Barnes and Co. sewing needles, a polished flint with an elegantly curved steel handle for sparking fires, a pair of tweezers for collecting specimens, and a brass instrument used to measure magnetic dip.

Farther along the survivors' route south, among the many more castoffs from the Franklin Expedition was a seaboot with a square toe and rounded at the top to fit a man's calf. Slightly torn at the back, top edge, where a sailor might have yanked on damp leather to pull the boot onto a swollen foot, it was also split along the stitching from the ankle about midway to the toe. The sole had almost peeled off. The boot was among shoes, pieces of Royal Navy uniforms, buttons, and other things discarded far to the south of the abandoned ships on the Adelaide Peninsula. At least some of Franklin's men had made it to the mainland, but they were stopped dead in their tracks. But by what? And when?

They were the strongest of strong men, the ones who had made it into at least one last summer, trudging ahead through the muck and the torture of frostbitten toes, patching tattered clothes while resting, sometimes dying, at campsites along the western shoreline, which was strewn with knife-edged limestone rocks, gravel, and sand. The dangers were many—whether from hunger, disease, polar madness, or polar bears able to pick up a tiny whiff of human scent from miles away and stalk their plodding prey for days before lunging to kill. The unseen, the ghostly sounds or fleeting, fractured visions, could have been the most frightening of the Arctic's threats. Inuit elders tell of spirits that wander King William Island and inhabit the seas that surround it. They must be respected and, if necessary, appeased. Their wrath is severe.

The most stubborn sailors may have decided they'd had enough and returned to *Erebus*. By then, she could have been drifting free, as *Terror* finally had done under Sir George Back a dozen years earlier, buffered against colliding floes by a rock-solid apron of sea ice. One way or another, she and the *Terror* were heading south just like the men who had forsaken her. There were signs that Neptune, the loyal Newfoundland dog, might have been among the last to die, with natural skills for survival if humans weren't able to provide. A pet built like a small long-haired bear before food became scarce, or maybe a newly found canine companion passed along from an Inuit team, apparently came with the *qalunaaq* to reboard *Erebus*, far from where the seamen first surrendered her to the ice. As they approached their once-invincible vessel, silent but for the incessant creaking of her timbers and the wind whistling through her masts, she must have towered over them like a ghost ship.

5

Lady Franklin's Mission

No one who knew ice expected *Erebus* and *Terror* to stay where their crews abandoned them. Even sea ice that looks solid as far as the eye can see, a frozen prison for two Royal Navy bomb ships closing in on two years, is almost continually moving. The exception is "fast ice," which grows out from the shore and remains attached to land. The Franklin Expedition vessels were far from the coast when they were abandoned, where wind, ocean currents, the shifting water surface beneath the ice, and internal stresses within the ice itself all caused the stranded ships to creep. *Erebus* and *Terror* not only moved, they separated from each other. The dynamics of sea ice, following unique habits and rules of a world modern scientists know as the cryosphere, made it all the more complicated to track them down.

Ice is an obstacle few outsiders even try to understand in its confounding, immaculate complexity. Knowing that it's cold, hard, and slippery, and chills food and drinks nicely, is good enough for most of us. Lady Franklin was different. Ice was on her list of things to figure out while recognized polar experts rattled on and stalled. She refused to wait around and worry about what might have happened to Sir John and his crewmen. Ross and Richardson tried to calm her, as Sir John had asked. The Admiralty mailed its own anodyne reassurances. But attempts to tamp down the fire in her heart, the counsel for patience over impetuousness, only infuriated her. If others refused to act, she herself would.

Jane set out to learn as much as she could, and to use that knowledge as power to shape decisions that might determine the missing men's fate. She ended up making some of the most important choices herself. Still, of all the places a Victorian woman didn't belong, the Arctic and the Admiralty were two of the toughest male bastions to penetrate. At the start of her own Arctic odyssey, the confounding realities of how seawater behaves when it cools to around 28 degrees Fahrenheit and freezes into crystals were the least of Lady Franklin's problems. Yet her first stop was to consult the man who was probably Britain's leading specialist in the arcane study of sea ice: William Scoresby Jr., for whom she had the deepest respect. His scientific knowledge and experience of the Arctic, his uncanny ability to read her capricious moods and understand the intricacies of sea ice, made Charles Darwin a fan. Even the fictional sailor Ishmael in Herman Melville's *Moby-Dick* quotes Scoresby on the complexities of cetology.

"He was always my hero," Lady Franklin said of Scoresby, a whaler-turned-scientist-turned-reverend.

By early 1849, Lady Franklin was "much out of health and in deep despondency," Sophy confided. Yet the women packed up some food and other provisions and went to meet whalers back home for the summer in Scottish ports to see if they knew anything useful and to spread word about the reward. Hoping to pass unnoticed, Lady Franklin and Sophy traveled north by sea with luggage tagged only by Sophy's last name, Cracroft. Although a tentative search effort was under way, experts were still engaged in a frustrating argument about where *Erebus* and *Terror* might be. Most were confident that Wellington Channel was the best place to look. They were wrong. Tired of the bureaucratic song and dance, Lady Franklin wanted to get a reality check and talk with seamen who had actually been in the Arctic recently. The Franklin Expedition's three years of provisions had either run out by now, or, as King had warned, survivors were starving and succumbing to scurvy.

The mass-circulation press was catching on in Britain. With well over a dozen newspapers competing for readers in London alone, and publishers defying regulations in a rush to print more, reporters were on the lookout for scandalous news to feed the public's growing appetite. A distraught Lady Franklin conspiring with scruffy whalers against the fusty Admiralty would make a good headline. She and Sophy had to keep a low profile in Edinburgh, so they stayed in squalid lodgings and dined with as much privacy as possible. The women slipped out to meet with Scoresby, who escorted them to Hull, a prosperous whaling port in northern England that was in the early years of steady decline. Her offer of more money for help in the Franklin search was welcome. A deal to get a whaling ship involved quickly made news in London, where editors of the highbrow *Athenaeum* put it at the top of its "Our Weekly Gossip" column.

"The whaler *Abram* is now being strengthened and equipped at Hull with the view of searching Jones Sound and vicinity. Lady Franklin offers a special reward for this service. The *Abram* will sail in a few days with a very effective crew. It is affecting to observe the restless energy with which Lady Franklin devotes herself to the task of soliciting aid in all directions for the effectual search of those seas to which her busy hopes and fears are unceasingly directed. The knight-errantry of the world is summoned by her on this path of adventure."

The *Abram* didn't have any better luck hunting by sea than Richardson and Rae had on land. Scoresby thought the Admiralty had blown its best chance of an early, exhaustive search effort. At Skaill, on the Atlantic coast of Orkney, Scotland, a returning sailor from the whaler *Truelove* tantalized the ladies with a tale of an Inuit sighting of Sir John and his ships in March 1849. There was even a hand-drawn map locating the expedition in Prince Regent Inlet. Sea ice prevented the *Truelove* getting close enough to check out the story, but the crew left a cache of food and coal that Lady Franklin had provided. Sophy was skeptical.

"My dearest Aunt bore the surprise almost better than I expected and was very able to cross question the sailor. I try to instill doubts into her mind of the truth of the *whole details*, tho' I think some must be true, and she receives very readily what I say."

Sir John was long dead by that spring. *Erebus* and *Terror* had been abandoned a year earlier. But confirmation of those sad truths wouldn't come for another decade, which left Lady Franklin and the British public vulnerable to all sorts of false leads and cruel hoaxes.

Scoresby aimed his disdain at the Admiralty. When it followed Lady Franklin's incentive and offered a reward to spur a private search effort, the Lords were a day late and a dollar short once again. In 1848, Lady Franklin had offered £2,000, which she raised to £3,000 (or more than $270,000 today) in the spring of 1849. The government put up £20,000 ($1.8 million today) as an inducement on March 23, 1849. That would have been an impressive sum if the naval command had put it on the table much earlier. Instead, they offered the reward "*after* most of the whalers had sailed, and were therefore without orders or authority for departing from the usual fishing grounds," Scoresby complained. "And, secondly, the reward was only claimable on the absolute condition of a successful search—a contingency so great as by no means to justify, in a commercial venture, the sacrificing of the interests of a voyage undertaken at so much cost and risk." If the Admiralty had done things Lady Franklin's way, and offered to reward extraordinary efforts or special searches remote from regular fishing grounds, "something effective would, no doubt, have been attempted," Scoresby concluded. Public sympathy, common humanity, and justice also demanded a better effort, he insisted, "*to the most liberal extent* possible consistent with reasonable practicability, remaining hope, and the fair prospect of safety to new adventurers."

That spring, Lady Franklin had raised establishment eyebrows by writing directly to US President Zachary Taylor. The son of a wealthy Virginia tobacco-plantation owner, Taylor was a career military officer who had fought in frontier wars against Native Americans. Known as "Old Rough and Ready," he was a hero of the Mexican War, which vaulted him into the Oval Office. Taylor also held scores of slaves, on two plantations in Louisiana and Mississippi, yet he butted heads with Congress over his insistence that new states in the West be slave-free. With anger boiling in the southern states, Taylor was still new in office and the threat of secession was only one of the urgent problems he had to juggle. That made it all the more audacious for Jane to insist on forcing onto his agenda a British expedition in the High Arctic.

Lady Franklin knew a few things about politics and persuasion, which took particular skill when trying to persuade an American leader with little schooling who had never voted in a presidential election until the one that put him in power. She played to the president's patriotism in a long letter she wrote in April 1849.

"I address myself to you as the head of a great nation," Jane began her appeal to him in the spring of 1849. To soften Taylor up a bit, she recalled her visit to the United States three years earlier and related how touched she was by Americans' appreciation for her husband's exploration. She provided the president a fairly detailed history of the expedition that was now causing so much worry. The Admiralty was trying to help and at great cost, she acknowledged. Yet valuable time had been lost, critical opportunities wasted. She now had more hope in American whalers "and the bold spirit of adventure which animates their crews. But I venture to look even beyond these. I am not without hope that you will deem it not unworthy of a great and kindred nation take up the cause of humanity which I plead in a national spirit, and thus generously make it your own."

Tweaking American pride, she let drop that the Imperial Russian government had offered to help, through its ambassador in London, by sending out exploring parties from the Western Arctic. Why not, Lady Franklin suggested, get the British, Americans, and Russians to cooperate together on such an important humanitarian mission?

"It would be a noble spectacle to the world," she tried to persuade the president, "if these three great nations, possessed of the widest empires on the face of the globe, were thus to unite their efforts in the truly Christian work of saving their perishing fellow men from destruction." Of course, if "American seamen had the good fortune to wrest from us the glory (as might be the case) of solving the problem of the unfound passage, or the still greater glory of saving our adventurous navigators from a lingering fate which the mind sickens to dwell on," then good for them. The Admiralty's critics suspected the Royal Navy and its chosen rescuers might be more interested in finding the Northwest Passage than dying men. Jane, with the skills of an adroit diplomat, was betting a strong dose of American competition could solve that problem.

Lady Franklin ended with an apology. She was, after all, a Victorian woman who was straining the boundaries of decorum and diplomacy with a personal appeal to an American president. She was also desperate, and she feared the tortured death of her husband and his men far more than being rebuked for trampling on official toes.

"The intense anxieties of a wife and of a daughter may have led me to press too earnestly on your notice . . . and to presume too much on the sympathy which we are assured is felt beyond the limits of our own land. Yet if you deem this to be the case, you will still find I am sure, even in that personal intensity of feeling, an excuse for the fearlessness with which I have thrown myself on your generosity, and will pardon the homage I thus pay to your own high character, and to that of the people over whom you have the distinction to preside."

The letter got Taylor's attention, which unfortunately didn't get Lady Franklin far. No fault of her own. The following year, after celebrating a sweltering Independence Day with a meal of cherries, raw vegetables, and milk at the unfinished Washington Monument, the president fell sick with acute gastroenteritis and died. But before Taylor's untimely demise, the president passed Jane's letter to his recently appointed Secretary of State, John M. Clayton, a Yale graduate, lawyer, and former senator from Delaware. He praised Jane's cri de coeur as one that "would strongly enlist the sympathy of the rulers and people of any portion of the civilized world."

Americans had watched "with the deepest interest that hazardous enterprise" that Sir John and his men had undertaken and were, he assured her, united in wanting their government to make every proper effort for a rescue. American navigators, especially whalers, would be called to action. Clayton promised that "all that the executive government of the United States, in the exercise of its constitutional powers, can effect to meet this requisition on American enterprise, skill and bravery, will be promptly undertaken." American and British newspapers gave it great play. Jane was thrilled that her gambit had worked. Yet more months passed. And nothing happened.

THE BUREAUCRATIC SHUFFLE was infuriating. The temporal world simply refused to cooperate. Desperate for something that would break her string of bad luck, Lady Franklin turned to the spiritual realm. The paranormal had a powerful attraction in the Victorian era, when science and religion were both swept up in rapid social, economic, and technological change. To the scientific establishment, superstition clashed with the effort to uncover and apply natural laws based on empirical evidence. But others eager to challenge orthodoxy, and explore any horizon they could imagine, insisted that talk of ghosts, seers, and astral travelers should be examined like any other unexplained occurrence. Among them were respectable writers and thinkers who argued that paranormal phenomena should not be dismissed unless investigated with the same rigor as anything else in the natural world.

If there was anything credible to it, sorting out good from bad was messy work. Scam artists and showmen used séances and levitations to profit from the gullible. The Franklin mystery was too popular for swindlers and sincere devotees of the occult to resist. Well over a dozen clairvoyants and seers in Britain, the United States, and Australia—at least ten of them known by name—claimed to have gleaned information about the lost Franklin Expedition through paranormal contacts. Skeptics abounded, but so did believers. Lady Franklin was on both sides of the fence, depending on how she judged the information and who was delivering it. That wasn't unusual among the Victorian upper classes, where publicly sniffing at the notion of communicating with the dead did not preclude a discreet night of table tapping at a séance. Even Jane's hero, the quiet and cerebral Scoresby, dabbled in experiments with animal magnetism, which he preferred to call "zoistic magnetism."

Spectral beings. Clairvoyants in trances leaving their bodies and flying like birds over great distances. The healing properties of animal magnetism. The whole supernatural world was the stuff of lively, entertaining debate in the salons of mid-nineteenth-century Europe. It filled many column inches in the popular press, and seats in theaters, which prospered from pseudoscientific spectacles, such as mesmerists claiming to treat patients on stage by manipulating invisible energy fields. The word *scientist* was less than two decades old when Jane attended séances in the hope of making contact with her husband. It couldn't have been an easy choice for the highly regarded wife of a devout evangelical Christian who was willing to sacrifice his life to advance scientific discovery. But to many of the era, there was no contradiction in that. Those who believed in communicating with ghosts just as strongly as they did praying to God found elements of the miraculous in the paranormal. Some thinkers attacked spiritualists with science while others used science to defend them. Whole journals were devoted to exploring the science of the supernatural. Others went into just as much depth debunking them.

The notion that energy could be naturally transferred from inanimate objects to animals, so-called animal magnetism, was born of medicine. German physician Franz Mesmer tried to cure serious illnesses in late-eighteenth-century Paris by unblocking this mysterious universal flow of energy that he believed was coursing through, and around, his patients. With a theatrical flair, he moved his hand about the body of a sufferer sitting in a large vat, holding iron rods. That was the basis of mesmerism, whose followers believed spiritualists could tap into invisible magnetic fluids that carried disembodied intelligence, the forerunner of hypnotism in Western medicine. Dr. James Esdaile, former assistant surgeon to the East India Company, swore by the healing powers of clairvoyant mesmerism, which he had studied in India. The physician published monthly newspaper reports defending spiritualism in his London practice and rallied popular support against attackers by denouncing what he called "the orthodox medical howl raised against me."

"These terrorists pretend that, because persons under the mesmeric influence cease for the time to be voluntary and responsible beings, and occasionally exhibit powers and acquire knowledge beyond their reach in their ordinary state of existence, therefore Mesmerism is synonymous with Atheism, seeing that it divests man of his responsibility, and invests him with powers hitherto supposed to be the exclusive attributes of God.

"These would-be leaders of the medical profession," Esdaile huffed, "and dictators of public opinion, are either grossly ignorant of various medical facts bearing upon and illustrating the subject, or willfully suppress the knowledge of them, in their eagerness to destroy those who differ from them in opinion."

Frustrated by officials, torn by conflicting expert advice, and suffering under intense emotional pressure, Lady Franklin was vulnerable to psychic suggestion, whether from well-meaning believers or from manipulative charlatans. She had worked hard to get her aging husband the command of the expedition that was supposed to rehabilitate him. Now, she realized, it may well have killed him. She couldn't just be the good navy wife and get on with life. Known for being high-strung in the best of circumstances, she was now becoming obsessed. For a woman determined to try anything to get her husband back, seeking contact through a clairvoyant seemed as good an option as any.

On a May evening, Jane went with Sophy and her sister Fanny's husband, Ashurst Majendie, to the Duke Street home of surgeon J. Hands on Grosvenor Square, where John Adams set up the late-eighteenth-century American mission to the Court of St. James. At 8 p.m., they had their first appointment with Ellen Dawson. The maid of another client described Dawson as "a young, pale sickly looking girl," but the clairvoyant could establish her bona fides with testimonials from satisfied customers. She had helped another client find a missing husband, just the sort of assistance Lady Franklin needed.

Another woman who attested to Dawson's skills provided a more detailed testimonial. The wealthy matron came for paranormal aid after losing an expensive brooch. She had told the story of her lost jewelry at so many dinner parties that it came to the attention of editors at *The Zoist: A Journal of Cerebral Physiology and Mesmerism and Their Applications to Human Welfare*. In its in-depth analysis of the bizarre case of the missing brooch, the magazine identified the owner only as Mrs. M. While convinced of "the real existence of true clairvoyant perception," she wanted to remain anonymous because she "does not court notoriety," the magazine explained.

The brooch stood out in her mind for its topaz center surrounded by brilliants. Sure that she had locked it up as usual in August, Mrs. M. was perplexed that she couldn't find it in November. Unfortunately, the names of likely suspects in the event of theft, the household servants, were less memorable for Mrs. M. She changed the help often and couldn't remember who was in her employ when she had last laid eyes on the cherished ornament. Bewildered, she contacted a mesmerist, a Mr. Barth, with whom she had no previous acquaintance. Barth, who insisted Mrs. M. not reveal to him what was missing, set up an appointment with Ellen Dawson at Hands's Grosvenor Square home, with the assurance that her powers included traveling clairvoyance, the ability to psychically visit another place.

"The result far, very far indeed surpassed my expectations," Mrs. M. recalled later. "Mr. Hands merely seemed to look at her, when her eyes closed and he said she was in a deep sleep, and after indulging in about ten minutes' repose would get into the sleep-waking state."

Hands left the room. Barth softened up the entranced clairvoyant with kind words and high praise, which, he had explained earlier to Mrs. M., was essential because "many persons fail in obtaining satisfactory replies from clairvoyants in consequence of their own rude and intolerant behaviour to them."

Barth asked Dawson if she knew why Mrs. M. had come to see her.

"About a loss—about something she has lost," the clairvoyant replied after a few minutes. At which point she knelt beside her client, held her hands and listened to Mrs. M. explain that she had lost something of great value. Dawson assumed she meant money. Hearing that was wrong, she decided the missing item must be property. Barth suggested she go out of body to Mrs. M.'s home for further investigation. After getting some directions, Dawson soon claimed to be standing in front of the place and described it to the owner's satisfaction. The clairvoyant entered the bedroom and gave accurate details of the furniture in "a very minute account."

"I then directed her attention to the place from where the article had been taken, and thus discover what I had lost, and she soon found out what I had lost. She first said jewelry; and when I asked her what kind, she answered, a brooch. I enquired then what it was like; to which she gave a wonderfully accurate answer: she said it looked like *amber* surrounded with white."

Asked what had happened to the missing jewelry, Mrs. M. continued, Dawson described the thief in such detail "no artist could have painted a more perfect resemblance; and it was a servant whom I never suspected."

If not for the gift of Dawson's paranormal powers, a flustered Mrs. M. insisted, she would have fingered an innocent washerwoman once on her household staff. The real culprit was a soft-spoken, fair-seeming woman who had a slightly troubling habit of rummaging about when she thought no one was looking. The clairvoyant saw the stolen item in "a queer place like a cellar with lots of other property—silver spoons and other things; but a cloud came and she could see no more." Dawson was certain the former servant kept the case in which the brooch was stored at her own house, in a trunk. And there were diamonds in it. At first, Mrs. M. was confused. She had a lot of jewelry to remember. Soon she realized "there were two diamond chains fastened to a small diamond ring, separate from the brooch, but for the purpose of attaching to it, and wearing as a locket."

The thief had pawned the brooch for a trifle and stashed the diamonds, which Mrs. M. had completely forgotten until the psychic jogged her memory. After Mrs. M. assured Dawson she didn't want the delinquent punished, the clairvoyant instructed her not to notify the police. The pincher would only clam up. Better to find her instead, and issue this stern warning: Not just God, but people here and now can see the wicked doing wrong when no one seems to be near, and happiness will be impossible unless she repents and confesses. Mrs. M. told the wayward servant precisely that. And the very pleased matron got her jewelry back. Along with a story she dined out on often, tempting Lady Franklin to find out if the clairvoyant's powers to find lost people and things reached across the world, all the way to the High Arctic.

Dawson was herself a patient of Dr. Hands, who claimed he discovered the young woman's psychic abilities by accident, while treating her for heart trouble and fits. Mesmerists often claimed to be able to cure women diagnosed with hysteria, a disorder attributed only to females, whose physicians decided their problem was the rejection of male authority. Hands allowed a few privileged guests to consult Dawson's paranormal powers. Once the doctor had lulled Jane into a trance, and apparently put her to sleep, the spirit medium embarked on her mental trip and revealed her visions to Sophy. With the gravity required of the psychic voyager, she spoke of crossing a great distance to sea and ice, where she saw a ship beset, with several people aboard. All were gentlemen, one rather old, stout, and dark, with a nice face.

"Is he quite well, or does he look ill or unhappy?" Sophy demanded.

"Oh no! He is quite well, and looks happy and comfortable"— which, upon reflection, Dawson saw as slightly anxious. She did not mention that Sir John was also quite dead at that point.

Sophy asked the ship's direction and when she might sail home, at which point Dawson's vision was obscured because "there was a cloud before her." Another ship was close by. Two others—*Could it be Sir James Ross's search expedition that was then searching the north coast of Somerset Island?*—weren't far from them. The men aboard the first ship were dining on salt beef and biscuits. They wore furs and smelled of brandy. Dawson peered into the nice old gentleman's cabin and saw two portraits of ladies, which Sophy took to be Lady Franklin's and the Queen's. They were in his cabin when *Erebus* departed England. Jane likely would have had more probing questions, but she was hypnotized in the next room. The medium refused to speak with her.

"You must tell her all I have told you," the seer instructed Sophy. "But if she heard me telling it, it would upset her—poor thing—she is very anxious. You stop with her—you are always with her now—you must do all you can to comfort and soothe her. . . —and all will be right. Make your mind easy, all is well, all is quite right."

THAT SAME MONTH, something happened, as ordinary in Victorian times as it was tragic, which set in motion a paranormal experience of a higher order: Captain William Coppin lost a daughter to typhoid fever. The family had no connection to Franklin or his crews, but the death of that child would have a significant impact on the search for *Erebus* and *Terror*. She was four-year-old Louisa, better known in her Londonderry home as Weesy. Coppin, a wealthy mariner around forty-five years old, had long experience and excellent credentials as surveyor to the Board of Trade and the Emigration Board, which oversaw migration to Britain's colonies. Born to English parents in Northern Ireland, he grew up living with relatives on Canada's Atlantic coast, in Saint John, New Brunswick. After working as a ferry captain, running between Londonderry and Liverpool, he built a very profitable shipbuilding company, owned his own shipyard, and employed seven hundred men.

Coppin had four children of his own, aged two to nine and a half. The captain and his wife shared a home with her sister and his father. Soon after Weesy was buried, Coppin left on business for three months, during which his kids saw a lot of Weesy. Her ghost was always about and especially liked to show up at meals, when a knife, fork, and chair were placed for her at the table so her spirit could enjoy mealtime with the rest of the kids. Louisa's favorite brother was William Jr., who frequently saw her ghost standing near or against walls of different rooms in their house. When he ran to hug his dead sister, the boy bounced off the wall, sometimes so hard he was left bleeding. By the family's account, Weesy's ghost wasn't the flowing-robe variety or the ghastly phantom made popular by modern-day movie lore. The children described seeing a ball of bluish light. Yet it didn't appear to any of the adults in the house, at least not that they were aware. At first it seemed adults' eyes couldn't pick up what the children's did. But when the captain returned, and his wife told him of the odd apparition, he soon saw it himself. To occult believers, there was a logical explanation: Coppin had psychic gifts, which he must have passed on to his children.

In the fall of 1849, when the public was rapt with the deepening mystery of the Franklin Expedition, experts were still pointing to Wellington Channel as the most likely place to find *Erebus* and *Terror*. Harriet Smith, an aunt of Coppin's children, asked his daughter Ann one October day to enquire of Weesy whether she had any thoughts on the matter, whereupon the spirit vanished. Almost immediately, Ann saw a vision of the Arctic on the floor, showing two ships surrounded by ice, almost covered by snow, at the end of a channel. Then another question: How could Sir John Franklin be reached? In a flash, words appeared on the opposite wall in large, round-handed letters some three inches tall: Erebus and Terror, Lancaster Sound, Prince Regent Inlet, Point Victory, and Victoria Channel. The girl acting as a spirit medium shivered, as if touched by the Arctic cold, and clutched her aunt Harriet's dress.

As child mediator to her sister's ghost, Ann drew a map so her aunt could see what Weesy had shown her. It included Victoria Channel, now called Victoria Strait, which was then unknown. The strait, which would become the focus of the modern Franklin search, didn't appear on any chart of the polar region until three years after Ann's vision, when John Rae's discovery of the waterway was reported in the *Journal of the Royal Geographical Society*. What's more, the child had never seen a map of the Arctic before, let alone drawn one. Yet, when the document recording the Franklin Expedition's troubles was discovered a decade later at Victory Point, the spectral apparition was proven remarkably accurate. Coppin got to work copying the map and recording the details of the ghost story to send in a letter to Lady Franklin.

It stayed on his desk for half a year while the captain dealt with heart trouble. But in May 1850, the captain and Lady Franklin finally met and he told her the startling details of Weesy's conveyance. As she listened, Jane recalled a crucial fact: Sir John had told her that if the expedition got in trouble, he would "go up by the Great Fish River and so get to Hudson Bay Territory." She believed Weesy had brought the truth. So did the Oxford-educated writer who analyzed the case for *Light: A Journal of Psychical, Occult, and Mystical Research.* He dissected the written account of Reverend J. Henry Skewes, who took heat from believers and skeptics alike for what many considered a sensationalist book.

One reviewer with faith in the occult hated Skewes's writing but was convinced he had a legitimate account of significant supernatural contact. The reverend "refuses to believe in what he calls 'the commonly accepted *modus operandi* of the spirit-workings of Spiritualism' (whatever that may mean), but he believes that his own pet 'revelation' came from the 'unseen spirit world,'" wrote the paranormal expert, identified only as M.A. (Oxon.), a Latin abbreviation for the University of Oxford.

"So do I: and that is one of the very many that Mr. Skewes evidently knows nothing of, and about which it would become him to write more modestly and cautiously. The fact is, when his book is divested of superincumbent speculation, crude opinion and irrelevant matter, there remains a record of mediumship that is valuable."

The only opinion that really mattered was Jane's. She took the Weesy revelations very seriously but was careful not to spread that around. She had too much to lose if the press portrayed her as a nut. Lady Franklin spent some eight years trying to get searchers to concentrate on the places Weesy's ghost had charted. She met discreetly with Coppin more than thirty times to discuss the revelations, according to Skewes, president of Liverpool's Mental Sciences Association. Among many questions raised was whether Ann saw words on the wall, or simply initials that adults later filled in with great meaning. Skeptics also asked why Weesy would neglect to mention a fact one might expect a ghost to bring up: Franklin had been dead for upwards of two years. Skewes's handling of the whole story only fed criticism that the reverend's book was sensationalist and unscientific piffle.

One reviewer, writing as the controversy still roiled in 1889, was so indignant that he attacked Coppin as "a remarkable man, a particularly successful shipbuilder, and the spoilt child of presentiments, coincidences, and benignant interpositions of Providence in his affairs generally." Chipping away at the story, the reviewer seemed suspicious that Lady Franklin's estate couldn't produce the original chart drawn according to Weesy's description. But there are large gaps in Jane's carefully kept records, which some suspect as evidence that they were culled after her death to protect her reputation. Skewes further undermined his case by writing "with pitiful want of command of English as she ought to be written." The furor forced a new edition of Skewes's book, which included more supporting evidence. That included letters among Coppin, Lady Franklin, and Sophy that showed Jane was willing to put more faith in the spirit of a dead girl than the assembled wisdom of Britain's polar veterans.

"It is a question capable of being judged by anyone who will give sufficient attention to it," Lady Franklin wrote to Coppin in June 1850, "and my own impression of its necessity is so great that were all the Arctic authorities collected together in one body against it (which, however, will never be the case), it would make no difference at all in my opinion. You who have other grounds for judging this matter will not wonder at my impressions, and may, perhaps, see that they came from a higher source than those which are founded on mere reasonings."

While Jane told trusted experts like Scoresby that she thought the search should focus farther south, in the area closer to King William Island, she didn't dare let on that the information came from the ghost of a toddler. She confided only in a close circle of trusted allies. One was the Admiralty's influential second secretary, Captain W. A. B. Hamilton, who met with Coppin and promised to inform the Lords in charge of the Royal Navy. She also told Charles Dickens and tried to persuade him to write an account in his new weekly magazine, *Household Words*, which sold 100,000 copies at its peak. A positive story from the era's most popular writer would have given the ghost story great credibility. But Coppin objected, insisting that "the hallowed memories of home life must be kept inviolate." Coppin didn't want to risk career-destroying ridicule. Even though Dickens was good with a ghost story, the captain had good reason to be wary: A regular column in *Household Words* mocked the paranormal under the headline "Latest Intelligence from Spirits."

Another psychic named Emma L. offered her own insights on the search. Captain Alexander Maconochie, who was Sir John Franklin's private secretary in Van Diemen's Land, set up that contact through mesmerist Joseph W. Haddock in Bolton, near Manchester. He had discovered Emma's clairvoyant powers after hiring her, at age twenty, as a domestic servant, whereupon he used her to try his hand at mesmerism. She solved some theft and missing-persons cases, which *The Zoist* reported on, and her fame as the woman known as "the Bolton clairvoyant" spread. Maconochie used his good offices to get the Admiralty to assist with handwriting samples from Sir John, his officers, and the commanders of search expeditions in the hope Emma might connect them. Haddock obtained Arctic charts from the navy so he could refine his questions and better understand her replies. He also got a lock of Sir John's sparse hair to improve the clairvoyant's chances of distant contact.

During one of her out-of-body trips to the Arctic in the fall of 1849, Emma marked the time between Bolton and Franklin's ships, which allowed a calculation of longitude. It placed *Erebus* and *Terror* in north-western Hudson Bay, where they never were. She later spotted Sir John in other places farther west, even though he was dead by then. After reading a letter from Maconochie, describing the visions for newspaper readers, Sophy concluded, "perhaps even more strongly than my aunt, that there was a diseased imagination, or even excited nerves, at work and therefore her statements should not be depended upon."

Paranormal sources were literally all over the map with their search tips. Useful leads were as rare as the South African quagga caged up at the London Zoo. Most psychic revelations about the fate of the Franklin Expedition were either too fuzzy to judge or too farcical to believe. A clairvoyant from London claimed from her trance that she had just passed another psychic from Liverpool in midair while astral traveling over the Arctic. By sheer accident, spectral intervention, or even sleight of hand that no one managed to see through, the information that Coppin's young daughter learned out of thin air was by far the most accurate. But who could be sure? What began quietly as a child's spectral vision in a Northern Ireland home was lost in the noise of what sounded to skeptics like spiritualist mumbo jumbo. Staid Arctic experts easily dismissed it all. Coppin petitioned the government to launch a search to the area on his daughter's map, but "all the arguments of the anxious Captain were but paper pellets on the hide of the rhinoceros," Skewes wrote.

Admiralty Lords loathed the letters from Haddock. The men at the helm of the world's greatest navy weren't accustomed to taking advice from magicians. Pestering them to take Emma's clairvoyance seriously, Haddock pointed out that her descriptions of officers she saw on various Arctic expeditions were "strikingly correct."

"Strikingly correct certainly—a perfect transcription of the description I wrote," retorted one Lord. Another was more blunt in his marginalia's assessment of the notion that spiritualists could find the lost Franklin Expedition when brave explorers found nothing but dead ends.

"Humbug!" he wrote.

JANE NEEDED to get nearer the Admiralty. She had to find a close perch to watch the adversary and plot better ways to get around the men standing in her way. She moved from an upper-class neighborhood lined with Georgian townhouses and took a suite of apartments at 33 Spring Gardens, next door to the seat of imperial naval power. Over the centuries, it had been a park for royals strolling from nearby Whitehall Palace, the site of a stable to house their horses, a refuge for aristocratic debt dodgers, and a quiet garden for people toiling in the Admiralty offices. By the time Lady Franklin needed a place from which to put more pressure on her missing husband's bosses, it was a posh enclave favored by politicians and civil servants.

The apartment became a comfortable bunker. Friends called it "The Battery." Jane spread out maps of the known Arctic, consulted experienced explorers on the latest rumors and theories, ruminated on her own thoughts about the best plans for more searches, and wrote to allies and the Admiralty, feverishly trying to get some results. When James Clark Ross told her a rumor was making the rounds that she had relocated to pressure the vaunted Royal Navy leadership, she told him the family home was simply too crowded with relatives and assured him dryly that, "if the great folks at the Admiralty think I am here for interfering purposes, they do my insignificance too much honour."

There was another, darker reason behind her move out of the five-story home she had shared with Sir John at Bedford Place. The all-consuming focus on finding him was splitting the only family Lady Franklin had left. With power of attorney from her husband, she could spend every last penny of the Franklin fortune if she chose.

Her father, sister Mary, and her husband John Simpkinson feared Jane was hell-bent on spending herself into poverty. They leaned on her to stand aside and let the Admiralty do what it knew best. Eleanor also turned against her stepmother, agreeing to marry without telling her. That left one ally whom Jane could really trust: Sir John's niece Sophy, whose devotion to her aunt was unshakable.

In Lady Franklin's defense, Sophy declared that she "is honoured and respected and sympathy for her has been expressed and conveyed to herself by all ranks, from the Queen down to the lowest of her subjects—and this notwithstanding the most shrinking anxiety to avoid notice, or comment or observation." Caroline Fox, an old Quaker friend of the Franklins, was worried the relentless stress would break Jane. "Poor Lady Franklin," Fox confided to her diary. "She is in such a restless excited state of feeling. . . . She spends most of her days in a room she has taken in Spring Gardens, where she sees all the people who can tell or suggest anything." She, like many who only saw Jane as a distraught woman, a widow lost in denial, severely underestimated her strength of will, stamina, and intelligence.

In an 1849 letter from Spring Gardens, Lady Franklin lobbied the Lords on the Admiralty's board to launch a search expedition in Wellington Channel and Prince Regent Inlet on the Gulf of Boothia. Both were far from where *Erebus* and *Terror* had been abandoned the previous year, but nobody outside the Arctic knew that yet, and Lady Franklin was repeating the consensus among veteran explorers. Change was coming. Sir John Barrow, who had pushed so hard to restart the Northwest Passage mission, died suddenly just six months after Franklin's men gave up their ships. The Admiralty must have hoped the Franklin headache would quickly pass with him. But no. Jane did everything she could to make sure the Arctic, and the plight of the men who had followed their orders, stayed front and center in the corridors of the naval high command.

She was, her lengthy letter made clear, well informed of the reasons for the Admiralty Lords' opinions and suffering "intense anxiety" over their procrastination. Embarrassing them with her own resolve, Jane stressed that she was sacrificing property, although not as much as she wanted to, and borrowing money to fund her own efforts. She asked the Royal Navy to lend her a couple of ships: two dockyard lighters, which normally transported provisions and stores from large ships anchored offshore. After what the Arctic had done to some of the navy's strongest vessels, a woman's suggestion that smaller, workaday transport ships could find *Erebus* and *Terror* must have sounded impertinent to some. But Lady Franklin had been convening with pros in The Battery and made her case like one.

"With some alterations in the rigging," she insisted with a sailor's certainty, they "would be well adapted for my purpose, and being very strong, they would soon be made ready for sea.

"It will not be, I trust, and ought not to be a reproach to me, that I use every means & argument I can think of, that is upright and true, to move you to the consideration of my request, and if you ever have cause to look back upon any part of your administration with regret, which I hope may never be, it will not I am persuaded arise from your having extended to me the assistance I seek on the present occasion," she concluded, signing: "Your obedient servant, Jane Franklin."

The Lords didn't dismiss her suggestion out of hand. By early the next year, a Dickens publication, *The Household Narrative of Current Events*, was reporting that the Lords of the Admiralty, with backing from the House of Commons, had approved a new search expedition under the command of Captain Horatio T. Austin. The brief story said the mission would consist of two steamers accompanied by two dockyard lighters. When Austin set sail in 1850, steamers went with him as backup, but his main vessels were two heavy barques specially designed for polar exploration. Lady Franklin's persistence was starting to pay off and she made sure William Penny the whaler was involved in the Royal Navy's next search. After several cold summers, the Admiralty was counting on a break in the Arctic chill to open search routes through the ice.

A long shot, but the Lords were now all-in.

6

The Arctic Committee

Two years after the crews of *Erebus* and *Terror* emptied their ships and set off on foot, the Royal Navy surrendered to pressure for action and launched the most ambitious attempt to find the lost Franklin Expedition. By the summer of 1850, there were thirteen ships, assembled in seven British and American expeditions, traversing the Arctic Archipelago, looking for some sign of the missing men. Lady Franklin's constant pressure and publicity campaign had not only kept alive demands for a major search but also spurred a new wave of exploration that would significantly expand the knowledge of the High Arctic. She had also ratcheted up the political risks. In just six years since Lady Franklin had offered the first reward to whalers, the mounting effort to find Sir John and his men would cost more than £760,000, or close to $70 million today. Most of that was public money that politicians had to assure taxpayers was well spent. But the first major mission mainly produced news of infighting, phony murder conspiracies, and wild-goose chases. The Franklin Expedition was a chronic headache that the Admiralty just couldn't shake.

On August 13, 1850, an alien clamor disturbed timeless silence as at least seven vessels—from magnificent three-masters to a humble single-sparred cutter—converged in the Arctic wilderness, on the northeast shores of Baffin Bay. The High Arctic hadn't seen anything like it before, and hasn't since. Sailors shouted from the decks and rigging as they hauled in sails, sounded the depths, and brought their mammoth vessels to rest. The resounding splash of anchors plunging into the sea followed a long whine of heavy rope anchor cables running through iron hawsepipes. The brassy clang of ships' bells marked the hours of the watch. This was an unplanned convergence of naval might far from any human settlement. The ships were supposed to be split up, navigating hundreds of miles apart and hunting for Franklin leads in different areas of the Arctic Archipelago, but pack ice squeezed them closer and into a more collaborative effort. As several expeditions dodged ice floes on the desolate northwest coast of Greenland, things got dicey in the dense fog and shifting floes. At one point, sailors landed on the ice, planted a hefty charge of gunpowder, and, on a signal, ignited a slow match. William Parker Snow watched from the smaller, eighty-nine-ton yacht *Prince Albert*.

Lady Franklin chose Snow for her first private expedition, under the command of Captain Charles Forsyth, who served with the Royal Navy's permission. Snow came aboard as surgeon, purser, and first mate. He brought his own paranormal revelation to the search. Born into a navy family, Snow suffered a serious head injury as a boy when he missed a crossbar in gym and cut his head open. The boy quickly developed what he believed were clairvoyant powers, and a Victorian-era magazine profile later called him "naturally psychic, living near the edge of the Fourth Dimension." He also had a visceral understanding of how cruel life could be at sea. Snow was severely abused as a child apprentice under a vicious captain who regularly had the boy flogged and tied to the mast. Snow was colted, or beaten with a knotted cord, three or four times a week until his back was a grotesque palette of bruises and suppurating sores.

"Day after day I was knocked about, rope's ended, thrown down and then kicked, mast-headed in bad weather, kept up from my watch below, and so brutally used that I was always sore in my body, and broken in my mind. My head at last got so affected and my old maladies so increased, that I often lay down all night writhing in agony."

The captain took twisted pleasure in watching the child sailor tormented and humiliated. Sometimes he ordered Snow roused from sleep and forced to sit on the highest yard, a horizontal spar attached to a mast, for two or three hours at a stretch. When that failed to break the boy's spirit, the trauma escalated to the bizarre.

"I was called up, stripped, and sent forward to be tarred, then stand in a tub while water was poured over me as a further punishment, and then, thus tarred, sent out to straddle the jibboom, to represent, as he said, a new figurehead."

Years later, when Snow volunteered to join the 1845 Franklin Expedition, the Royal Navy rejected him as unfit. He had bad eyesight, stammered incessantly, and his memory or consciousness would all of a sudden fail him. So he moved to New York to write for a newspaper. It was there, at 3 o'clock in the morning on January 7, 1850, that he had a vision, a sort of waking dream, when "the curtains of my sleeping-room were drawn aside from the bottom and a picture appeared before my eye."

Snow saw a flat, ice-covered triangle that included what he took to be King William Island and an area to the northeast around the North Magnetic Pole. At the bottom was the continental coast around the estuary of the Great Fish River, and the Boothia Isthmus. Crossing King William Island, and along its shores, Snow spotted "a few men, while several bodies lay seemingly lifeless on the ground." More white men were farther south at the mouth of the Great Fish River, and near the Salmon Lakes, Boothia Isthmus, and the gulf. To the west, there were other parties of white men in the apparition.

"It seemed to me in my waking dream that they were calling aloud to me for aid, and their call appeared to be strongly sounding in my ears. This so thoroughly startled me, that, as my wife well remembers, and often expresses how it woke her, I sprang out of bed shiv-

ering with fright, horror and pity, towards the sitting-room. I found
the curtains closed as we had left them, but I promptly threw on my
attire, and with the candle I had lit, proceeded to my desk. The early
morning was cold, yet I did not appear to want a fire; I was like as
though heated enough by what my dream or vision had pictured me.
Thus I commenced writing and copied what I wrote."

Those elements of the image conjured in Snow's rattled mind
might simply have been a good guess for a seaman obsessed by the
Arctic and possessed of an active imagination. But there were other
details in the manifestation that were far more prescient—and much
more difficult to explain away.

"Two apparently deserted ships were to be seen, one embedded in
the ice south west of the magnetic pole and north west of Point Victory," which James Ross had named, on the northwest tip of King William Island. "The other ship was away down in a bay—MacLoughlin
Bay—or close to O'Reilly Island."

Today's charts show it as McLoughlin Bay, and it lies just southeast of O'Reilly Island, in eastern Queen Maud Gulf. It's the general
area where Inuit oral history told of a three-masted ship, where men
had lived with a dog, until they went off one day, leaving footprints
in the snow, never to return. Later searchers reported those details in
their journals from interviews with Inuit, long after Snow claims he
saw it all in New York as it was unfolding high in the Arctic in 1850.
That was nine years before the discovery of the Victory Point note
that described where and when *Erebus* and *Terror* were abandoned
to sea ice northwest of King William Island. The experience was so
powerful that Snow sat down at his desk the same cold January morning and wrote a letter to Lady Franklin. According to the *Saturday
Review*, a respected London weekly of the era that reported arts, literature, science, and politics, Snow's letter was "printed in the Parliamentary papers respecting the Arctic expedition for that year."

He told Lady Franklin that the search needed to shift farther south, without mentioning that his information came from a clair-voyant vision. He was afraid that would sound crazy. Now Snow was in the hunt aboard the *Prince Albert*, biding his time, waiting for the right moment and place to ask Forsyth for permission to check the eastern Queen Maud Gulf.

Standing on the *Prince Albert*'s deck, watching the ice explode, he didn't have the buffer of the big ships' reinforced hulls to cushion the shock. The water suddenly roiled with ice exploding "in convulsive movement, as though shaken by a volcanic eruption, until piece upon piece was sent in the air, and the larger bodies were completely rent into innumerable fragments." The blast barely nicked the Arctic's armor of ice, but it opened enough water for the ships to advance.

Once safely through the obstacle course of ice, the ships anchored off Cape York. Most impressive were the Royal Navy's barque-rigged exploration vessels specially outfitted for another run at the Northwest Passage. HMS *Resolute* was the flagship of Captain Horatio T. Austin, commander of an expedition that totaled four vessels. Her sister ship was HMS *Assistance*. Two steam-powered tenders, *Intrepid* and *Pioneer*, were along to tow the sailing vessels when necessary and to penetrate deeper into the archipelago if sea ice or weather conditions made that too risky for the others. William Penny would also rendezvous there with HMS *Lady Franklin* and HMS *Sophia*, whaling brigs brought into Royal Navy service under the whaling master's command. Gold-braided naval officers normally sniffed at such unpedigreed merchant seamen. Now they had no choice but to work with Penny because Lady Jane Franklin wanted it so. Her campaign of newspaper editorials, supported by sympathetic readers' letters to the editor, had shamed the Admiralty into financing his ships and his crew.

Sir John Ross added another fuse to the powder keg. He was back in the Arctic, finally getting his shot at a rescue attempt, spending some of his own money with backing from the Hudson's Bay Company. It helped fund his voyage on a private schooner, the 120-ton *Felix*, which led the way for Ross's own yacht, the 12-ton *Mary*. She came along as an unmanned tender in case the explorers had to abandon the main vessel. Neither ship was strong enough for an aggressive hunt, yet Ross would still end up in the middle of another ugly fight over his lost friend Franklin.

The morning started off calm and quiet. Snow had been up in the crow's nest, scanning a coast that struck him as endlessly dreary, looking for any hint of people or wrecks. He craved conversation. After breakfast, he boarded the *Assistance* with a parcel of newspapers sent by the proprietors of the *Morning Herald*. He thought Austin's officers might like a chance to catch up on the headlines. Crewmen spotted Inuit in the distance, standing on snow beneath cliffs, and Snow returned to the *Prince Albert*, where Forsyth was eager to launch a shore party to ask if anyone had seen *Erebus* or *Terror*.

Several men from different ships headed for the ice that formed a sort of beachhead offshore. As they approached, Snow marveled at massive glaciers, many miles long, with "solid streams of frozen snow, rushing occasionally with the force of an avalanche into open water." Curious, mostly smiling Inuit dressed in sealskin came closer to greet the visitors. Snow took a shine to the last to arrive, a chubby-faced boy, and pulled out a blue cotton pocket handkerchief, spotted white, to tie it around the child's neck. Snow thought of taking the boy, named Aladoongà, home with him to England.

"But, poor little fellow! it was not so ordained. Away he went from me with his handkerchief round his neck as I vainly tried to call him back; and the rude hut, and the state of life, half human, half beast, was to remain his lot. I looked long and anxiously after him, and began to reflect. But, after all, said I mentally, perhaps he is really happier where he is. Increased knowledge but increases sorrow."

Around 8 p.m. that night, everyone was back aboard ship, catching up after a long day. A steward named John Smith, who had learned some Inuktitut during his time with the Hudson's Bay Company, chatted with Adam Beck, Sir John Ross's interpreter. His English struck others on the expedition as weak, which caused serious problems. Smith was so startled by what he heard that he took Snow aside: Beck was reporting a massacre of Royal Navy sailors. That's what the friendly Inuit had told him earlier in the day, Smith relayed to Snow. Two ships had wrecked farther up the coast, and the men who made it ashore, including officers with gold bands on their caps and other naval insignia, were later killed. Snow couldn't believe what he was hearing, took out his Inuktitut pocket phrase book, and did his best to interrogate Beck. The interpreter used a piece of chalk to write "1846," the year of the alleged murders, "in a clear and good scholar-like hand," on the ship's gunwale. As alarm spread, and Beck faced more questioners, more details emerged. He insisted Inuit had told him that two ships arrived in the winter of 1846, when snow was falling, and got crushed by ice near Cape Dudley Digges. White men made for shore. Some drowned. The survivors, some armed with guns but without ammunition, camped for a time in white tents or huts, separate from the Inuit, who eventually killed the exhausted and weak sailors with darts or arrows.

Horrified, Snow reported the gruesome details to his commander, who reported it up the chain. Sailors fired a howitzer, and hoisted the colors, to get Austin's urgent attention. Penny went back ashore with his interpreter, a Danish official named Carl Petersen, who spoke a Greenland dialect of Inuktitut. He listened to the Inuit repeat their story and said they made no claims of any killing at all. The only confirmed dead white man was a sailor from the *North Star*, which had wintered at Wolstenholme Sound the previous winter. He fell off a cliff. Petersen called Beck a liar and tried to intimidate him into silence, but Ross's interpreter pushed back, insisting he was telling the truth. Beck later swore to his account of the murder in a signed deposition, made in front of a magistrate at Godhavn, on Greenland's Disko

Island. While Austin and other senior officers made a plan to investigate what, if true, would be a major crime against the Royal Navy, Beck spent hours below with the lower ranks, trying to persuade the seamen with pleas that they heard only as gibberish.

"He had been much pained by their laughing and jeering him about his miserable looks," Snow recalled, "and when he sufficiently explained himself to let them understand 'ships lost,' and 'all men speared,' they told him that he *lied*, and this made him cry, saying nàà mee, nàà (not me, not me)."

Few believed Beck from the start. But his story had to be checked out, which forced a risky, late-season delay in the expeditions' search efforts farther west in the archipelago. Austin was angry and would make Beck, and his strongest supporter, Sir John Ross, suffer for it later. With so many ships joining the hunt, there was finally a chance to make real progress in finding either *Erebus* or *Terror*, or at least to get closer to figuring out what happened to the Franklin Expedition. Yet, once again, petty politics, bickering, and recriminations eclipsed all that really mattered: the lives of 129 lost men.

WHILE THE BRITISH jostled and maneuvered, Americans saw an opening. Lady Franklin's Washington gambit had run into a political wall in Congress, which New York shipping tycoon Henry Grinnell breached by offering financing and two brigantines, *Advance* and *Rescue*. President Taylor's government endorsed the expedition and provided Navy Lieutenant Edwin De Haven to lead it. His surgeon and scientist was Dr. Elisha Kent Kane, a short, thin naval officer whose daring overcame the frailty of a rheumatic heart and the notoriety of marriage to a young woman who communicated with ghosts. She was Margaret Fox, one of the three traveling Fox Sisters from Rochester, New York, who sparked a spiritualism craze across the US by claiming to communicate with the dead by rapping on walls and tabletops. Although Kane thought the séances were some kind of unexplained parlor trick, he still couldn't resist Margaret's allure.

The US Navy ordered De Haven to sail through Lancaster Sound to Wellington Channel and then west to Cape Walker. Franklin had been told to follow the same course. If De Haven reached the cape without finding the missing British seamen, and the route farther west was blocked, he was to make his way to Jones and Smith Sounds. They lie far to the northeast, in the opposite direction of where *Erebus* and *Terror* were abandoned. The US government wasn't taking such a big financial and political risk just to do a worried wife's bidding. Commanders were curious about the possibility of navigable waters closer to the North Pole, and the Franklin search allowed them to put a humanitarian spin on a much more important mission: a belated quest for the mythical Open Polar Sea. The Americans, like the British, were convinced the sea would be warmer at the top of the world.

"This opinion seems to be sustained by the fact that beasts and fowls are seen migrating over the ice from the mouth of Mackenzie River and its neighboring shores to the north," Secretary of the Navy William Ballard Preston explained in De Haven's instructions. "These dumb creatures are probably by their wise instincts to seek a more genial climate in that direction, and upon the borders of the supposed more open sea."

Preston was explicit that De Haven not try looking farther south for Sir John and his men, along the North American coast, where survivors had headed under Francis Crozier's command.

"Nearly the entire Arctic front of the continent has been scoured without finding any traces of the missing ships," the navy secretary wrote. "It is useless for you to go there, or to re-examine any other place where search has already been made. You will, therefore, confine your attention to the routes already indicated."

The stretch of cold summers didn't break as hoped, and heavy sea ice stymied the expeditions at several turns. But in mid-August, word

reached William Penny that men aboard *Assistance*, commanded by
Royal Navy Captain Erasmus Ommanney, had found traces of the
Franklin Expedition at Cape Riley, on the southwest tip of Devon
Island. The site overlooks the southern entrance of Wellington Channel, and Penny assumed crewmen from *Erebus* and *Terror* must have
stopped there in retreat. Searchers walking the shoreline found a
bottle, scraps of newspaper, rifle shot, and other items several miles
north of Cape Riley, at Bowden Point. They read those as evidence
that some of Franklin's men, perhaps a hunting party, had camped
there. Restricted by sea ice, Penny joined up with the American ships
Advance and *Rescue*, and Ross aboard the *Felix*. Ross loathed Penny.
Austin, the most senior Royal Navy commander there, didn't have
much time for either man, nor they for him.

Suspicious, and at times openly hostile to one another, expedition leaders brought their ships together in a bight on the northwest
side of Beechey Island. There they agreed that the Americans under
De Haven would try to pick up the Franklin men's trail by continu-
ing northward along the east coast of Wellington Channel. Penny
headed eastward. Leading a party of his officers, the whaler found the
first solid evidence that the Franklin Expedition had run into serious
problems. They discovered the weathered wooden markers, pounded
into the permafrost, above the Beechey Island graves of John Torrington, John Hartnell, and William Braine. Austin concluded that
the expedition must have spent its first winter nearby and "that there
was circumstantial evidence sufficient to prove that its departure was
somewhat sudden." Penny and his group searched for any kind of written record, but they found none. It was a bad sign, but still a major
break, yet the whaler would soon be fighting to defend himself in
front of an Admiralty board of inquiry, with all the tension and insin-
uation of a criminal trial.

Snow reluctantly headed home that same August, boiling with
resentment of his own. Once the *Prince Albert* neared the area where

his vision told him to look for *Erebus* or *Terror*, Snow summoned the courage to ask Forsyth to pause. Snow asked permission to borrow a boat to check the Boothia Peninsula. He also wanted a small group of men from the ship's crew. They had eagerly volunteered in a meeting on the ship's deck, despite the obvious risks. The captain waffled, then flatly refused, and suddenly set sail for England.

TROUBLE AWAITED the British commanders of the first full-scale Franklin search when they reached home port in 1851. After resisting a mass hunt for as long as it could, the Admiralty had spent stacks of the public's money. To quiet skeptics, they needed something equally big to show for it. The discovery of three graves, but no rescued sailors, ships, or written records of their whereabouts, was not the news the Lords wanted to hear. Wild rumors of a massacre didn't help. Someone had to suffer, but the Royal Navy would deflect as much blame as possible. As a whaler, William Penny had a target on his back anyway, so the Admiralty took aim at him first.

Letters forwarded from the ships still at sea provided ample ammunition. A specially convened Arctic Committee led the investigation, headed by Rear-Admiral William Bowles. A career Royal Navy man with white nimbus eyebrows and muttonchop sideburns that framed pinched lips like a pair of hatchets, Bowles had an unremarkable war record. That didn't matter. His Conservative Party connections were impeccable, which ensured he was well on his way to becoming Admiral of the Fleet. His five-man board of inquiry was dominated by three former Arctic expedition commanders, luminaries of the Royal Navy's polar pantheon: George Back, Frederick Beechey, and William Parry. The main issue in front of the august panel stemmed from an argument in the High Arctic on August 11, 1851, when Penny and Austin were aboard their ships in Cornwallis Island's Assistance Bay. But Lady Franklin suspected the Admiralty was really looking for payback. She didn't trust Back, for one, and thought the committee was stacked against Penny, the most vulnerable member of her team.

Penny and Sir John Ross had wintered at Assistance Bay, beset by sea ice. It got so cold that on February 24, 1851, a sunny day with little wind, the thermometer's mercury froze solid at –41 degrees Fahrenheit. By late summer, leads opened in the ice, allowing a rendezvous with Austin. They debated whether to head up Wellington Channel and try to find Franklin's trail on one of the optional routes the Admiralty had given in his written instructions. Sir John had gone that way with *Erebus* and *Terror* in his circumnavigation of Cornwallis Island, before wintering at Beechey Island. But the ships were far to the south, if not already on the seabed, by the time Austin and Penny butted heads over where to go looking for them. An officer of Her Majesty's Royal Navy normally wouldn't stoop to debate a whaling captain. But this was already far from a normal naval operation.

"It was sort of a rambling conversation of which I could make nothing," Austin huffed after one exchange with Penny and Ross.

While the naval commander insisted he was trying to be polite and attentive, "I was pained to the extreme. How I was able to maintain myself as an officer and a gentleman under the circumstances I cannot tell."

The dispute stayed on a steady boil through the day, carried out in letters between ships, heated discussions face-to-face, even with a shout from the stern as Austin told Penny, when the whaler passed beneath him in a small boat: "Go up into the Wellington Channel, and you will do good to the cause." In one letter, Penny was worried about the risk of sailing into sea ice drifting fast and hard in stiff currents farther north. Winter was about to slam the search window shut, and Penny wasn't eager to get his neck caught by sticking it out too far. He warned of "the fearful rate at which the tide runs (not less than six knots) through the sounds that divide the channel, dangerous even for a boat, much more to a ship, unless clear of ice, which from its present appearance would not be so that season."

Austin thought his expedition teams' searches to the west and the south proved there was no point going farther north. Of course, unknown to him, the Franklin Expedition survivors already had gone south. If a search there had failed to find anyone alive, at least it might have found evidence of what happened. Later, under fire from all sides back home, Penny insisted he was eager to proceed north into Wellington Channel, and he asked Austin for a steamer, only to be refused. The Arctic Committee concluded that Penny had changed his story after "he found everybody disappointed" on his return to England and faulted him for not staying a couple of weeks longer to at least gauge ice conditions in the channel. The panel agreed that both Penny and Austin were fully justified under their orders from the Admiralty to avoid the risk of getting stuck for another winter. But the investigation's final report, and its lavish praise for "the zeal, energy, intrepidity, and perseverance" of individual searchers, did not placate growing public frustration with one of the country's most revered institutions. To a highbrow *Athenaeum* commentator, Austin's slight against Penny, who deserved to be celebrated for finding the Franklin crewmen's graves on Beechey Island, was a disgraceful example of British naval snobbery.

"The Royal Navy captain scorned to take information or advice from the captain of a 'mercantile' Expedition, though sailing like himself under Admiralty orders, and engaged, with him, at great national cost, on a common work of humanity. Sir John Franklin and his gallant companions might lie and rot in 'thick-ribbed ice'—and the yearnings of a generous country after its long lost sons be spurned and disregarded—rather than the former commander of a whaler should show the way to the rescue."

The committee also probed Adam Beck's chilling claim that Inuit had murdered the crews of *Erebus* and *Terror*. The provenance of the story wasn't great to begin with, and searchers had wasted good time just trying to get the basics straight. Now the experts wanted their kick at the can. Despite initial doubts, John Ross testified, he was convinced that Beck was being completely honest. He had been "raised up to Christianity by missionaries," Ross told the committee, and understood the severe consequences of lying under oath.

"I should add that the class of persons to whom he belongs are perfectly insane when drunk."

Ross didn't elaborate. He didn't have to. What were savages if not crazily drunk liars? Yet Ross remained defiant under sharp questioning of Beck's actions and his own. As the panel dug deeper into the Franklin "murder mystery," Admiral Bowles wanted to be sure Ross and the other searchers hadn't missed something, perhaps a note that would provide a more promising account of the Franklin Expedition's fate. In one line of questioning, the chairman zeroed in on a Beechey Island cairn built from tin cans. It seemed the perfect place to stash one or more notes about the expedition's status. But the cans were all empty. Bowles suspected the searchers had slipped up and missed important clues. Ross, now a rear admiral himself, assured the inquiry that the whole area was checked very carefully. It was possible, but not probable, that something was overlooked, he conceded under questioning. His own experience confirmed that.

"There is a tin containing some lines of poetry that I left on the top of the hill above Leopold Harbour, and although a hundred men have been there since it has never been found, and it is there yet. Almost all the ships companies of the *Investigator* and *Enterprise* have been there, and have never found it."

Ross saw an important clue in the dearth of them, which he "considered a proof that Sir John Franklin had given up all hope of proceeding further, had determined on proceeding home, and was lost." For the many desperate to see something good come from the search, Ross fanned a flicker of hope.

"I think he was lost by getting into packed ice as Sir James Ross got into. That is one reason why I think Adam Beck's story probable. I agreed with Sir John Franklin before he went away that if he advanced he was to leave notices where he was going, and to make deposits [of food and supplies]. I did not require that the Government should make these deposits, but that Sir John Franklin should make them out of his own resources, as I did.

"I said to him, 'I shall most likely be the person to come out for you if you are missed, so that we will understand that you are to leave deposits at Cornwallis Island and Melville Island. State what your intentions are. If you do not leave anything I shall conclude that you are returning home, and that you consider it would be of no use to leave notices.'"

But there was an elephant sitting in the staid hearing room. False leads plagued the investigation into the missing expedition. Plenty of them. Every time expectations of a rescue were raised, only to be dashed, the missing men's distraught families suffered more. Ross's name was attached to a recent, especially crushing disappointment that went unmentioned at the hearing, even though, or perhaps because, it had made headlines. Aboard the schooner *Felix*, he had two homing pigeons donated by a Miss Dunlop of Annanhill, near Ayr, Scotland. In the fall of 1851, when sea ice caught Ross's ship in Assistance Bay, he cupped the pigeons in his hands and slipped them from their cage to attach a message and send them aloft.

The birds were supposed to fly off and find people—with any luck, sailors on a whaling ship far to the east, or at a Hudson's Bay Company outpost deeper south. Instead, the pigeons circled over a desolate expanse of snow and ice and returned to the *Felix*. Several attempts failed to persuade the birds to fly toward one of the whaling ships in Davis Strait. When scaring the pigeons with rifle fire didn't work, Ross improvised. He floated the birds skyward in a small paper box, dangling from two big, gas-filled balloons, measuring six feet by eight.

A slow match mechanism was designed to open a trap door and release the airborne messengers twenty-four hours later. The contraption floated southward until it disappeared from telescope view.

Within two weeks, Scottish newspapers reported that at least one of the pigeons had flown some two thousand miles across the North Atlantic and alighted near its home roost in Ayr. Others said both of the flying messengers had come back. One of the more outlandish news stories, in the *Dundee Advertiser*, had a rifleman with a good eye blasting off the birds' legs. Which sent headline writers aflight: "Latest news from Sir John Ross—extraordinary flight of carrier pigeons" and "Sir John Ross's letter-carriers." Except that no one could produce any notes that proved any of Ross's carrier pigeons had reached Scotland—or anywhere else beyond the lethally cold High Arctic. The birds probably froze there, either trapped in the drifting balloon box or after landing on ice or frozen tundra, where pecking around for food wouldn't have got them far.

No matter. Like anything to do with the increasingly bizarre circus surrounding the slowly unfolding Franklin tragedy, the public couldn't get enough of it. People were now watching the sky, hoping for airborne messages from *Erebus* and *Terror*. Just days after the earlier sightings, when a passenger pigeon was spotted in a ship's rigging in Dundee, people tried to catch it. The bird flew off to the railway station with an excited crowd in pursuit. Eventually, more sober voices prevailed, including an expert who wrote to the *Manchester Guardian*, pooh-poohing the notion that Ross's pigeons could have flown so far as "a clumsy invention of some wag desirous of practising upon the credulity of the public."

In short, it was a sick prank. Not the first surrounding Franklin and his men. Not the last. Precisely the sort of public silliness the Admiralty, and its revered polar explorers, did not want associated with their good names. Instead, they went after John Ross at the inquiry in a nasty fight over a more plausible claim. William Parry, who had made it halfway through the Arctic Archipelago and shown how to survive a killer winter, asked Ross what he knew about a piece of wood and tin that Adam Beck said he had picked up on shore. The interpreter swore that he found it near the place Franklin and his men were thought to have spent their first winter.

"The piece of wood was four feet nine inches long, and three inches by four square," Ross replied. "On the top it had been cut with a saw, and in that was a piece of tin. I saw that piece of tin. Adam Beck was carrying it along, when the tin dropped out and sunk into the snow which was very deep at the time; it could not afterwards be found. The man has sworn that on this piece of tin was 'September 1846.'"

"Did I understand you to say you saw the tin?" Beechey asked.

"Yes, I saw him bringing the tin along with my spyglass. I was about a quarter of a mile away. This was on the north-east side of Union Bay. I considered it to be a meridian mark. There was a cairn that it had fallen from."

The tin sign was never found, even though several people had looked for it in the snow. Once again, Ross's credibility was in doubt. In his career-ending error of 1819, he had seen a mirage of mountains blocking Lancaster Sound. Was he now imagining a message on metal left by the lost Franklin Expedition? If the explorer and his interpreter had in fact seen "September 1846" on a sign in the High Arctic, they had discovered a stunning clue. It marked the month that *Erebus* and *Terror* were beset, a fact that wouldn't be known for certain until the note at Victory Point was discovered some eight years after Ross testified. True or not, that lead had slipped out of fumbling hands, only to be hidden by the Arctic, as so many others had done.

Ross didn't help his own damaged credibility. He seemed slightly confused himself on an important matter concerning his interpreter. At first, Ross didn't believe Adam Beck's murder story because Carl Petersen contradicted it. But Ross boasted of being the only officer in the Royal Navy who could understand Danish, and he thought that gave him unique insight into whether Petersen or Beck was telling the truth. He suspected Petersen was the liar and changed his view on the alleged killing in front of the very skeptical Arctic Committee. It took more pleasure in the testimony of Captain Horatio Austin, who had a very low opinion of Beck and didn't like the Inuk making his own decisions, acting outside the chain of command. The chairman's first question to Austin on the third day of hearings concerned his complaints about Beck and his tale of murder, which Austin lodged in writing on the same day of the Wellington Channel quarrel.

"And do you still entertain the same opinion as to that story?" Bowles asked.

"I do, precisely," Austin replied. "I consider that everything was gone into, and that every one who was present agreed that the conduct of Adam Beck was most discreditable."

"To what circumstances do you allude that have not been detailed in reference to Adam Beck?"

"Everything has since been borne out by the conduct of Adam Beck."

"What do you allude to?"

"I allude to his stopping back, and to what passed when he was landed, which Captain Ommanney can speak of better than I can—to his conduct when with Sir John Ross. He was a man in whom no faith could be placed from his irregular conduct and I believe drunkenness. I think he was about the worst description of a civilized savage I ever saw."

Dismissing Inuit testimony didn't require a lot of argument. Racial prejudice toward indigenous people made disregard for what they said and thought almost automatic for many Europeans certain of their superior moral fiber and intellect. They also regarded as suspect the Inuit tradition of recalling history through telling stories instead of books. For people who put great faith in the written word, indigenous people recalling the past from memory were only spinning legends, entertaining perhaps, but unworthy of an educated expert's time. Mistakes, misunderstandings, and contradictions, the unavoidable flaws of any account told and retold over years, even generations, made Inuit stories all the more suspect to listeners who either weren't willing, or didn't know how, to distill truth from the fog of memory or embellishment.

Besides, compared to a lot of what passed for news of the Franklin Expedition in Europe, Inuit stories were quite cautious. The mystery bred false leads, paranormal tips, and cruel hoaxes like mushrooms on moist manure. Hunters in Spitsbergen noticed reindeer with notched ears. A German expert contacted the Admiralty to suggest it might be Franklin sending a message by way of wild caribou, since other explorers had tried sending notes in collars attached to Arctic foxes. Mysterious bottles floating in the Russian Arctic were thought to be carrying reports from *Erebus* and *Terror*, but they turned up empty. About the size of soda bottles, these were round, made of dark glass, and, after Admiralty analysis, found to be of foreign origin. They looked exactly like Norwegian fishing-net floats, the experts decided. Which is exactly what they were.

Mistakes born of hope were understandable. But the Franklin frenzy went far beyond that. A letter to the *Dundee Advertiser* described how a whaling captain named J. Robb wintered over on the *Flora* in Lancaster Sound. Acting on an Inuit lead, a dozen crewmen found the bodies of four men, "frozen like icicles." One had "H. Carr" tattooed on his arm. The shocking news made it into several newspapers, and all the way to the House of Commons, where members of Parliament shouted, "Hear, hear!" to assurances of a full investigation. The result: "Customs reports that upon enquiry, the whole has proved to be a fiction,—no such vessel as the 'Flora' of Hull being in existence."

Arctic hallucinations abounded. The crew of the English ship

Renovation reported to the Admiralty a sighting of two three-masted, square-rigged ships on an iceberg on the Grand Banks, off Newfoundland. One ship was upright, the other on her beams. The captain, Edward Coward, was sick in his cabin at the time, but the crew watched the trapped vessels through a telescope for close to three-quarters of an hour. Seeing no life, they didn't go in for a closer look, apparently fearing phantoms were aboard. A headline in Canada's *Kingston Whig Standard* declared: "Captain Coward—how appropriate the name!" The Admiralty investigated again, in a three-month probe that included the Foreign Office, the Colonial Office, the Coast Guard, consular officials in Venice, shipping firms in Britain and Newfoundland, and customs collectors in England, Ireland, and Canada. It all came up blank. The apparition of the ghost ships was never explained.

THE SEARCH FOR the Franklin Expedition could have ended with the Arctic Committee's cross-examinations and conclusions drawn from the comfort and safety of naval headquarters. It had been six years now since *Erebus* and *Terror* departed, with roughly three years' worth of food in their stores. Large sums of money, public and private, had been expended, ships and sled parties had crisscrossed thousands of miles in the Arctic Archipelago and found few helpful traces. All that the latest hunt had turned up were graves and a piece of English elm thought to be from one of Franklin's vessels, which only produced more grief and argument. But the committee served an important purpose by looking to the future. It asked its witnesses and other experts for written opinions on whether any of Franklin's men might be alive, and if so, how best to continue looking for them. William Scoresby's coldly rational view was persuasive:

"That Sir John Franklin or some portion of his associates *may* still

survive is a position which cannot be controverted. It follows, therefore, that *some degree of probability*, whatever that degree may be, does
exist. Such probability, it appears to me is involved in or supported by
a variety of considerations.

"Sir John Ross was absent and unheard from for *four years* and
some months (though never at a greater distance from positions often
visited by the whalers than 250 miles), and returned with nearly all his
crew in health."

Since *Erebus* and *Terror* carried "incomparably superior equipment
and resources," Scoresby continued, they "might yet survive." Then
reason failed him, defeated by mere hope and pride. Inuit lived in similarly cold and desolate areas for their whole lives: "Why then may not
hardy enterprizing Britons, sustained, over and above, by the moral
courage and Christian hope which preserved the same Franklin, a
Richardson, a Back, and others, when the ordinary powers of life in
men experienced in like hardships, Canadian voyages, failed. Why may
they not be yet surviving amid the desolateness of Arctic solitudes, and
the wreck of the hopes of the timid and doubting?" The only rational
possibility of a catastrophe wiping out every man in the expedition was
a gale so powerful that both ships overturned near the seaward edge of
ice, Scoresby argued. Two ships had never gone down, taking all men
aboard, during decades of Arctic voyages by tens of thousands of whalers, he added. It made no sense to him that Franklin's ships, "among
the strongest ever sent out to the Arctic seas, should be so completely
annihilated as to leave not a wreck behind."

Austin and Ommanney thought it impossible that anyone in the
Franklin Expedition was still alive. But the consensus among other
polar veterans gave enough hope, however faint, that someone might
need rescue. The Arctic Committee recommended another mission,
with some caveats. The Admiralty couldn't have been pleased. The cost
to its budget, and its prestige, was mounting. Now some of the coun-

try's most revered explorers were insisting on another major effort, including significant improvements to mariners' clothing, before the Royal Navy sent any more men into the extreme cold.

Francis McClintock, who served under Austin, wrote extensively on the clothing and equipment issue, with detailed drawings of improved tents, lists of gear with calculated weights, and daily rations of food, including a quarter pint of rum to get each man ready for the cold each morning. An Irishman described as "short, slender, but wiry and (with a) muscular frame well fitted for the endurance of long-continued exertion and hardships," he had spent more time than most with Inuit and helped pioneer explorers' long-distance travel over land. He developed the system of half a dozen seamen, led by an officer, dragging sledges, with help from sails in favorable winds. Out of twenty sledge parties deployed in the spring of 1851, McClintock's covered the most ground, some 760 miles in seven weeks. His polar experience and extraordinary stamina, and the equal determination of an officer under McClintock's command, would be the key to finding the first solid evidence of what happened to Sir John and his men.

McClintock suggested searchers should be outfitted with fur in place of woolen seamen's sweaters, called jumpers, which would be tailored on board after purchasing cured sealskin in bulk from Inuit. A firm believer in traveling light, McClintock felt the ideal Arctic kit should consist of: "1 flannel shirt or Guernsey frock, 1 pair drawers, 1 blue serge or knitted frock, 1 pair breeches, waistbelt, 1 pair worsted stockings, 1 pair cloth boots, comforter, Welsh wig [a woolen cap that covered ears and neck], southwester, mitts, veil, jacket or sealskin jumper—the latter is much preferable, being longer, less bulky and cumbrous, much lighter and impervious to wind, snow, or wet."

A. R. Bradford, surgeon on the *Resolute* and second-in-command of the western search parties, gave the most detailed analysis of the standard clothing and equipment's flaws. It is easy to feel the pain and discomfort Franklin's men must have suffered—getting worse the longer they lived as their clothes and boots fell apart—through the doctor's response to the committee. The outdoor "clothing was not in the least adapted to the exigencies of an Arctic travelling party," he wrote, "more particularly so in the colder season, when the cold winds, loaded with a fine drift, penetrated through every garment that was in the most minute degree open in its texture, such as woollen and cloth fabrics." Bradford switched to sealskin pants but preferred the leather trousers and frock coats from the Hudson Bay territory because fine, drifting snow didn't collect on the smooth surface. Second best was Inuit sealskin, in Bradford's view, which he said was too tight on British crews when purchased readymade.

"Clothing should never be tight fitting in an Arctic climate, as any impediment to a free circulation in a limb leads to its readily becoming frozen. The only objection to the sealskin is that the very fine drift lodges under the hair, which the most careful brushing will never entirely remove. The consequence is, when the man has turned into his bag, and becomes sufficiently warm to melt this fine snow, a great accumulation of damp takes place, and the bags become saturated with wet when the men are in them, or frozen hard a few minutes after they get out, no opportunity offering to dry damp or wet articles until the season is well advanced."

Bradford wanted the Royal Navy to toss its canvas boots, which were supplemented with "blanket feet wrappers" and said they should be replaced with Inuit sealskin boots. He found them well suited to both dry and wet weather. The navy's canvas boots only got wet and froze, all the way through to the blistered, perhaps frostbitten skin of the poor man trying to walk on what must have felt like sharp needles.

"The canvas boots occupied a long time in clearing the inside of ice, which had to be scraped out with a knife. They were occasionally frozen so hard and stiff that the men had to take them into their sleeping-bags for one or two hours between their legs to thaw them, before they could be got on."

John Richardson, Franklin's close friend and surgeon on his earlier expeditions, suggested replacing winter shoes made of canvas with ones of soft tanned leather. "They should be made in shape of the Canadian moccasin, and roomy enough to hold three socks of white fearnought [thick wool]," he recommended. Scoresby added another, more radical thought to improve travel on the snow and ice: Do as the local people do and make more use of sled dogs, as Penny had done to great advantage.

In its final report, the committee didn't completely bury Beck's murder claim. But it advised that if the Admiralty's Lords decided further inquiry were necessary, they should keep it separate from any renewed search. Enough valuable time had been lost on that wild-goose chase. The experts recommended a renewed hunt for *Erebus* and *Terror* in the summer of 1852, which should include an effort to find the tin sign that Ross said he saw Beck drop in the snow. But the next expeditions to go looking for Franklin and his men should focus on the upper part of Wellington Channel, "as far beyond Mr. Penny's north-western advance as possible," the committee's final report suggested.

After all the arguments and finger pointing, the sober study and considered advice, the explorer establishment was determined to keep looking in the wrong place.

7

Ghost Ships

Polar explorers who knew what Franklin and his men were up against assumed they had gotten stuck somewhere around midway through the Northwest Passage. But the Royal Navy hadn't given up on the chance they had reached the Western Arctic, where Sir John had hoped to start making his way home by way of Russia. HMS *Enterprise* and HMS *Investigator* were assigned that search area and had to take the long way, sailing around Cape Horn at the tip of South America and up the coast through the Bering Strait. Lady Jane Franklin kept the hunt alive in areas farther east, where survivors were most likely to be found. This time she chose a Métis, William Kennedy, to lead. Kennedy was just five years old when he met Franklin as the novice explorer prepared for his first overland expedition to the Arctic at Cumberland House, the Hudson's Bay Company's fur-trading post on Pine Island in the Saskatchewan River. Kennedy's father, Alexander, was chief factor. During long winter nights, Franklin taught the boy, the fifth child of a Cree mother and a Scottish father, how to read and write. Inspired to learn, William went off to school in northern Scotland's Orkney Islands. He followed his father into the fur trade but quit the Hudson's Bay Company the same year that Franklin sailed with *Erebus* and *Terror* for the Northwest Passage. Kennedy refused to sell liquor to indigenous people, knowing it ruined and frequently ended their lives.

Lady Franklin offered him command of the *Prince Albert* on the recommendation of a former fur trader and Métis rights activist A. K. Isbister, Kennedy's nephew. More than a century later, the connection among Isbister, Kennedy, and Cumberland House, where both men once lived, would prove another serendipitous turning point during the modern search for the Franklin Expedition. William Kennedy interviewed and chose his crew for the ketch, most of them rugged Scots from the windswept Shetland Islands, with Lady Franklin's approval. The expedition took along seven carrier pigeons, marked with specially developed ink, in another attempt to send airborne updates, good or bad, from the Arctic. Sophy explained the method in specific instructions:

"A Cross on the breast (either in red or black ink, according to the color of the bird) to be used *only* in the event of good news, not necessarily implying the safety of Sir John Franklin individually, but that the missing Expedition has been found."

The sighting of a special pigeon, named for the purpose, would signal especially good news:

"The bird 'Lady Ross' to be sent off *only* under the joyful circumstances of Sir John's *individual* rescue and safety. It must besides, as a guarantee that it has been *sent* off, and has not escaped, have the red or black cross upon the breast and be marked No. 7."

Heeding guidance from the spirit world, Lady Franklin bucked the polar experts and instructed Kennedy to take the search south rather than via Wellington Channel. Her commander felt just as strongly that the supernatural messages were real. Kennedy was a friend of Captain William Coppin and had spent three days with him in Derry during the months of planning for the 1851 expedition. To be sure, Kennedy sat through three sessions to make contact with Weesy's ghost. He heard the same four place names, including the still-undiscovered Victoria Strait, and the location of *Erebus* and *Terror* off Victory Point, revealed in the original apparition two years earlier. Coppin even saw the *Prince Albert* off from Aberdeen.

Kennedy declared her a dry ship, with only a small amount of rum for medicinal purposes. On their way into the Arctic, the crew bought six sled dogs, sealskin boots, and other warm clothing from Inuit. The expedition covered some 1,100 grueling miles overland, in conditions so extreme they often couldn't build a fire, forcing them to eat ptarmigan, frozen and raw. At Peel Sound, where Kennedy should have made a turn south for the magnetic pole as Lady Franklin had instructed, he became confused. Just as an Arctic mirage had fooled John Ross years earlier in Lancaster Sound, Kennedy saw a land block between Somerset and Prince of Wales Islands that didn't exist. Convinced there was no navigable route, he headed farther west, where heavy ice and a lashing snowstorm made the hunt for an exit impossible. During the blizzard, air, land, and sea melded into an opaque smear. So close to the magnetic pole, a compass wasn't much help.

"In our own case our course was guided almost entirely by the wind, the direction of which was indicated by a dog-vane carried in the hand. The weather had been exceedingly cold for the last few days, and to-day excessively so, and we were all suffering severely from snow-blindness; the pain from which, aggravated by the sharp particles of the snow-drift dashed against our eyes by a furious head-wind, was absolutely excruciating."

They pushed on, followed for a while by a starving wolf. One of the sled dogs fainted and took twenty-five minutes to catch its breath. After several frustrating days, surviving on pemmican and snow to save water and fuel, Kennedy saw signs of scurvy and ordered a retreat. Tantalizingly close to picking up the missing men's trail, Kennedy pulled up short.

The Admiralty stuck to its view that Wellington Channel was the place to be, far to the north of where Franklin's men gave up their ships. For the next run at the wrong place, the Royal Navy chose Sir Edward Belcher, a tough taskmaster born in Halifax, Nova Scotia, who moved with his family to England when he was a boy. He volunteered for the navy at age thirteen and later served under Frederick Beechey in the Western Arctic. After Belcher developed a reputation for being too harsh, the Admiralty didn't give him a command for several years. But in 1852, the navy put him in charge of an expedition of five ships to look for Sir John and his crewmen. Belcher made no apologies for demanding the most of his men. At sea in the Arctic, there was far too much to lose to settle for anything less.

"Men who command must feel for the lives entrusted to their keeping," was the way he saw it. "And good men do not follow mad-brained fools."

HMS *Resolute* and her tender, the *Intrepid*, went west through Barrow Strait to Melville Island. Their main achievement was finding the stranded, starving, and stir-crazy men of HMS *Investigator*, a beat-up remnant of the navy's 1850 push to find the Franklin Expedition. She had spent months sailing to the Western Arctic with HMS *Enterprise*, by way of Cape Horn, then northwest through the Pacific to what is now Hawaii, and northeast from there into the Bering Strait. Another costly, high-risk deployment of two Royal Navy ships, and the payoff was minimal.

Investigator's captain, Robert McClure, discovered Prince of Wales Strait between Banks and Victoria Islands, but he almost lost everything in the gamble. In a storm, a massive ice floe snagged *Investigator* and shoved her back down the strait. The pressure was so intense that it snapped nine-inch-thick hawsers (the ship's heavy rope mooring lines) like threads and ripped off six ice anchors. The crew thought it was curtains, and, defying orders, broke into the liquor stores, hoping to dull the pain. The storm passed, and *Investigator* was still upright, so McClure sailed on, made it through another close call, and then decided to seek safe harbor. He chose a spot off M'Clure Strait, which he called Bay of God's Mercy, to winter over in 1851. As ship's surgeon Alexander Armstrong later griped: "It would have been *a mercy had we never entered it.*"

Grounded on a shoal, the ship was soon trapped in ice. During three winters of torture in Mercy Bay, temperatures dropped to –65 degrees Fahrenheit, at times forcing sixty-six men surviving on two-thirds rations to go without fresh water. Their stores were frozen solid. When the air finally warmed just above freezing in late June 1852, the sailors waited and watched for the sea ice to break up. Instead, its grip only tightened, growing by three inches over the previous month to seven feet, two inches thick. As the moans of his men mixed with the equally pained groan and creak of massive timbers squeezed by ice, McClure ordered his crew to abandon *Investigator* more than once, only to rescind and hope again that the Arctic would show mercy and free them.

When Belcher reached the archipelago with his five ships, he sent Henry Kellett with HMS *Resolute* and its steam tender, *Intrepid*, west to Melville Island. Belcher sailed north up Wellington Channel with HMS *Assistance* and the steamer *Pioneer*, while HMS *North Star* anchored off Beechey Island as a depot ship. On a twenty-two-day sledge trip across Melville Island, Lieutenant George Mecham stopped at Winter Harbor, where William Parry and his crew had struggled to survive decades earlier. There he found McClure's cached record of proceedings, which described his expedition's stranding at Mercy Bay. It also claimed McClure had discovered the final link in the Northwest Passage, which he had seen but not transited because ice blocked the way. Arriving too late in the year to attempt a rescue, Lieutenant Bedford Pim led a mission hauling two sledges early in the spring of 1853. The bigger one broke down, and Pim continued with two men by dogsled. After twenty-eight days covering 160 miles, in nasty cold, they managed to find *Investigator* just as McClure and his starving, addled, and disabled men were about to abandon the ship. The rescue left him speechless.

"The heart was too full for the tongue to speak," McClure recalled, thankful that he and his men had narrowly escaped the same catastrophe that befell Franklin and his crews.

Once warmed up and fed, McClure wanted to complete the Northwest Passage. Four of his men were dead, some survivors were blind, others were unable to walk. All had scurvy. Yet McClure insisted to Kellett that there was no reason to give up. Kellett won the argument, *Investigator* was abandoned, and everyone aboard moved to the Belcher Expedition's ships. Then they proceeded to get stuck in various places. Determined to keep morale as high as possible, Kellett got everyone who could stand outside and playing. On the ice, in −15 degrees Fahrenheit, the sailors batted balls and ran the bases in matches of rounders, a version of cricket considered an ancestor of baseball. The constant running kept them warm and gave them less time to think about being miserable. Kellett also put the men to work "snowing the deck," which provided a level surface on a ship listing several degrees to port and also helped keep the interior decks warmer.

Ship's surgeon Dr. William T. Domville led classes, starting with chemistry. The crew chose an abridged version of Shakespeare's *The Taming of the Shrew* for their first winter theater entertainment. Officers staged a popular one-act farce, *The Two Bonnycastles*. The play rollicks on from an opening scene in which a gentleman walking in the park snatches a watch from a man he thought had stolen it from him, only to find the timepiece in question was on the dressing table at home, and that the victim was in fact the perpetrator. All of which required a lot of preparation aboard *Resolute*: altering of dresses, rigging chandeliers, retouching drop scenes. Mr. Dean, the ship's carpenter, spent ten days making fifes, a guitar, and a key prop: a leg of mutton fashioned from wood and canvas.

But it wasn't all good times in the High Arctic. A ship's mate named Sainsbury, rescued from *Investigator*, had been growing weaker by the day. He and everyone else knew he was going to die. Emaciated, the sailor held on until half past midnight, then slipped away without a struggle. Two days later, Kellett led a somber service in the mid-November cold and mist. Then crewmen sewed Sainsbury's body into a rough shroud, carried him 250 yards from the ship to a hole cut in the ice, and let Arctic waters take his corpse. Sainsbury's burial in an ice-covered sea seared itself into the memory of George McDougall, the *Resolute*'s master.

"And never shall I forget the scene on the ice, as the body, sewn in canvas, with weights attached, was launched through the narrow opening, and disappeared to our view. Within an hour, Nature had placed an icy slab over the grave of our departed messmate."

Things only got worse. Storms pounded the vessels. The ice grew thicker. More men died.

In the spring of 1853, the Admiralty dispatched the *Breadalbane*, an old merchant ship pressed into naval transport service along with the steamer HMS *Phoenix*. Their mission was to resupply the Belcher Expedition in the hope that they had made enough progress to keep up the Franklin search. *Breadalbane*, a three-masted barque, hauled clothes, coal, food, and rum and anchored to sea ice off Beechey Island. Belcher's orders were to get the supply ship turned around quickly, before ice caught her, and to send any sick men, along with an update on his mission, back to Britain. Most of the cargo had been moved to shore when, not long after midnight on Sunday, August 21, 1853, *Breadalbane*'s timbers, which weren't properly strengthened for the Arctic like Royal Navy discovery ships were, began to squeal and wail. She was crying out in pain. Setting sea ice grating against her hull was about to crush it.

Phoenix quickly began to tow her out, as gently as possible, and by 3 a.m. the floating tandem fleeing the expanding ice sheet was halfway between Beechey Island and Devon Island's Cape Riley. Everything seemed under control, so William Fawckner, government agent aboard the *Breadalbane*, retired to his quarters. He was trying to sleep when the pressure of ice squeezing the hull popped his cabin door open around ten after four in the morning.

The lifeboats, he thought.

At least get the lifeboats off before she goes under! Fawckner hurried to get dressed and hustled on deck, in his slippers, to find his crew trying to lift the boats off to at least keep them in one piece. But they were like dry nuts in a nutcracker. Compressing ice instantly splintered them. Fawckner headed for the bow to send an emergency signal.

"I went forward to hail the Phoenix, for men to save the boats, and whilst doing so, the ropes by which we were secured parted, and a heavy nip took the ship, making every timber in her creak, and the ship tremble all over. I looked in the main hold and saw the beams giving away."

Down below, Fawckner's men didn't realize their ship's end was nigh. He rushed back to his cabin and hauled out his portmanteau, a leather chest, "and roared like a bull to those in their beds to jump out and save their lives." When Fawckner reached topside himself, the men on the ice shouted for him to jump. *Breadalbane* was going over. He ditched the portmanteau and leapt, losing his slippers in the descent to the broken ice. Within five minutes, the ship began "cracking up like matches would in the hand. When the destruction suddenly paused, Fawckner and a few others went aboard to salvage some belongings. He measured the water pouring into the hold. It was five feet deep.

While "in the act of sounding, a heavier nip than before pressed out the starboard bow and the ice was forced right into the forecastle." Everyone abandoned ship, with the few clothes they could save.

"The ship now began to sink fast, and from the time her bowsprit touched the ice, until her mastheads were out of sight, did not occupy above one minute and a half. It was a very sad and unceremonious way of being turned out of our ship. From the time the first nip took her, until her disappearance, did not occupy more than 15 minutes."

Everyone got onto the ice before *Breadalbane* went down. No one died, but other crews suffered fatalities, and little trace of Sir John Franklin and his men had been found. Belcher finally decided to cut his own losses. He ordered all the ships abandoned in the summer of 1854. Everyone would have to go home on *North Star*, still waiting at Beechey Island. This time Kellett, among others, was the one arguing to stay the course. McClintock, who was in charge of Kellett's tender, *Intrepid*, traveled six days by dogsled to argue with Belcher. They went back and forth for two days until, Belcher thought, "it can hardly be imagined that the case was not thoroughly sifted in all its bearings." The bullheaded commander wouldn't budge and delivered his final order in writing:

"This *abandonment* goes mightily against the grain. If we could save even 'Intrepid,' it would be something; but your *distance off-shore* precludes any movement before the 22nd of August, and that is too late for operations at Beechey Island. *No! All must come*; no volunteering will satisfy me!"

A final sledge party sent to move provisions from *Investigator* ashore to a cache reported in April 1854 that she was still beset, heeling slightly to starboard at an angle of 10 degrees. She eventually sank.

Early in the month after *Investigator* went down, Kellett and his crew made careful preparations to give up on *Resolute* and abandon her, too. It was a routine spelled out in Royal Navy training, one the men of *Erebus* and *Terror* likely followed almost six years earlier before heading ashore. Sailors coiled cables, hoisted boats and secured them, stowed booms, tied up the topsails, raised the rudder, and either stored below anything else that moved or lashed it down on deck. After each group completed its tasks, the men embarked on the roughly five-day trek to Beechey Island, until, after several days, only the commander and a few men were left. Anyone too sick to walk was carried—one lying on a cot, another in a makeshift palanquin. Kellett ordered that seamen could only carry thirty pounds of clothes and necessities. He allowed officers to carry forty-five pounds. After witnessing Kellett burn *Resolute*'s secret signals, McDougall had to decide himself what personal effects he should pack and what he would leave to the Arctic.

"There were a thousand and one things we would have desired to save, such as souvenirs from those we loved and respected, had our weights permitted; forty-five pounds is, however, too low a figure to indulge in luxuries. With a sigh, therefore, we were obliged to set aside the ornamental, and choose something more useful, but less romantic, in the shape of shirts, flannels, drawers, and such."

Down to the last compulsory steps of abandoning a Royal Navy ship, *Resolute*'s men hoisted the pilot jack, with a letter D, at the fore-topmasthead and displayed the red ensign and pendant. That was to ensure, as the ship's master put it, "in the event of her being obliged to 'knock under' to her icy antagonist, she might sink beneath the wave, as many a gallant predecessor had done, with colours flying." In the final countdown, the mournful ring of the ship's bell sounded across the ice to mark each hour. Smoke billowed from the galley stove's chimney as signal books turned to ashes in the fire.

Carpenters caulked down the gunroom skylight and after-companion, leaving the main hatchway the last entry and exit between the lower deck and the outside world. Only half of that remained open. After the captain and a few men dined in the darkened gunroom, Kellett inspected the lower decks and holds. Then he toasted his ship and the men who sailed her with a glass of wine. The last aboard drained their glasses and the commander ordered everyone topside. A carpenter sealed the main hatchway and at 7 p.m. on Saturday, May 13, 1854, the last men of the *Resolute* bid her a final good-bye and left on four sledges.

Embedded in a huge ice floe, *Resolute* slowly drifted while Kellett and others made their way to the rendezvous with *North Star*. When Belcher brought his expedition home, the Admiralty was displeased with his decisions. The Royal Navy court-martialed him. Belcher tried to intimidate witnesses, but respected voices lined up against him. They not only questioned his judgment as a Royal Navy commander but also accused him of frequently being drunk at sea, unable to make sound decisions if he wanted to. In a rambling defense, Belcher cited the Admiralty's own instructions, insisting he ordered the four ships abandoned within the leeway the naval command had granted him. Refusing to be the Lords' fall guy, Belcher effectively spit their charges back at them.

"I have now been nearly 43 years in the Naval service of my country, 36 years a commissioned officer and for periods of nearly 20 years, I have been entrusted with more important commands and exercised greater powers than, I believe, few of my rank have ever held," he told the court-martial.

"Next to the approbation of my Sovereign, and of my Lords Commissioners of the Admiralty, I value the honourable approval of my professional brethren. Jealous of my honour, and sensitively alive to the remotest shadow of blame, I confidently repose in your hands that character which during a long and trying service in every clime, and in the remotest regions of the Earth, has, I trust, not now been tarnished by obedience to the wishes, as well as the commands of my Lords Commissioners of the Admiralty."

Belcher was acquitted but not exonerated. The Arctic had ruined another reputation. McClure and his men fared better. They picked up Parliament's £10,000 prize for finding the Northwest Passage, although Lady Franklin would later insist that Sir John had found it. Despite the official claims of mission accomplished, however, there was still more humiliation to come for the Royal Navy. Just as Kellett and McClintock had predicted, the sea ice opened and *Resolute* broke free on her own. Arctic winds and currents delivered her to Baffin Bay.

James Buddington, an American whaling captain who sailed out of New England on the barque *George Henry*, had his crew corral her in September 1855. After *Resolute* spent some fifteen months surviving on her own, a ghost ship making her own way to safety, the Americans found her in remarkably good shape.

"The ropes, indeed, were hard and inflexible as chains; the rigging was stiff, and cracked at the touch," the *Illustrated London News* reported. "The tanks in the hold had burst, the ironwork was rusted, the paint was discoloured with bilge-water, and the mast, and topgallantmast were shattered; but the hull had escaped unscathed, and the ship was not hurt in any vital part. There were three or four feet of water in the hold, but she had not sprung a leak."

Buddington towed the vessel to New London, Connecticut. The Admiralty sent its thanks and offered to waive its sovereign rights over the ship and let him keep *Resolute*. If Buddington preferred, he could let the British consul in Boston sell her and he and his crew could take cash. Lady Franklin asked that the ship be put at her disposal to go looking for her husband again. But the US Congress voted to fix up *Resolute*, and return her whole, to Britain. For their skill and bravery, Buddington and his men pocketed $40,000, or more than $1 million today, from Congress.

The gesture made Queen Victoria so happy that she went to Cowes Harbour, on the Isle of Wight, to receive *Resolute* when US Navy Captain Henry Hartstene presented the vessel to her on December 16, 1856. The British were suitably impressed by the exquisite fix-up job by American workers at the Brooklyn Navy Yard. Not only was everything on board preserved, "even to the books in the Captain's library, the pictures in his cabin, and some musical instruments belonging to other officers," but the US navy yard made new British flags to replace the ones that had rotted in the Arctic.

"Sir, I thank you," the queen told Hartstene after he delivered a message of goodwill from the American people.

Years later, when *Resolute* was decommissioned, Queen Victoria returned the favor and presented a desk made from her oak timbers to President Rutherford B. Hayes in 1880. With a few exceptions, every US president since then has used it, either in the study in the private residence or in the Oval Office. Only Lyndon Johnson, Richard Nixon, and Gerald Ford eschewed a seat at a rich piece of Arctic and Royal Navy history. Franklin Roosevelt asked that the desk be remodeled to include a modesty panel, carved with the presidential seal, so people couldn't see the leg braces of a leader disabled by polio. He died too soon to see the work done, but Harry Truman had it completed. The Resolute Desk became iconic when President John F. Kennedy's son, John Jr., opened the kneehole panel and peeked out at a photographer while his dad was at work.

The barque *Breadalbane*, on the other hand, could easily have been lost to time in the uncharted depths of the High Arctic. She was just a supply ship, a misfortunate sacrifice of the merchant marine, left to slowly decay on the seafloor. Without an HMS in front of her name, she was long forgotten. Then an explorer, doctor, and inventor—a twentieth-century swashbuckler cut from the same cloth as the men who sailed her, hoping to help save other men like them—discovered the sunken wreck.

That unlikely moment would be the first big break in the modern hunt for *Erebus* and *Terror*.

8

Starvation Cove

Two paths crossing in the winter void finally broke the Arctic's obstinate silence surrounding the Franklin Expedition's disappearance. That historic turning point arrived in 1854, when physician and fur trader John Rae had a serendipitous encounter, in the middle of nowhere, with an Inuk hunter. Lady Franklin had been trying for months to persuade Rae to look where dissident voices, and the paranormal, convinced her *Erebus* and *Terror* could be found. The Hudson's Bay Company trader, a veteran Arctic explorer, was a hard man to convince. During Lady Franklin's 1849 visit to Scotland with Sophy to speak with whalers and William Scoresby, Rae was away in the Arctic with John Richardson, looking for Lady Franklin's husband. Jane visited Rae's mother and sipped some cherry brandy with her, an excellent opportunity to offer some thoughts on how her Sir John might be found. Later that same year, after Rae returned empty-handed, she tried to nudge him toward the area south of King William Island.

"I do not know whether you consider that the mouth of the Great Fish River should be examined," she wrote to Rae, dropping an obvious hint. But on matters of the Franklin search, the Hudson's Bay Company took instructions from the Admiralty and required Rae to do the same.

"Lady Franklin also says that a growing opinion prevails in England that the long-missing expedition is icebound somewhere in the direction of the magnetic pole, or towards Back's River, and to search in the neighbourhood of these places was the principal object of the small expedition under Captain Forsyth," Rae wrote to fellow physician and Franklin friend Richardson in April 1851.

"It is very proper that those parts should be examined, but I have very little expectation that any traces of those looked for will be found in that quarter."

Rae was convinced that if *Erebus* and *Terror* weren't way to the northwest, between Cape Walker and Cape Bathurst, they were likely at Melville Island. That is a very broad region, one that Franklin and his crewmen could have passed through only if the Arctic had allowed them to take the route the Admiralty specified in its orders. Rae would have to eat his words. But before finding proof he was wrong, he discovered evidence that suggested he was right. The fur trader was far to the east of where Jane had hoped he would go when, in the late summer of 1851, he stumbled across two pieces of wood in Parker Bay, about fifty miles east of Cambridge Bay, on Victoria Island. The shore where he found the debris overlooks the western end of Queen Maud Gulf, near the bottom of Victoria Strait. Currents and sea ice could have carried broken pieces of *Erebus* or *Terror* there. Less than three years earlier, Franklin's men had abandoned the ships roughly 150 miles to the northeast, at the top of Victoria Strait.

The pieces Rae picked up must have come from at least one Royal Navy ship. The first was round with a square base, five feet, nine inches long, and appeared to be the butt end of a small flagstaff. It was marked with what seemed to be the initials S.C. The proof that the object was Royal Navy property came from a looped piece of white line, which was nailed onto the wood with two copper tacks. A broad arrow stamped on the tacks, and a red worsted thread running through the attached line, marked them as government property. Half a mile away, Rae discovered the second piece of wood, which was lying in the water but touching the beach. It was three feet, eight inches long, and made of oak. Rae thought it was likely the remains of a stanchion that had been turned in a lathe, and once fit into a clasp or band of iron. The Admiralty consulted various experts, including polar mariners, who couldn't conclusively say what ship they came from.

The most experienced and successful *qalunaaq* traveler in the Arctic, John Rae won the highest praise from the Royal Geographical Society for that 1851 journey. In awarding him the Founder's Gold Medal, it noted that "he set out accompanied by two men only, and, trusting solely for shelter to snow houses, which he taught his men to build, accomplished a distance of 1,060 miles in 39 days or 27 miles per day including stoppages—a feat which has never been equaled in Arctic travelling." Rae had learned well from Inuit how to travel long distances in the Arctic and come back alive. But he had loved the outdoors since he was a boy, exploring the moors of Scotland, sailing small boats, and learning how to handle a rifle. A crack shot by the time he reached the Canadian wilderness, he once winged a wolf in a circling pack preparing to eat him. They hightailed it instead.

At age forty, the acknowledged master of Arctic exploration, Rae still wanted more. He was eager for a fourth and final expedition to map what he believed were the last three to four hundred unexplored miles of North America's Arctic coast. But the Admiralty no longer had any need for the peacetime mission that John Barrow, and Arctic exploration, had provided following the Royal Navy's victory in the Napoleonic Wars. Almost four decades of peace in Europe ended in October 1853 with the outbreak of the Crimean War between allied powers and Russia. Weeks earlier, Rae had set off from Chesterfield Inlet, on Hudson Bay's western shore, on a mapping mission that the Hudson's Bay Company bankrolled at his request. It would take Rae to precisely the area that Franklin Expedition survivors had set out to reach five years earlier. It was the same place where dissident voices and spectral visions had said searchers should look. Rae didn't expect to turn up anything useful.

"I do not mention the lost navigators," he wrote in a published letter to *The Times* on November 27, 1852, "as there is not the slightest hope of finding any traces of them in the quarter to which I am going."

Barrow, still devoted to his Arctic project, provided Rae with what the explorer called "a very valuable Halketts Boat for the Service of my party," for his final expedition. But a screwup with the railway baggage trains between London and Liverpool meant the portable boat didn't reach Rae before his steamer left the dock. That didn't affect his plans much. He would make most of this grueling journey with a small team of men hauling heavy sledges over the snow and ice by rope. Rae's goal was to reach the Castor and Pollux River, about fifty miles northeast of the Chantrey Inlet, where what is now called the Back River flows into the Arctic sea.

In late August 1853, Rae and seven of his men, who included Métis, a Cree hunter, and an Inuk interpreter, packed up a small boat with food and supplies and headed north for the mouth of Back River. For eleven days, they paddled through wicked currents and rapids and portaged around waterfalls, including one about twenty-five feet high, only to be blocked by terrain covered in rocks and stones for miles. It wasn't impossible to haul a boat over the long obstacle, Rae judged, but that was too arduous a job for so late in the season. So the men headed for Repulse Bay, on Hudson Bay, to spend the winter there. To stock up, they killed 109 caribou, a musk ox, fifty-three ptarmigan, and a seal. They also netted fifty-four salmon. Rae shot the musk ox and twenty-one of the caribou himself.

That got them through a very cold, stormy winter in good shape. On the last day of March 1854, Rae took four men and the interpreter, William Ouligbuck, to journey across land for a survey of the Boothia Peninsula's west coast. He planned to finish work that John Ross and his nephew James had begun during their hellish years stranded in sea ice a quarter-century earlier. Rae's team had 865 pounds of provisions for a sixty-five-day expedition. Every man dragged a sledge: Rae's weighed 110 pounds, while the others had to pull 160 pounds. The Inuk faced the same risks and hardships that Rae did, but the payoff was significantly less: an annual salary of £20, or some $380 today. To Inuit, hauling heavy sledges was dogs' work. Ouligbuck soon tired of it and tried to bolt, which proved fortuitous to the Franklin search.

Rae was suspicious of his interpreter. He thought Ouligbuck was sulky and derided him as an "incorrigible thief" and "one of the greatest rascals unhung." But the explorer's preferred interpreter, William's father, wasn't available. Known simply as Ouligbuck, he died in 1852. It was a great loss. The elder Inuk had given many years in loyalty to the fur-trading-company explorers he assisted, dating back to Franklin's early years in the Arctic. Franklin was a captain when he met Ouligbuck in 1824, when a Hudson's Bay Company post assigned the Inuk to go with Franklin on his second overland expedition to the northern coast, by way of the Mackenzie River. The elder Ouligbuck couldn't speak English then, but he accompanied the Inuk interpreter Tattannoeuk as a hunter on the journey, for wages of fifty beaver pelts per annum.

At the Mackenzie delta, the group split and Ouligbuck went east with John Richardson, the doctor and friend who would be an important ally to Lady Franklin as she pressed for rescue missions. The Inuk climbed the ranks from hunting seal and weeding the turnip garden at Hudson's Bay Company outposts and became a skilled interpreter. His ability to win the trust of other Inuit helped the fur-trading company to open up new trade links. His son didn't prove so reliable, or quite as valuable, to Rae. At least not directly. After William tried to flee, a chance encounter with an Inuk hunter in the middle of nowhere changed the course of the Franklin search forever.

As Rae's sledging party moved northward, they were pounded by winter gales from the west and had to slog through ankle-deep snow, advancing a little over one mile each hour. Exhausted, they built a small snow house, had some tea and frozen pemmican, and got a few hours of rest. When they started moving again, a bigger storm hit, dumping another thick layer of snow that made walking even more difficult. By the time they reached Pelly Belly (now the hamlet of Kugaaruk), in the Gulf of Boothia, Rae was so far behind schedule that he decided to take a detour on his journey to the Castor and Pollux River. Instead, he set a course for the magnetic pole, but soon he had to give up on that too, after seeing rocky, mountainous terrain to the north. So the group headed south, and, after a couple of days' slogging, Rae spotted fresh footprints in the snow. Assuming they must be Inuit, he sent William Ouligbuck and another man to track down the people who made them. Eleven hours later, they returned with seventeen Inuit, five of them women. Rae remembered several in the group from his stay at Repulse Bay five years earlier.

"Most of the others had never before seen 'Whites,' and were extremely forward and troublesome, they would give us no information on which any reliance could be placed, and none of them would consent to accompany us for a day or two, although I promised to reward them liberally. Apparently, there was great objection to our travelling across the Country in a westerly direction.

"Finding that it was their object to puzzle the Interpreter and mislead us, I declined purchasing more than a small piece of Seal from them, and sent them away, not however, without some difficulty, as they lingered about with the hope of stealing something, and notwithstanding our vigilance, succeeded in abstracting from one of the sledges a few pounds of Biscuit and Grease."

The next morning was clear. With such good weather, Rae got the men up and sledging at 3 a.m. While they were caching the seal meat Rae had bought, Ouligbuck made a run for it. He tried to rejoin the Inuit the explorer had shunned, but he "was overtaken after a sharp race of four or five miles."

"He was in a great fright when we came up to him, and was crying like a child, but expressed his readiness to return, and pleaded sickness as an excuse for his conduct. I believe he was really unwell, probably from having eaten too much boiled Seals flesh, with which he had been regaled in the snowhuts of the Natives."

The Inuk interpreter's excuse didn't seem to explain his suddenly erratic behavior. He was frightened, not sick, so afraid of the place Rae wanted to visit that a grown man was reduced to tears. The reason was too sensitive to discuss with *qalunaaq*. The spirits must be respected. It would take a long time, and the probing work of an Inuk historian, to reveal what Ouligbuck was really thinking that day, and why. Rae was satisfied with what he heard and had his men unload some of Ouligbuck's sledge, hoping to make the arduous journey easier on him.

The group had barely started moving again when they bumped into an Inuk hunter. He was more relaxed, even eager to answer Rae's questions. Their conversation revealed other dark truths of horrible suffering and death that soon shocked a waiting nation.

Rae recorded the man's name with a different spelling, likely a phonetic version, but history has settled on In-nook-poo-zhee-jook. He was driving a dogsled, piled with musk-ox or caribou meat, when Rae and his men appeared early on the morning of April 21, 1854. The hunter struck the explorer as intelligent and willing to speak freely with outsiders, even though he had never met *qalunaaq* before. The Inuk also had a remarkable memory for precise details, which would remain the same in follow-up interviews with visitors who came looking for him years later. Rae noticed he was wearing a gold cap-band around his head, which obviously wasn't traditional clothing. It was part of a Royal Navy uniform, likely worn by an officer. Rae asked where the hunter got it, and he replied that it came from "where the dead white men were, but that he himself had never been there, that he did not know the place, and could not go so far, giving me the idea that it was a great way off." In his rough notes, Rae said the Inuk guessed it was ten or twelve days' journey to the west, beyond two large rivers, but he did not know the place.

Then began a gruesome story: In the spring of 1850, two years after the sailors of *Erebus* and *Terror* gave up their ships, Inuit families hunting seals on the north coast of King William Island saw about forty *qalunaaq* men walking south over the ice. The travelers were thin and all but one were dragging a boat and sledges by ropes. The Inuit described the man in charge as tall, stout, and middle-aged. None could speak Inuktitut, but, using hand gestures, they managed to get across that a ship, or ships, had been crushed by ice. Short of provisions, they bought either a small seal, or a piece of seal, and then pitched tents to rest.

Later that same spring, but before the sea ice broke up, Inuit discovered the corpses of some thirty dead white men. The graves of others were on the mainland, and five more bodies were buried on an island nearby. That was "about a long day's journey to the northwest of the mouth of a large stream, which can be no other than Back's Great Fish River (named by the Esquimaux Oot-koo-hi-ca-lik), as its description, and that of the low shore in the neighbourhood of Point Ogle and Montreal Island, agree exactly with that of Sir George Back," Rae reported.

The site of mass death would later be named Starvation Cove. It is near Richardson Point, which is roughly twenty miles southwest of Gjoa Haven, across the eastern end of Simpson Strait. The graveyard Inuit described to the south was on Montreal Island, which lies off the western shore of Chantrey Inlet, not far from the mouth of what is now called the Back River.

"Some of the bodies were in a tent or tents; others were under the boat which had been turned over to form a shelter, and some lay scattered about in different directions," Rae wrote to company headquarters in London. "Of those seen on the Island, it was supposed that one was that of an Officer, (chief) as he had a telescope strapped over his shoulders, and his double barrelled gun lay underneath him.

"From the mutilated state of many of the bodies and the contents of the kettles, it is evident that our wretched Countrymen had been driven to the last dread alternative, as a means of sustaining life. A few of the unfortunate Men must have survived until the arrival of the wild fowl, (say until the end of May,) as shots were heard, and fresh bones and feathers of geese were noticed near the scene of the sad event."

Rae concluded that the dying Franklin Expedition survivors had more than enough weaponry to hunt for food if they had been physically, and mentally, able to do so.

"There appears to have been an abundant store of ammunition, as the Gunpowder was emptied by the Natives in a heap on the ground out of the kegs or cases containing it and a quantity of shot and ball was found below high water mark, having probably been left on the ice close to the beach before the spring thaw commenced.

"There must have been a number of telescopes, guns, (several of them double barrelled,) watches, compasses &c. all of which seem to have been broken up, as I saw pieces of these different articles with the Natives, and I purchased as many of them as possible, together with some silver spoons and forks, an order of merit in the form of a Star, and a small silver plate engraved Sir John Franklin K.O.H."

Rae knew that the grisly story, especially the claim that mariners in Her Majesty's Royal Navy had resorted to cannibalism, would cause a storm when it inevitably made the newspapers, so he tried to gather any solid evidence he could. He made In-nook-poo-zhee-jook an offer:

"I bought the cap-band from him, and told him that if he or his companions had any other things, to bring them to our winter quarters at Repulse Bay, where they would receive good prices for them."

Along with the silver plate, the relics he brought back to London were Sir John Franklin's star of the Hanoverian order of knighthood.

The silver spoons and forks were engraved, or, in at least one case, scratched with a sharp instrument to show the initials of other officers from *Erebus* and *Terror*, including second-in-command Crozier, Gore, the surgeon Goodsir, and his assistants Peddie and McDonald. Also among the artifacts were two pieces of a gold watch case etched with the name James Reid, *Erebus*'s ice master, plus several coins, a surgeon's knife and scalpel, a pocket compass box, part of an optical instrument, and a small silver pencil case.

The stories and objects "prove, beyond a doubt, that a portion, if not all, of the then survivors of the long lost and unfortunate party under Sir John Franklin, had met with a fate as melancholy and dreadful as it is possible to imagine," Rae wrote in a letter to the company secretary, dated September 1, 1854.

The place where so many of Franklin's men were said to have met their deaths was far to the west. Rae didn't speak to anyone who had actually been there or seen for themselves what their accounts described. The Inuit claimed to have heard from others who lived west of them and saw the men traveling across the ice. Rae had no doubt they were telling the truth, so he decided to hurry back to London to inform his bosses, who then told the Admiralty. He had been heading southeast for the top of Hudson Bay and ruled out a detour to try to find what would have been the first major discovery in the mystery of the lost Franklin Expedition.

"The information was too vague to act upon, particularly at this season, when everything is covered with snow," he explained in his notes.

Evidence of a baffling disaster, which may have included logbooks, diaries of dying men, or other written records, would be left to scavengers and the ravages of nature for several years to come. What Rae took to be conclusive answers just raised more questions, doubts, and fresh theories in what became a cottage industry of trying to solve a mystery that only became more tangled as people pulled at threads.

Long before Rae could reach London and report that he believed the last men of *Erebus* and *Terror* were dead, Lady Franklin's life was unraveling. The Admiralty informed her by letter on January 12, 1854, that it would strike from the Royal Navy's books the names of all men serving in the lost Franklin Expedition. The announcement was to be made in the official gazette that carried government announcements on March 31, three weeks before Rae happened upon his crushing discovery. Jane was officially being declared a widow. She was incensed as much as heartbroken. It took her a week to recover from the shock, get her gumption back, and write a disgusted reply. She declared the navy's death notice "presumptuous in the sight of God, as it will be felt to be indecorous, not to say indecent (you must pardon me for speaking the truth as I feel it) in the eyes of men."

Lady Franklin politely told the navy to stuff its widow's pension. She wasn't going to go easy on the Admiralty and accept money for the death of a husband without incontrovertible proof he had actually died. Jane found new strength in defiance, a transformation of spirit that her stepdaughter Eleanor described: She "changed the deep mourning she had been wearing for years for bright colours of green & pink as soon as the Admiralty notice was gazetted," making the notice public, official, and final.

"I made no enquiries what other officers' wives would do, considering that I was privileged to judge for myself and if every individual belonging to me or belonging to the ships were to put on the habiliments of despair, it would make no difference to me...," Jane explained to Sir John's anguished sister.

"It would be acting a falsehood & a gross hypocrisy on my part to put on mourning when I have not yet given up all hope—still less would I do so in that month & day that suits the Admiralty's financial convenience."

After a stormy return across the Atlantic, Rae reached London in late October 1854 and went straight to the Admiralty. He briefly filled in naval command on the bad news and filed a more complete expedition report to his employers. The Admiralty released to *The Times* a written account he had sent in July, including sketches of the artifacts he bought from Inuit. The newspaper broke to the British public the shocking story of cannibalism and the long, suffering deaths of dozens of men, setting off a furor that raged for months. Charles Dickens led the charge with a two-part diatribe in *Household Words*.

Dickens not only condemned the cannibalism claims as an affront to his countrymen's honor and high Christian morals but also dismissed Inuit testimony as "the wild tales of a herd of savages." Dickens angrily pointed an accusing finger at the bearers of bad news, people who history would prove were telling the truth. Like one of the misanthropes in his novels, an armchair detective determined to make the facts serve his prejudices, the writer spun the few Inuit-reported facts that served his purpose. The mutilated bodies they described could easily be explained as the ravages of scurvy or scavenging bears, wolves, or foxes, Dickens insisted. He found more telling the body of what appeared to be an officer, the large man with the telescope slung over his shoulders, lying facedown on a double-barreled rifle. That struck Dickens as strong evidence Franklin's men were murdered.

"Lastly, no man can, with any show of reason, undertake to affirm that this sad remnant of Franklin's gallant band were not set upon and slain by the Esquimaux themselves," he wrote in a two-part *Household Words* screed in December 1854. "It is impossible to form an estimate of the character of any race of savages, from their deferential behaviour to the white man while he is strong. The mistake has been made again and again; and the moment the white man has appeared in the new aspect of being weaker than the savage, the savage has changed and sprung upon him.

"There are pious persons who, in their practice, with a strange inconsistency, claim for every child born to civilisation all innate depravity, and for every savage born to the woods and wilds all innate virtue. We believe every savage to be in his heart covetous, treacherous, and cruel; and we have yet to learn what knowledge the white man—lost, houseless, shipless, apparently forgotten by his race, plainly famine-stricken, weak, frozen, helpless, and dying— has of the gentleness of Esquimaux nature."

While Dickens was stoking public anger, Rae discovered there was a £10,000 reward, or more than $900,000 today, on the books for any- one who the Admiralty board determined was the first to ascertain the Franklin Expedition's fate. Rae was in a salary dispute with the Hud- son's Bay Company, which was withholding judgment on his bonus for wintering over. The board wanted to see if the government would pay him its reward. Linking the two—one a matter of service to employers, the other a very big thank-you from his country—was to Rae "perfectly beyond my comprehension." He quickly applied for the reward.

After weighing the evidence, the Admiralty ruled that Rae should get the money in early 1856. Lady Franklin, who was seriously ill at the time, wrote a scathing letter of protest three months later, when she had partially recovered. She complained that no bodies or doc- uments had been found to prove beyond doubt the Inuit accounts of mass death. Jane insisted that the Admiralty board's decision was premature. She also criticized a follow-up mission sent out the previous year to check Rae's information. Headed by James Ander- son and James Green, after Rae declined to lead it, the expedition descended the Back River to Chantrey Inlet and Montreal Island. It was a rushed operation, without a proper interpreter or supplies to overwinter.

They made it past eighty-three rapids in birch-bark canoes, which doubled as shields against the frigid wind at night, even though the bark was almost worn out. With winter approaching fast, the men could only spend nine days looking for evidence to back up Rae's report. Ice floes made travel dodgy through the inlet. One of the voya- geur paddlers claimed years later that he saw the masts of a partially submerged ship poking through the ice to the north, but he kept quiet because he wanted to get south before freeze-up trapped the men. The expedition came up blank except for some wood and metal fragments, including a chip bearing the name of *Erebus* crew member "Mr. Stanley." Lady Franklin was livid. She blamed the Admiralty for putting concerns of cost before the lives of Royal Navy men when Rae's report required a major investigation.

"There was but one feeling in the country on this sad occasion," she wrote on April 12, 1856, eight years after *Erebus* and *Terror* were surrendered to the sea ice. "No amount of expense would have been grudged to make a final expedition of search complete, for it was felt that after six long years of failure and disappointment, the clue which we had asked and prayed for was now in our hands, and that England's honour and credit were concerned in holding it fast and following it up till it led to the solution of the mystery.

"My Lords, I shrink from recalling the pain and woful [sic] disappointment I felt, and which many others felt with me, when the response to this generous excitement in the public mind, and the sole result of your deliberations, was no more than a birch bark canoe expedition down the Great Fish River, confided to the Hudson's Bay Company, but unsustained by any naval resources."

She begged the Admiralty not to close the file on Sir John or his men.

"I would entreat of you, before you place an extinguisher upon the light which has arisen in that dark corner of the earth, whither we have been directed as by the finger of God, that you will, as you have done before, call together those Arctic officers, and obtain their individual and collective judgment in this emergency."

If the Admiralty refused to send a final search mission, Jane concluded in her letter, it should at least assist her in mounting a private expedition to look for her husband, whom she now accepted was dead, and his crewmen.

"My funds, since the settlement of my late husband's affairs, are equal to the ample equipment of the Isabel schooner, which is now lying in dock, waiting, at a considerable expense to me, her possible destination; and, unless these my independent funds should become exhausted, which I do not forsee, I shall not even ask your Lordships for the ordinary pension of a rear-admiral's widow, to which I presume I am entitled. My request to your Lordships will be limited to such assistance as is entirely independent of money, and indeed, to such as I have been assured, on the highest authority, will not be denied."

Leading scientists and members of the polar pantheon, including Frederick Beechey, Collinson, and Ross, rallied to Lady Franklin's side. Thirty-six signed a hastily prepared petition to the prime minister, Viscount Palmerston, which included the names of eighteen more dignitaries who couldn't be in London to sign. It called on the government to launch one more search for *Erebus* and *Terror* to "clear up a mystery which has excited the sympathy of the civilized world."

"Although most persons have arrived at the conclusion that there can now be no survivors of Franklin's Expedition, yet there are eminent men in our own country and in America who hold a contrary opinion," the petition pointed out. It cited Dr. Elisha Kent Kane, the American physician and explorer who had gone the farthest north in search of *Erebus* and *Terror*. He had recently received the Royal Geographical Society's highest honor. "By dogs—the great blessing of arctic travel—this whole area could be scoured; and we must remember that Rae had these animals at Repulse Bay, and, but for his return (to London), could, in a single month, have cleared up the mystery," Kane suggested to his financier, Henry Grinnell, anxious to go where Rae hadn't.

Only a Royal Navy man-of-war would be capable of reaching the death sites the Inuit described, the petitioners insisted. The risk to that ship would be low because another had already "passed to Cambridge Bay, within 150 miles of the mouth of the Back River, and returned home unscathed—its commander having expressed his conviction that the passage in question is so constantly open that ships can navigate it without difficulty in one season."

In a pleading letter asking the prime minister to approve the request, Lady Franklin argued that the country owed one last effort to mariners who, quoting Sir John's friend and physician John Richardson, had "forged the last link of the North West passage with their lives." She suggested that the prime minister order the *Resolute*, kindly repaired by the Americans and ready for Arctic service, to carry out the mission.

"Surely then, I may plead for such men, that a careful search be made for any possible survivor, that the bones of the dead be sought for and gathered together, that their buried records be unearthed, or recovered from the hands of the Esquimaux, and above all, that their last written words, so precious to their bereaved families and friends, be saved from destruction.

"A mission so sacred is worthy of a Government which has grudged and spared nothing for its heroic soldiers and sailors in other fields of warfare, and will surely be approved by our gracious Queen, who overlooks none of Her loyal subjects suffering and dying for their country's honour. This final and exhausting search is all I seek in behalf of the first and only martyrs to Arctic discovery in modern times, and it is all I ever intend to ask."

The petition failed. The Admiralty considered the matter closed. It didn't even bother to respond to Lady Franklin's impassioned April letter. The government said, with great regret, that there was no chance to save any lives so there was no reason to expose more men to potentially mortal danger.

"It is not extraordinary that those who are disposed to form a low estimate of the value of scientific research, should also entertain doubts as to the propriety of hazarding human life in its behalf," Lord Wrottesley, a disgusted signatory and president of the Royal Society that represented Britain's best scientific minds, told members.

Doubling down, he said: "In the late discussions on the expediency of undertaking another Polar Expedition, it seemed to be assumed by some, that the well-grounded anticipation of valuable contributions to physical and geographical science, would not alone be sufficient to justify the exposing of the lives of gallant men to peril, not even of those who were most willing and anxious to be so employed, emulous of such distinction, and regardless of the risk."

Lady Franklin, however, refused to concede defeat. Beaten down by years of fighting powerful men who could not abide the notion they might be wrong, she was exhausted, and her finances almost were too. At times, she was weak, her moods dark, her health failing. It must have been tempting to cut her losses and live the simpler life of a lost hero's widow. But Jane had come too far to give up now. Once again, she picked herself up and stood tall. She seized the lead from men too timid to stomach all the things they imagined could go wrong, not least the political heat that would flare if more sailors were lost. Putting the rest of the family fortune, and her own reputation, on the line, Lady Franklin launched the expedition that found the only written record of what happened to her husband and his ships.

"Your leave is granted," she telegraphed Francis McClintock in Dublin on April 23, 1857, soon after he applied for leave from the Royal Navy. "The 'Fox' is mine; the refit will commence immediately."

Lady Franklin bought the ship from the estate of Sir Richard Sutton, a master of foxhounds who became undersecretary of state. Before his death in 1856, he had sailed the *Fox* on a single voyage to Norway. Jane bought the lightly used screw yacht for £2,000, or more than $180,000 today. The expedition, including upgrades to the ship, was expected to cost more than eight times that. She raised some of the money from donations, as small as a single shilling coin to £500, which came from the expedition's sailing master, Allen Young. He had made a small fortune as a merchant mariner and volunteered his time to look for Sir John and his men. Lady Franklin was still some £7,000 short when McClintock was about ready to sail. Jane let him off the hook for any liabilities and future expenses by signing a deed of indemnity.

At 177 tons, the *Fox* was smaller and lighter than *Erebus* and *Terror*, and right in the polar exploration sweet spot, which Scoresby had defined more than half a century earlier when he wrote: "The class of vessels best adapted for discovery in the Polar Seas, seems to be that of 100 to 200 tons burden. . . . They are stronger, more easily managed, in less danger of being stove or crushed by ice, and are less expensive." Under the gun to get the *Fox* ready to sail by July 1, 1857, refit workers in Aberdeen did what they could to make her ready for harsh Arctic travel. Workmen pulled down the yacht's velvet hangings. They reduced the skylights and roomy hallways to conserve warmth, which had to come from smaller stoves that replaced a larger furnace to make room for a crew of twenty-five.

"Internally, she was fitted up with the strictest economy in every sense, and the officers were crammed into pigeon-holes, styled cabins, in order to make room for provisions and stores; our mess-room, for five persons, measured 8 feet square," McClintock wrote in his journal.

Yet he had no trouble finding men eager to join the search for anyone still alive in the Franklin Expedition or any remains, documents, or important artifacts searchers could turn up.

"Expeditions of this nature are always popular with seamen, and innumerable were the applications sent to me; but still more abundant the offers to 'serve in any capacity' which poured in from all parts of the country, from people of all classes, many of whom had never seen the sea."

The *Fox* was bolstered with heavy planking, crossbeams, and "the slender brass propeller replaced by a massive iron one." That was the expedition's salvation several times when ice floes closed in and the *Fox* steamed free, as occurred on August 19, 1857, in Melville Bay: "Continued strong S.E. winds, pressing the ice closely together, dark sky and snow; everything wears a wintry and threatening aspect; we are closely hemmed in, and have our rudder and screw unshipped." As the weather cleared, the crew worked thirteen hours to get "the ship out of her small ice-creek into a larger space of water, and in so doing advancing a mile and a half." Even still, McClintock noted, the expedition was making slower progress than Sir James Clark Ross had made on HMS *Enterprise* in 1848, when some of Franklin's men were still alive.

On the last day of June, Lady Franklin and Sophy boarded the *Fox* to see the expedition off. "Seeing how deeply agitated she was on leaving the ship," noted McClintock, "I endeavoured to repress the enthusiasm of my crew, but without avail; it found vent in three prolonged hearty cheers."

At McClintock's request, Jane sat down to write instructions to her expedition commander on the eve of departure. She couldn't bring herself to influence his judgment, since she was certain they agreed on what should be done. But Lady Franklin did remind him: If no survivors could be found, then her greatest hope was "the recovery of the unspeakably precious documents of the expedition, public and private, and the personal relics of my dear husband and his companions." Finally, she asked him to find any evidence that Sir John and his crewmen, not John Rae, had found the last stretch of the Northwest Passage.

"I am sure that you will do all that man can do for the attainment of all these objects; my only fear is that you may spend yourselves too much in the effort; and you must therefore let me tell you how much dearer to me even than any of them is the preservation of the valuable lives of the little band of heroes who are your companions and followers."

McClintock planned to focus his search efforts on King William

Island and the area along the continental coastline between the Coppermine and Back Rivers. Rae's information from the Inuit made the latter essential. Paranormal revelations had helped put the former on the list. Rae had only recently discovered the strait, named after him, that showed what until then was called King William Land to be an island. That was some four years after William Snow claimed he saw it separated from the mainland in his waking New York dream. Had anyone asked the Inuit, there couldn't have been any doubt. What John Ross had named King William Land, and later explorers called King William's Land, Inuit knew as Qikiqtaq, which means "island."

Things didn't start out well for McClintock's expedition. The Arctic cycle had turned extremely cold again. No one could remember the sea ice being so bad in late summer at the eastern entrance to the archipelago. Whalers had left without even trying to penetrate the pack ice. McClintock threw the *Fox* into it, hoping the steam-powered propeller would get her through, but sea ice quickly locked her up. The ship was stuck for 250 days, drifting with the heavy ice across Baffin Bay and into Davis Strait, an agonizing journey in frozen shackles of more than 1,190 miles. He sent a letter to Lady Franklin with the bad news, and the bright side of it:

"It is true that a year, an unfortunate year, has been lost, but it is a great consolation to know that we have more reason to hope for success now, in as much as we are very early in the field and are ready to follow up this advantage."

The Arctic finally freed the *Fox* on Easter Sunday in 1858. Emotionally and physically drained by their winter of torment, the men were anxious to get to work looking for whatever remained of the Franklin Expedition. The good news was that McClintock had picked up dogs in Greenland to haul sleds, which would allow the searchers to split up, cover more ground, and speak to as many Inuit as they could find for leads. McClintock had another advantage: To be sure he had a highly skilled interpreter, the commander telegraphed Copenhagen to engage the services of Carl Petersen, the Danish official who had done the job so well for Penny and Kane.

McClintock dogsledded along King William Island's southern end, making magnetic observations as he went, while his second-in-command, Lieutenant William Hobson, took the northern end. Soon after crossing to the eastern shore of King William Island from Matty Island, next to the Boothia Peninsula, McClintock met thirty or forty Netsilingmiut Inuit living in what he called a "snow village."

"I do not think any of them had ever seen white people alive before, but they evidently knew us as friends," he wrote. "We halted at a little distance, pitched our tent, the better to secure small articles from being stolen whilst we bartered with them."

The captain traded for items the Inuit told him were from a shipwreck, five days' journey away: one up the inlet and four overland to the western coast of King William Island, where "they added that but little now remained of the wreck which was accessible, their countrymen having carried almost everything away." The ship had no masts, the Inuit assured him, laughing at the question and talking to each other about fire. "There had been *many books* they said, but all have long ago been destroyed by the weather; the ship was forced on shore in the fall of the year by the ice."

Although McClintock was eager "to get away from these good-humoured, noisy thieves," they repeatedly tapped him gently on his chest and assured him in Inuktitut: "We are friends." They also sold him six pieces of silver plate, bearing the crests or initials of Franklin, Crozier, Lieutenant James Fairholme (a veteran of the Syrian War in 1840 who was also briefly captured by the Moors while serving aboard a captured slave ship), and Dr. Alexander McDonald, an assistant surgeon aboard the *Terror*. The Inuit also traded bows and arrows they had crafted from what McClintock called "English woods," along with buttons from uniforms and other clothing, and silver spoons and forks, which cost him four sewing needles each. When he had all the relics, McClintock swapped some of his sled-dog puppies for food: seal meat, blubber, frozen venison, and some dried and frozen salmon.

The Inuit told McClintock they had not visited the shipwreck he sought during the past winter and pointed out a boy and an old woman who were the last to see her. "Petersen questioned the woman closely, and she seemed anxious to give all the information in her power." They had last seen the wreck in the winter of 1857–58, she told Petersen, which would have been a decade after *Erebus* and *Terror* were given up to the ice.

"She said many of the white men dropped by the way as they went to the Great River; that some were buried and some were not; they did not themselves witness this, but discovered their bodies during the winter following."

McClintock would soon discover why, when he picked up Hobson's trail and saw the stunning notes the lieutenant had found at Victory Point, in which survivors, including Crozier and Fitzjames, briefly detailed Franklin's death, their ships' long imprisonment in sea ice, and the decision to abandon them to try to make it to Back's Great Fish River. McClintock and Hobson studied the large, heavy boat attached to a sledge, which was pointing back toward sea, on the northern coast of King William Island where crewmen from *Erebus* and *Terror* made landfall.

"The total weight of boat and sledge may be taken at 1,400 lbs.," which amounts to a heavy load for seven strong healthy men," McClintock calculated.

Portions of two skeletons inside were, McClintock estimated, "of a slight young person; the other of a large, strongly made, middle-aged man." The latter might have been an officer, the commander guessed, but it was impossible to tell because "large and powerful animals, probably wolves, had destroyed much of this skeleton." Lying near it was a fragment of a fine pair of slippers, embroidered in a pattern of tiny diamond shapes with dots in the middle.

"The lines were white, with a black margin; the spaces white, red, and yellow. They had originally been 11 inches long, lined with calf-skin with the hair left on, and the edges bound with red silk ribbon. Besides these slippers there were a pair of small strong shooting half-boots. The other skeleton was in a somewhat more perfect state, and was enveloped with clothes and furs; it lay across the boat, under the after-thwart. Close beside it were found five watches; and there were two double-barrelled guns—one barrel in each loaded and cocked—standing muzzle upwards against the boat's side."

McClintock noted that neither skeleton's skull was found, except for the lower jaw of each. The direction the boat was pointing helped convince him that it was supposed to return to the ships stranded off-shore. The two dead men likely couldn't keep up, and were left behind until others returned with fresh supplies. If McClintock was right, they apparently died waiting.

Their remains weren't buried until twenty years after McClintock found them, when US Army Lieutenant Frederick Schwatka rediscovered the skeletons.

Other artifacts included half a dozen small books, most of which were Christian works, including *Christian Melodies*. The exception was *The Vicar of Wakefield*. The reader of a small Bible had underlined whole passages and made several notes in the margins. There were also silk handkerchiefs and "an amazing quantity of clothing" that included several pairs of boots, towels, soap, a sponge, toothbrush, and combs, along with sailmakers' leather palms, bayonet scabbards cut down into knife sheaths, some tobacco in a tin, twine, nails, saws, and lots of silverware and plates, eight of which bore Sir John's family crest. The only provisions were tea and roughly forty pounds of chocolate.

McClintock summed up the hodgepodge of things the escaping crewmen hauled from *Erebus* and *Terror* as, "in short, a quantity of articles of one description and another truly astonishing in variety, and such as, for the most part, modern sledge-travellers in these regions would consider a mere accumulation of dead weight, of little use, and very likely to break down the strength of the sledge-crews."

Farther south, where at least some of the Franklin Expedition survivors made their way southward along the west coast of King William Island, McClintock was walking along a gravel ridge shortly after midnight when he spotted a bleached skeleton, partly exposed, with a few fragments of clothing poking through the snow. Lying face down, the victim was a young man, slightly built, who seemed taller than normal, McClintock thought. The dead man was wearing a blue jacket, with slashed sleeves and braided edging beneath a pilot-cloth greatcoat with plain buttons. His neckerchief was tied in a loose bow-knot, which told McClintock the young man must have been a steward or officer's servant.

"This poor man seems to have selected the bare ridge top, as affording the least tiresome walking, and to have fallen upon his face in the position in which we found him," McClintock concluded, which reminded him of what an old Inuit woman had said, "They fell down and died as they walked along."

The searchers also met Inuit on King William Island who said they had seen two ships, "one of them was seen to sink in deep water, and nothing was obtained from her, a circumstance at which they expressed much regret; but the other was forced on shore by the ice, where they suppose she still remains, but is much broken."

They called the area where the second ship, a great source of wood for their families, met her end Oot-loo-lik. McClintock spelled it as he heard it, but the modern version is Ugjulik, meaning "it has bearded seals." He thought the Inuit were talking about the west coast of King William Island, but they meant the eastern end of what *qalunaaq* named Queen Maud Gulf.

The Inuit had spoken with McClintock weeks earlier and didn't mention any ship wrecking on shore. He thought they were holding out on him and only started talking, under anxious questions, after a young man let the tantalizing information slip. He "also told us that the body of a man was found on board the ship; that he must have been a very large man, and had long teeth: this is all he recollected having been told, for he was quite a child at the time." The Inuit "told us it was in the fall of the year—that is, August or September—when the ships were destroyed; that all the white people went away to the 'large river,' taking a boat or boats with them, and that in the following winter their bones were found there."

McClintock bought both of the two families' dogs and a hunter's knife, and moved on. After two and a half months of sledding, he returned to the *Fox* to find Hobson very sick with scurvy. The expedition had already lost three men in the course of making the biggest breakthrough yet in the long, fruitless hunt for *Erebus* and *Terror* or any survivors, so the commander decided it was time to head home to inform his sponsor and the nation. When the *Fox* reached England, Lady Franklin was in the Pyrenees under doctor's orders, decompressing from the stress of waiting for word of her husband. An urgent telegram, sent through the British consul at Bayonne, informed her: "Succes full return of fox important letters for Lady Franclin," which were waiting for her at the riverside spa town of Bagnères-de-Bigorre. In the most important one, McClintock matter-of-factly informed her that Sir John was without question dead. He tried to soften the blow with a postscript that said Franklin would not have suffered long and had died with reason to hope his mission would succeed. "I cannot help remarking to you what instantly occurred to me on reading the records [left at Victory Point]," he wrote. "That Sir John Franklin was not harassed by either want of success or forebodings of evil."

Jane hurried home, where the newspapers trumpeted her as a heroine. Under the headline "The Good Wife's Expedition," the *News of the World* declared:

"Since the beginning of the world, it has been considered that a good woman is the best thing to be found in the world. . . . This is not a frothy compliment, for the world has before it at the present moment the living woman who deserves it, to contemplate, to admire, and to bow down with all the homage and devotion that a human being may bestow. There is a Lady Franklin to extol. . . ."

Other papers attacked the government, blaming it for bungling years of search efforts. The Royal Geographical Society awarded Jane's tireless campaign with the Founder's Gold Medal, making her the first woman to receive it. But what she enjoyed most was the vindication of her husband by the people who really mattered in the world of exploration. The society's commemoration said it was "testifying to the fact that his Expedition was the first to discover a North-West Passage."

The world soon turned its attention to war again, this time in the United States, where the horrors of civil war reached new heights.

The smoke barely settled, President Abraham Lincoln was assassinated in 1865, and his towering legacy met, at least for a moment, the Franklin lore. In April, a hearse drawn by six horses carried Lincoln's coffin to New York's City Hall, where it was placed beneath the rotunda on a bier covered in black velvet. Thousands of people, from dignitaries to newsboys, filed by to pay their respects. Just before the coffin was closed for the president's burial, Captain William Parker Snow handed General John A. Dix, commander of the New York military district, what the Franklin searcher claimed were expedition artifacts to inter alongside Lincoln. They included a tattered page of a prayer book. The first legible word was "Martyr."

THE FRANKLIN EXPEDITION gradually faded into history, but never from Lady Franklin's mind. Still searching for answers, she finally made her own voyage to the Arctic.

A brief report in *The Times* rekindled Lady Franklin's determination to make the journey north, even though McClintock's expedition had proved Sir John was long dead.

"Dr. Hall, the Arctic Explorer, arrived at New Bedford [Massachusetts] yesterday from Repulse bay, after an absence of five years," read a paragraph in *The Times*. "He discovered the skeletons of several of Sir John Franklin's party at King William's Land, and he brings numerous relics of the Franklin expedition."

The brief news story played to Jane's deepest anxiety: Even if everyone in the Franklin Expedition was dead, they might still speak, and answer the many lingering questions, through their writing. She fired off a telegram to Charles Hall's sponsor, Henry Grinnell, asking if the American explorer had recovered any documents, whether journals, letters, or even manuscripts for books.

"None," the financier replied.

Lady Franklin needed to speak to Hall directly. She even offered to pay his travel expenses to England. Jane was bent on persuading Hall to return to King William Island to look for documents, but under the supervision of a British officer. Hall didn't like the idea of serving under a foreigner, but he told Franklin's widow he would consider it. He invited her to visit him in the United States while he awaited government support for his proposed journey to the North Pole.

"Having failed in my last effort to get any experienced Arctic officer to cross examine him personally we are compelled to feel we must go now to America ourselves," Jane wrote.

She and Sophy set off in 1870, accompanied by a maid and a manservant, overland to the West Coast by way of Panama and then on by boat around Cape Horn. Dr. David Walker, an Irish surgeon aboard the *Fox*, had joined the US Army and was stationed in San Francisco, where he welcomed the women and their servants to a country still trying to regain its feet, less than five full years into Reconstruction after the end of the Civil War. Just under three years earlier, the Russian Empire had sold Alaska to the United States for $7.2 million. The physician offered to arrange passage to Sitka, Alaska, on the *Newbern*, a steamer around two hundred feet long that carried troops and supplies. Hoping Franklin Expedition documents might have made their way into Russian hands, and might still be found in the newly American territory, Jane jumped at the chance to visit an area of the Arctic her late husband had first seen some forty-four years earlier, before they were married. Lady Franklin was seventy-eight years old and still following her wanderlust. Despite the ship's tendency to roll with the waves, the women and their servants reached Alaska without incident. But apart from some souvenirs they bought, including what Sophy described as "a horn spoon with an ornamental handle, and some rather handsome moccasins," they left empty-handed.

To the end of her life, Lady Franklin kept trying to find her lost husband's final words. Early in 1875, her health frail at age eighty-three, she reminded whalers once again that she was still offering a £2,000 reward to anyone who discovered records from *Erebus* or *Terror*. That generated good coverage in the American press, including at the *New York Herald*. Its publisher, James Gordon Bennett Jr., cooperated with Jane to finance an Arctic expedition by Allen Young to search for Franklin Expedition records. Young, who had served under McClintock on the *Fox*, sailed aboard *Pandora*, a former Royal Navy gunboat, but heavy sea ice in Peel Sound blocked her and forced her to turn back. By the time Young got back to England, Lady Jane Franklin was dead.

PART III

THE DISCOVERY

9

An Inuk Detective

Step through the doorway, out of the snug warmth and into the midday winter twilight, and *whomp*. The High Arctic comes at you hard. No electric space heaters and diesel furnaces to comfort you now. If the sun rises at all, it isn't high enough in the sky to feel. The pale disk, in a halo of suspended ice crystals, only teases. Your body is your only source of heat, which is only a fragile cocoon of air trapped beneath a heavy parka, lined with the highly prized Hutterite down of white geese and a hood rim of coyote fur. The wind never stops piercing any crack or hole it can find in that flimsy defense. It constantly bites at any unprotected flesh, such as earlobes, fingertips, or a bit of nose poking through a wrapped scarf.

At –37 degrees Fahrenheit on an early February day in Gjoa Haven—a mind-numbing –68.8 degrees Fahrenheit in a moaning wind—parched Arctic air is your closest enemy. In a matter of minutes, it can turn life-threatening. The weather office has issued an Extreme Cold Warning, and cold has to be *very cold* to set off alarms way up here. This alert warns anyone venturing outside, even just for a few minutes, to pay attention to shortness of breath, irregular heartbeats, or chest pains, along with changing skin color and stiff, swollen, or painful muscles. In the Arctic stillness, they are alarms screeching: *Get back inside. Escape the cold that can kill you.*

Like a hungry predator that feeds on epidermal cells, the cold wind sniffs out any unprotected skin and bears down. The attack escalates as seconds pass from stinging to numbing to a burning sensation. At first, there's no pain, no body distress signals to say the deep freeze is inflicting serious damage. Then suddenly your skin is so cold it feels hot.

Old wounds, forgotten long ago, hurt again.

In just over four minutes, Arctic air can turn exposed skin from blush pink to itchy patches of pale white, quickly chilling it down to grayish-yellow as bodily fluids begin to freeze and ice crystals form in cells. By now, those cells are dying fast. For you, it is too late. Warming the skin at this point just produces throbbing red blisters. Frostbitten body parts swell up like dark red balloons. The excruciatingly painful bubbles eventually deflate, but if final-stage frostbite grabs hold, the damaged skin turns as hard and black as cooling tar. Without urgent treatment, infection can seep in. What started as a shivering chill is now gangrene. By that point, the cold has won. Your best hope is probably amputation.

But in those first steps outdoors, nothing feels better. Your heart races with the thrill of an Arctic high. The rush comes from crystal-clear quiet, pure beauty, and the exhilarating freshness of air that, on a whim, might just suck the life out of you. So you walk, feeling warm and cozy, like there's no better place to be on the planet. With each step in all those layers of thermal protection, a sweat builds. Soon the scarf covering your face, and the edge of the wool cap pulled down tight, are as stiff as brittle wood and covered with frost and tiny icicles. They grow from each breath as the warm air from your lungs instantly freezes, turning eyebrows into ice sculptures. The long polar night is over, yet the sun only manages to climb above the horizon for some six hours a day. Just barely. It ekes out a pale yellow glow, cutting a low arc across the skyline, straight from sunrise to sunset. In mid-afternoon, it sinks again, drawing a curtain of frigid darkness behind it. The range between the day's lowest and highest temperatures is only a few degrees. Some days the mercury doesn't move at all. Light or dark, up or down, it's pretty much the same: fiercely cold.

On this morning, wind that rattled walls in the night has dropped to a breeze out of the northwest, enough to send feathers of snow crystals dancing along the ice, like wisps of sand skittering across the desert. The wind is mercifully light, yet it still lands a heavy punch to the chest. The first, untested breath zaps the nerves in your teeth, sending pulses across the top row like mild jolts of electricity. Your nostril hairs instantly freeze in clumps, and as the cold air invades warm lungs, they stop in a midbreath shock. The fluid in your eyes is getting gluey. It's a fight just to keep your eyelids from freezing shut.

That is a hint of winter in Gjoa Haven, a hamlet of around thirteen hundred people on the southern coast of King William Island. It's the only settlement on the world's sixty-first largest island. Most who live here are Inuit who know well how to brave the cold. They have been doing it for centuries, long before foreign explorers sailed in to a world they saw as barren and threatening. In one of the planet's most hostile environments, adaptation is survival. For humans, that hasn't been easy. We, and the modern comforts we crave, aren't built for this place. It's a constant struggle to keep everything, including our bodies, from breaking down.

Cars and trucks sit empty, with engines idling, for hours each day so they aren't seized up when someone steps out to drive a short distance across the settlement, which is all most people dare try in a car or truck. There are no roads linking Gjoa Haven to anywhere else. Most residents walk through the hamlet on snow-packed gravel roads or buzz around on snowmobiles. Layered in wool, nylon, fur, and down-filled parkas, they glide silently on *kamiik* boots hand-sewn from sealskin, or clomp around in heavy moon boots with rubber soles as flexible as frozen tire treads. With each step, the wind-hardened snow squeaks and pops, as if they were walking on slippery Styrofoam. Yet passing eyes seem to smile as people peer out from the cone-shaped tunnels of hoods drawn tightly round their heads. Inuit not only have learned how to live with lethal cold, they've also come to love it.

That affection for our world's northern extremes is something most visitors have to learn. Many give up trying. It's not just the cold that gets to them, but the weeks of constant darkness with flickers of twilight, and the gnawing sense of isolation. At first, the High Arctic is exhilarating. But it can quickly wear down a newcomer. People who need each other to succeed, even to survive, can turn on each other, inviting failure, courting death. Inuit have always known that the Arctic demands collaboration and respect, not only among people but also with the environment that sustains humans, and the spirit world that can destroy them. Few Franklin Expedition searchers heeded that lesson in the nineteenth century. Others repeated their mistakes into the twenty-first. Then lines of fate converged, a potent alliance of Inuit traditional knowledge and modern science triumphed, and the Arctic couldn't conceal one of her best-held secrets any longer.

LOUIE KAMOOKAK was born on the tundra to a mother whom missionaries had christened Mary. She wanted him to grow up strong, become a good hunter. When Louie outgrew crawling, and stood upright on the land, his Inuk father noticed something different. George was sure Louie walked like a *qalunaaq*. Irish genes, inherited from a legendary fur trader, might explain that. But there was something more special passed down to the child through his Inuit ancestry. His great-grandfather was a very respected shaman, an *angakkuq*, who played an important role in educating Norwegian explorer Roald Amundsen about Inuit culture and the lay of the land during his historic first transit of the Northwest Passage in the early years of the twentieth century.

The child was also the great-grandson of a renowned storyteller named Hummahuk. In a slightly creased snapshot, she is an elder happily sitting on the floor with family. A spark lights up her eyes. The dark lines of tattoos fan out across her cheeks, like the whiskers of a cat. Thicker markings stripe her chin and forehead. They are an ancient form of body art that archaeologists have found on centuries-old, mummified remains of Inuit. In Hummahuk's day, the facial tattoos were made with very basic tools. Netsilingmiut women were tattooed with an initial prick from a large metal needle. Then a second, smaller needle made of wood, and dipped in soot from a cooking pot or an oil lamp, was inserted in the hole. The press of a fingertip sealed it. In another technique, said to be more common, an Inuk had to endure a kind of facial sewing as a needle and thread made from caribou sinew, blackened with soot, pierced her skin to be tugged and drawn through, over and over again, as if she were a doll embroidered by a seamstress's hand. A girl was usually tattooed on her chin at puberty, and then more markings were added at marriage. They also served a spiritual purpose: to show she was good when her soul entered the next life.

Hummahuk knew what many have long forgotten: A story well told is eternal. Generations of listeners revered her as a captivating narrator of Inuit tradition and oral history. Louie Kamookak heard her magical stories as a child, lying in a caribou-hide tent in the soft, dancing light of the soapstone *qulliq*, a seal-oil lamp. She was helping a boy live up to his inheritance as a modern shaman, with the strengths of a wise storyteller, a leader's close ear to the spirits, and a drive to search for answers from the past. One night, as Hummahuk lay dying, and the rest of Louie's family hunted caribou far away, he listened to his great-grandmother speak quietly in the glow of a day when she was a girl and stumbled upon strange metal objects scattered on the ground. The story took hold of Louie and wouldn't let go.

He grew up to be a round-faced bear of a man, with the deep, entrancing baritone of a born raconteur. His hands are broad and leathered from a lifetime in a tough, unforgiving land. In the gray twilight of a High Arctic afternoon, his eyes sparkle, as if from some inner light. Warm and welcoming one minute, they seem wary the next. By Inuit tradition, when an extended family welcomes a new-born, elders often look to nature for the traits they hope the child will emulate. A polar bear must have come to mind when the Kamookak family considered baby Louie: powerful but stealthy, even elusive. He cautiously feels out a newcomer, making sure any knowledge he chooses to share will be safe. He guards his emotions just as carefully.

In Hummahuk's stories, the boy picked up the scent of people and events that continue to reshape his people's Arctic homeland. Kamookak has been following it, even when the hunt threatened to kill him, his whole life. His meticulous work gathering Inuit oral history proved a crucial point, which took well over a century for the outside world to accept without challenge: The Netsilingmiut knew what happened to the Franklin Expedition. That truth was lost for generations in the cultural haze between *qalunaaq* and Inuit, as thick as the banks of icy mist that roll in off a cold sea on a warm day. Relying on translators, whose own precision and accuracy were questionable, only clouded things more. For decades, outsiders were terrible at sorting out good information from bad. In some cases, what sounded like encounters with survivors desperately trying to reach the mainland were actually descriptions of men searching for them. Many would try to untangle false or broken leads from fact. No one worked harder at it, spent more time listening to elders, coaxing out more details, cross-referencing local names with foreign ones, puzzling out locations from vague descriptions, than Louie Kamookak.

"I'm like a detective," he told me, and his eyes flashed with a mystical glint.

Kamookak's grandfather was another great shaman who helped

Knud Rasmussen, the Greenland-born Danish anthropologist who carried out the most respected early study of Inuit, to understand a culture deeply rooted in the spirit world. The first European to cross the Canadian Arctic on a dogsled, Rasmussen spoke an Inuit dialect and traveled with two Inuit hunters. Starting off from Greenland in 1921, he mushed a team of a dozen dogs some twenty thousand miles to Nome, Alaska. Rasmussen spent more than three years living off the land, and nearly dying on it, to trace the origins and development of the Inuit, their culture, and the spiritualism born of one of the cruelest places on Earth. Mass death was not unique to the Franklin Expedition, he learned. The Inuit, too, had suffered similar horrors.

Elders spoke of the Ukjulingmiut, the People of the Great Bearded Seal, an Inuit group who spent their summers on King William Island and the Adelaide Peninsula. When sea ice covered Queen Maud Gulf, they moved there to hunt seals. One winter was so severe, with constant blizzards howling across the gulf, that their suffering was legendary, told and retold down the generations as a warning of what could happen when the spirits were enraged and the hunt failed. Once numerous, the Ukjulingmiut were nearly wiped out by famine: "Some froze to death, others starved, and the bodies of the dead were eaten by the living—in fact many were killed to provide food, for these poor people were driven almost mad by their sufferings that winter," Rasmussen wrote. The few survivors fled south to the Back River, the same place Franklin's men tried to reach after he died and they surrendered *Erebus* and *Terror* to the ice.

In his ten-volume account of the Fifth Thule Expedition, Rasmussen wrote that Netsilingmiut survived by spending most of their lives in small family groups and making brutally hard sacrifices. Their hunting bands could grow to dozens of people until the return of winter, and the inevitable shortage of food, dispersed them again. Getting by on the little that the Arctic grudgingly conceded left no room for the complications of larger social groups. So they had no permanent settlements, no rigid clans, no institutionalized chiefs, and no formal government. In winters, when the sea ice froze up to seven feet thick, and temperatures plummeted to –40 degrees Fahrenheit or lower, they hunkered down in igloos. Summer gave them more freedom to move with their animal-skin shelters to follow their preferred prey, mainly seal, caribou, musk ox, and polar bear. There is also evidence that they were drawn by discoveries of driftwood, pieces of iron, or other items brought by the outsiders in large ships. The Inuit shaped them into tools or hunting weapons. Driftwood was hard to find in the eastern heart of their territory, so the arrival of *qalunaaq* explorers, and the wrecked ships they left behind, were a magnet attracting the Netsilingmiut to the western shores of King William Island, where Inuit witnessed dying survivors of the Franklin Expedition struggling to make their escape. When survival left no other choice, they, like the Inuit, resorted to cannibalism.

The *qalunaaq* still judged Inuit as savages who needed to be civilized. But the Netsilingmiut already had an ancient social code, a value system that is their source of individual and community strength in an environment where no one can stand completely alone and survive for long. They call it *Quajimajatuqangit*, which comprises eight basic, guiding principles: respect and caring for others; consensus decision-making; leadership and commitment to serving the common good; being open, welcoming, and inclusive; working together for a common purpose; solving problems through innovation and resourcefulness and respect; and care for the land, the animals, and the environment. The eighth element, known as *Pilimmaksarniq*, calls on each person to build the capacity to acquire skills and knowledge.

Living constantly on the edge often required hard choices. Infanticide had to be one of the hardest for any heart to bear. Like other Inuit groups, the Netsilingmiut often killed newborn babies or let them die. They were usually girls. Fathers normally made the decision, soon after birth, but it fell to the babies' mothers to make all the preparations. The Arctic usually did the actual killing. In winter, the baby could be left by the short, narrow tunnel of an igloo's entrance, where she quickly froze to death. In summer, a mother could dig a shallow grave in the permafrost and leave the newborn there to die a slower death, normally within hours. Or the mother could suffocate her child by covering its face with the thick fur of an animal skin. It shocks the modern mind, but for centuries in the Arctic, infanticide was a necessity of life in the High Arctic: Some had to die so that others might live.

"These murders of newborn girls are not at all committed as the outcome of crudeness of mind nor because they underrate the importance of the female to the community; they are quite well aware that she is indispensable," Rasmussen wrote. "When it happens, it is only because the struggle for existence is so hard, because the experience of generations is that the individual provider is unable to feed more than the most necessary members of the family."

When Rasmussen did his census of the Netsilingmiut in 1923, he reported a total population of 259, of whom 42 percent were female. To do a detailed study of infanticide, the Danish anthropologist visited a settlement at Malerualik Lake, on the south coast of King William Island. He visited every tent and "asked all the women how many children they had borne and how many girls they had put out of the way," and he recorded thirty-eight girls killed out of ninety-six total births. A shaman named Samik gave Rasmussen an example of how starvation forced a grisly sacrifice, a choice meant to spare the child from prolonged suffering while giving its mother a better chance of living.

"Once when there was a famine Nagtok gave birth to a child, while people lay around about her dying of hunger," Rasmussen quoted him. "What did that child want here? How could it live, when its mother, who should give it life, was herself dried up and starving? So she strangled it and allowed it to freeze and later on ate it."

In a place of great suffering, which constantly tests the extremes of what a human being can endure, spirits are a source of both strength and great fear. Inuit rely on shamans and their helper spirits to mediate with the malevolent forces that punish through powerful storms, failed hunts, long famines, or other calamities all too common to King William Island. When Rasmussen reached its southeast coast, he was so close to the North Magnetic Pole that his compass was useless. A blinding blizzard left him even more disoriented. His sled made little headway, and often slid ahead of the dogs, which "were creeping timidly forward over the ice, fearing to be blown away. Face, eyes, nose, mouth and hair were so encrusted with fine snow that we could barely see. Now and then we could find the trail by lying flat down and scraping the snow away."

The sled dogs eventually sniffed out a camp of igloos that Rasmussen and his Inuit guide had spent days trying to find. The anthropologist was eager to get started building his large collection of amulets, a delicate task under the circumstances because he wanted to ensure that, "when I was gone, they would have no occasion for blaming me for the misfortunes that might visit the settlement." To persuade people to trade the talismans that protected them from evil spirits, he went from home to home, accepting Inuit hospitality, eating "as many festive meals of frozen salmon, the contents of caribou stomachs and seal meat as I could manage at all." His aim was to build trust without betraying any ulterior motive. Then he brought out the trinkets: "Shining sewing needles—removed from the packets to look more imposing in bulk; there were knives, files, thimbles, nails, tobacco, matches—all of those trifles that are so natural to us, but of great value to people out of touch with civilization."

That night, Rasmussen went to work on the group's oldest man, a shaman whose face glistened with blubber that he smeared on his skin for the occasion. Talk turned to religion, and Rasmussen tried to impress the old man with knowledge of the amulets' power. When a crowd later showed up with various furs to trade, the anthropologist quoted what he called the local oracle to convince them that giving up their charms would not leave them defenseless.

"I emphasized as strongly as I could that, in the opinion of their own shaman, the owner was not deprived of the protection of his amulet even if he lost it. The power of an amulet was magically attached to the person who wore it since he was a child."

The next morning, a girl named Kuseq arrived with a small animal-skin bag. Its moldy contents included a long, black swan's beak, which the girl shyly explained that she kept "so that the first child I have may be a boy." Next was the head of a ptarmigan tied to its foot, to make sure her future son could run fast, and not tire easily, while hunting caribou. There was also a bear's tooth to guarantee a good bite and healthy digestion, and the skin of an ermine, its skull attached to the head, for strength and adroitness. A small flounder amulet was meant to protect the girl against the dangers of meeting strange tribes. Rasmussen took all of those and more. He skillfully got what he wanted. But he had effectively tricked vulnerable Inuit, in the depths of a threatening winter, into surrendering objects that gave them hope against the vicious Arctic. And more than any white man bearing gifts, he knew it.

"The religion of these people is based upon a constant fight against evil, invisible spirits who interfere in their daily life in a variety of ways, but especially by means of sickness and bad hunting," he wrote. "To protect themselves against all these perils they have only their amulets in combination with their taboo and their magic formulas."

LOUIE KAMOOKAK was born a little over a generation after Rasmussen visited King William Island. Inuit life was still very hard when Mary gave birth to her second of ten children on August 26, 1959, in a tent pitched on the windswept Boothia tundra. Survival was never certain. Mary's first husband had died, and now, laboring to bring a new life into the world, she risked her own. After remarrying, she had traveled from King William Island to Boothia to visit her mother. Louie was born that summer, at a sealing camp near Spence Bay, which is now called Taloyoak. It was a bad year for hunting. Caribou were scarce, which meant the newborn's parents were struggling to feed themselves when he arrived. The baby was another hungry mouth. His mother was too sick to breast-feed, so Louie started life sucking up the broth from boiled caribou meat. He needed a special strength to survive, a force of will he would have to call on again and again. What name would suit such a resolute boy, wailing against the Arctic's indifference?

A mother might learn the name of her baby in a dream, when ancestors whispered. She could also get help from an elder like Hummahuk, who knew the ancient ways of shaping a child's destiny. To give a singer a good start in life, she rubbed a baby with the skin of a loon. If there was any concern the child might grow up to be a lightweight, she stuck a big, heavy rock on the afterbirth. Hummahuk would then have a say in choosing the infant's name. But by the end of the 1950s, southerners were pressuring Inuit to give up their traditions. Missionaries traveling the Canadian Arctic called them to a Christian god. Father Henry, a Catholic priest, baptized the newborn and suggested he be named Louie. His parents obeyed. They chose their son's second name, Qayuttinuaq, from a relative on his mother's side, a shaman who wrote songs for drum dances. He asked that it be so. By making the boy his namesake, he was expressing a wish: that the child would grow to be at least as good, but hopefully better than himself before he died. To government officials who decided Inuit fate from the south, none of that mattered. They would know the boy by a number, not a name.

White authority—the doctors, nurses, teachers, administrators, and Royal Canadian Mounted Police from the south—had trouble pronouncing and remembering Inuit names. The Mounties suggested fingerprinting as a solution. That was deemed too complicated, not to mention unsettling for Inuit, who would wonder what they had done wrong to be standing in front of the cops, having their fingers rolled in dark ink and pressed on white paper. Following the military's example, a medical officer in Pangnirtung, on Baffin Island, decided in 1935 that handing out dog tags was a better answer. Six years later, Canadian federal authorities made it official: All Inuit must be registered, and each Inuk was assigned a four-digit number. Known as Eskimo Numbers, or E-numbers for short, they were stamped on pressed-fiber disks about the size of a quarter. Those were called Eskimo Identification Tags. Lest the Inuit miss the weighty importance of their numbers, their tags bore the regal imprimatur of Canada's coat of arms, with a crowned lion above another lion and a unicorn wielding lances, on a wreath of roses, thistles, shamrocks, and lilies. Each Inuk got one, along with a cheap chain so they could wear the tags around their necks or wrists.

Inuit had to carry their ID tags only when they came in contact with white officialdom, such as doctors and nurses who made annual stops on a medical ship to check for tuberculosis and treat other ailments. A mother would get out her tag, and put one on each of her kids, so the *qalunaaq* could address them by number. For the thousands who lived under the system for about three decades, until it was abolished in the early 1970s, the E-number was a shadow identity, a kind of ghost-self stirred to life whenever white people showed up. So many times had Louie heard authorities call the number they knew as his, so many times had he stated it, that it became deeply etched into his psyche. When I asked, it came to him as quickly, and clearly, as the date of his birth, a hurtful absurdity spoken without a hint of bitterness. Free of the humiliation now, he could even smile as he recited the identity stamped on a tag that once dangled from a chain around his neck as though he were someone's wandering pet.

"E-4826," he said.

That was how Canada's government knew the child destined to help rewrite history.

Inuit put up with the indignities of rule from the south just as they tolerated many other threats they couldn't control. Stand your ground if you can, give way if you must, is often the Inuit way. Parents teach it to their children when they speak of *tunngaq*, ghosts. Stay away as long as possible, they learn, but if spirits come, try not to fear them. Some may be there to help. Others are evil and can cause great harm. Those spirits are *amayuqruq*, which roughly translates as "taken away." Their preferred prey are younger children.

Louie may have felt one's terrifying grasp in the cold of early summer—a night that seared itself in Louie's memory. As he remembers it, the extended Kamookak family was huddled against a bitter wind in two igloos, joined by a tunnel shaped from blocks of snow. It was just big enough to crawl through, with grandparents on one side and the rest of the family on the other. He has relived the most chilling seconds countless times in a recurring nightmare: Everyone is in the neighboring igloo, in the light, but the boy is alone, sleeping in the blackness of night. Then *it* grabs him.

"There was something pulling me and it was dark. And my head was on fire."

For years that was all he knew. Something unseen, a dark presence, had snatched hold of him and pulled, something with a touch so hot that he felt aflame. It took Louie years to work up the courage to speak to anyone about that night. In his late teens, he told his parents about it. They recalled a similar night, when they were camped out with his mother's uncle. Louie was an infant, too young to walk.

"They were sleeping in an igloo and I was in a tent. It was in the summer. And I was sleeping between my mom and my dad. My mom's uncle was sleeping on the side, behind my father. They heard him shout, and then I started crying, and I was halfway out the entrance of the tent. They said something pulled me out—some kind of spirit. They said in the past sometimes kids would disappear."

The explanation only left him with new questions. One whispered insistently: If a spirit came for him that night, whose was it?

As he grew, the boy also learned about curses, especially one particular to King William Island. Elders have long warned that it came with the hideous deaths of Franklin and his men. Some believed Louie's grandfather, on his mother's side, fell victim to it.

WILLIAM "PADDY" GIBSON, an Irish transplant to the Arctic, was born in Kells Parish, County Meath, about forty miles from Dublin. In World War I, he served in the Imperial Overseas Forces of the British Army. After a brief stint in the Royal Irish Constabulary, he spent five years in the Royal Canadian Mounted Police, working mainly on the Western Arctic's Herschel Island, just off Yukon's Beaufort Sea coast. Then he moved east to become trading-post manager for the Hudson's Bay Company on King William Island's south coast, overlooking Simpson Strait, a narrow gap between the island and the northern coast of mainland Canada. By 1927, he was running the new trading post at Gjoa Haven. Gibson's arrival marked a turning point for the Inuit, when a nomadic people began to settle. They were brought into a trading economy that almost always favored the *qalunaaq* buyer over the Inuk seller. Paddy Gibson got around, logging six thousand miles a year by dogsled. He knew the land and its people well and fused with the place, like a ship beset. To Inuit, he was an odd, sometimes frightening presence.

"The first white man I encountered was a man by the name of Gibson. I was terrified of him," Emily Haloktalik recalled years later.

Inuit hunters used to gather each spring outside the door of Gibson's small house, which still stands as the original building on King

William Island. They brought stacks of frozen carcasses of Arctic foxes, their winter fur still snow white. Buyers prized the pelts for their downy softness to make glamorous hats, stoles, mufflers, and coats. Taken dead from traps, the bodies were stacked on wooden *qamutik* sleds pulled by dog teams to the trading post. Louie's grandmother, Irene, was with the other women, on the cold ground, skinning stiff, dead foxes and cleaning the pelts, when she met Gibson. He was soon sleeping with her, but they never married. She wasn't the fur trader's only Inuk companion. In his own travels, Kamookak met other Inuit who were Gibson's progeny, including a son in Cambridge Bay and a daughter in Kugluktuk. They bonded over stories of the dogsledding fur trader who spawned an Irish–Inuit bloodline.

"Gibson didn't have any wives up here," Kamookak told me, chuckling at the thought. "Just kids. Gibson just got around. Having kids here and there."

As the fur trader worked his routes, he followed in the tracks of European explorers, including those of the dying members of the Franklin Expedition. In 1931, Gibson set out from Gjoa Haven on his own expedition to see if he could figure out what happened to Franklin and his men. On the Todd Islands, four islets near the southern coast of King William Island, he found the partial remains of at least four skeletons. He picked out obvious signs that they were once Royal Navy seamen.

"Two of these were found embedded in the soft sand of a low spit running out from the most southerly islet in the group," Gibson reported in *The Beaver*, then a popular magazine published by the Hudson's Bay Company. "One was almost intact and lying in an extended natural position, evidently that of a slight young man. The teeth of both jaws were complete and remarkable in their flawless perfection.

"These skeletons had been well preserved in the moist sand and patches of the blue naval broadcloth held together and were taken

Fig. 1 Sir John Franklin, the commanding officer of the doomed Franklin Expedition, in 1840.

Fig. 2 Lady Jane Franklin, wife and staunch supporter of Sir John Franklin, in a drawing made in 1816.

Fig. 3 The HMS *Erebus* and HMS *Terror*, departing from England in search of the fabled Northwest Passage, in 1845.

Fig. 4 A daguerreotype of Franklin, made on the day before the expedition set sail from England.

Fig. 5 James Fitzjames, captain of the HMS *Erebus*.

Fig. 6 James Reid, the ice master on the HMS *Erebus*.

Fig. 7 Belgian painter François Etienne Musin's 1846 depiction of HMS *Erebus* surrounded by ice.

Fig. 8 British painter W. Thomas Smith's 1895 depiction of Sir John Franklin and his crew dying alongside their boat.

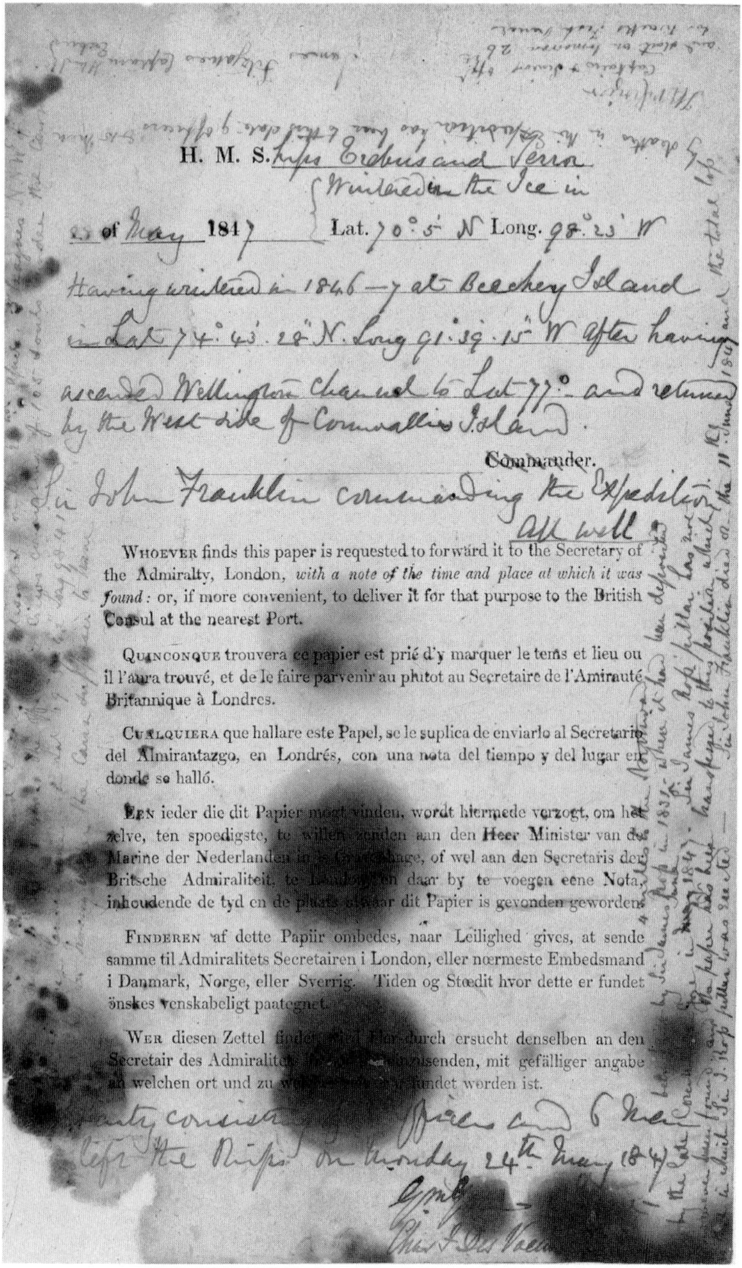

H. M. S.hips Erebus and Terror
Wintered in the Ice in
of May 1847 Lat. 70°5' N Long. 98°23' W
Having wintered in 1846–7 at Beechey Island
in Lat 74°43'28" N. Long 91°39'15" W after having
ascended Wellington Channel to Lat 77° and returned
by the West side of Cornwallis Island.
Commander.
Sir John Franklin commanding the Expedition
All well

Whoever finds this paper is requested to forward it to the Secretary of the Admiralty, London, *with a note of the time and place at which it was found*: or, if more convenient, to deliver it for that purpose to the British Consul at the nearest Port.

Quinconque trouvera ce papier est prié d'y marquer le tems et lieu ou il l'aura trouvé, et de le faire parvenir au plutot au Secretaire de l'Amirauté Britannique à Londres.

Cualquiera que hallare este Papel, se le suplica de enviarlo al Secretario del Almirantazgo, en Londrés, con una nota del tiempo y del lugar en donde se halló.

Een ieder die dit Papier mogt vinden, wordt hiermede verzogt, om het zelve, ten spoedigste, te willen zenden aan den Heer Minister van de Marine der Nederlanden in 's Gravenhage, of wel aan den Secretaris der Britsche Admiraliteit, te London, en daar by te voegen eene Nota, inhoudende de tyd en de plaats alwaar dit Papier is gevonden geworden.

Finderen af dette Papiir ombedes, naar Leilighed gives, at sende samme til Admiralitets Secretairen i London, eller nærmeste Embedsmand i Danmark, Norge, eller Sverrig. Tiden og Stædit hvor dette er fundet önskes venskabeligt paategnet.

Wer diesen Zettel findet, wird hier-durch ersucht denselben an den Secretair des Admiralitets in London einzusenden, mit gefälliger angabe an welchen ort und zu welcher zeit er gefundet worden ist.

Party consisting of ... Officers and 6 Men
left the Ships on Monday 24th May 1847
Gm. Gore
Chas F Des Voeux

Fig. 9 The Victory Point Record, notes detailing the fate of the Franklin Expedition found by the McClintock Expedition in 1859.

Fig. 10 The members of the Arctic Council—including John Ross, John Richardson, John Barrow, and William Parry—planning a search for the missing Franklin Expedition.

Fig. 11 In March of 1849, the British government offered a reward in a belated effort to encourage a private search for the lost Franklin Expedition.

Fig. 12 Hunger stalked Inuit into the early 20th century on King William Island, where shifting migrations of caribou, musk ox and other large mammals often left hunters without prey.

Fig. 13 Louie Kamookak, a descendent of Inuit shamans, became fascinated by the Franklin Expedition after hearing stories from his great-grandmother while growing up on King William Island. He's pictured here with the Governor-General, the Queen's representative in Canada, after receiving the inaugural Polar Medal in 2015 for his essential role in the discovery of the HMS *Erebus*.

Fig. 14 Canada's first professional underwater archaeologist, Walter Zacharchuk (left), with Parks Canada head archaeologist John Rick (right) in 1967.

Fig. 15 David Woodman in 1994 at Victory Point, where the McClintock Expedition found the note confirming that members of the Franklin Expedition had perished.

Fig. 16 Cast-bronze bell from the deck of HMS *Erebus*, found with the rest of the ship in 2014.

Fig. 17 The stunning sight of an almost perfectly preserved double-wheeled helm helped an Arctic Research Foundation crew confirm they had found the wreck of HMS *Terror* in September 2016.

away by us. Digging in the vicinity of the other remains—which were very incomplete—the vivid colour only of the broadcloth was discernible, the fabric having entirely disintegrated."

High tides often washed up the low spit where Gibson was standing, and he thought more human remains might be buried there beneath sand deposited over more than a century. A very experienced Arctic traveler, he concluded that the Franklin survivors were confused and followed the King William Island shoreline too far east, where the distance to the North American mainland broadens to a huge gap of several miles. Farther west, from where the men apparently came, the crossing over Simpson Strait is just two miles. Gibson gained a deep understanding of Inuit accounts of the dying sailors' movements, which he didn't take at face value. They convinced him of a key fact, one that would take decades, and hard work from his Inuk grandson, to prove. Gibson's own analysis of Inuit stories that one of Franklin's vessels ended up far south of where both were abandoned in 1848, at the top of Victoria Strait, was prescient.

"They discovered the ship, which was possibly the *Erebus*, for she was larger and more strongly built than her consort, would appear to have drifted out of the heavy ice in Victoria Strait during the late summer or fall of the same year in which her crew abandoned her. That would mean that it occupied the vessel approximately three years to drift at a slow rate to the open water south of that belt of heavy ice which was the prime factor in the destruction of the expedition.

"It is an ironic contemplation that had the crews only remained with their ships for another few months, one of them at least was actually to escape undamaged to those same ice-free coastal waters for which Franklin was striving three years previously when he was fatefully beset. Carried south by the current the vessel was brought to a stationary position near the mainland where the natives found her, by the freezing over of the sea again at the onset of winter."

On another search two years later, Gibson was fascinated by a

marker, left by earlier explorers, which the last remnants of the lost
Franklin Expedition might have been seeking in the desperate push
south. In the High Arctic desert, dead reckoning can be tough when
the horizon disappears. A winter sky melds into ice-covered sea and
land in a uniform palette of gray. One long, flat stretch can seem the
same as the last. Ice fog and other phenomena deceive sharp eyes, let
alone those dulled by hunger or sickness. It's so easy to get lost that
Inuit learned long ago the necessity of building their own landmarks
to save lives. They stack flat slabs of rock into towers that perform
a variety of functions, such as pointing travelers on the right path,
marking cached food, even acting as decoys to confuse caribou. What
Inuit call an *inuksuk*, which roughly means "to act in the capacity of a
human," northern explorers called a *cairn*, from the Gaelic for "heap
of stones."

Under the white light of a full moon in January, Gibson came off
the frozen Simpson Strait on a January night, his dog team hauling
toward Cape Herschel on King William Island's southwest corner,
when he saw the dark outline of a cairn on the crown of the ridge.

"Following preparations for camping, and while my Eskimo companion set about building the snow hut, I climbed the ridge to inspect
the conspicuous landmark without even a neighboring boulder to
lessen the contrast of its loneliness."

Gibson had found a cairn built a century earlier by two fellow Hudson's Bay Company explorers, Thomas Simpson and Peter
Dease. Together they completed the map of North America's northern coast from the Coppermine River to Chantrey Inlet. That same
inlet was the spot Franklin Expedition survivors were aiming for, just
across from the southern tip of King William Island, as they tried
to reach the mouth of Back's Great Fish River. The explorers' report
described two straits (which they named after themselves) that were
sheltered from sea ice. The cairn's north side stood about four feet
high, "while the south side is reduced to a mass of tumbled rock," Gib-

son recalled from his visit. McClintock had found it in the same state in 1859 and speculated that Inuit had pulled the stones down to search for something inside, perhaps a note in a canister from Franklin's men.

Standing next to the crumbling monument, Gibson imagined "the perishing crews of HMS *Erebus* and *Terror*" must have passed it "on their death march to Back's Great Fish River and the Hudson's Bay territories during the year 1848." He also lamented that "an untimely death cut short a promising career" for Simpson. The explorer allegedly killed himself with a double-barreled rifle after murdering two Métis on the American prairie. Witnesses told investigators that Simpson was deranged and suspected the men were plotting to shoot him as the group headed for New York, where he planned to catch a ship back to London. Simpson was apparently worried that Dease would steal credit for their discoveries, and frustrated because the Hudson's Bay Company had rejected his pitch to lead an expedition to finish mapping the coast. The company's governor doubted he was fit for sole command.

Nine years after paying homage at the cairn, Gibson himself would die at the hands of the Arctic that had become his home. On February 22, 1942, he boarded a Noorduyn Norseman IV, a Canadian-made, single-engine bush plane, in Yellowknife. The Canadian Airways flight was bound for the Victoria Island hamlet of Cambridge Bay, around 530 miles northwest. From there, Gibson planned to travel another 230 miles by dogsled, hauling supplies for the trading post and mail for the RCMP. Norsemans were early workhorses of the region. They were mostly used by Mounties, mining companies, and other pioneers working in the rugged, unforgiving North, where a Norseman could land on water, ice, or a reasonably flat stretch of dirt to drop off workers, equipment, and supplies.

With rounded wings constructed from wood covered in fabric, they were a fire hazard. The aircraft carrying Gibson was just over four years old, the fourteenth off the Montreal assembly line. The pilot and his mechanic were the only others on board for just another routine Arctic flight by the seat of a bush pilot's pants. Until this Norseman caught fire.

Descending toward the wilds, flames and smoke spreading fast, the pilot needed a relatively level, open place to land. It had to be far enough from the forest of stunted, bristly trees poking up like large pipe cleaners from the virgin snow that he wouldn't clip the wings and break up in a ball of fire. But this was no time to be choosy. At some point in the crisis, a load of ammunition exploded, riddling the aircraft with bullets. By chance or choice, the pilot set the aircraft down on Dumas Lake, 270 miles north of Yellowknife. The small lake was named after Pierre Dumas, a member of Franklin's disastrous first overland expedition.

Franklin's guides were voyageurs, the French Canadians who formed the backbone of the fur trade as expert paddlers and outdoorsmen. They knew the woods as well as the native people who inhabited them. Dumas was one of sixteen voyageurs who had joined the expedition at Cumberland House, the last trading post in Saskatchewan, before Franklin set off into the Barren Lands, destined for the Arctic coast. So Gibson, an Irishman who had taken his own stab at solving the Franklin mystery, came to his end on the ice and snow of a lake that honors one of the Royal Navy explorers' first Arctic guides. It was a connection arcing across one century to another, one among many in the epic hunt for the lost Franklin Expedition. Another link, this one to the supernatural, may have been what took his life in the first place.

Gibson was the only one of the three men aboard the downed plane who didn't survive. The pilot managed to pull his burned body from the wreckage before the fire reduced it to a scorched frame. With no shelter and nothing to salvage, the pilot and his mechanic had to get by, in the dead of winter at −40 degrees Fahrenheit, on wits alone. Rescuers found them nine days later. Gibson's obituary, which ran in the southern establishment's preferred newspaper, *The Globe and Mail*, briefly described his work in the Arctic. It also noted he was a fellow of the Royal Canadian Geographical Society, a member of the Masonic Order, and he had four surviving sisters, three in Toronto and one in Ireland. There wasn't a word, not even a hint, of his Inuit family. Up in the Arctic, a fellow fur trader talked of a curse killing his comrade.

"If there is any place in the far north that is haunted by ghosts it is certainly King William Land," cautioned Lorenz A. Learmonth, who had managed the Hudson's Bay Company on the island and across the Arctic.

Local legend had it that an Inuk named Aglooka was walking one day along a beach on the southern shore of Simpson Strait, near Starvation Cove. Inuit oral history says dozens of men from the Franklin Expedition died there. The Inuk stumbled on "a large piece of much-weathered spar, which had drifted in from some shipwreck of long ago, possibly from Franklin's *Erebus* or *Terror*," Learmonth wrote. Aglooka turned it into a fine sled, the envy of everyone, but soon fell sick and died. In his final moments, Aglooka told his family and old hunting friend Neovitcheak that he wanted to be buried with his prized sled. They obliged, but Neovitcheak gave in to temptation, dug into the grave, and stole it. He too became ill, decided Aglooka's spirit had hexed him, and reburied the sled with his old friend. Neovitcheak's illness got steadily worse anyway. His family was plagued by bad luck. So he hung himself from a line of seal sinew in his igloo, hoping to free the others from the jinx.

Learmonth duly reported the suicide to RCMP Sergeant Henry Larsen, himself a legend of the North. The Mountie defied Inuit warnings of a double curse and went by dogsled to Neovitcheak's grave, at the bay named after US Army Lieutenant Frederick Schwatka, who led a search for the Franklin Expedition in the late 1870s. During Larsen's investigation, the Mountie disturbed Neovitcheak's burial site, and, when he got back to Gjoa Haven, a storm struck and buried the place in black snow. The snow may have been darkened by fine dust carried thousands of miles north from the United States, but it was such a rare event, and lingered for so long, that Inuit saw it as an evil omen. They blamed Neovitcheak's curse. Larsen returned the following year, and after he passed by the grave again, the Mountie's sled dogs got distemper or some other disease. Most died.

By 1941, Larsen was commanding the *St. Roch*, the first ship to complete the Northwest Passage from west to east. First a gale battered her. Then she was beset by sea ice. While frozen in for nearly a year, Larsen sent Constable "Frenchy" Chartrand on patrol to the King William Island post. Back at the ship, Chartrand died. Larsen and acting Corporal Pat Hunt went to ask a priest to bury him, but were told to wait for spring. They sledded on to Gjoa Haven, where they waited with Learmonth for a delivery, part of the cargo Paddy Gibson had planned to bring from the landing strip at Cambridge Bay. It was all lost with him in the crash.

"Neovitcheak had again been at work," Learmonth was certain, "and all Larsen's and Hunt's mail and the rest of the *St. Roch* and Western Arctic mail had been destroyed in the plane, with Paddy on board, which fell flaming from the sky between Eldorado and Coppermine."

LOUIE KAMOOKAK was seven years old when he heard for the first time about the *qalunaaq* visitors who had come in big ships long ago. Hummahuk told him the story when they were together where the boy loved to be, out on the land, living in a tent with his maternal great-grandmother. His parents and older brother had gone in pursuit of a caribou herd. Louie stayed behind with instructions to make sure the sick, frail elder was comfortable and not hungry or thirsty. He also kept her and the tent clean, doing regular chores like emptying her toilet bucket. Their hunting camp was near the Kaleet River, on the northern edge of mainland Canada. The family traveled the roughly seventy miles from Gjoa Haven by dog team before the summer melt. They wouldn't return until the ocean froze over again and the sea ice gave them a new bridge back to King William Island. They stayed not far from the river mouth that Franklin's dying crewmen had struggled to reach more than a century earlier. After all that had passed over the generations since, the wilderness around the Kamookak camp wasn't much different from what the Royal Navy sailors would have found if any had lived to see it.

Including Louie, a dozen Inuit camped by the Kaleet. At its mouth, where the river became more of a stream as silty fresh water spilled into ocean, the surrounding land was largely flat and rocky. Stone *inuksuit* stood like dark, silent sentries whose pointing arms helped travelers find their way to the caribou and then back home again. In those days, the caribou didn't come all the way to Gjoa Haven. The long-haired, usually shy musk ox were also staying away from the island. There could have been reasons for that other than human activity or even shaman's curses. Migrations of the Arctic's largest mammals have always changed with a mysterious cycle of nature. They still do. But elders said the coming of the *qalunaaq* added a new twist: Caribou and musk ox stayed away from King William Island during the time when white men visited in tall ships. Years later, Kamookak found evidence that suggests the British sailors hunted eider ducks. There were wooden remnants of what appeared to be man-made duck blinds by a lake not far from Victory Point. As the sick and hungry sailors trekked farther south, it got harder to find fresh meat, just as Louie's family was having trouble in this hard season, as they made their desperate move south.

"Franklin's time was a bad time," he told me. That is what the elders' stories taught.

Louie and his family made up eight of the hunting party, which totaled fourteen people. His parents were there. So were their parents, and their parents too. Parents, grandparents, great-grandparents, all together on the land, with children watching, learning, and working, just the way Inuit families had fed, clothed, and cared for each other for centuries. Each night, Hummahuk lit the *qulliq*, which sat on the ground with smooth, curved edges—like lamps southern kids read about in exotic tales of genies—burning oil pounded from seal blubber. Lying in the dim light that cast moving shadows on the tent wall, when darkness was falling earlier each August evening, Louie couldn't have been more content, drifting toward sleep, safe and warm on a mattress of caribou hides, stacked several thick, with his head resting on a rolled-up parka. The squawk and screech of gulls, buzzing mosquitoes, and the rising wind outside the small, square tent were nature's lullaby. His great-grandmother knelt on the side of the small space that she shared with her husband. She spoke softly as the boy fought to keep his heavy eyelids from shutting, captivated by the elder's voice that spoke of things, places, and beings he could only imagine. Hummahuk told of a time when she was a girl, around six or seven years old, with her father searching the shore for driftwood. They stumbled upon strange things by a big bay.

They didn't know what they were, she said, but the shape of some stuck in the girl's mind. In Hummahuk's description, one piece of metal she saw sounded like a table knife, not sharp and pointed like one a hunter would need to gut a freshly harpooned seal. More oddly rounded. The details weren't precise, but other items sounded like forks and spoons and muskets. Hummahuk and her father filled their mitts with the lead balls of musket shot. At first glance, they appeared to be the scattered droppings of an Arctic hare. But these were made of metal, which made them useful. It seemed they had been lying anywhere from a mile to a three-mile walk inland, on a small hill or ridge, in fine gravel. But where? The question gnawed at Louie for years.

As the boy grew and traveled, asked questions, read books, and learned more about the white man's ways, he thought about that story many times. He wondered if the blunt knife was one that a Royal Navy officer used to butter his toast at breakfast. Louie's great-grandmother remembered one thing for certain: She and her father didn't try to take everything they saw. Only what was necessary. Things they were sure could be put to good use. That was the Inuit way.

Hummahuk had already heard from her father the stories of encounters with *qalunaaq* men. She knew the strange things scattered about at their feet must have belonged to them. Nervous, she also knew the owners were dead and gone. That demanded extreme caution. Who could say what spirits might guard this place? Suddenly the girl saw something larger hidden in the gravel. Hummahuk described it to her great-grandson that night in their tent.

"It was the length of a human being. And at one end, there was a stone with some strange markings on it. It was a grave. And they wouldn't go near it. They were afraid. They were pretty sure somebody was under there. So her father grabbed a few items and one of them was a butter knife, or a dinner knife, which she later on turned into an ice chisel."

After years of research, Kamookak concluded that Hummahuk's encounter took place roughly two decades after the Franklin Expedition's men made landfall on King William Island's northern shores. Early on, the historian thought it was Collinson Inlet, which cuts deep into the island's northwest coast, on the same route that Francis Crozier had led survivors south. After some more sleuthing, however, he realized the place in Hummahuk's story was actually Erebus Bay, where archaeologists have found a number of Franklin artifacts, including a bone toothbrush and sailors' buttons.

Now there was no doubt: The items his great-grandmother had described came from *Erebus* or *Terror*. They must have come with the mariner whose body lay buried beneath rocks by the beach, where Hummahuk saw many musket balls and other items scattered near a large mound.

10

He Who Takes Long Strides

Louie Kamookak's strength as a self-trained historian comes from his innate understanding of two eras bridged by his own life. Born into the traditional Inuit world, he grew up in an era of forced modernization as part of the "Settlement Generation." Its oldest roots run back to the late 1950s, when Canada's government began its most determined push to change Inuit subsistence culture. That was justified as a civilizing mission, but it had political advantages for a nation worried that Soviets or Americans might encroach on Canada's Arctic if permanent settlements weren't set up to establish sovereignty. The strategy relied on drawing people who had always lived in concert with the rhythms of nature, and the animals they hunted and trapped on land and at sea, into a more jarring, sedentary life. Then they could be integrated into a new economy based on trade, jobs and wages for the fortunate minority who could find paid work, and social welfare for the rest. To quicken the break from the past, children would be civilized in the ways of the south.

If the strategy succeeded, it would cleave the Inuit soul from the Arctic's.

They are still living, and dying, with the mistakes of that policy today. But it was a change that had been coming, with the inevitability of a round rock rolling downhill, since the arrival of the white sailors in big ships, propelled into their hidden world by the wind and currents. A century after Sir John Franklin and his men died during the most technologically advanced expedition of the day, most Inuit were still living the traditional way. Whether they sheltered in tents in the summer or igloos in the winter, their homes were designed for people constantly on the move. Structures adapted to the Arctic over the centuries had the added advantage of natural insulation, which made them relatively easy to keep warm with a mix of body heat, portable kerosene stoves, and seal-oil lamps.

Moving nomads into fixed homes was a crucial step in building permanent hamlets. At first, Inuit built their own shacks, usually out of scrap wood and metal. They improvised insulation with cardboard, paper, and wool, filling in cracks with moss and lichen in the hope that would seal out the gale-force winds that regularly blow from the pole. The government came up with a slight improvement: It shipped prefab homes north by barge. That remains the only way to move heavy freight into the vast majority of Canada's Far North because there are no road links to the south.

The new homes, a uniform twelve feet by twenty-four feet, were officially called Plan 370 houses. But the tiny structures, which extended families had to squeeze into, were quickly known by a more apt name: Matchbox Houses. Inuit had to buy them for $1,000, half the government's cost of building and transporting each unit. Families who didn't have that much cash on hand, a fact of life for most, could pay back the government over a decade. That was hard enough, but a heavy, hidden cost made paying off that debt virtually impossible: Matchbox Houses were so poorly built for the extreme Arctic climate that it cost around $500 a year to heat each one, far more than most families earned.

Gjoa Haven got its first Matchbox Houses in 1967. Federal author-

ities had conceded in the mid-1960s that selling substandard prefab
housing to people who couldn't afford it wasn't a good idea. So bureaucrats decided to make them pay rent instead of taking out loans. The
government also offered larger houses, called 512s because of their
square footage. A subsidy of 20 percent of a household's total income
was capped at $100 a month, which meant the fundamental prob-
lem didn't change: Few Inuit families could scrape together enough
income to pay for housing that was a basic necessity. That made it
almost impossible to turn down anything officials offered as an incentive to settle in organized hamlets. This created some hard choices
for parents like Louie's, who were torn between the old life they knew
and a new one they couldn't completely trust—or fully afford. Relief
came each summer for the family when they headed back out on the
land to hunt. Camping in the pure air, and hunting for what the Inuit
call country food, was the way life should be. As Louie would soon discover, the government had a plan to fix that, too.

The drone of a circling bush plane was a sound that could send
shivers through Inuit children. As soon as they were old enough to go
to school, they knew to fear the noise from above as much as the eerie,
throaty growl of a polar bear. A good hunter, maybe even the intervention of a fine shaman, could protect them from predators on the
tundra. Against the *qalunaaq* who came from the sky, they were pow-
erless. As late summer days grew shorter, the wind colder, Inuit parents knew the planes could descend at any moment, without warning.
Like some strange winged beast, come to life from an elders' myth,
they landed and disgorged white people who searched hunting camps,
looking for kids to snatch. The first day of school was approaching,
which meant Louie's life on the land with his family was about to come
to an abrupt end—at least for now. It didn't matter how far into the
wilderness a family moved. If a plane could land, the *qalunaaq* would
come, take school-age kids, and fly off. Some ended up in residential

schools run by the Catholic Church, others boarded with relatives who had enough trouble feeding their own families. No one asked permission. No one signed, or applied thumbprints, to any official documents. In many cases, Inuit parents didn't understand what the people effectively stealing their offspring were saying. All their protests, the crying, and shouts of "Leave my children alone!" fell on deaf ears. Frightened kids were strapped into plane seats. Engines revved. And they were gone.

It was a relentless system, built on the premise that indigenous people had to be civilized by assimilating their inferior culture into the Euro-Christian traditions of white Canada. By force if necessary. When the last residential school was closed in 1996, an estimated 150,000 First Nation, Inuit, and Métis kids had been taken from their families and forced to live in conditions that still plague their communities. Many suffered physical and sexual abuse. The Truth and Reconciliation Commission that probed the secret history of the system found that 4,100 aboriginal children died in 130 schools across the country. Most lost their lives to tuberculosis and other diseases that spread easily in overcrowded residential schools. Others killed themselves or died in accidents, including fires and drowning.

The dreaded day of the plane dawned for Louie in late August 1969, at the same Kaleet River hunting camp where he was caring for his sick great-grandmother, Hummahuk. Louie's younger sister, Rosie, was with grandparents in another tent. His parents and older brother, Raymond, were maybe two days away on foot, hunting for the larger caribou herd. Minding Hummahuk kept Louie busy, but some days he went out with his grandfather to hunt one of the small number of caribou that had come to graze that far north. One morning, the boy's grandmother woke him up, all excited, telling him to hurry and look. Staring hard across the river, Louie wasn't really sure what it was he was trying to make out. At first, he could only see four small black blobs. His grandmother, who had been south as far as Edmonton, figured they might be train cars. His grandfather peered through his binoculars.

Musk ox. Just hearing the word got the pulse going.

One of nature's most intriguing, and enduring, mammals, musk ox shared the grassy northern steppes at the end of the last Ice Age with mammoth, woolly rhino, and mastodon. The others fell to extinction as the climate warmed, and migrating hunters helped decimate their populations. Yet thousands of years later, musk ox are still struggling to survive against all sorts of modern threats. Much like Inuit themselves, who hold musk ox in very high regard. Netsilingmiut legend even told of musk ox that could speak to humans. But it had been so long since King William Island elders had seen any of the animals that spotting a herd so close was like an encounter with the wandering spectres of a lost species.

For a boy who knew these animals only through elders' stories, their arrival was riveting. Telltale details quickly came into focus: the freakishly long shag rug of a fur coat, covering a layer of down called *qiviut*, some of the warmest fiber growing on any animal anywhere; the sharp horns, curved like a sixties flip; on the bulls, a thick, heavy crown called a boss. Their behavior was even more fascinating. Powerful, yet mostly docile, a frightened herd usually runs first and then forms a circle, with their heads and horns lowered. At times, they are willing to die trying to protect any young hiding behind them from wolves or other predators. Or they may break and run again, leaving the weakest exposed and easily picked off in the stampede. These four musk ox were adults, but still easy prey for Louie's grandfather and great-grandfather, who brought down the small herd with sharply aimed rifle shots. The kill provided hundreds of pounds of good meat, and warm bedding, for the coming winter.

That mesmerizing moment played over and again in his mind for days, like a spell of nature. Only the distant hum of an approaching aircraft could break it. The floatplane landed on the river in the afternoon. A nurse, a teacher, an Inuktitut interpreter, and the pilot got out and walked toward the tents. Louie knew this day would come. He had been warned. He was resigned to accept whatever happened when it did. But instead of the excitement of going to school that a child should feel, he had a twinge of fear. His parents were still off hunting. He thought of his mom and dad coming back to the camp only to find he was gone. Would he ever see them or his older brother again? And how could he leave Hummahuk? She was sick and getting sicker. His parents had told him she was his responsibility. She *needed* him. With no way to communicate, Louie's parents only knew what they heard on returning to the camp: Their children had flown off in the white man's plane. They would live with the sadness, and the unanswered questions, for a few months until the sea froze again and the dog teams took them back to Gjoa Haven.

The *qalunaaq* did not tolerate objections or resistance. They did not pause to explain or ask permission. The rules didn't require that, and the schedule demanded otherwise. They took Louie and his little sister Rosie, assuming their parents would figure out that the children were taken because it was time for school. They wanted Raymond, too, but he was beyond their reach in a floatplane that couldn't land on the tundra. His younger brother and sister were dropped off in Gjoa Haven, a community of just over a hundred people in those days. There they lived with their mother's cousin, his wife, and their three kids. That made seven people sharing a Matchbox House just 228 feet square. They were poor and could scarcely feed their own kids properly, let alone two more dropped on their doorstep by white authorities.

In school, Inuit children, many of them snatched from their parents just as Louie and his siblings had been, learned that the government did not err. Louie's teacher used to bring out a record player, drop the needle in the vinyl groove, and lead him, his cousins, and their friends in dutiful song. An ear worm bored into his mind for a lifetime, a tune he can still hum, which told Inuit children the authorities were never wrong.

For many Inuit, settling turned life upside down. Those who didn't leave Gjoa Haven to hunt had to rely mainly on dried fish and the little they could afford to buy at the local store, which didn't sell fresh meat. So Louie and his little sister, the children of skilled hunters who were brave and determined providers, were reduced to charity and a diet of porridge, bannock, and tea, with a smear of butter on a good day. They often went hungry and wouldn't be reunited with their own family until long into the winter. When Raymond was old enough for high school, Gjoa Haven didn't have one. So he had to leave for a residential school far to the west in Inuvik, near the Mackenzie River Delta and the Beaufort Sea. He might as well have been on the other side of the planet. Even when the brothers were older and saw each other again, Raymond didn't tell Louie much about what had happened there.

Being torn from his family by strangers ripped a hole in Louie's heart. He dreamed of seeing his great-grandmother once more, lying under an animal-hide blanket, listening to her stories and legends in the lamplight. But he would never get to hear her voice again. Later that winter, a group of hunters came through Gjoa Haven to trade furs at the Hudson's Bay Company post. They brought bad news of Hummahuk. She was very ill and probably wouldn't be able to travel back to the hamlet. They had a message from her, a final wish: She desperately wanted to see her son, David Aglukkaq, before she died. He braved the December cold and managed to reach her by dogsled. When the group was spotted coming back, Louie rushed out onto the ice, excited to see his family again. In the commotion of barking and jumping sled dogs, and travelers happy to be safely home, he looked for Hummahuk. She wasn't there. They had waited for her to die out on the land and then left her where she wanted to rest, wrapped in a caribou-hide shroud.

The next summer, during the family's hunting trip, Louie passed near their old camp, but taboo said he couldn't stay. By tradition, everyone had to avoid the area where someone had died for at least a year. Permafrost is too solid year-round to dig a deep grave, so Inuit developed unique funerary rites over the centuries. The Netsiling-miut wrapped their dead in animal hides and laid them on the ground, framed by rocks, allowing wild scavengers to dispose of the body according to the cycles of nature. Keeping a respectful distance for a good length of time made gruesome discoveries less likely. All Louie could see as he and his family passed was a wooden cross that his grandfather had planted next to Hummahuk on a hill where her body lay. Years later, Louie returned to the Kaleet River with a friend. The cross had toppled, and there were only rocks placed in the outline of a body. As she had wanted, Hummahuk left this world the way Inuit had for centuries. Piling rocks over her body would have protected it from scavengers. But that would have restrained her soul from flying free, either to return to nature or to be reincarnated as another person, inhabiting the body of a namesake.

The plane soon came again to take Kamookak to school. This time, they let his mother travel with her children to Gjoa Haven. As they settled in for another winter on King William Island, he couldn't stop thinking about his great-grandmother. He wouldn't hear her stories again, but the mystery of the white men that she entrusted him with wouldn't let go. It never did. He spent decades trying to answer the questions that grew from the things she told him in her final days. No matter how frustrating that got, or how hard the work became as his own health faltered, Kamookak kept searching for clues. That was how he would play the cards life had dealt him: standing alone, show-ing respect for elders and their stories by making sure they were care-fully recorded, studied, and never lost to time.

Hummahuk had given him a mission and he would risk his life more than once to complete it.

Kamookak was just entering his teens, nearing a forced end to his schooling, when he first heard the name of Sir John Franklin. He was a kid at a desk with a bench seat, listening to a teacher talk about white men who came from far across the sea. To other kids shifting in their seats, wishing they were somewhere else, it was just another story from a foreign culture that meant little to them. In Kamookak's mind, there was a mental spark. As though live wires had met, touch-ing off an arc of bright light, he immediately saw the connection between written *qalunaaq* history and the stories Hummahuk had told him years earlier in the tent. Now he understood where the strange objects his great-grandmother had described must have come from. He had to learn more.

The school text told Kamookak little, so he went looking for bet-ter books on Franklin and his men, and those who had tried to find them. He was stuck with the schoolbook because there wasn't much else in Gjoa Haven to read on the subject. So he went out on the land, where Inuit have always relied on the strength of traditional knowl-edge to find answers to big questions. He hitched a ride with his father as he worked his trap line. That ended around Cape Crozier, King William Island's westernmost point, named after Sir John's second-in-command. While his father caught Arctic fox, Kamookak pressed farther north on a snowmobile until he was roughly eighty miles northwest of home. There he stood on Victory Point, alone and per-plexed. More than a century after Franklin's men had made their way from stranded ships to leave a note in the stone cairn that John Ross's nephew James had built, Kamookak was consumed by the same ques-tion: *Why?* Why would sailors give up the vessels that were their best shelter? Why would they go south by land when the men they counted on looking for them would likely retrace a similar route through the northern archipelago by sea? Why, with so many weapons and supplies, so much power and knowledge, was not a single man able to survive?

Kamookak knew early that he was onto something important in his research, but it wasn't until he hit a dead end in school that he really committed to the work of recording oral history from the many stories elders were eager to tell whenever a young visitor sat patiently, eager to listen. Just as he was ready to leave home to continue on to the next grade, the government briefly stopped sending kids to the residential schools that were their only chance for secondary education. His teacher told him, and most of his classmates, that they were too old. The system wouldn't allow Kamookak past ninth grade, so it was time to earn his keep at home instead. In months when his father couldn't find construction work, the two would go out trapping, and when his father couldn't get out on the land, the teenager worked the trap lines with his uncles instead.

Louie Kamookak didn't set out to solve one of naval history's most enduring mysteries. His early work focused on tracing the family trees of four main groups that made up the Netsilingmiut. As the lines of those family trees became clearer, Kamookak also got a better understanding of contacts that Inuit had had with the foreign explorers. *Qalunaaq* names didn't make any more sense to them than Inuit names registered in white men's ears. So Inuit gave the outsiders nicknames. A common one was Aglooka, from the Inuktitut description of the long strides they saw foreigners taking. The problem is that Inuit knew several nineteenth-century visitors by that name, including James Clark Ross and Crozier. That makes it hard for someone accustomed to the conventions of European history to untangle the various strands of it in Inuit oral history. But if an Inuk tells a story of an encounter with Aglooka from an old relative, and a listener like Kamookak knows the source's family group, he can figure out where they normally lived and hunted. That gave the Inuk historian a distinct edge over experts from the south trying to figure out the Franklin mystery. Traveling across Netsilingmiut territory, he listened and learned, deciphering elders' stories to figure out which groups of *qalunaaq* various Inuit family groups likely met, and when. In time, Kamookak found that one of the most obvious mariners in the elders' stories was Franklin's loyal friend John Ross. Those accounts came from the years when the Ross Expedition was trapped on the Boothia Peninsula, and Netsilingmiut helped the sailors survive, sealing their place in local legend.

Catching Arctic fox turned out to be a cinch compared to tracking Franklin leads. Over the years of crisscrossing Netsilingmiut territory, Louie Kamookak amassed an encyclopedic list of local names. From those, he meticulously drew family trees and mapped out each group's traditional hunting grounds across vast stretches of the High Arctic. Like any detective on a very cold case, he dismisses nothing. He has scribbled notes from every elder he interviewed into several notebooks. Kamookak hauls around a small reference library of notes and old books as he works to sort out solid details from sketchy ones. During one of our chats, his knapsack sat at his feet, bulging with books. He showed me a few, including explorers' journals and a 1971 volume: *Human Osteology: A Laboratory and Field Manual of the Human Skeleton*, by William M. Bass, MD. The spine was broken and pages fell out when he opened it.

Another time, Kamookak's portable library was crammed with stacks of old photographs and binders full of notes chronicling Inuit oral history. He riffled through the snapshots, looking for those that told important stories. He stopped to linger on ones that meant the most to him. A foggy black-and-white image shows his grandfather Paddy Gibson in a Mountie uniform on horseback. Another is a picture of a shaman's bone amulets, strung into a belt that he found under a rock. He reached in again and slipped out a binder with a clear plastic cover and a black back. It was labeled *Franklin Oral History 1998.*

Scanning the pages, Kamookak paused at an account from elders he visited on the mainland, near the mouth of the river that the Franklin Expedition survivors were trying to reach. In 1832, after some three years of silence from the Ross Expedition, the Admiralty was under pressure to launch a search mission. Commander George Back made plans to head for the Boothia Peninsula area with relief supplies, by way of what indigenous people called the Great Fish River. Before he set off, Back received a letter that Ross had already been rescued and had safely returned to England. Back's orders were to make the voyage anyway and explore the northern coast. He took a treacherous, undiscovered route some 605 miles northeast from Great Slave Lake, in what is now Canada's Northwest Territories, to the Arctic Ocean. That's where Back met a group of Inuit near Franklin Lake, not far from the mouth of the river that now bears his name. The encounter turned so nasty that Inuit were still talking about it generations later when Kamookak sat down with me for interviews in Gjoa Haven.

Back reported that some of his men, who had separated from the main group, got in a fight with Inuit and killed three of them. The Inuit threw rocks and an elderly shaman ran after the visitors. Back also recalled that the man was angry and shouting during the August 31, 1834, encounter. Then the explorer felt the need to mock what he didn't understand: "We perceived, infinitely to our amusement, that this was the conjurer, or wise man of the tribe . . . thinking no doubt to charm us away." Knud Rasmussen heard the Inuit side of the story almost ninety years later, when they described how one of their oldest shamans "spoke a magic verse that was intended to charm the white men away, far away. . . ."

Kamookak sensed a link when an old Inuk woman told him a story that she heard from her elders about ancestors who kept a few white people in an area near the Back River. By the sound of it, they weren't guests.

"It might have been a true story," Kamookak explained, "but it's too short to do much with it. There's not enough there to back it up."

Yet he doesn't dismiss the possibility altogether. He has heard a lot of weird things over the years, not only from Inuit. Some details he could chase down and confirm as facts. Others remained in the ethereal dimension of legend. By figuring out the difference, he developed a gut feeling about where the last survivors of the Franklin Expedition spent their final hours. Kamookak suspects they made it to the mainland and got pretty close to escaping the Arctic by moving off the rocky tundra of King William Island, perhaps reaching the thicker grass and flowering sedge to the south. If they did, the men somehow died before they could get far enough south to reach the nearest outpost. Traces would be very difficult to find today.

"I think some may have got further down the Back River," Kamookak speculated. "But as you search further down, it gets harder to find evidence because there's more growth on the mainland to hide things. Where up here, nothing much grows on the limestone."

On a trip to gather Inuit oral history, he also developed a theory about at least some of the King William Island spirit stories.

"Three elders told me: If you travel on King William Island, do not ever travel alone because there's bad spirits there," Kamookak said. "I think they're referring to the Franklin men starving and dying. When people saw them in their terrible condition, the cannibalism, I think they thought: 'These guys are not human. They're bad spirits.'"

Reading from his binder of oral-history interviews, Kamookak filled in more details that explained how the friendly atmosphere of the Ross days had turned lethal. The trouble began as a misunderstanding over a woman's knife. Inuit women use the broad-bladed *ulu* for doing a variety of things, such as scraping animal hides, butchering meat, or even cutting hair. By strict custom, an *ulu* shouldn't be sharpened in the summer, when fish were running up the river to spawn. But Back, or one of his men, saw an Inuk woman struggling to cut fish with her blunt tool. So he took it from her to sharpen it. He meant to be kind, but the grab came across as a deep insult—more *qalunaaq* arrogance.

Blood was spilled. Any hope of trust was destroyed. And, at least among the area's Inuit, the reason was never forgotten.

SHAMANS, the wise men and women of their Inuit clans, weren't always accommodating to white visitors. They had to produce results to maintain their high status, which sometimes required at least a show of hostility. If the Netsilingmiut world seemed to go wrong when outsiders came in, it was up to the shaman to make things right. People's lives depended on it. They turned to those with the most power whenever life was confounding, illnesses didn't pass, or strange threats, such as white explorers, suddenly upset their lives. A group followed the best hunter to food. But if caribou, musk ox, seals, or other prey were nowhere to be found, Inuit suspected a curse. When a hunt failed and hunger set in, the shaman danced to a drumbeat, singing mournfully into a trance, and appealed to helper spirits, called *tornait*, for rescue. If someone fell sick, the shaman worked to heal her with rituals and traditional medicines. A shaman wearing an animal-hide band tied across his forehead, and a belt of bone and ivory amulets, could summon his spirits and seek a cure, sometimes assisting with lichens and plants brewed into medicinal teas.

Among the most coveted Inuit amulets were objects that shamans used to cure the sick. They usually collected these from the land. A lemming snatched from among the rocks was skinned. Its fur, pressed onto a boil, could drain the pus and, one hoped, whatever evil power was producing it. But first, the sick person had to confess all her wrongdoing. Hold anything back, and the shaman's power was useless. If spirits refused to abide, there was no other hope in those days. Netsilingmiut hunters who reached the northwest shores of King William Island might have stumbled on the Franklin crew's abandoned medicine chest, with its tiny frosted bottles containing various powders and elixirs. But they would have seemed useless next to the iron and wood that Inuit prized most. Those could be transformed into weapons, tools, sled parts, or other items practical in the physical world. When Inuit came across widely scattered artifacts from *Erebus* and *Terror*, a shaman would have had an eye for anything that seemed useful in summoning the power of spirits among the hollow brass curtain rods and clay pipes, soup tins and blue-tinted snow goggles. Perhaps she would have pondered the utility of a Victorian toothbrush, a beaded silk purse, a sextant and telescope, porcelain teacups or pocket chronometers. If something looked like it might transfer *qalunaaq* power, even if it was just a scrap of a Royal Navy officer's cap, or brass buttons emblazoned with an insignia, scavengers picked it up.

Decades later, hunting for what was left along the Franklin Expedition's escape route, Kamookak turned over a rock and found the shaman's amulet belt. Notched pieces of bone, carved into slivers, were strung together. They looked like tiny knives, or animal claws, and hung next to a pair of rusty, blunt-tipped pocket scissors. The scissors looked like they came out of the nineteenth century, maybe something from a navy seaman's sewing kit or a surgeon's case. By stringing them with animal sinew next to more traditional amulets, the shaman may have sought protection from spirits that had come from an unknown world. They had conjured a powerful curse, recalled in elders' stories that told of exceptionally cold years on King William Island, when game were scarce, after the dying white men came ashore.

Sometimes Kamookak unwittingly retraced the steps of those who had come looking for the Franklin Expedition long before him. Judas Aqilriaq, an elder from the Back River area, told the historian a story he heard from his grandfather, who was living in a hunting camp when a group of four or five *qalunaaq* arrived, looking for white men who had survived a shipwreck. They gave him a metal tube that, by his description, sounded like one of the canisters Royal Navy ships carried to seal location reports, just as *Erebus* and *Terror* had. They were tossed overboard at regular intervals to help map ocean currents, or in the hope of leaving a trail in case they went missing.

"They told him to guard it and keep it. If they didn't return, it was something that would speak for them. Then they went. From time to time, his grandfather would wonder: 'How's it gonna speak? If it opened, would it speak out that way?' Once in a while, the old man would open it and his wife would say, 'You are not told to tamper with that.' When the white men came back, they gave gifts to people. But they never gave this old man nothing."

Louie followed the lead as far as he could and concluded that Aqilriaq's grandfather must have met Lieutenant Frederick Schwatka, the US Army officer who led a private hunt for the Franklin Expedition in the late 1870s. An Inuk elder getting the cold shoulder for his curiosity from a huffy American soldier was an amusing anecdote but only a small, peripheral piece of a very complex puzzle. Kamookak was no closer to solving it. Yet the bond he formed with Aqilriaq proved crucial to a more important search. In 2002, the elder went missing himself during a late-September day trip out on the land, when the looming night would easily be cold enough to kill. His wife, Mary, went on local radio to spread the word that he hadn't come home, and a search-and-rescue team quickly jumped into action. Ten ATVs fanned out and looked for Aqilriaq all night. The next day, around noon, Kamookak found the old man, twenty-five hours after he had left home.

"He wasn't doing too good," Kamookak said at the time. "He was really thirsty and his boots were really wet because he had been falling all over trying to walk."

Aqilriaq got stranded on the tundra while driving his ATV slowly over the slushy snow. The rear wheels lost traction and he was stuck. The elder waited there for a time, moving around to keep warm, hoping someone would find him. Then he gave up and tried to save himself, walking with his rifle as a kind of crutch. Aqilriaq was a mile away from his ATV, and some seven miles outside Gjoa Haven, when he saw Kamookak's four-wheeler humming toward him on the horizon. The missing hunter's legs and feet were badly swollen, but his faith in salvation was unbowed.

"I wasn't too worried. . . . I knew that the people who were searching for me were being guided," he told a reporter. The news report said he was talking about God. *Tornait* might have been more to the point.

A common thread through some of the elders' stories of encounters with explorers was the kindness of "a great leader of the ship" toward the Inuit he met. They recalled the gifts he gave—cherished, useful items made of metal, such as needles and scissors. Kamookak believes that leader was Franklin. After all, his instructions from the Admiralty were precise on the need for benevolence toward any natives his expedition encountered: *You are to endeavor by every means in your power to cultivate a friendship with them, by making them presents of such articles as you may be supplied with, and which may be useful or agreeable to them.*

Inuit believed that such a generous leader, who came to them afloat a mighty vessel that rode wind and waves through ice, must have been a strong shaman. Their stories, which became legend, recounted his burial. They described a very great and powerful leader who, on his death, when his people laid him on the ground, this shaman turned to stone. To Kamookak's ear, that was a crucial clue. Inuit ancestors were intrigued that this *qalunaaq* was not wrapped in animal hide and left on the surface, as Inuit custom dictated. They must have gone for a closer look, he supposes, and seen the outline of a stone tomb, perhaps sealed with rudimentary cement. Once Kamookak knew that, he knew what he must find, neither *Erebus* nor *Terror*. Even if he were inclined to go poking around underwater, which he definitely wasn't, Kamookak saw no reason to go looking for sunken wrecks when Inuit stories told generally where they went down. Kamookak was determined to find something much more important: Sir John Franklin's grave.

Another lead came from a story he heard of a man and his uncle taking away part of a large wooden structure to make a sled. The nephew described "big, flat stones in that spot and one of the stones had kind of lifted in one corner," Kamookak recalled. "And he could see that it was hollow, and dark, inside. The theory now is that was a (burial) vault and they used flat stones to cover it." Later, according to yet another story, Inuit came to remove the remaining, largest piece of wood. They had a hard time knocking it down. An elder told Kamookak in the 1980s that he was hunting caribou in the same area of King William Island and thought he spotted some in the distance. He put his binoculars down on the sled and started walking until stumbling onto what he described as "a big, old copper rod sticking out of the ground, bent. At that time I asked him, 'Was there flat stones there?'

"He said, 'Yeah.'

"He asked me if I'd seen it and I said, 'Only up here,'" Kamookak told me, gently tapping his large head.

The historian, it seemed, had seen in a vision what he thought was Sir John Franklin's burial place. Kamookak tempted fate, and the spirits, trying to find proof of it. He thinks the rod in the elder's account was an anchor for the largest piece of wood, which once stood in a prominent spot, on high ground, along the island's northern shore. Whoever went to so much trouble wanted the structure to be seen clearly from the sea. The wooden base stood straight up in the rocky, frozen ground. The smaller attachment was secured horizontally, held so firmly in the frozen ground that the hunter who saw the copper rod couldn't pry it loose from the permafrost.

"So it's out there. Bent," Kamookak assured me. "The flat stones are there. Franklin's body is in there. And the documents."

It couldn't be clearer in his mind: The Inuit stories were describing a large cross, anchored firmly into the permafrost, marking a tomb made of stone that ancestors believed was the transformed corpse of a great white shaman who came to them on a ship bearing gifts. His lifelong quest for the spot Hummahuk told him about in the tent on the tundra as a boy now had a companion compulsion.

"My first wish is to see the spot my great-grandmother found," Kamookak told me. "The second is to bring Franklin home. I think that's going to bring a lot of peace—in life and spiritually."

LOUIE KAMOOKAK's catalogue of Inuit oral history was growing steadily thicker, but he wasn't filling most of his notebooks with detective work on the Franklin mystery. Trying to find Sir John's remains had become a sideline. The Inuk historian's primary mission was to preserve as much of his people's traditional knowledge as one man's life, the Arctic, and her spirits allowed. Arctic geography had become a tangled knot of names that was making it difficult, at times impossible, for Inuit and *qalunaaq* to understand one another's history and learn from each other. The first thing foreign explorers did when they came to the archipelago was rename the places they saw to honor themselves, their backers, or some dignitary in line to be enshrined on a map. Those toponyms gradually obliterated the names Inuit had used for centuries to identify places important to them for completely different reasons. By the early 1980s, official bulldozing of Inuit geography and its crucial links to ancestors and oral history was virtually complete. Kamookak was determined to rebuild at least a solid foundation from the linguistic rubble. Traveling around Netsilingmiut lands, he spent hours sitting with elders, listening to the original names of places and the Inuit legends behind them, and writing it all down in his notebooks.

Understanding the why behind an old name was critical to seeing history more clearly, including answers Kamookak still sought to the riddles of the Franklin Expedition. European explorers ignoring indigenous geographical names and creating their own was all about ego, honor, and power, and some sense that having someone speak your name while pointing to an island or a strait was the closest one could get to everlasting life on Earth. In the relentless drive for discovery, the planet seemed to be their plaything. Inuit saw their world differently. In those days, they didn't name any part of the land or sea after people, not even to memorialize a revered shaman or some other powerful figure. Naming landmarks was more utilitarian, usually based on descriptions that could help people find their way around, which was essential to their survival. That changed when Inuit settled and began to copy the *qalunaaq*. They started having competitions to name hamlet government offices, schools, and streets after Inuit, hoping to assert their own identity with as much pride as Europeans had had in trampling it.

"The feedback we started getting from the elders was they didn't really like that," Kamookak told me. "They didn't like places named after someone deceased or after any person—even if it was a building."

He didn't question their doubts, but he suspects they had a superstitious fear. The spirits still commanded their respect. It was unwise to tempt their wrath. Kamookak knew that if he didn't learn and record the old names, most would die out with the elders who knew them best. Others in his generation, and younger people coming up, didn't seem to care. Louie's wife, Josephine, joined the cause, and together they gathered around four hundred local names. Interest grew in reviving many that foreign explorers had overwritten by fiat.

Inuit not only have a more practical view of naming places, they also like to have fun with it when they can. Since they were also less puritanical about human sex and the requisite body parts before Christian missionaries arrived, asking for directions can get a bit risqué. A small island with no English name, which sits in the Sherman Basin near the mouth of the Kaleet River, has two distinctive hills. So Inuit call it *Igruq*, which means "two testicles." Other toponyms were more significant to history and the way Europeans rewrote it. Norwegian explorer Roald Amundsen, the first European to transit the Northwest Passage early in the twentieth century, mapped The Royal Geographical Society Islands and named them after one of his expedition's sponsors. Inuit already knew them as *Hiurarjuaq*, which means "the big sand." Montreal Island, where relics and Inuit stories suggest some of the last survivors among Franklin's men spent their final hours at the mouth of the Great Fish River, was *Qaiqturaarjuit*. That describes the place precisely, not for one tragedy but for the way the land has always looked to travelers. It means "many little bedrock outcrops."

When he chatted with elders about names and places, Kamookak also asked if they knew any stories about early *qalunaaq* visitors. They had many to tell, but a key detail was always missing: Inuit didn't know the foreigners' names. There was no Inuit calendar to pin down years or dates. Since the nicknames that elders passed down in their stories were either descriptive, or approximations of what Inuit heard in the original encounters long ago, it was hard to be sure who they were talking about. Kamookak kept digging. On his trips to the top of King William Island, he often found tantalizing clues. Sometimes they were lying in plain sight in abandoned camps. In Terror Bay, about midway up the island's west coast, Kamookak found a piece of wood and some old rope in a circle of stones, which was an old Inuit tent ring. The wood and rope were obviously foreign. The historian's gut told him they were Franklin relics, which teased him deeper into the search.

As Kamookak got older, he got bolder. He was even willing to break the Inuit taboo against going near human remains, which had kept him waiting to see Hummahuk's grave when he was a boy. Now, when he saw a human skull or other bones poking out of the permafrost, he moved in close. Any signs of burial told him they were almost certainly *qalunaaq* remains. Careful not to disturb a potentially significant archaeological site, he scanned the area for anything that might tell him more. Near Cape John Franklin, where Franklin's crewmen passed on the exodus south, Kamookak saw a skull lying on the ground. Hard as he tried, the budding detective was still stuck skirting the enigma's edges. He knew Inuit history and was filling in blanks all the time. But the accounts of foreign explorers and searchers were out of reach. In a hamlet high in the Arctic, he couldn't get his hands on the detailed journals that they had published in the nineteenth century.

The answer to that problem came from the sky, when a helicopter landed in Gjoa Haven one early summer day in 1995. It dropped off Royal Navy Lieutenant Ernest Coleman and his Canadian guide, Cameron Treleaven, owner of Aquila Books, a small antiquarian store in Calgary, Alberta. In an age when the digital revolution is strangling many bookstores, Treleaven's is a sanctuary squeezed between a dental office and a parking lot on a six-lane boulevard. With jazz playing softly in the background, and comfy antique armchairs facing each other on a red Afghan carpet in a corner nook, it has the feel of a modern adventurer's den. High shelves packed with books line the walls and aisles amid an eclectic mix of native art, military memorabilia, and nineteenth-century scientific instruments. Antique kayaks hang from the ceiling, suspended on filaments, as if they were gliding through air instead of sea. The rare-book specialties in Treleaven's collection, which draws an equally eclectic mix of buyers from around the world, include polar exploration, mountaineering, hunting and fishing, the history of the oil industry (a struggling mainstay of Alberta's economy), and Lucy Maud Montgomery, most loved for her first book, *Anne of Green Gables*.

Treleaven himself is rare among Franklinophiles. While many others pore over books, antique charts, and original source material to spin various theories about what happened to the men of *Erebus* and *Terror*, the bookseller prefers looking for answers out on the land. An adventurer with an archaeology degree who keeps fit running and playing squash, Treleaven is no bookish, armchair Franklin expert. His skills and accomplishments as an explorer drew the attention of Britain's prestigious Royal Geographical Society, where Treleaven has been a fellow for more than two decades. That is why Lieutenant Coleman wanted to team up with him. The Royal Navy recruiting officer needed a good guide who understood King William Island, and how to survive it, as well as he knew Franklin history.

Coleman had visited Netsilingmiut territory at least once before. In 1992, he found what seemed to be two man-made burial mounds about four miles south of Cape Felix, on the island's northwest coast. His report of that trip, which noted that the apparent graves had a rectangular depression paved with stone slabs, raised speculation that he might have discovered the burial sites of Franklin Expedition men, perhaps even of Sir John himself. Peter Wadhams, who went on to head Cambridge University's Polar Ocean Physics Group, excavated the mounds during the Lady Franklin Memorial Expedition in 1993 and found that they were natural formations. Coleman later claimed that he told Canadian authorities where one of Franklin's missing ships could be found underwater, but "no one would believe me."

Coleman contacted Treleaven with an ambitious plan. He wanted to replicate at least part of the Franklin Expedition's doomed retreat. That meant walking from the spot on the northwest coast where 105 survivors under Francis Crozier's command landed in 1848, all the way south to Gjoa Haven—a journey of more than 140 miles, following the shore. It is an arduous journey even for physically fit, experienced

Arctic trekkers like Treleaven. Sizing up the retired naval officer, the antiquarian bookseller doubted his traveling companion would make it to the end. Coleman reached his limit long before that. Treleaven was shaking mad.

The walk started at Cape Jane Franklin, where a plane dropped off Coleman and Treleaven. After five days of hiking, they stopped at the edge of a flooded river valley. Once warm in his tent, Coleman wouldn't get out of it. He complained of a bad back. Treleaven offered to show how they could walk through water that was just below waist high and about half a mile across. The seaman refused to budge. Treleaven had a handheld personal locator beacon, which he said he packed to ease his wife's nerves. But Treleaven was damned if he was going to call in a rescue. He passed the device to Coleman and told him to press the button if he wasn't going to get moving. The lieutenant quickly did, instantly beaming an emergency signal up to an orbiting satellite.

An RCMP Twin Otter answered the call and buzzed over their campsite to confirm their location. Then a mining-camp helicopter arrived to airlift the hikers. The chopper dropped them off at Gjoa Haven just before midnight, when a very tall Mountie, who looked a good six foot six to Treleaven, came out to meet them. While Treleaven cowered in embarrassment, Coleman impressed upon the Mountie in no uncertain terms the need to get him on the earliest flight off the island. Treleaven happily let him go. With enough supplies for three weeks, the bookseller decided to pitch his tent outside the RCMP detachment. He and the tall constable became quick friends. When the Mountie heard what had brought Treleaven to the island in the first place, he offered some serendipitous advice.

"Talk to Louie Kamookak," the Mountie told him. "He's the local Franklin expert."

They met at the housing coop's maintenance building, where Kamookak worked at the time, and hit it off immediately. Treleaven became Kamookak's houseguest for the rest of some six days in the hamlet. When Treleaven got back to his bookstore, he thought: "I have one of the greatest Arctic libraries in the world. And Louie doesn't have anything, really. Just a few modern, junky paperbacks."

"So I brought up a whole whack of books for him," Treleaven told me. "He didn't care that they were collectible copies, but he got first editions. I built up a 'Franklin search library' for him."

The bond between the two men, forged by a mutual love of the Arctic, respect for Inuit culture, and a fascination with things Franklin, was quick, strong, and lasting. Treleaven would undertake a total of five expeditions with Kamookak over the years. Soon after their first meeting, they made a date for the following year to explore the island on all-terrain vehicles. As a team, they were the first to cross the island in four-wheelers in summer, when the risks of flipping or getting stuck are high. A couple of times, they did the journey on snow machines. They even lived in an igloo through a snowstorm in April 1998 in order to place a plaque honoring the dead of the Franklin Expedition, on the 150th anniversary of Crozier's landing south of Victory Point.

But Treleaven's most important contribution to advancing the Franklin search turned out to be his gift of books. The first few arrived by mail. As Kamookak read, the packages kept coming with more volumes of Franklin history. They were like stones in a bridge connecting past and present. In their pages, Louie found the missing links among Inuit oral history, their family trees, and traditional place names. The nineteenth-century Franklin searchers wrote phoneticized versions of the names of Inuit they interviewed. From his own research into family trees, Kamookak knew the hunting grounds of each clan, which gave him a better sense of places they were describing or sketching out in rough maps, which outside experts had debated for decades. That led him to hidden nuggets, which proved the Inuit oral history he was gathering had been consistent on key points from the beginning. Something else revealed itself, a deeper arc between then and now:

Just as chance had made the crucial connection between John Rae and
In-nook-poo-zhee-jook, serendipity helped Kamookak tell an important truth about why Rae's interpreter ran off that day in 1854.

Reading the books Treleaven provided, Kamookak saw a serious
flaw in Rae's account of why his interpreter, William Ouligbuck, was
so reluctant, along with other Inuit, to help him check the stories of
many dead white men to the west. Rae believed the Inuk's claim that
he was sick. A later explanation suggested Ouligbuck was afraid the
Inuit to the west would kill the men if they went there. Kamookak
saw the basic elements of the same story elders had recalled when he
was researching Inuit oral history. With a significant twist, and in
the context of Inuit culture, it seems to fit the Inuk interpreter's rash
behavior better. Elders told Kamookak it was fear of the dead, and the
revenge their angry spectres might wreak, that sent Ouligbuck running. The historian concluded that Rae's interpreter, and the Inuit
who were so reluctant to head west with the *qalunaaq*, were afraid of
the ghosts of Franklin's men wandering the icy landscape. They didn't
dare let on to Rae about spirits. They were a deadly serious matter
that Inuit only trusted their shamans to deal with. Speaking of evil
tunngaq to the wrong person could be enough to summon them.

The problem played out in the pages of one of the books Treleaven
sent, *Narrative of the Second Arctic Expedition made by Charles F. Hall*,
published in 1879. Hall was an eccentric, small-time American publisher, a man with little formal education who made a passable living in
the seal-engraving trade and by publishing the unremarkable *Cincinnati
Occasional* and *Daily Press*. Hall heard the voice of God telling him to go
to the Arctic, where, the Almighty assured him, he could find the men
of the Franklin Expedition still alive. Now obsessed with the Arctic,
Hall read all he could find about its geography and history. Rae's and
McClintock's revelations couldn't shake Hall's conviction that some
of Franklin's men were living somewhere with Inuit. After persuading
Henry Grinnell to back him, he sailed for the Arctic in 1860, expect-

ing to reach King William Island with the help of whalers. Despite the benefit of an unusually warm summer, his boat was destroyed before he could reach his destination. Hall's salvation was an Inuit couple—a woman named Tookoolito, or Hannah, and her husband Ebierbing, whom whalers called "Eskimo Joe." She was the younger sister of Eenoolooapik, who had died of tuberculosis after William Penny took him to England, hoping to win government support for exploring new whaling grounds.

One of Penny's English competitors in Cumberland Sound, John Bowlby, had bought the *Lady Franklin* and the *Sophia* from the Admiralty and turned the exploration ships into whalers. After a good hunting season, he took Tookoolito and Ebierbing to England, where they enjoyed a meal with Queen Victoria and Prince Albert. The queen was amused:

"They are my subjects, very curious, & quite different to any of the southern or African tribes, having very flat round faces, with a Mongolian shape of eye, a fair skin, & jet black hair . . . ," she wrote in her diary.

During twenty months in England, Tookoolito developed a taste for tea, took up knitting, and became fluent in English. They sailed back to Cumberland Sound in the summer of 1855 with Penny, aboard the *Lady Franklin*, which he now owned. From then on, Tookoolito and Ebierbing were an unbeatable team: she the interpreter, he the guide and hunter. Five years later, Hall was writing in his cabin on an early November morning when he heard a soft, refined voice say, "Good morning, sir."

"As Tookoolito continued speaking, I could not help admiring the exceeding gracefulness and modesty of her demeanor. Simple and gentle in her way, there was a degree of calm intellectual power about her that more and more astonished me. I felt delighted beyond measure, because of the opportunity it gave me for becoming better acquainted with these people through her means, and I hope to improve it toward the furtherance of the great object I had in view."

Hall spent two years in Frobisher Bay, getting nowhere in his godly quest to find Franklin survivors. But he learned enough from the Inuit to write a book about life with the Arctic's indigenous people, and he grew close to Ebierbing and Tookoolito. Hall took them to the United States, where he was determined to find a way back to the Arctic to pick up the search. But he had to raise money to do it. The Inuit couple, their son Tukerlikto, and their two dogs Ratty and Barbekark were valuable assets in Hall's fundraising effort. As exotic human and canine curiosities, they were a big draw at the gate. Hall had the Inuit dress up in their sealskin clothes and display hunting tools like trident-tipped spears used to catch fish and the bows and arrows the hunters used to bring down bigger prey. Hall showed them off at a lecture, after which Tookoolito graciously answered questions. Then he exhibited the Inuit family at Barnum's American Museum in New York, where they were held over for a two-week run due to popular demand. In a later visit, President Ulysses S. Grant eventually met with the Inuit couple and was so impressed he supported Hall's effort to get backing from Congress for a new expedition, this one to the North Pole.

Tookoolito proved very good at helping Hall interview Inuit by gaining their confidence and avoiding the trap of all translation: influencing interviewees' thoughts or massaging their answers. During a second mission to reach King William Island, the Inuit couple introduced Hall to In-nook-poo-zhee-jook, who retold stories Rae had heard about cannibalism and sunken ships, but with more details. No doubt, Tookoolito deserved credit for that. The Inuk leader also drew a map of the island where the second ship went down, south of King William Island. The spot was roughly a hundred miles from where the Victory Point Record, the name historians gave to the notes that

Lieutenant William Hobson found in 1859, had said Franklin's men abandoned their ships.

A witness told Hall of seeing the survivors with a small boat they carried wrapped up in a pack, carried on one of the men's shoulders. By the Inuit description, it had places on the sides that held air. It sounded exactly like Halkett's portable boat that the Royal Navy issued and Franklin had brought to test in the Arctic. Other Inuit whom Hall interviewed described four larger boats hanging from the sides of the ship that had come south and said a plank extended from it down to the ice. The first to visit the ship found it locked up tight and had to break a hole in the hull to get in. The vessel soon sank, but sections of the tall masts poked above the surface. Various Inuit estimates put the location from five to eight miles off Grant Point, on the Adelaide Peninsula's west coast.

They "were sure some white men must have lived there through the winter," Hall wrote in his field notebook. "Heard of tracks of 4 strangers, not Innuits, being seen on land adjacent to the ship." Others described smoke coming from a chimney and said, judging from the last tracks they saw in the snow, the men aboard had a dog. People assumed they had gone off hunting.

Wherever they went, they never came back.

11

Operation Franklin

Louie Kamookak wasn't the only one thinking that Sir John Franklin's body was likely entombed somewhere in the High Arctic—perhaps mummified in ice like his sailors buried in the permafrost on Beechey Island more than a year before their commander lost his life. Some experts have long assumed that Franklin would have been buried at sea—a challenge, since he died when the ice was so thick and solid that two Royal Navy bomb ships with steam engines couldn't break free. Another theory suggests Sir John was bundled up in *Erebus*, his flagship, where the knight of the realm's remains waited to be brought home for a hero's funeral. By 1967, belief in Franklin's Arctic tomb had spread to senior ranks of the Canadian military. For decades, that was a closely held secret, buried in a manila file the Department of National Defence marked CONFIDENTIAL. Released to me under Canada's Access to Information and Privacy Act in digital format, the file is titled, in bold letters penned in dark ink:

DND CENTENNIAL PROJECT
SEARCH FOR SIR JOHN FRANKLIN, GRAVE

The comma and the word GRAVE, in bold writing, look like they were added later. They were written with a black felt marker, like the one used to draw a line across the cover of volume one, from the bottom left corner to the top right. The word DEAD declares the file closed. Inside are 299 documents that track preparations for a search that deployed fifty-one Canadian soldiers and civilians, including a small unit of army scuba divers, to the High Arctic in 1967.

Princess Patricia's Canadian Light Infantry, a storied regiment that fought bravely in two world wars and Korea, was tasked to lead Operation Franklin. The troops camped out in the cold, supported by two Boeing CH-113A Voyageurs, twin-rotor helicopters fitted with long-range fuel tanks to get them several hundred miles from their Edmonton base to the main camp and back. William A. McKenzie, a London, Ontario, history buff and insurance broker, came up with the project and pitched it the previous fall to the then-Liberal government's minister of defence, Paul Hellyer.

The $140,855 mission, which would unfold over three weeks that August, was a costly political gamble worth more than a million dollars today. The government marketed it to taxpayers with high-blown rhetoric that harked back to Sir John Barrow in the nineteenth century. The centennial operation "takes on a very special significance when we are just beginning to understand what potential wealth for Canada these northern territories represent," declared John Fisher, commissioner in charge of the celebrations for Canada's centennial. "This project should be an epic that will stir the imagination, not only of Canadians, but of the entire world."

Captain James M. Hoffman, an army artillery officer assigned to lead the mission, felt the pressure to deliver results that justified the cost, just as Royal Navy officers had done, generations before him.

"We'll give her hell," Hoffman assured McKenzie, who served as civilian project adviser.

In the great tradition of Franklin searches, the two men would soon clash over how and where to look. Others would take sides amid second-guessing that was rife. As always, people could argue all they wanted because the Arctic would have the final word. An April 1967 Teletype message announced planning for the project, under the subject line WARNING ORDER SEARCH FOR SIR JOHN FRANKLINS GRAVE AND RECORDS. At the start, there was no mention of *Erebus, Terror,* or shipwrecks in general. Chasing shadows over vast, inhospitable areas of the Arctic is not something the military normally warms to, and at one point in an arcane debate over theories and speculation that had been going in circles for generations, Major General Roger Rowley, a decorated World War II infantryman, reminded McKenzie that the army "dealt in facts."

To which McKenzie responded: So does the insurance industry.

A planning memo, addressed to the Army Survey Establishment in Ottawa, noted that the search area would focus on King William Island and the Boothia Peninsula, adding: "OF PARTICULAR INTEREST IS THE LOCATION OF NORTH MAGNETIC POLE IN YEARS 1831, 1847 AND 1859. CAN YOU ASSIST?" Those were significant milestones in polar exploration: The first was when James Clark Ross discovered the North Magnetic Pole; the second marked the year that the Victory Point notes were left at the cairn that Ross built, and was also the year of Franklin's death; the third was when Francis McClintock and William Hobson found the notes and other conclusive evidence that the expedition's men had perished.

Hoffman later explained his interest in the ever-shifting North Magnetic Pole in a July letter to ABC television's John Secondari, a pioneering documentary producer in New York. He came recommended by Lord Mountbatten, a great-grandson of Queen Victoria, as a good source because the American journalist was researching a film on the Franklin Expedition. Since *Erebus* and *Terror* were locked in ice not far from the North Magnetic Pole, Hoffman reasoned, it might have drawn the trapped seamen "for the purpose of conducting scientific observations on terrestrial magnetism which was planned when the expedition was formed."

Mission-planning documents included excerpts from the National Intelligence Survey's chapter entitled "Military Geography," which detailed the terrain that the soldiers would face on King William Island. Franklin Expedition survivors were up against the same bleak landscape as they walked southward: mostly low, flat land covered with clay and glacial debris, all dotted by numerous lakes and eskers. Those are serpentine ridges of layered sand and gravel, likely formed by rivers that flowed inside and underneath ancient glaciers. Moving inland from the low terrain that forms the continental coast, the searchers would encounter "a scarp of hills 20 feet or more high" and countless pingos, hillocks of peat and gravel, as much as forty feet high, often topped with ponds in craterlike depressions. Drainage is poor, so few streams take hold, the intelligence report advised. Vegetation is very sparse near the coast, where it seems most of the Franklin Expedition survivors walked. Farther inland, the lowlands are more alive in summer with grasses, wildflowers, heather, and dwarf willow.

Any of the Franklin Expedition sailors who made it to the southern coast, beaten down by months of extreme cold, hunger, disease, and hopelessness, wouldn't have had anything to celebrate as they looked out across the land that stood between them and their last chance to get out alive. Once beyond the treeline in summer, the thawing tundra is wet, spongy, swampy, and "in *general a serious handicap to movement*," the intelligence report warned. "Very little surface can be traversed by anything but small boats. Canoe travel is the customary—in fact, aside from the airplane, the only means of travel through this country in summertime."

As planning progressed in the spring of 1967, Brigadier S. C. Waters, commander of 1 Canadian Infantry Brigade Group, urged in a testy, handwritten memo that his men study previous searches and consider bringing in a dozen specialists from a reconnaissance platoon.

"Will such untrained, untutored eyes recognize an artifact or object from the 18th/19th century, particularly after weathering for over 100 years?" he asked. "Will they need some training in *what to look for, what signs and indications are significant,* etc.?"

The government permit authorizing the search for artifacts was issued to David Hughes, a physical anthropologist at the National Museum of Canada, who brought a trained eye to the military team. But the soldiers doing the hunting didn't get much guidance, certainly nowhere near the knowledge and experience that local Inuit already had. A request to the Hudson's Bay Company for any useful documents from its own searchers produced little beyond a suggestion from librarian Shirlee A. Smith that the military contact Lorenz Learmonth, the onetime fur trader who wrote about Neovitcheak's curse, "who knows the King William area well and has his own theories on Franklin."

"Most interesting but not very encouraging," the brigadier wrote in blue pen in the letter's margin. "I am more than ever convinced that our military search needs scientific members."

Waters made no mention of turning to Inuit elders, even though they knew more than anyone about important Franklin sites, including the area of eastern Queen Maud Gulf, where their oral history recalled the sinking of a large ship. Learmonth, whom McKenzie had dismissed as "a mystic" who would be neither cooperative nor interested in the military's efforts, was the first to suggest that the military reach out to the Inuit. Captain Hoffman went to see him at his home in Georgetown, west of Toronto, on May 27, 1967. Calling their meeting "the highlight and most valuable of the research I have conducted on Franklin," Hoffman told Learmonth: "You are one of the most interesting men I have ever met."

The captain had arrived that afternoon more interested in finding Franklin's grave and any fresh expedition records that might be discovered with his body. Learmonth, who knew the frustrations and dangers of the Franklin search well, urged the artillery officer to think again and focus on locating a shipwreck instead.

"I told him that so far as my experience permitted me to say, the only probable useful thing left for him to do about that sad affair would be to try to locate the O'Reilly Island vicinity under-water-wreck remains and identify them," Learmonth reported to P. A. C. Nichols, manager of the Hudson's Bay Company's Arctic Division.

The best place to start, Learmonth told the captain, was at the Perry Island trading post, on the central gulf's southern coast. There he would find Angulalik, an Inuk who had helped both the Hudson's Bay Company and its fierce rival, the Canalaska Trading Company, set up posts in an area rich with Arctic fox. Angulalik had traveled far in the fur trade, and knew Inuit in many places, so Learmonth expected he would be an excellent source on where Inuit believed at least one of Franklin's ships went down in eastern Queen Maud Gulf. He also recommended listening to Inuit elders of Perry River on the Adelaide Peninsula, the ancestral home of the Illuilirmiut, and on Sherman Inlet, which separates the Adelaide and Klutschak Peninsulas.

Some of their "forefathers were the *only* Eskimos who actually met and spoke with the retreating crews," Learmonth claimed.

"They are also the *only* Eskimos who have any proper idea of where their traditional stories have it one of the ships positively went down and from which, before it sank, their forefathers salvaged many things. If Angulalik cannot pin point the spot he and other older members of his clan will certainly know the approximate location of what may remain of the wreck (if it has not been scattered far and wide long ago by heavy ice floes driven down from McClintock Channel and which to this day frequently go hard aground and pile up in these shallow O'Reilly Island waters after break-up each season . . .)."

With the experience of more than thirty years living and working on and around King William Island, the retired fur trader also assured Hoffman that claims that Inuit had massacred Franklin Expedition survivors on Taylor Island, which lies west across Victoria Strait from King William Island, were unfounded. McKenzie pushed back, citing the Royal Navy's Rear-Admiral Noel Wright, a British naval historian, who believed Inuit violence was the best way to explain why none of Franklin's men survived. Inuit accounts to the contrary were sheer fantasy, McKenzie assured the army captain. Like others before him, the insurance executive put more faith in wild speculation and prejudice than Inuit oral history.

"These present day tales which have been told hundreds of times are really legends and can hardly be regarded as factual," McKenzie assured Hoffman.

AS IT TURNED OUT, someone at the local Hudson's Bay Company post told Hoffman that Angulalik "wasn't able to help in this matter." But, "as a result of the Northern equivalent of the Bamboo Telegraph," the army captain wrote, he got a call from the Gjoa Haven post. Folks there offered to have several Inuit speak with him at the start of the operation that August. Their ancestors had also had contact with men from the Franklin Expedition, Hoffman was told. Hoffman reported everything up the chain of command, including word that a trapper had found "parts of a wrecked boat about 1,000 yards inland on Stewart Point [near Perry River] which he never reported to anyone." The captain recommended that the information from Learmonth and the Inuit receive high-priority consideration in Operation Franklin.

The mission's main base was at Gladman Point, on the southwest coast of King William Island, overlooking the entrance to Simpson Strait. It was the site of a US Air Force radar station in the Distant Early Warning, or DEW Line, built during the Cold War to track

Soviet bombers that might try to strike the homeland in flights over the pole. Operation Franklin search teams deployed from Gladman Point in five-person tent groups, each one armed with a shovel, a pickax, oil lamps, a naphtha-fueled cooking stove, and three plastic jerry cans of water. The searchers also had mine detectors, which turned out to be useless. Instead of uncovering artifacts, they were constantly set off by ferrous deposits. Their magnetic waves couldn't penetrate more than two feet into the permafrost anyway. The teams' PRC 125 radio sets weren't much more effective, leaving some cut off from communication with the Gladman Point base for days.

Bad weather, including heavy fog, low clouds, cold rain, freezing drizzle, and snowfall on several days, blew holes in a plan that was months in the making. Even when the weather cooperated, mechanical problems sometimes grounded the helicopters. Gravel kicked up by rotor wash in the landing zones fouled the chopper engines early in the mission. A C-130E transport plane had to fly in two replacement engines, delaying the operation still more. They were grounded again when the wind direction sent blasts straight up the helicopters' exhaust pipes, risking what chopper pilots call a "hot start," which could have damaged the engines.

The soldiers survived on basic combat rations that included powdered potatoes, preserved ham, and canned meat, along with tinned juice, vegetables and fruit, assorted soups, bread, flour, tea, and sugar. The Arctic supplement consisted of two chocolate bars and a package of cocoa powder. Things hadn't changed that much for troops slogging it out in the High Arctic since Franklin's day, except the Canadian rations excluded an important Royal Navy comfort: alcohol. When Canadian military planners pushed food services to toss in some fresh eggs and oatmeal, the Teletype response pointed out dryly that standard RP4 ration packs "are designed for combat and they express disbelief that the ref[erenced] project requires a more concentrated effort than combat."

The late-summer weather was so bad in 1967 that Operation Franklin troops had to kill time waiting for it to clear. They organized fishing parties. They challenged the Americans employed by the Federal
Electric Corporation to operate the DEW Line radar station at Gladman Point to a tug-of-war match. The Canadians won. The first air
and ground searches began August 7, and conditions were far from
ideal. The military called sea-ice conditions on the east and west
coasts of King William Island "impossible—the ice has not broken up
and still fills the straits." Winter was coming early, the commander
decided. He was ready to cancel operations at any moment.

Two of the tent groups deployed to the northwest coast of King
William Island started the walking searches between Capes Felix and
Jane Franklin, a stretch of coast that had been checked many times
over the decades. Since Ross had named a cape after Franklin's wife,
Hoffman reasoned in his letter to Secondari, "sentimentalists of the
Franklin Expedition might have thought it suitable for the burial of
Sir John." Two other tent groups were assigned to the Boothia Peninsula, in the area where James Clark Ross discovered the North
Magnetic Pole in 1831. A fifth group was ordered to check the Clar-
ence Islands and then join the Boothia Peninsula operation. While
helicopters did aerial searches along the island's Albert Edward Bay,
another land group looked for Franklin's grave on Mount Matheson,
the hill northeast of Gjoa Haven.

McKenzie won the argument over Taylor Island, which ended up
at the bottom of five targets on the Priority One list. Bad weather
delayed a ground search there until too late in the operation for soldiers to do more than a cursory check. Helicopters spotted nothing
untoward. They shifted their aerial hunt to Gateshead Island, farther
north in McClintock Channel, and again came up empty. The ground
search ended at two cairns forty miles north of Gjoa Haven. The military got expert advice on cairn spotting from Michael Marsden, a
geography professor at Sir George Williams University, which later

merged to form Montreal's Concordia University. Marsden, who had had long experience in the Arctic and was also a Franklin buff, advised the searchers to keep eyes peeled for three types of stone cairns. Navy marker cairns were usually circular, around three feet across at the base and normally built tall enough for someone to see from the deck of a ship offshore. Even if a cairn had crumbled, or been dismantled, the remaining foundation circle of stones could mark the spot.

"An item to look for here is an old spar as messages were frequently placed in a plugged hole in the base of the spar which was then placed on end in the top of the cairn," a summary of Marsden's tips advised. "The possibility of finding one is fairly remote as the wooden spar would be very attractive to the Eskimos."

A second type of cairn, built to cache Royal Navy food, had a larger base, built up two or three feet and ten to twelve feet in diameter. A tall cairn rose above that storage area. Finally, Marsden described Inuit food caches as "usually just a pile of stones placed over the food they wanted to protect. The Eskimo cache will always be found where stones are available whereas the Navy cairns may be as far as two miles from the nearest stones and built on gravel or sand."

The professor suggested that soldiers be briefed "to think like sailors," and focus on places such as headlands, capes, and points, where seamen would logically erect a marker cairn so that it could be seen from a passing ship. Deploying a small army assault boat to cruise offshore might help direct the land search to the best hunting grounds, Marsden suggested. Then he had some final advice, on handling Inuit guides and cutting costs, passed along in the military memo. The federal government's Department of Northern Affairs (DNA) set an Inuit guide's wages at $12 a day, but: "Should you give an Eskimo a lift by helicopter to the west coast of the island or any other place so that he can do some hunting, he may provide some guiding at no charge as you have then assisted him rather than him assisting you. The DNA is very firm on the wage scale though and it would not be wise to try to pay less than the scale. (They cannot work for bully beef.)" The troops ended up searching without the benefit of Inuit guides because, as Operation Franklin's after-action report concluded: "It was felt that whatever information they could have provided would have been colored by time and legend."

E. F. Roots, head of the Polar Continental Shelf Program that still operates a Resolute Bay logistics base for scientists and government agencies on Cornwallis Island, had advised the military not to expect too much of Operation Franklin. Two years earlier, his survey team had searched for magnetic anomalies around O'Reilly Island, hoping the iron in *Erebus* or *Terror*'s locomotive engines, or the bow sheathing, would trigger a magnetometer. They hauled the device on a sledge and got some intriguing hits. But Roots was convinced the biggest one was "purely geological—too big to be man-made," and was likely "iron and manganese deposits in the serpentine."

They did find a nail, with the telltale broad-arrow marking that identified Royal Navy property, along with some bits of wood. Roots described the place, in a letter to McKenzie, as "a low, hook-shaped island about half a mile long lying a couple of miles off the north east corner of O'Reilly island." Roots seemed to accept Inuit testimony that the wreck of a large ship, possibly one of Franklin's, was in the rough vicinity. He warned that heavy floes of sea ice, driven by powerful northerlies, often piled up "to tremendous heights along the island coasts and even form grounded masses of ice in mid-channel. Such action makes it quite unlikely that a foundered ship would have remained intact in this from 1847 to the present unless by some chance it had been pushed into a deep hole." The area was well-traveled by Inuit, so the chances "of your finding any significant relics in this area above the shore-line would appear to be remote," Roots cautioned.

"However, we wish you good hunting!"

BARELY A WEEK into the mission, soldiers searching the Boothia Peninsula were running out of rations and down to one meal a day. Captain Hoffman declared their situation critical and ordered them back to base.

Five army divers from 1 Field Squadron, Royal Canadian Engineers, deployed southwest of King William Island under the command of Lieutenant J. G. Critchley. Their mission was to follow up on Learmonth's tip about Inuit testimony and a submerged wreck near the Klutschak Peninsula, which thrusts up from the North American mainland. The divers had no sonar or other equipment to look underwater. They only had their eyes, staring down at the seabed as they were towed by a rope, dodging ice floes in water around 29 degrees Fahrenheit. Their hooded wetsuits were marginally thicker than the standard for scuba diving, but the divers cut holes in their booties to keep from inflating into black balloons as they were dragged through the ocean. As a result, the icy water constantly flowed over their skin like a damp draft through a meat locker, never resting long enough to form an insulating layer. Instead, it constantly sapped the searchers' strength.

Bob Shaw, a twenty-five-year-old corporal, could see ice crystals floating past on the current when he was down around twenty feet. The smallest were like the first few snowflakes of a flurry in the early winter twilight. Others were closer to tiny ice cubes, Shaw thought. He held onto a towboard, about three feet long, with a depth gauge, dive watch, and compass fastened to the top. The army called the device an underwater sled. Diving plank would be more like it. Army engineers cut it from a piece of plywood in their workshop. Two holes jigsawed out of each side served as handgrips. A length of five-eighths-inch nylon rope, knotted through holes at the top of the board, ran more than a hundred feet to the transom of an inflatable boat that was about twelve feet long and propelled by an 18 hp outboard motor. The throttle never got much higher than idle—just enough to keep the boat barely moving forward against any currents, or to cut around ice floes. In effect, it was trolling, with a soldier on a rope instead of a lure on a fishing line.

Holding on with elbows slightly bent, a diver tilted the front edge of the plywood down to descend. He'd point it up to glide back toward the surface. To signal, in the event he spotted something interesting, the diver let go of the board altogether. When it popped up on the surface, a spotter shouted for the boat to stop. That did not happen often during Operation Franklin. At maximum depth, between forty and fifty feet, divers could see only around twenty feet in front of them, which was considered good visibility. As clear as diving in the Caribbean, Shaw thought. Just a helluva lot colder. The most promising object that caught his eye on the sandy bottom was a rusting tin can, which wasn't nearly old enough to be from a Royal Navy expedition. Learmonth had warned that a lot of fur-trade wrecks, and their rubbish, were scattered across the Canadian Arctic. Shaw might have been examining one piece of that trash. Realizing it wasn't anything significant, he stopped for a moment anyway to watch a little fish swim in and out. It was a diversion from the monotony and numbing cold. For frogmen trained to carry out clandestine combat operations in the Cold War, this was more like cold water torture. Before long, Shaw couldn't think about much more than being in a nice, warm sleeping bag. The freezing water sapped his body heat and his strength, stiffening his fingers and joints until he could barely function.

The only places to try to warm up were in the team's two ten-person tents, which had hexagonal walls of canvas and an inner lining of nylon. One was reserved for drying wetsuits. The other was the divers' home. With limited stores of fresh water in jerry cans, a camping stove, and heavy winds clawing to tear holes in the thin walls, it took a wet diver straight out of the frigid sea some imagination and concentration to feel warm enough to stop shivering. At the start, they were able to search the seabed, working lines perpendicular to the shore, for fifty-five minutes at a stretch. The inflatable towed one diver out at a time in a straight line, until his shift was over and the boat took him back to the island to warm up. Then the next man went in the water on a parallel track. On Shaw's first run, he surfaced to grab hold of the boat, buffeted by waves, for a belt of hot coffee from a Thermos. His hand was shaking so badly he couldn't get the drink to his lips without spilling it.

"Hell, just pour it into my glove," Shaw told a buddy, who promptly did just that. Steaming hot from the container, the coffee was barely tepid against the corporal's hand. The touch of warmth, followed by a sip and a jolt of caffeine, was enough to steady his hand for a proper gulp or two of coffee before heading underwater for a few more minutes.

By the third week, shifts were down almost by half to an average of just thirty minutes. When ice floes closed in, the frogmen did their best to use them as dive platforms and plunge off, attached to lifelines. Dive operations had to shut down completely just two days after they began, because a storm blew so many ice floes south that they packed the narrow channels around the cluster of islands. They couldn't go back underwater until three days before Operation Franklin was called off altogether on August 21. So the divers spent most of their time on land, eyes down and scanning the ridges and shorelines, where they had better luck.

After completing less than two of the hunt's scheduled three weeks, the land, sea, and air mission hadn't found Franklin's grave, any of his expedition's records, or either of his ships. The soldiers did, however, collect a few artifacts: an old spoon, likely Inuit-made from wood and brass, lying near a tall, unidentified cairn on the Boothia Peninsula; the remains of a foot near Two Grave Bay; the sole and heel of a boot, with wooden hobs, at Cape Felix; shreds of canvas, an Inuk's skull and bones, believed to be a female's, along with harpoon tips and spearheads, and a Hudson's Bay Company snow knife. Divers found nothing important underwater, but they did pick up several artifacts during the island searches. On O'Reilly, Shaw walked a ridge overlooking the shore while teammates tracked roughly parallel to him down to the waterline. The corporal stumbled upon a piece of splintered wood, about two feet long, with a join in the middle. He cut it down to the length of his forearm, square and flat at one end and tapering to the other. The wood was light. Maybe fir or pine, Shaw guessed. Whatever it was, he knew it came from somewhere outside the treeless Arctic. Polished up later, it had a rich grain, befitting a Royal Navy officer's cabin, maybe even the commander's. The diver kept it as a souvenir.

The objects the soldiers photographed, in black-and-white images, included a slightly weathered, solid-wood belaying pin, with a curved handle and a cylindrical pin. Just the right size for clubbing someone, it was intended to secure running rigging on the bulwarks of a large sailing ship. The dive team also found two round iron bars called drift pins, one snapped shorter and slightly bent. They likely held together heavy parts of a big ship that had to withstand a lot of strain, as the keel or stern of a Royal Navy bomb ship would under the intense compression of winter sea ice. Among the other artifacts were pieces of a small boat's gunwale, the rusted remnants of four rectangular cans, torn and twisted bits of copper sheeting, along with fragments of wooden timbers, a barrel stave, and dowel pins. There was also a three-quarter piece of wooden disk, identified as a wood coverplate from a block. It resembled the plug for a deck hawsehole leading down to the iron pipe that channeled the anchor's heavy rope cable into its locker. One that looked very similar turned up on another island decades later—a critical clue in the hunt.

The soldiers had good reason to believe the things they discovered had come from a Franklin vessel, even though they were far to the south of where the expedition members had abandoned their ships

in 1848. Either *Erebus* or *Terror* seemed tantalizingly close, just as the
Inuit had always said. But where? The answer to that gnawing question was still as elusive in 1967 as it had been for close to 120 years.

WAITING FOR A RIDE out on a Voyageur helicopter, which was
grounded with engine problems, the divers had to stretch a week's
rations for another five days. Even after the memo fight with the
supply clerk months earlier, there was little choice: mainly canned
meats, sausages, sardines, instant potatoes, and candies and coffee for
pick-me-ups from the sugar and caffeine. There was also something
resembling jambalaya, which the team had set aside for just such an
emergency. When the chopper finally got in to take them out, the
exhausted soldiers were down to their last can of the stuff. The long
wait left Corporal Shaw time for some tinkering with his piece of
wood. He heated up a coat hanger over a Coleman stove and gradually
burned a small depression, shaped like a black eye, to make an ashtray.

"O'Reilly Is. N.W.T.," he wrote next to it. (The site was in the
Northwest Territories then. It is now part of Nunavut, a self-governing,
mainly Inuit territory.) Shaw also etched in each teammate's name: Vic,
John, Ken, Bob, and Larry.

In its after-action report, the dive team concluded that "time has
erased any signs on land left by Franklin's expedition." They only thing
left to do, their final report recommended, "would be to locate Franklin's ships and locate from them the records that would have been left
on ship." The concentration of debris they found was mainly on the
southern tip of a small finger-shaped island, and on the nearby shores
of O'Reilly. Critchley's hand-drawn map unofficially named the narrow strip Critchley Island after himself. Tipping his cap to the rest of
the team, there was also Shaw Bay to the east, then Butler Bay, just
southeast of Nail Island, where the 1965 search found the spike with
the Royal Navy's broad arrow, and, farther east and south, Davidson

and Marks Islands. Small X's marked the location of each discovery. The map was attached to the military report, which concluded that the scattering of objects "indicates that an old wooden ship is in the close vicinity."

Army searchers working on the northwest tip of King William Island found another intriguing clue at a cairn on Cape Felix. It was in a message left by Sergeant Henry Larsen, the RCMP inspector, during his transit of the Northwest Passage in 1959.

"We note two small islets off this cape. . . . It is believed that Sir John Franklin's grave might be on one of these islets."

A helicopter couldn't even confirm the islets still existed above water because so much ice had piled up in the early freeze that summer.

12

The Hunt Goes Underwater

No chain of islands on Earth is more vicious than the Arctic Archipelago. Like teeth lining colossal jaws, some ninety-four large islands, and 36,469 smaller ones, stretch across a territory about half the size of the contiguous United States. They can bite down and swallow ships whole. Even the earliest, most hopeful searchers, who mapped large parts of the archipelago as they looked for *Erebus* and *Terror* and their crews, knew it would take a miracle to find anyone in that gargantuan maw. Large Royal Navy sailing ships, driven by favorable winds, could make fast, early progress on a current flowing east to west only to hit a powerful opposing flow, or struggle for headway against circling gyres as they navigated deeper into the archipelago's myriad channels. They could sail calmly across large basins gouged by ancient glaciers to a depth of more than 1,900 feet and then suddenly run into shoals, hiding just beneath the surface, waiting to tear into a ship's hull.

For decades, searchers looking for *Erebus* and *Terror* only turned up promising scraps: a splintered piece of wood here, some fragments of copper or other metal sheeting there. Proof of origin was extremely hard to come by. Experts knew to look for telltale markings, especially the broad arrow, also known as a crow's foot. The Royal Navy stamped it on bits of ships big and small. Even seemingly insignificant items, like a tack or a screw, bore the broad arrow to counter the many thieves who tried to walk off with whatever they could sell from dockyards and other opportune places to pinch things. Finding Inuit with obvious artifacts from the Franklin Expedition hadn't brought searchers any closer to finding Sir John's ships. Their trail remained stone cold until the hunt moved beneath the water's surface.

Marine archaeology wasn't born until the early 1960s, some two decades after Jacques-Yves Cousteau and his partner, Émile Gagnan, invented the Aqua-Lung, which they renamed with the acronym SCUBA (self-contained underwater breathing apparatus). Imagined riches had drawn divers to shipwrecks long before Cousteau and Gagnan made it easier with scuba gear. Dressed in bulky helmets and canvas suits, tethered to clattering air pumps in boats bobbing on the surface, earlier wreck explorers had grabbed what they could, even if that meant hammering and prying at a historic site to pull pieces off. Scuba gear freed divers to go deeper inside wrecks and strip them of gold ingots, scattered coins and jewels, and other valuables. Archaeologists who saw the potential for significant discoveries underwater first worked through divers as their eyes and hands. But there was more frustration than success, prompting one early practitioner to complain that "it is far easier to teach diving to an archaeologist than archaeology to a diver!"

CANADA BECAME a pioneer in underwater archaeology through the tenacity and invention of Walter Zacharchuk, the country's first professional marine archaeologist. Born in Poland to ethnic Ukrainian parents who escaped the Soviet Union before they could be imprisoned during the Bolshevik Revolution, Zacharchuk was only eight when the Nazis forced him to work. His small fingers were ideal for poking into the tiny spaces of a gas-fired machine producing medicine vials in the small, east-central German town of Grossbreitenbach. For two years, he sweated in the factory, standing in shorts and kneesocks that he darned himself with scorched, blistered fingers. He slept in a bunk in a drafty barracks, barely surviving on starvation rations of buttermilk and cornmeal, supplemented with cauliflower and turnips when they were available.

After liberation in 1945, the Red Cross pieced his family back together. Two years after the war ended, Zacharchuk's brother-in-law, an official in the French Ministère de l'Aire, the Air Ministry, took him south to Toulon, for centuries a major French naval port on the Côte d'Azur. One day at the beach, looking out on the Mediterranean where Admiral Horatio Nelson's Royal Navy fleet had imposed a blockade during the Napoleonic Wars, Zacharchuk spotted men in green wetsuits emerging from the water.

They were French military frogmen. Watching them trudge up the beach, dripping water trailed from a hidden world, the twelve-year-old was hooked hard. Zacharchuk eagerly asked if he could look through one of their diving masks. They obliged, and he ran to the water's edge and jumped into the sea. One second, the boy was waist-deep in water near a rocky outcrop, standing in a hurtful world where dreaming of a future usually led to disappointment. The next, he was submerged in an enchanting universe, floating in a soothing, almost weightless place where sounds were muffled and life seemed magical, even as the ocean seeped into the diver's mask that was too big for his head. It was a revelation: There, in the hypnotic ballet of swaying sea grass, moss, and darting fingerlings, a child saw his destiny.

In 1948, the family moved to Montreal. Zacharchuk, now fourteen, worked a part-time job riding a bicycle route to pick up rolls of film from drugstores and deliver them for developing at his landlord's photo shop. He was still trying to figure out how to get back to the undersea world that the French frogmen had let him see. Zacharchuk couldn't afford diving gear, so he went to work building his own.

Fortunately, John Date, an English coppersmith and brass molder, had started making deep-sea diving equipment in Montreal in 1853. Date manufactured the big, round diving helmets with small glass face plates that were attached to air hoses and crankshaft pumps on the surface. Zacharchuk started hanging around Date's Concord Street factory, pestering staff for information and examining the bulky crankshaft pump, with cast-iron cylinders, that still did the job long after scuba tanks were commonplace. Zacharchuk figured he could reverse engineer Date's system for next to nothing. Which was almost more than he could afford.

Working through the winter, in their basement workshop in a rented Rosemont duplex, Walt and his father, Cyrille, built the air pump out of two large apple-juice cans. They put a piston in each and a rocking beam across the top. Then they attached one-way valves to control the airflow in and out. Two copper tubes leading to a one-gallon paint can served as a reservoir. Twenty feet of stiff, red-rubber garden hose completed the contraption. The pump lever was a broomstick. Zacharchuk didn't dare try constructing a helmet. Cyrille made a face mask from quarter-inch plate glass, cut in an oval, attached to a piece of car-tire inner tube, bound together with string, and held onto Walt's face with inner-tube straps and water pressure.

Zacharchuk tried it out from a pier on a summer day in 1951, in Saint-Paul-de-l'Île-aux-Noix, which sits across from a 210-acre island in the Richelieu River, about ten miles north of the US border. Since the late eighteenth century, it had been a strategic post on the main route from Montreal to New York. Zacharchuk's diving platform looked out on Fort Lennox, which the British started building as a bulwark against American invaders in 1819—the same year Sir John Franklin began his first overland expedition to the Arctic. During World War II, it housed Jewish refugees who escaped the Nazis. The marina's pier gave Zacharchuk an ideal spot for his tin-can air pump, down close enough to the water for the garden hose to reach his mouth and stay there. His girlfriend Doreen, who not only stuck with the experiment but eventually became his wife, worked the broomstick pump handle.

When Zacharchuk stepped into the river, his lips pinched around the garden hose, he could barely dunk his head below the surface without stopping the airflow. The tin-can piston couldn't overcome the surrounding water's pressure. He got glimpses of sunfish and rock bass hanging around rusting bicycles, soft-drink bottles, cans, and other trash. Which was enough to tempt him back to the drawing board. In an early modification, he strapped a hot-water bottle to his back and ran the garden hose through that, which provided a reservoir of air at ambient pressure. The improvisation got him down four feet, with a lead-weight belt. His ears were painful at five feet until, on his mother's advice, Zacharchuk put a button under his tongue and cleared his eustachian tubes from throat to ears with each swallow.

A simple philosophy ensured Zacharchuk never gave up: "You gotta live with what you're getting."

It helps to have a Plan B. Zacharchuk was still hanging out at John Date's dive shop, cleaning floors and doing other odd jobs to work off the price of an imported regulator, made by the French company La Spirotechnique. The shop was happy to get rid of the thing because scuba still hadn't caught on with its customers. Now he had a regulator but no air tanks, which usually hold compressed air at 2,200 psi. After watching Cousteau's specials on TV, and voraciously reading dive magazines, an idea dawned on Zacharchuk: Fire extinguishers are rated at 1,800 psi. Not perfect, but close enough, he thought. Why not turn them into scuba tanks? He bought a fire extinguisher for around $5 from a scrap dealer outside Montreal, cleaned it up, and then scrounged for a European gooseneck valve to attach the regulator. That only left him with a bigger problem: No compressed-gas company would touch it. Zacharchuk went from one to another, trying to find a sympathetic staffer to fill his fire-extinguisher scuba tank with air. Everyone looked at him, a gangly seventeen-year-old kid, about 120 pounds wet, as though he were nuts. They were afraid the thing would blow up under pressure, with the blast force of up to several hundred pounds of TNT.

In 1953, Zacharchuk ended up at Liquid Air, a subsidiary of France's Air Liquide in Montreal. This time, the person he talked to at the front desk was more helpful. He called someone out to take a look. It was Émile Gagnan, the same French engineer who had invented scuba with Cousteau. He had immigrated to Canada six years earlier, fearing postwar France would go to the Communists, and set up shop in Montreal to produce the Aqua-Lung for the North American market. Zacharchuk had no idea who he was talking to until later. But the guy sure seemed to know a lot about diving equipment when the kid explained he was having trouble getting his French regulator to fit his fire-extinguisher air tank.

"It's very easy," Gagnan assured him.

He showed Zacharchuk how to add a pressure reducer and an adapter. The engineer suggested he go to a hospital and ask for a mouthpiece, made of rubber and plastic with a tilt valve, used to help patients breathe during seizures. It was elegantly close to a diver's mouthpiece. Within days, Zacharchuk had one. The modifications cost around $75, more than what he took home in a month working the graveyard shift as a newsroom copy clerk, who spoke seven languages fluently, at CBC Radio's English service. Liquid Air agreed to fill the makeshift tank, which worked perfectly, giving Zacharchuk just over an hour in as much as thirty feet of water. That was enough for him to start freelancing as a diver, mostly searching for outboard motors, anchors, fishing gear, and other items that had fallen off boats at the marina, for a few bucks per salvage. Zacharchuk quickly discovered that the riverbed was rich in historic artifacts. He found old English mallet bottles that once held wine and liquor, and ornate metal badges from British troops' tall, cylindrical shako hats. There were lots of buttons, including one made of pewter from a soldier's eighteenth-century uniform. In the silt and weeds, he uncovered anchors, muskets, more cannonballs than he could count, and cans filled with sawdust impregnated with animal-fat tallow or wax and small, cast-iron balls. Warriors of the day called them canister shot.

More lucrative contract work soon came his way. He got paid to install flow meters in city sewers, recover bodies from river accidents and suicides, and repair municipal water-filtration works. Finally he saved up enough cash to buy factory-made diving gear. He bought sheets of neoprene rubber and glued together his wet suit. In 1958, Zacharchuk met another self-made diver named Sean Gilmore. They teamed up just as the YMCA was about to ruin their business plans by turning out scuba divers by the dozens. While George Bass was laying the foundation of underwater archaeology in the United States, Zacharchuk and Gilmore were becoming skilled amateurs dabbling in a new scientific discipline that few even knew existed.

They dove in the summer, usually at night when the contrast made things easier to spot on the riverbed. In winter, they searched the archives, learning more about the stories behind the objects. Months spent poring over historical records and books revealed parts of the rich human stories behind the retrieved objects. Zacharchuk and Gilmore schooled themselves on archaeological techniques that were standard practice on land and adapted them under water. Instead of just scooping up relics, they carefully plotted their positions on a grid first, and they recorded other details that could explain how they ended up on the riverbed. The divers also read up on artifact conservation. Letting wood that had been submerged for more than a century dry naturally usually meant watching history turn to dust. The team experimented and got good results by slowly soaking the wood in linseed oil, and, later, in a sugar solution. Zacharchuk turned the family bathtub into a restoration vat, which was constantly filled with soaking relics—from smaller items like buckles and buttons to bigger daggers, swords, and muskets. His wife, Doreen, took their newborn baby to her mother-in-law's tub for bathing.

The divers soon had more artifacts than space—enough of history's detritus to fill a five-ton truck. Museum curators and historians turned up their noses. The divers couldn't find anyone to even consider taking the objects off their hands. The head of a big tobacco company was interested in their pitch for funds to donate the trove for public display on Montreal's Île Sainte-Hélène. Until he got lung cancer and died. Antique dealers listened politely, mostly because they were interested in old bottles. But they were more helpful with historical details, and conservation advice. No one, Zacharchuk figured, was going to take a couple of scavenging divers seriously.

"Number one, it's because we don't have degrees," he thought. "Two, we're men in black, wet, rubber suits. Who the hell would believe we'd have such an amount of important artifacts? They have divers coming out of their ears. These days, everyone with a Rolex watch is an archaeologist."

Things suddenly changed on a summer day in 1964, when Zacharchuk and Gilmore duckwalked out of the river, dripping harbingers from the deep. They bumped into John Rick, head of archaeology at Parks Canada, who had set up a field school on Île aux Noix, just outside Fort Lennox, where an instructor and students were digging trenches and sifting the dirt to pick out broken bits of pottery and shards of glass. Rick was stunned at the exquisitely preserved objects the divers carried out of the water.

"This is what a whole bottle looks like," one said. "This is what a musket looks like."

Rick was more than impressed. The pipe-smoking intellectual, in tweed jacket with elbow patches, to Zacharchuk's leather-clad motorbike rider, the archaeologist sensed this was one of the rare moments in science when amateurs leapfrog experts. Rick spent evenings with the divers, listening intently, imagining the possibilities. Zacharchuk brought him a small truckload of old bottles in a Renault R-4 hatchback as a hint of what they had in storage, and a clue to the even bigger treasures waiting on the riverbed. What really changed the world as Rick saw it was a map the divers showed him. They had taken a navigation chart and meticulously drawn a grid across the sections where they dove, each one lettered along with the specific locations of objects marked in subsections.

These weren't just scavengers hauling up treasure, Rick realized. They were marine archaeologists, ahead of their time. The only important work they hadn't done was stratigraphy, a technique borrowed from geology that records objects' precise positions in sedimentary layers to provide more clues and context. Otherwise, the divers were doing the science of archaeology without formal training or title, which Rick was eager to bestow. Why not come and work for him at Parks Canada, the federal agency that oversaw national historical sites, he suggested? Gilmore passed. He had a more lucrative offer from a telecom company. Zacharchuk jumped at the chance. He started out on a one-year contract in the fall of 1964, with a $500 advance and a $1,500 limit on expenses.

As the first head of Canada's marine archaeological unit, and its only staff member, Walter Zacharchuk was boss, employee, and supplier. He even had to provide a boat, with diving equipment that he had bought—a humble, uncertain beginning for what became the team of scientists who led the hunt for *Erebus* and *Terror*. Decades later, Zacharchuk's own place in history was secured when Vice-Admiral Mark Norman of the Royal Canadian Navy not only called him "the father of underwater archaeology in Canada" but also compared the diver who got his start with a tin can and a garden hose to Jacques Cousteau himself.

ZACHARCHUK soon had a staff member, hired on contract. In a cable-knit sweater, looking at once the windblown and aristocratic gray-beard, Robert Grenier fits what became the Cousteau archetype. But that is a comparison underwater archaeologists tend to resist. They see Cousteau, who was not a trained scientist, as more of an enlightened treasure hunter, showman, inventor, and environmental activist than a pioneer of their profession. Even in the early 1960s, before Cousteau had filmed the prime-time special that led to an eight-season run for *The Undersea World of Jacques Cousteau* on American TV, Grenier was a diver with a degree in archaeology and classics from Quebec's Laval University. He also has the pedigree of old French blood in North America. His ancestor, Captain Claude François Grenier, arrived in the early 1790s, when it seems the Catholic officer deserted during the French Revolution to escape a religious pogrom.

In 1978, Robert Grenier had led a wreck search that moved under-water archaeology into subzero North Atlantic seas off Labrador, where the current flowing south from the Arctic carries icebergs, like mythical castles calved from glaciers in western Greenland. Grenier's extraordinary discovery of a Basque whaling boat called the *San Juan* on the bottom of a remote bay rewrote early North American history. She sank, with a cargo of whale oil, in a fall storm in 1565. Grenier's find shed new light on North America's first industrial-scale whaling opera-tion, a lucrative but dangerous industry that Basque sailors established in the sixteenth century to feed Europe's growing demand for lamp oil. The crush of a thrashing bowhead whale's fluke may have killed some of the 125 Basque sailors found buried nearby in unmarked graves on Labrador's Red Bay. They were laid to rest on the same windswept shore where comrades flensed whale carcasses and rendered the blub-ber in large vats each summer before making the treacherous voyage back across the North Atlantic. Some of the dead men were covered only in a thin layer of sod, suggesting they may have been trapped by a brutal winter that killed them. The ground was frozen so hard that survivors, likely near death themselves, couldn't dig proper graves. Franklin's men suffered a similar fate a few hundred years later, and Grenier's work in the icy waters of Red Bay was an essential step toward finding out what happened to their lost ships farther north.

The six-year underwater excavation of the *San Juan*, which helped set new standards in the field, ended in 1984. The wreck stayed on the ocean floor, but Grenier and his team raised a chalupa, one of the small boats that the whalers used to chase and harpoon their prey. Piece by piece, archaeologists reassembled the centuries-old craft. After several years soaking in a vat of polyethylene glycol, the restored vessel was put on permanent display at a museum in Red Bay.

The year after the pioneering underwater project ended, Grenier took over as head of the underwater archaeology department from Zacharchuk, who moved on to private consulting. Grenier also became president of the International Committee on the Underwater Cultural Heritage (ICUCH), which aims to inventory, conserve, and promote interest in the world's underwater cultural heritage. He played a key role in negotiating an international agreement that sets out rules on how to treat hundreds of thousands of shipwrecks around the world.

Called the Convention on the Protection of the Underwater Cultural Heritage, one of its most important principles holds that wrecks are usually better left where they lie.

UNESCO's underwater cultural heritage agreement, which came into force in 2009, commits countries to leave shipwrecks *in situ*, or in the place where they lie underwater, as the first option. That emphasizes the need to preserve historical context as well as the scientific importance of leaving a ship where it sank. But exceptions are allowed to the *in situ* rule if the purpose is to make a significant contribution to the protection or knowledge of underwater cultural heritage. The

backdrop of the logo symbolizing that global commitment is the chalupa that the Basque whalers left behind on the bottom of Red Bay.

A LEGENDARY DIVER, inventor, and explorer—a more brash Canadian
version of Cousteau—was determined to show that humans could,
and should, be working undersea in the Arctic. Joe MacInnis, who
included physician, poet, photographer, author, scientist, and aqua-
naut on his résumé, kept powerful company. The first man to swim
and photograph beneath the ice cap at the North Pole, he also walked
upside down under Arctic ice with Britain's Prince Charles for half an
hour, carrying an umbrella.

MacInnis took iconic CBS News anchorman Walter Cronkite
beneath the waves with him, as well as fellow Canadians Pierre Trudeau, who was prime minister at the time, and Hollywood director
James Cameron. They worked together exploring the wreck of the
RMS *Titanic*, the luxury cruise ship that hit an iceberg southeast of
Newfoundland in 1912 and sank about 12,500 feet to the bottom of
the Atlantic. Another ally was Canada's Dome Petroleum, which saw
mutual benefit in MacInnis's exploration and innovation underwater
in the Arctic. In his prime, the diver was so adept at influencing the
influential that his own friend—canoeist, artist, and filmmaker Bill
Mason—marveled at his ability to hit up anyone for money to fund the
next big idea.

"Well, you can call him anything you want. But I know MacInnis
as well as anybody," Mason said wryly. "And I'll tell you right now: He's
a con man. Joe starts talking about the Arctic and whales and sunken
ships. Before you know it, you're reaching into your pocket, or worse
still, pleading to go along. If that guy had been born a couple of hundred years ago, he'd a been on one of those [Royal Navy] ships. And
knowing MacInnis, he probably would have been in command."

In the late 1960s, when the US Navy put aquanauts in a yellow steel tube called *Sealab III* to see what would happen while they lived for twelve days on the deep sea floor, the military brought in Mac-Innis as a consultant. He then decided cheaper was better and built an underwater habitat of his own for just $10,000, which he drew from his personal bank account in 1969. MacInnis came up with the idea while doodling on a napkin in a New York restaurant. A young engineer in the city noticed that the rough sketch looked similar to a railway ore carrier. So they modified one, sprayed the insides with a two-inch coating of plastic foam insulation, and attached a bottom filled with ten tons of iron-ore ballast to weigh down the structure underwater. Painted yellow and blue, it looked like a giant version of a backpacker's propane stove, with a small window and a dome, both made of plexiglass. MacInnis called his prototype *Sublimnos*, which he made up from the root word *limnology*—the study of inland waters as ecosystems interacting with their drainage basins and the atmosphere. The world's first freshwater habitat, *Sublimnos* was also the only one operating beneath ice when Lake Huron froze over each winter.

MacInnis lowered it thirty-two feet to the bottom of the lake's Georgian Bay. The site is near Tobermory, Ontario, where thousand-year-old cedar trees top the cliffs of the Bruce Peninsula. There are more than twenty historic shipwrecks in the clear waters off the town, several protected in a national marine park. The area, including Big Tub Harbor, is so rich with easily accessible archaeological sites that it has been called the freshwater diving capital of the world. MacInnis had an "open hatch policy." Anyone with a booked spot could get into his diving bell, which *Popular Mechanics* called "a bargain basement habitat." The cover art of the 1971 edition featuring MacInnis's project imagined an amphibious jet dropping off campers at a dock for their vacation in a submersible the size of a Volkswagen. Thousands of people accepted the invitation to use *Sublimnos*, including a fashion designer, medical students, engineers, and a kid in junior high who wanted to go deep on his science project.

MacInnis chafed at government regulation. In one speech, he compared lawmakers and civil servants to a fat seal wriggling clumsily across ice in a film. He wanted slow movers out of his way, where they couldn't impede progress. Deep-sea divers, MacInnis boasted to a club of well-heeled businessmen, are "rugged individuals who are in the front ranks of free enterprise." Like many explorers before him—people like Franklin and Ross, with little patience for the petty games of politicians and bureaucrats—MacInnis saw conquest in the High Arctic as the ultimate prize. To him, sixty-three hours at the North Pole, on an ice cap fifteen feet thick and 450 miles from the nearest land in April 1974, was the bliss of something close to pure freedom.

"My colleagues on this expedition, and in all of the nine expeditions to the north, have the same motivation that fires an exploring businessman," he once told a lunch gathering at Toronto's tony Empire Club of Canada. "They both start with a dream and follow it with vision and perseverance. At the North Pole, we were extremely fortunate. We had no overburden of bureaucracy.

"There was no one to tell us what to do and how to do it, and none of us was concerned about welfare payments or pension cheques."

The centerpiece of MacInnis's push for undersea work in the Arctic was *Sub-Igloo*, which he launched at the end of 1972. MacInnis and his team built the habitat out of transparent acrylic and placed it on the seabed at Resolute Bay as a divers' refuge and communications station with 360-degree visibility. He pitched the unit as semiportable and deployable without heavy equipment. Filled with air, with eight tons of upward buoyancy, it would provide shelter, safety, and contact with the outside world. MacInnis installed a red, Canadian-designed Contempra telephone, which he used to call Trudeau. The walls were so transparent that it was easy to forget the pulsing jellyfish and anemones were outside. Divers' companions sometimes tossed water on the inside of the station as a reminder there was something between them and a sea so cold that it could kill with just five minutes of exposure. MacInnis envisioned *Sub-Igloo* as critical to the coming legions of cold-water divers as small tents are to mountaineers.

"Tomorrow's ocean world includes exploratory [oil] well heads, sub-sea production platforms, pipelines and an extraordinary amount of work for scientific and industrial divers," he predicted. "If we are to understand, use, and effectively manage this part of Canada, almost half the territory of the nation, then we must develop the capability to actually work and when necessary, live under the ice."

Neither *Sub-Igloo* or *Sublimnos* survived. MacInnis's vision of developing a new subsea economy in Canada's Arctic is still largely that. He then turned to a new dream, one nagging at most divers' minds. Mac-Innis was going to discover a shipwreck, but not on some reef or rocky shore in tropical waters. He would do it in the Arctic Archipelago, where no one had done it before. The idea came to him on Cornwallis Island in April 1975, while standing on a hill overlooking Resolute Bay, waiting for Prince Charles, then twenty-six and an officer in the Royal Navy. MacInnis landed first on the snow in a Twin Otter bush plane with skis, beneath the cliffs of Beechey Island that once towered above Franklin and his men. Prince Charles was following in another plane, which couldn't land in a buffeting wind. MacInnis tromped up a steep slope through knee-deep snow to a cairn with a marble tablet that Francis McClintock had erected on behalf of Lady Franklin. The monument she commissioned was made in New York, under Henry Grinnell's direction, and dated 1855. The American expedition tasked to erect it couldn't reach Beechey Island, so the memorial waited in Greenland until McClintock picked it up to fulfill Jane's wish in 1859. Alone with his thoughts in the Arctic cold 116 years later, MacInnis read the epitaph:

To the Memory of

FRANKLIN

CROZIER, FITZJAMES,

and all their gallant brother officers and faithful companions
who have suffered and perished in the cause of science and the
service of their country.

THIS TABLET

is erected near the spot where they passed their first Arctic
winter and whence they issued forth to conquer difficulties or

TO DIE.

It commemorates the grief of their
admiring countrymen and friends,
and the anguish, subdued by faith,
of her who has lost, in the heroic
leader of the expedition, the most
devoted and affectionate of husbands.

"And so He bringeth them unto the
Haven where they would be."

Back down the slope, near the bush plane, MacInnis joined Stu
Hodgson, the federal official in charge of the Northwest Territories.
A former union boss on the Vancouver docks, Hodgson was staring
out to sea, deep in thought.

"There's a ship out there somewhere, Joe, lying on the seafloor,
buried under all that ice. . . ."

MacInnis had his next mission: figuring out where to search for a
wreck. He flew to London to get advice from Clive Holland, archivist,
deputy librarian, and museum curator at the Scott Polar Research
Institute in Cambridge. Holland was skeptical. No one had ever found

a wreck that far north, he reminded MacInnis, who didn't budge. They went for drinks in a local pub.

"Ideally, we need a ship in water deep enough for her to be below the ice scour, but shallow enough to be accessible," MacInnis said. "Something in the seventy to one hundred meters would be perfect. Think of it. A ship buried in freezing waters for such a long period of time would be preserved beautifully. It would be like finding a time capsule."

"There are times when I think you must be joking," Holland replied, "and then there are times when I think you are daft. You want to find something less than 40 meters long, buried under thousands of square kilometers of ice. In water that is ice-free for only a few weeks each year. Where winds are dangerous and unpredictable and where icebergs weigh up to a million tons."

By now, though, Holland knew MacInnis wasn't one to take no for an answer.

"There are, however, several remote possibilities," Holland finally conceded. "And I stress the word remote. What is needed is an eye-witness account, preferably a log entry made by an officer. It will be difficult, perhaps impossible, and may take a considerable amount of time."

Months later, MacInnis received a typed note from Holland, briefly shortlisting ships that sank in the Arctic Archipelago with a rough location of where they went down. Top of the list was the histo-rian's recommendation of the wreck most likely to be found.

It was *Breadalbane*.

MacInnis next turned to Phil Nuytten, a cigar-puffing diver, scien-tist, and inventor based in Vancouver. His deepwater diving creations include the Newtsuit, a lightweight atmospheric system that allows the operator to work at depths of up to a thousand feet, under extreme pressures, without having to decompress on the way up. It looks like a yellow Michelin Man with pincers, ideal for exploring *Breadalbane* if

MacInnis could only figure out where she was. Nuytten was a valuable ally on that front, too. He had another, inner skill: an extraordinary knack for finding things lost deep beneath the sea.

"Why can't you look for a ship in the Bahamas?" Nuytten, his feet propped on the corner of his desk, asked MacInnis after hearing the pitch. "It might have some gold on it. If nothing else, we could come away with a suntan."

He joined MacInnis's small team that headed north in the summer of 1978. Working around ice floes in two Zodiac rubber boats, they had a search window of just a few days. Their side-scan sonar device was shaped like a slender torpedo and about six feet long. Affectionately known as a towfish, it picked up nothing interesting beyond deep scours that sea ice had carved out of the seabed for millennia. MacInnis tried, and failed, again the following summer. By 1980, the money was running out. Interest was drying up. He had one last chance. This time, CCGS *John A. MacDonald*, the same icebreaker that had helped escort the oil supertanker SS *Manhattan* on a pioneering voyage through the Northwest Passage just over a decade earlier, would haul the towfish. The searchers put it in the water around 8 p.m. on August 13, 1980, and before long the recorder pen was furiously scratching, as sonar hits pinged off something big on the bottom. At first, the lines traced another deep ice scour, around one and a quarter miles south of Beechey Island, some 320 feet down. Then the ghostly image of a ship appeared.

"That's it! I think that's it!" blurted Gary Kozak, the side-scan sonar operator.

"You're kidding."

"No, dammit. That's it! Look, there's her hull. I can't believe this! She's intact! Even her masts are still standing!"

Late in the winter of 1981, MacInnis tried to return with a team equipped to dive under the thick ice, but pressure ridges jutting up at all angles above the wreck site like a miniature mountain range made landing a bush plane impossible. It was even worse the following year. He finally got to explore *Breadalbane* three years after finding her. Robert Grenier joined the team of two dozen as the supervising archaeologist required by the federal permit. Feeling bad vibes, and suffering from a nasty bout of flu, Grenier tried to back out at the last minute. But several cultural directors pleaded with Parks Canada to participate to prevent wholesale looting.

"It was made clear that this was not to be an archaeological expedition with artifacts recovery, unless in the case of justifiable samples as judged by the permitted archaeologist—me," Grenier told me.

Dome Petroleum helped fund the project. Explaining its support, the oil company said information that MacInnis's team gathered would have "industrial applications." In the 1970s and early 1980s, Dome was one of several firms that drilled 176 offshore wells in the Beaufort Sea in Canada's Western Arctic. They weren't developed, in part because there was growing disagreement over whether there was a safe way to get any oil and natural gas out. MacInnis's plan for deepwater diving on the *Breadalbane* seemed a good showcase for technology that future undersea workers might use for tapping enormous reserves.

Two holes blasted in sea ice several feet thick gave a remotely piloted vehicle access from the bow while divers were lowered to the stern. Nuytten worked in shifts with Doug Osborne in a yellow WASP suit, a largely glass-reinforced plastic cousin of the cast-aluminum Newtsuit. With a big domed top, four thrusters, articulated arms with bulbous wrists, metal claws, and an enclosed leg area shaped like an insect's abdomen, it floated above *Breadalbane* like a hovering alien shining beams of light on a newly discovered world.

A remotely piloted vehicle (RPV), not much bigger than a portable generator, descended first to assess the wreck. Its camera caught sight of the ship's wheel, an iconic piece of any wreck. Marine archaeologists wouldn't think of touching such a sensitive wreck without precisely mapping the vessel and the positions of its artifacts. But MacInnis wasn't an archaeologist. He also wasn't willing to wait. With a black watch cap pulled tightly down to his ears, Grenier sat slumped in a chair across from MacInnis, scribbling notes on a large pad and watching the monitor closely as a robotic arm reached out for a wooden relic, about the size of a dessert plate, ringed by metal and with a large pentagonal hole in the middle.

"Snap that sucker," MacInnis said, and the claw pinched shut to lift the object from the rocky seabed, inches away from the ship. "That's great. Oh yah! Fabulous!"

"Drop it," said Grenier, cutting through the happy chatter with the sharp tone of a store detective stopping a shoplifter in mid-snatch.

"Drop it? *Why?*" MacInnis asked sternly.

"Well, I said we'll have a discussion," the archaeologist replied, steeled for a fight. "And we'll have a discussion."

"Your concern is to position this," MacInnis replied more collegially. "Is that right?"

Grenier was feeling the legendary MacInnis squeeze. Neither man looked at the other. The archaeologist flicked at the tip of his nose a couple of times, pen squeezed between his fingers like a cigarette, and tried to assert federal authority.

"We were going to have a conversation tomorrow," MacInnis pressed, arching his eyebrows as Bill Mason's movie camera rolled for a documentary. "We're about to have it now."

The RPV operator kept a grip on the artifact while Grenier and MacInnis argued. MacInnis insisted the object didn't "look particularly valuable." Grenier disagreed. MacInnis was especially interested in the metal, which appeared to be copper alloy. Archaeologists had agreed the expedition would collect artifacts to study how different materials deteriorated over long periods submerged in cold water. That offered a payoff for Dome and other oil companies that needed to know how wellheads or pipelines might react over decades in Arctic seas. As Britain's *New Scientist* magazine explained in an advance story on the *Breadalbane* dive operation, "the Northwest Passage will probably be used to carry oil to southern markets, and this kind of information could prove essential in planning, regulating and operating such trade." The RPV had a tight hold on something MacInnis thought was the perfect size for the analysis needed. He wasn't in the mood for a debate. Transformers had been blowing left and right. The ice might suddenly freeze and close the dive hole.

"We may not be able to get back to this thing," MacInnis said, almost pleading.

"I agreed to one thing," Grenier countered, "which was to lift a few artifacts when they are located." He meant in the archaeological sense: being sure where it lay in relation to the ship, the debris field, and other items to provide provenance that might prove telling in later research.

"But this *has* been located," MacInnis insisted.

"No, not this one. We don't know where it is."

Grenier shifted in his chair and bit his lower lip.

"This may be the only thing we take off the ship," MacInnis said. "And I can't tell you what it's taken to get this far, to get that. That's a million dollar shot if you want my, ah. . . . And I don't want to put the heat on you. But I'll take responsibility. We gotta make a decision and I'm gonna make it."

Grenier was overruled.

"Go ahead and pick it up," MacInnis told the RPV operator.

With a few nudges of a black joystick, the robotic arm lifted the round piece of *Breadalbane*, pivoted right to a cage that had delivered the vehicle to the depths, and dropped it through a triangular hole between wooden struts. Then it grabbed a larger artifact, which looked like one of the wooden blocks used as pulleys in the ship's heavy rigging, and did the same. After Phil Nuytten got his WASP suit assembled, he went down for a recon trip. Soon he was hovering over the ship's wheel, floating past a tall mast, getting a better sense of the layout, currents, and anything that might snag him. That went off without a hitch, including a close look into the deckhouse, where Nuytten saw some more things he wanted to bring up.

The team convened in the mess tent, where a hand-painted sign above the door declared: RAIDERS OF THE LOST BARQUE. Grenier sat at the edge of the group, the shunned outsider, a notebook with a ringed spine and about the size of an organizer open on his lap. Nuytten said he wanted to take a compass off the wreck, another iconic piece of any ship. The atmosphere snapped taut again as Grenier explained the absolute need to ensure the safety and integrity of any artifacts. This time he was standing behind MacInnis, who spoke with his head leaning on four fingers, as a teacher might while scolding a pupil. Both men looked at the ground, spitting words like daggers.

"I can't see how this operation can take place safely," Grenier said, his fingers interlaced and thumbs touching, as if in prayer.

"Safely for the artifacts?" MacInnis asked.

"For the artifacts, yes."

"Well, if I understand correctly, the objective in marine archaeology is to bring them back to the surface with the minimum of damage." There was a long silence while both men fumed. "That correct?"

"Not only to the artifacts," Grenier explained, "but to the surroundings."

"They're all artifacts," MacInnis shot back. He repeated his question. Grenier agreed.

MacInnis turned to Doug Osborne, the next diver in line, and told him to get suited up, with instructions to discuss what he saw at the wreck site with Grenier, and then suggest what he wanted to do. Osborne navigated to a wheelhouse cabinet with several rows of large rectangular openings. A signal light and at least one of *Breadalbane*'s compasses sat on shelves, where they held their positions during the ship's fall through the sea ice and on her final, jolting drop to the seabed. With the WASP's manipulator claw, Osborne tapped the object that experts on the surface were confident was a compass.

"It's intact. It's solid," he said.

Then the diver warned Nuytten that the cabinet was fragile and might fall off the ship's wall if he proceeded. The compass was allowed to remain where it was. Osborne moved over to the ship's wheel. Grenier told MacInnis he was concerned about the mineral concretions on the wooden base. A thick layer as hard as concrete, it could break the wheel if it were moved. MacInnis wanted to make an attempt to raise it anyway.

"No, in this condition, I would stop it there, Joe," Grenier said. "I cannot go in for this."

"Maybe you can tell me why you don't want it moved. That wheel," MacInnis countered.

"Because . . ."

"Just let me finish this," MacInnis interrupted, answering his own question before the archaeologist could. "The reason we would like the wheel, and anything else off the ship, is really for the people of Canada to appreciate this kind of history. So maybe you could tell me why you don't want it moved."

Grenier glanced back over his shoulder at the movie camera, removed his watch cap, and ruffled his hair in frustration.

"Reasonably concisely," MacInnis added. "Understanding that there might be some damage. But we're looking at, really, a one-in-a-million opportunity."

Osborne would be gentle, MacInnis assured Grenier, who said he didn't like the damage that was already done to the archaeological site. He expected more if the diver didn't stop.

"In my perception, we have done enough," Grenier said. "I don't figure that it's archaeologically sound to go any further than that at this point."

On the grainy video feed, Grenier could faintly see that a steel rod seemed to still be tying the wheel to the steering mechanism. The archaeologist thought it might be a valuable specimen for lab analysis that could provide many samples to study how Arctic seawater degrades a single object. So he acquiesced in the retrieval of *Breadalbane*'s wheel. Then disaster struck. Grenier saw the steel rod break, and, before he could say anything, the binnacle hanging above the wheel came crashing down onto the deck below it.

"That was it; the deal I had made was off and I called off the operation," Grenier told me. "At that point, any communication with the diver was cut off. I had lost control. The operation continued without me, illegally, in a destructive manner."

Osborne pinched the ship's wheel with both claws, yanked it away from *Breadalbane*, and brought it to the surface, hugging it with one arm. When the wheel was secured, yet still in the water, Grenier saw MacInnis step away with a filmmaker shooting for *National Geographic*. They had a picture in mind, something dramatic enough to make the magazine's cover, an iconic image of the wheel framed by ocean and sea ice, at the moment the nineteenth-century world connected with the twentieth. Grenier decided to lift the wheel to the surface and slide it over a panel of plywood. MacInnis was furious when he saw the "money shot" was blown. That set off a new dispute as Grenier tried to stop him from putting the wheel back in the water for the shoot, which would have violated a basic rule of preserving artifacts moved from saltwater to air.

"No!" Grenier insisted. "Only over my dead body."

The anger still lingering decades later, Grenier stressed that he was impressed by Nuytten's work on the site but had to try to draw a firm line when he saw the wreck suffering: "I had conditionally acquiesced to the lifting of the wheel under clear condition of no damage: when damage occurred, I said no more and MacInnis went ahead anyway."

The archaeologist won the argument over whether to put the wheel back in the water. Grenier built a wooden box and spent half the night gently securing the *Breadalbane*'s fractured wheel in it, trying to prevent further damage. He flew to Ottawa the next day and delivered the precious artifact to Parks Canada's conservators, who had to figure out how to keep it from disintegrating into dust. They immersed the wheel in a vat of cold water bubbling with a stream of nitrogen, which cut off the oxygen for microorganisms that had been feasting since the nineteenth century on the deteriorating composite of different types of wood and metal. An X-ray revealed empty spaces where the original screws once held the wheel intact. Conservators had to tie it together with plastic bands.

More than three decades later, *Breadalbane*'s wheel was still locked up in a crate in Parks Canada's Ottawa headquarters, bound together with ties and too fragile to be left in the open air for long, let alone put on display. The bill for the unfinished conservation work on it was well over $100,000 and climbing, with no end in sight. The never-ending cost of dealing with a wheel, from a merchant resupply ship, was a cautionary tale when talk inevitably returned to the real quarry, the elusive wrecks of *Erebus* and *Terror*.

13

Skull Island

To Inuit who knew elders' stories about the two huge ships—the "strange houses" that delivered dying white men and vanished beneath the waves—there wasn't much left to learn. The basic facts were well known, and had been for a long time. Sea ice crushed one, and some stories said that ship went down in water so deep off the north end of King William Island that no one could say precisely where she ended up. Other, often tangled, accounts suggested both ships may have moved south. Inuit had boarded at least one, had seen a dead man, and carried off countless useful items before she also went down. Oral history told of that wreck's rough location, in a cluster of islands at the eastern end of Queen Maud Gulf. Louie Kamookak, as he told one interviewer, "wasn't about to go out there and stick my head in the water." He was focused on trying to find Franklin's body. So, for a time, the frontline search for *Erebus* and *Terror* was left to southern adventurers, mostly treasure hunters, documentary film crews, or wealthy travelers who had the budgets and equipment to launch modern search expeditions.

None had the impact of David Woodman. Like Kamookak, he came to the Franklin search by following a compulsion that wouldn't be silenced. Blunt and built like a cask, Woodman has a closely cropped gray beard and a talent for storytelling, the traits of a man shaped by the sea—first in the Royal Canadian Navy, then as a harbormaster, and finally as a captain at the helm of West Coast car ferries. Some who go on about life on the water are more wind than sail. Not Woodman. He has a restless, Type-A mind hungry for hard facts and no room for fools or phonies. More important to history, he has a subtle power to make the outrageous request seem perfectly reasonable. Listening to him talk about all the arms he gently twisted, persuading military pilots to fly low over the High Arctic with a magnetometer, or getting a loaner towed slowly over the ice by a whining snowmobile, all in the off chance of detecting the submerged metal in a Franklin wreck, you get the sense Woodman could coax leaves down from a tree if he set his mind to it.

Archaeologists dig and dive for artifacts that reveal old truths. Woodman waded deep into the weeds of Inuit oral history, as recorded by Franklin searchers in the nineteenth century. While Kamookak was listening to elders for clues, interpreting them with an innate understanding of the culture and the environment that sustains it, Woodman was focused on the written word. Both spent uncounted hours winnowing out the chaff by meticulously cross-referencing details, trying to figure out which of many accounts were the most credible. Depending on the Inuit accounts one believed, or how a historian read the often-distorted versions from explorers who wrote them down, the southern Franklin wreck must be close to O'Reilly Island or thirty miles to the west. Then again, it should be seven miles to the northwest of Grant Point, five miles due west of it, or any number of other places. Inuit knew where the wreck was. The problem was figuring out who had it right.

It didn't take long for Woodman to see why Inuit knew *Erebus* or *Terror* ended up in eastern Queen Maud Gulf. What occupies his mind are the Inuit stories of seamen living aboard that ship, with a dog, long after she was originally abandoned. There were anywhere from about five to seventeen men on the vessel, according to various descriptions. If proven by archaeological evidence, that would suggest some of Franklin's crew sailed the ship there. If the vessel's hull was encased in a huge ice pan, perhaps those same men simply went with the flow through the maze of ice and islands. If a wreck could be found far south of where the Victory Point Record said she was left ensnared in ice, as firmly as an animal in a trap, then objects, records, or even human remains might answer a crucial question: Did some of Sir John's men sail her there? If they did, all sorts of fascinating possibilities arise. Maybe mutineers defied orders and returned to their ship. Perhaps fortunate survivors saw her passing, slowed by ice floes, and somehow managed to scramble aboard and ride the wind and currents with her to their destiny.

As a student at the University of Toronto, Woodman had spent weekends at Robarts Library, fourteen stories of sharp angles in precast concrete, considered one of the continent's standout examples of Brutalist architecture. On a Friday night in January 1975, he was on his way out and walked past the reshelving bin. A thick volume on top of the heap practically called out to Woodman. It was *The Voyage of the 'Fox' in Arctic Seas*, Sir Francis McClintock's narrative of his historic expedition for Lady Franklin. All Woodman knew was the words *voyage of* sounded like a trip worth taking. He read it through twice over the weekend. He lingered on the words one of Franklin's men wrote in the Victory Point Record on May 28, 1847. In Woodman's mind, the longitude and latitude reported for *Erebus* and *Terror* lined up like arrows pointing to a big X on a map.

"This'll be easy," Woodman judged. "We'll drill a hole there, dive down, one bounce dive, find ships, come back up and I have a bar story forever. I actually figured, if I put some effort into this, in two years I can do it."

Heavily in debt, Woodman ended up in the Royal Canadian Navy instead, training as a diver, a career cut short by a leg infection. He served a dozen years on navy ships and submarines instead, reaching the rank of lieutenant. During the Cold War, he logged many dull hours in the White Sea, off Murmansk in the Soviet Arctic in a diesel submarine, going in hundred-mile circles. Running in stealth mode on battery power, the sub towed an array of hydrophones, recording the sound signatures of Soviet boomer boats, the subs armed with nuclear missiles, as they left port. After a stint as harbormaster in the northwest coast port of Prince Rupert, he became a BC Ferries captain. The whole time, Woodman read Arctic explorers' journals, studied Inuit testimony, and plotted ways to get up to the Arctic to search for the Franklin wrecks that had been on his mind since that fateful Friday night in the university library. He was a low-budget explorer: negotiating to piggyback on other expeditions, lining up sponsors to back his own, trying to wangle freebies for equipment and supplies, or at least employee discounts when that was the best he could get, and usually hearing: "No." Franklinologists can be an insular lot. Woodman was an untutored outsider. Instinct and a life at sea told him to heed Inuit witnesses, which accepted experts had largely dismissed.

"Everyone kept telling me, 'There are Inuit stories out there, but they are so confused and confusing that they are basically useless.' So every narrative is built on the Victory Point Record. This is all they gave us: 138 words, and there are arguments about almost every word on that page."

Woodman headed to Washington, DC, to pore over Charles Francis Hall's papers, a trove of diaries, journals, notebooks, scrapbooks, letters, ships' logs, and other documents preserved at the Smithsonian Institution. Apparently the first person to request the documents in a century, Woodman worked through the jumble of notes, searching for gems among the scree. One of the many things that kept him reading was a description of the encounter at the ice crack in Washington Bay, considered one of the most credible accounts of Franklin survivors meeting Inuit. A *qalunaaq* carrying a rifle identified himself as Ill-kern, according to the Inuit story Hall wrote down. But Hall died before he could turn his notes into a book, so the Senate directed Joseph E. Nourse, a professor at the US Naval Observatory, to do it. In that edited version, Nourse rendered the Inuit retelling of the sailor's name as Tierkin. Imagining Inuit trying to get their mouths around a British sailor's name, likely one spoken by a man who was hungry, sick, or dying, Woodman checked the Franklin Expedition crew lists. To his ear, it sounded like the Inuit were saying the name of William Pilkington, one of five Royal Marines aboard *Erebus*. With careful study, which Woodman built up in spreadsheets and notes that filled many file folders, facts began to corroborate the Inuit oral history.

"It convinced me that the Inuit have very good memories for detail, which should have been self-evident," Woodman recalled. "That's their life. If you want to get home from a hunt, you have to remember almost every black rock from you to the caribou and back. This encounter was like a UFO landing to us. It was so out of the ordinary to meet strangers, *white people*, that it would make a deep impression. This was something they were going to remember, and tell on the long dark nights, over and over again."

Woodman was a second officer, and navigator, on the navy's oceanographic research ship HMCS *Endeavour* when he finished writing the book that is his biggest contribution to the Franklin search. He stashed it in his filing cabinet in 1986 and left it there, afraid the acknowledged Franklin experts would think he was an idiot if he tried to get it published. There it sat, unwanted, for two years—until his wife, Franca, got tired of listening to him bicker about how other writers had it all wrong. She sent her husband's manuscript to publishers. To Woodman's astonishment, his analysis of Inuit testimony passed peer review by an academic book publisher. Archaeologists were soon carrying around dog-eared copies of *Unravelling the Franklin Mystery: Inuit Testimony*. Scholars called it seminal and made it an essential citation in their own work. The gruff sailor's name was now part of highbrow conversation, oft-repeated in the phrase that is music to any academic's ears: "As Woodman has shown, . . ." He was all the more interesting for challenging Old World myths that had long outlasted

the Royal Navy's power over the world, including the almost canon-
ical certainty that Franklin's men had moved as one, advancing sto-
ically against the Arctic despite heavy losses, as Her Majesty's troops
would do against any foe. Instead, by piecing together Inuit accounts
over decades, Woodman argued that the sailors must have broken up
into smaller, disorganized groups as they fought for survival, hobbled
by the weaknesses all humans share against the power of nature.

"They didn't march heroically, with Queen Victoria's flag in front
of them, and the weakest one dropped, the next one and the next
one," he said. "That's the narrative that had been carried for more
than 100 years."

About a year after leaving the military, Woodman decided it was
time to go Franklin wreck-hunting in the Arctic. It wasn't as though
he suddenly had nothing to do or extra money to blow. What he did
have was potentially more valuable: a few good friends in the right
places. He knew he had to pitch them before they moved on, or rose
too high in the ranks to bother answering his calls. He was selling a
shot in the dark. The best place to look for *Erebus* or *Terror*, the area of
eastern Queen Maud Gulf that Inuit call *Ugjulik*, is almost fifty miles
long and twenty miles wide. That is roughly a thousand square miles,
or three times the size of New York City, covered by thick ice most
of the year. From his submarine days, Woodman had an idea how to
cover a lot of distance fast. The Royal Canadian Air Force hunted subs
with the Lockheed CP-140 Aurora maritime patrol aircraft, a Canadian version of the US P-3 Orion. The aircraft carried a magnetometer
as an airborne metal detector. Woodman called an old friend to ask
whether the same device could detect the iron cladding on a smaller
wooden ship sitting underwater.

He was soon talking to Brad Nelson, the expert at Defense Research
Establishment Pacific, who did the math. An Aurora equipped with a
magnetometer, flying two hundred feet above the surface at an airspeed
of just 100 knots would have about a 60 percent chance of success, he

estimated. Not the best odds, but Woodman got to work persuading commanders that trying to find *Erebus* or *Terror* with an airplane would be an excellent project to hone aircrew skills. He needed what in military jargon is known as a "corollary benefit." The 1978 Canadian Arctic crash of Kosmos 954, a Soviet reconnaissance satellite powered by a nuclear reactor, was a compelling one. To find the wreckage, the United States and Canadian militaries launched a joint mission, called Operation Morning Light. Searching for months on foot and in the air, troops covered forty-eight thousand square miles before finding a dozen pieces of the downed satellite, most of which were radioactive. The thought that it was bound to happen again, likely more than once, made Woodman's idea of practicing on a lost Franklin ship attractive. He also highlighted the risk of an airliner crashing on its way over the pole. Very thinly spread search-and-rescue teams would have to find the wreckage quickly for any hope of saving lives. Wreck hunting would also give the Canadian military a friendly way to show the flag in the Northwest Passage. Canada considers the route internal waters, whereas several other maritime nations, led by the United States, insist it is an international strait.

The air force only committed to one flight, lasting no more than half a day in 1992, which meant Woodman would have to be very lucky to find anything. He put his chips down on the area around Grant Point because that's where the most specific Inuit testimony pointed. Wood and other ship debris found farther south on O'Reilly Island could be explained by the natural drift of ocean currents and sea ice. After finishing only half of the planned search lanes in the allotted time, members of the aircrew were chatting on the way back to base at Yellowknife. Woodman, in the back, was oblivious. The crew decided to return the next day, a rest day, to finish the job. In the end, they covered 155 square miles, identified sixty-one "magnetic anomalies," and marked five of those High Priority. That was nothing to get too excited about. That part of the Arctic is very magnetic by nature.

"That's what all of our hits turned out to be—geological features," Woodman said.

He refused to give up. Over a dozen years, Woodman either led or took part in nine search expeditions, including a brutal hike of some twelve days through knee-deep sucking mud and banks of melting snow on the high ground. He drained some $200,000 from his savings account, with little to show for it except some marvelous stories. In 1997, the 150th anniversary of Franklin's death inspired an ambitious, privately led attempt to find the wrecks of his ships for ten days. Woodman joined with Eco-Nova Productions Ltd., a film company out of Halifax, to work with a team that included several federal agencies, based on the icebreaker CCGS *Sir Wilfrid Laurier*. Robert Grenier was there too, reliving the dark days of the *Breadalbane* documentary shoot. Woodman was given the honorary title of Search Coordinator, which was really just a bit part in the movie.

"Whenever I said, 'Alright, this is where I want to go,' they'd say: 'No, no. That's out in the middle. We can't get good film there. Let's go closer to the land so we can at least get the boats going past the land.'"

But Inuit oral history said the wreck was a three-mile walk across the sea ice, Woodman pointed out. He was overruled. The best-equipped search expedition yet focused on waters off O'Reilly Island, where army divers had come up dry thirty years earlier in eastern Queen Maud Gulf. Federal hydrographers, who normally suffer the unheralded slog of surveying the bottoms of rivers, lakes, and oceans to produce navigation charts, searched with side-scan sonar. Single-beam echo sounders and a magnetometer put more electronic eyes on the ocean bottom. Just like the military divers in 1967, the only useful things the team found were on land, this time on a string of islets north of O'Reilly. At first, the most exciting were fragments of copper-alloy sheathing. Copper sheets covered the Franklin ships' hulls to prevent fouling by marine life, such as barnacles or seaweed that created drag or warm-water borers such as shipworm and the teredo, which sailors called gribbles.

The metal debris, which still had oakum sealant on the back, was found on an island Inuit call *Puvittuq*, which means "Copper Sheet Island." The Canadian army had found similar bits in the same area. The Eco-Nova expedition also found a small copper-alloy disk. Grenier took it south for analysis and tests seemed to show it was the bottom of a Britannia coffeepot. The Royal Navy issued them for roughly a decade, which included the year *Erebus* and *Terror* sailed on their final voyage. But several years after what seemed a promising find, Woodman was told the coffeepot theory had been ruled out.

On the growing list of Franklin Expedition artifacts, these latest weren't much. Years later, senior underwater archaeologists Ryan Harris and Jonathan Moore studied the metal sheeting and other objects in detail, carefully examining the nailing patterns and the composition of the metal, and poring over historical records in England. They confirmed that copper sheeting, installed on Royal Navy hulls since the 1780s to ward off shipworm, a warm-water mollusk, and other organisms that fouled hulls in tropical waters, had been removed from Franklin's ships before they sailed for the Arctic.

"We know for a fact they didn't come from *Erebus* and *Terror*," Moore told me.

The objects weren't Franklin relics, but they still served a crucial purpose. They spurred a closer study of the Inuit oral history. Before the artifacts' provenance was proven, the federal government hired Kamookak and Darren Keith, another expert in Inuit traditions, to show examples and photographs of them to elders and ask where the items might have come from. The team's lengthy report added a new wrinkle to *qalunaaq* confusion over Inuit accounts. In the nineteenth century, Inuit used the wind and the sun's movement to reckon direction. What they called north referred to where the wind blew from,

which is actually northwest. South to them was the origin of the southeast wind. That left a lot of room to get lost in translation for early
expeditions trying to find Franklin and his men, using compasses that
pointed unreliably to the North Magnetic Pole. Kamookak and Keith
wanted to give any who followed a heads-up to course-correct instead
of going astray with more assumptions based on fundamental cultural
misunderstandings.

"If searchers were given information in oral testimonies as to the
location of the shipwreck, it would be important to realize that the
Inuktitut north is actually northwest," the report stressed. "Their
south is to the southeast and their west is to the southwest."

The report also cited Woodman's belief that the seabed close to
Kirkwall Island might be prime hunting ground for *Erebus* or *Terror*.
He pinpointed it as the island Inuit knew as *Umiaqtalik*. Woodman
turned out to be wrong, but not far off. Kirkwall is actually *Haturuaq*
to Inuit, or "Big Flat One," and lies at the top of a string of tiny islands
gently arcing down toward the Adelaide Peninsula, like rough-cut
gemstones on a necklace. The Kamookak–Keith study identified
First Island as *Umiaqtalik*. It is roughly five miles southeast of Kirkwall. Not a significant difference as the crow flies. But at that point
in the epic hunt for *Erebus* and *Terror*, after 150 years of failure, much
depended on who was right about this because of that Inuktitut name.

Kamookak translated it as: "There is a boat there."

"An *umiaq* was a large boat in the Inuit world of the 1800s but it
was usually used for a boat the size of whaleboat or dory," the report
pointed out. "A ship was and still is referred to as *umiarjuaq* or
'big boat.'"

In the last hour on the final day of the Eco-Nova expedition,
archaeologist Margaret Bertulli was walking the shore of an islet
that Inuit testimony placed in prime territory for a submerged wreck.
She came across a human skull. Without a permit to collect human
remains, she had no choice but to try to learn what she could from a

distance, with time running out. The archaeologist took photos, from every possible angle. Then she left the skull where it lay, exposed to whatever ravages of wildlife or weather might come.

In her report to Douglas Stenton, a veteran terrestrial archaeologist and Nunavut's director of culture and heritage, Bertulli credited the find to Ivan Campbell, a leading seaman on the *Laurier*. She didn't see any grave or other feature in the vicinity. Dr. Anne Keenleyside, a bioarchaeologist specializing in human remains, studied photographs of the cranium and identified it as Caucasian. She found several similarities, especially in the eye orbits and the shape and size of the nasal cavity, with the skulls of five Franklin Expedition crewmen found on the south shore of King William Island's Erebus Bay. Bertulli suggested the latest skull could be confirmed by aging and possibly measuring the lead level.

"The discovery of remains of a Franklin crew member near O'Reilly Island may point to the surrounding waters as the general location of one of Franklin's ships, H.M.S. Erebus or Terror," Bertulli added in her 1998 report.

Four years later, back on what he calls Skull Island, Woodman searched again with a borrowed magnetometer, a Scintrex Smartmag 4 towed on a wooden sled. Designed mainly for workers trying to locate underground pipelines, it wasn't built to bounce on a snowmobile, along twenty-kilometer search lanes, crawling forward at about four miles an hour. Woodman and his team made it work by soldering things back together, and tightening screws, each night after a day of heavy rattling. They had to play out at least a hundred feet of rope to separate the sled from the snowmobile and isolate the magnetometer from metal that would throw off its readings. Sapped by the severe cold, the batteries lasted no longer than two and half hours. When searchers failed to notice the point where the device went dead, they tried to calculate the missed distance, pop in a fresh battery, and retrace their tracks. A computer processed about fifteen pulses per second, sniffing along the magnetic field for any anomaly that hinted *Erebus* or *Terror* might be lurking beneath the thick sea ice. Bundled up in metal-free caribou parkas and sealskin boots, the team managed to cover 120 dreary square miles in those two short seasons. Still, no joy. One day during the 2002 expedition, while the rest of the team members were eating lunch, Inuk head guide Saul Aksoolak, from Gjoa Haven, did a quick circuit along the sea ice on his snow machine and returned to the tent to soberly announce:

"I found the head."

Everyone rushed to follow him back to the skull. This time, only the bleached white crown was sticking out of the snow, about the size of a man's palm and perfectly camouflaged, white against white. Yet a skilled hunter's eyes had seen it from afar while moving at a good clip. Animals, wind, waves, ice, or some other force had moved it about ten yards since Bertulli's discovery. But as the snow slowly melted over the next week, more and more of the skull was exposed, leaving no doubt that it was the same one she photographed. Woodman was seething. If Bertulli had her hands-off assessment right, a critical clue was staring him in the face and he couldn't pick it up for experts to analyze in a lab. The skull had already moved, and it was only a matter of time before Arctic waters crept up and snatched it for the rest of time.

"If it turns out to be a 25-year-old white man, from 100 years ago," he thought, "then forget what the Inuit stories say about the ship being manned. What's he *doing* here?"

Within ten yards of the skull, Woodman found a hint at a possible answer. It was a piece of glass sitting on a rock. Sandblasted by decades of wind-blown sand, it appeared to be a prism, perhaps part of a scientific or navigational instrument. There were also remnants of old rectangular campsites on the islet, which suggested several *qalu-*

naaq had stopped there for some time. The glass Woodman saw, but could only photograph, seemed to be a lens. Maybe it was a remnant of a sextant that a lost mariner pointed toward the stars, hoping they would lead him out of the Arctic. Or it could have come from a telescope that an officer might have held up to his eye, searching for a way home. Only expert analysis could say. Since Woodman wasn't allowed to move the object, he marked the spot with small piles of stones in the hope that an archaeologist could get there before the glass artifact vanished forever.

14

Fast Ice

Around the time that David Woodman was working on Skull Island, Louie Kamookak began to sense that his own tortuous search was drawing close to Franklin's grave. He could feel it in his heart. From Inuit descriptions and his amateur detective's deductions, he imagined what a burial vault built of stone and camouflaged among the slabs and shards of rock that cover King William Island would look like. Kamookak described it to a local artist, who made a sketch so the historian could visualize Franklin's burial place without the heavy weight of it constantly on his mind. He could also show it to trusted people to see if it tripped anything in their memories. In 2004, Sir John's resting place suddenly seemed within reach.

"I thought I had found some stuff," he said, cautious with clipped words. "And I got pretty sick. Had to have heart surgery. Ten percent chance of survival. Some people told me it's bad luck. Getting too close to Franklin."

Kamookak had to be flown some twelve hundred miles southwest to Edmonton, Alberta, to reach the closest hospital that had the skilled doctors and equipment with any chance to save his life. He was on the operating table about nine hours while cardiac surgeons replaced one heart valve and repaired another. He likes to think the new valve came from a polar bear, which brings a big, broad smile to his face.

"I was in the hospital for four months," he said. "I barely made it through."

Elders and others who knew of the *qalunaaq* curse on King William Island thought Kamookak should heed fair warning. Instead, when he was back on his feet, he tried to pick up the trail of Franklin's tomb again. So many skeletons of Sir John's men have been found since the middle of the nineteenth century, including by Kamookak's own grandfather, that he couldn't ignore descriptions of two unique burial places. The other men were either buried in very shallow graves, or left to decompose where they dropped. If only one or two of the dead were worthy of musket salutes, and tombs made from carefully laid stones, one with a very large wooden cross built to last, Kamookak needed to know why. Even if it killed him.

THREE YEARS AFTER his near-death experience, the first in a quickening series of serendipitous turns gave new life to the hunt for *Erebus* and *Terror*. In what ordinarily would be an unremarkable shift in the civil service, marine biologist Martin Bergmann took charge of the Polar Continental Shelf Program in the hamlet of Resolute, on Cornwallis Island's south coast, overlooking a High Arctic leg of Northwest Passage. Inuit know it as *Qausuittuq*, the "Place with No Dawn," because, from late April to mid-August, the sun never sets. From late November to mid-January, the sun doesn't rise. A biologist by training, Bergmann was now responsible for a logistics hub that supported scientists from around the world doing research in the High Arctic.

When a NASA-led research effort needed to test equipment such as robots, mining technologies, extravehicular activities, and other essentials for putting humans on Mars, its Haughton-Mars Project relied on Bergmann and his staff for complex logistics support. The harsh environment and rugged geology in the poorly mapped polar desert on Devon Island, about 165 miles north of Resolute, was an ideal stand-in for exploration of the red planet. In 2006, the logistics center supported a team of American paleontologists that discovered a fossilized "missing link" in the evolution of sea creatures to land animals buried in a river delta on Ellesmere Island. *Tiktaalik roseae*, which lived some 375 million years ago, was covered with bony scales, had jaws like a crocodile's, but swam with front fins that were developing the elbows and wrists of arms. When the scientists, led by Edward Daeschler and Neil Shubin, discovered the fossil of another lobe-finned species on Ellesmere, they wanted to honor Bergmann for providing "essential support to a wide community of Arctic researchers" and for making the Arctic relevant to a global audience. So they named the toothy Devonian predator *Holoptychius bergmanni*.

The paleontologists were celebrating a mission that Bergmann shared with another scientist and longtime friend, oceanographer Eddy Carmack, who headed the federal Three Oceans Program studying Canada's Pacific, Atlantic, and Arctic waters from top to bottom. Each summer, marine scientists crisscrossed the Arctic Archipelago on two icebreakers, taking water samples, collecting mud from the sea bottom, capturing microscopic marine life, and conducting other long-term studies to see more clearly how climate change is affecting the planet's most rapidly warming region. When beds opened up for a few days between crew changes, Carmack and Bergmann filled them with up to twenty VIPs, leading research scientists, businesspeople, government policymakers, experts in Inuit culture, and others on what were called Philosopher Cruises. The guests hosted seminars on whatever topic they thought important while absorbing the Arctic messages that Carmack and Bergmann were determined to spread. Singing Stan Rogers's ballad *Northwest Passage*, with its lyrical longing "to find the hand of Franklin reaching for the Beaufort Sea," was a required ritual.

It was part of a plan Bergmann and Carmack discussed Sunday nights, separated by more than a thousand miles of prairie and western mountains, when they each poured a glass of Scotch, got on the phone, and schemed about how to advance their Arctic agenda. They talked about how to encourage responsible northern development based on solid science, not hypotheticals, political slogans, or outright myths. The best way to achieve that, they decided, was to get more people up to the Arctic to experience a precious place for themselves, whether they were tourists, businesspeople, or scientists. Master of the elevator pitch, Bergmann never stopped plotting to win over influential people he thought would advance the cause. If that meant attending a dull function just to chat up a diplomat on his list, Bergmann jumped at the chance. If a research scientist was important to the plan, Bergmann coaxed her into the fold. He eventually built a core group of around twenty, including young people Bergmann mentored, knowing they were the ones who would carry on the work long after he was gone.

In a German airport lounge, Bergmann spotted a new target. Peter Mansbridge knew the Arctic, but not the bureaucrat who was becoming an evangelist for the North. The national news anchor for the Canadian Broadcasting Corporation (CBC) has been called Canada's Cronkite. When Disney needed a convincing voice for the animated moose news anchor in its hit film *Zootopia*, Mansbridge got the call. He became Peter Moosebridge. Long before he was a name, Mansbridge was based in Churchill, Manitoba, a port that links Hudson Bay to the transnational railroad. *Kuugjuaq* to the Inuit, Churchill is best known for watching polar bears. They developed the habit of wandering into town to feast on a garbage-dump buffet before it was shut down. Mansbridge began his CBC career there and made frequent reporting trips higher into the Arctic.

In the spring of 2006, Mansbridge was between flights, heading home from interviewing Israeli Prime Minister Ehud Olmert and broadcasting live from Jerusalem, when the journalist sat in what seemed a quiet spot in Air Canada's lounge at Frankfurt Airport. He was jet-lagged, all talked out, and hoping the world would leave him alone. Out of the corner of his eye, Mansbridge spotted a bear of a man striding purposefully toward him. He had that look on his face, the one where ordinary folk recognize a celebrity and zero in.

"Oh, boy," the anchor thought, bracing himself.

"Peter Mansbridge!" the interloper blurted.

"That's right."

Bergmann launched into what was by then a well-honed pitch.

"This is the story you need to be covering, Peter: You need to be talking about the Arctic and climate change."

Bergmann lured Mansbridge north again with the promise that he would be the first to broadcast the national news live from the Northwest Passage. Which wasn't easy.

At Resolute, the farthest point north on their icebreaker voyage, the CBC crew was roughly a thousand miles from the North Pole. To keep their satellite signal from dropping out, technicians had to move the dish by hand, nudging it tiny fractions of an inch as the ship moved. Push too hard, or not enough, and viewers across the country would be shouting at their screens. Instead, they were part of a historic first. No one had ever watched a live broadcast from as far north in Canada's Arctic. It pulled in a good audience, especially for the summer doldrums of TV news, and allowed people to see that climate change was not a fuzzy theoretical threat in the Arctic.

"In areas where we'd normally be still crunching through ice at the end of July, it was wide open," Mansbridge recalled. "We were basically sunning on the deck. It was unbelievable."

A new leader had just taken power in Canada, and he had his own designs on the Arctic, including a strategy to market his broader conservative agenda through heroic tales of the North. Prime Minister Stephen Harper immediately began to ratchet the bolts on what quickly became an excruciatingly tight information-management machine. He set it to work gagging federal scientists, especially experts warning of human-driven climate change, and anyone else who might think of challenging his plans. Harper wanted the Arctic to be the shiny white wrapping around his government's darker policies. Those included loosening regulations on private enterprise, weakening environmental controls over resource development, and taking a more bellicose stand on Canada's ownership claim not just over the Arctic Archipelago but also over the seabed all the way to the North Pole. The territory is thought to hold a bonanza of fossil-fuel and mineral resources. In an extremely sensitive environment battered by storms, they would be extraordinarily difficult, if not impossible, to extract without causing severe damage that could ripple around the world. But with scientists predicting the Arctic could be ice-free in summertime within a generation, pressure was building to open up the High Arctic to more fishing trawlers, shippers, and resource companies.

Just as John Barrow had done in the mid-nineteenth century, Harper saw power in taming the Arctic. He had just the plan to join two eras of Arctic promise in voters' minds. A new, more ambitious search for the lost ships of the Franklin Expedition became a central part of his strategy to mold public opinion. As a propaganda piece, the Northwest Passage was just as good at stirring Canadian nationalism in the twenty-first century as it was with British imperial pride in the nineteenth. Environment Minister John Baird announced the revived Franklin hunt in the summer of 2008, a hard sell in the depths of the worst global financial crisis since the Great Depression. Baird pitched the projected $75,000 cost as an affordable adventure with what he called "the allure of an Indiana Jones mystery." The prototype had been set in 1997: A Coast Guard icebreaker would be a floating base, but several agencies would cooperate in the search. The government committed to three summers of searching, led by Robert Grenier's underwater archaeology unit at Parks Canada. After more than a century and a half of failed attempts to find *Erebus* and *Terror*, Kamookak might make the difference this time, Baird suggested.

"His research has provided incredibly valuable insight that will help contribute greatly to this search," the environment minister said, predicting success within two years.

Douglas Stenton, Nunavut's heritage director, also praised Kamookak's groundwork, which helped narrow the search blocks to two main areas: where the ships were first abandoned at the top of Victoria Strait, and in eastern Queen Maud Gulf. Staged from the icebreaker CCGS *Sir Wilfrid Laurier*, the first season of Stephen Harper's vaunted shipwreck search had a sputtering start. Search teams had to stand down when higher priorities, such as looking for lost and stranded Inuit hunters or assisting ships stuck in ice, bumped them down the tasking list. The scheduled six-week focus on eastern Queen Maud Gulf was quietly cut to just over half a week of scanning the seabed for *Erebus* and *Terror*. Bathymetric mapping of the zone where the ships were abandoned in 1848, which archaeologists sometimes call the point of desertion, showed a depth of more than 410 feet. Heavy ice is also common in the area in summer. Finding a wreck there was going to be tough. Without knowing it, that first expedition got very close to hitting pay dirt north of O'Reilly Island.

Nothing happened the second year because Parks Canada couldn't book time on a Coast Guard or a military vessel. Harper was pressing for faster progress on a much bigger priority: a detailed study of the continental shelf to back up Canada's claim over a vast stretch of the Arctic seabed, straight up to the North Pole. Moscow had upped the ante on Arctic territorial claims by sending two submarines more than two miles beneath the ice-covered pole to plant a titanium Russian flag on the Lomonosov Ridge. This undersea mountain range, which bisects the Arctic for nearly twelve hundred miles, holds reserves of oil and natural gas worth billions of dollars. If drilling ever happens, scientists say it would only accelerate catastrophic climate change.

Tom Zagon has the round, smoothly bald head of a pro wrestler or a clean-and-jerk weight lifter. But the physical forces he knows intimately are the pressures of ice against the hulls of ship and the power that wind and ocean current exert on floes. In the nineteenth century, William Scoresby wowed the scientific world with exquisite drawings of ice crystals, works of art that revealed myriad microscopic forms that he used to explain, among other things, why cirrus clouds are sometimes iridescent. When Zagon looks at ice, he doesn't see a solid object, but rather a dynamic process that can move as fast as a flash frost spreading across a windowpane—albeit on a vastly bigger scale. In six months, from the height of summer to the depths of winter, the Northern Hemisphere's ice cover can grow by some 3.8 million square miles.

"If you do it as a back of the envelope calculation, sometimes the rate of freeze up is around one square kilometer (or just under half a square mile) a second," Zagon explained.

At that speed, ice is like a charging beast that can easily pounce on unsuspecting mariners. Zagon has fallen prey himself. In November 1995, he was ice adviser aboard M/V *Arctic*, a 725-foot ship owned by Canada's Fednav Group, which carried Arctic oil and ore through the Northwest Passage. The ship was beset for four days until an icebreaker freed her. If anyone could imagine how *Erebus*'s ice master James Reid must have felt when Franklin's ships ran into similar trouble at the north end of Victoria Strait, it was Zagon during those long days in winter darkness on the Arctic.

"You are the most hated man on the ship," he said. "The captain realizes it's not your fault. But everybody else says it is your fault."

Reid, *Erebus*'s ice master, relied largely on gut instinct and hard-won experience to advise Franklin as he circumnavigated nearby Cornwallis Island a year before getting stuck. Sir John passed within sight of the future mine to the northwest. Zagon helped the *Arctic* reach its destination by studying images beamed down from a chartered Challenger jet that flew in front of the ship once or twice a day, reporting regular updates on ice conditions as the winter freeze-up began to close the passage. The bill was tens of thousands of dollars a day. Four years later, when Zagon's mind turned to the Franklin Expedition, he realized the sea ice must have been very light in the late summer of 1845 for two Royal Navy barques to make it around Cornwallis Island so late in the season. It was one of several eureka moments that drew him into the search.

"Why can't ice information be used to understand what happened to Franklin's voyage, or any voyage for that matter?" he wondered.

Zagon stored the thought in the back of his mind until the fall of 2009. He was at work on a new job as an analyst at the Canadian Ice Service, the federal agency that provides navigators the Daily Ice Chart, detailing sea-ice conditions by region. He was alone on the evening shift in downtown Ottawa, waiting for the latest images to come down from an orbiting satellite equipped with synthetic aperture radar that can see through the thickest clouds. Banks of monitors on several desks glowed in the half-light of the operational area, more than a thousand square feet of fourth-floor office space where weather data is integrated with satellite imagery into ice charts. He had made a mental note to keep an eye on a TV program coming up. Peter Mansbridge was interviewing Robert Grenier, head of the marine archaeology unit, on his half-hour show *Mansbridge One on One*. The subject was the lost Franklin Expedition, which first had caught Zagon's interest six years earlier as a geography major doing fieldwork at an ice camp in Barrow Strait. He had packed classics of the Franklin genre for off-hours reading. When the opening credits rolled on the Ice Service's big-screen TV, Zagon turned up the volume.

Grenier began talking about the importance of Inuit stories, and how outsiders have trouble interpreting that oral history in time and space. He mentioned Louie Kamookak's research, and islands Inuit call "the fingers," and how the Inuk historian showed they must be far south of where *Erebus* and *Terror* were abandoned because he traced the nineteenth-century sources to their home territory.

"White men like us cannot understand this," Grenier told Mansbridge. "I think what's fascinating in this expedition, this project, is that we link archaeological research with this oral history tradition."

He showed a piece of the copper sheeting that had been found in eastern Queen Maud Gulf and said it would have been relatively easy for someone using primitive tools to remove it from the hull of a Royal Navy ship. That person could have carried it an unknown distance, so the copper only hinted that a shipwreck might be nearby.

"If you find them—and I think, in your mind, you've got a pretty good idea where you think at least one of them may be on the bottom—what kind of shape would it be in after 160 years?" Mansbridge asked.

"It's a ship that would have sunk in fresh ice, according to the Inuit testimony, indicating that it's not a place where the ice crush accumulates, like we see when a river freezes up in the spring. It could be a ship very well preserved, that one."

Ice was Zagon's business. Without a detailed understanding of its peculiar habits, he figured, accurately diagnosing problems like lost ships in Arctic seas was impossible. He thought about what Grenier was saying and sensed that the archaeologist was out of his depth. The instant the thought crossed Zagon's mind, a desktop machine began to whir, slowly spitting out one of about twenty fresh satellite images produced each day for different parts of Canada's Arctic.

This one was especially timely. Zagon was looking at Victoria Strait.

"What happened here?" Zagon asked himself, staring at an image from space of the spot where the Arctic closed her fist on the Franklin Expedition. "I can take some historical evidence and use satellite imagery to either support it or refute it.

"And if I can do that for one piece of evidence, why can't you do it for other pieces of evidence? Why can't I do that for *all* the evidence?"

After a timely transfer to the Ice Service's research department, Zagon pitched his new bosses on a plan to study every relevant satellite image from the first one Radarsat-1 made in 1995. They eventually greenlighted Zagon to spend 10 percent of his time scrutinizing thousands of satellite images. He meticulously mapped areas of pressure, shear lines, patterns of breakup and freeze-up, and other sea-ice characteristics, gradually building a case to explain what the Arctic did with *Erebus* and *Terror*. The more Zagon saw in the patterns of sea ice spread over decades, the more he believed in a theory of what doomed the Franklin Expedition. Some years, the area where they were stranded is completely covered in ice; in others, it is wide-open water. Those conditions often remain the same, even after a storm.

"But in just a few years, and this is obviously the condition that Franklin's ships would have had to be in, it's light enough for them to enter—so there's some open water—but obviously something caused that open water to close, to become compacted pack ice," Zagon said. "In those cases, storms are the reason. They actually start around mid-September, which is when the ships became beset."

Franklin became an obsession. He seeped into Zagon's dreams. The ice analyst would find himself bolt upright in the middle of the night, compelled to go check a fact on his computer about some element of Arctic weather or ice. He went into work on weekends to look at more satellite images, often flicking back and forth to see ice movement, with the concentration of a conspiracy theorist moving through frames of the Zapruder film. As he got traction on his study, he read David Woodman's books on Inuit accounts, and the picture grew steadily clearer. In the summer of 2010, another newsbreak drew him even deeper into the Franklin mystery.

Parks Canada's marine archaeologists found the wreck of HMS *Investigator*, the ship McClure reluctantly abandoned during his failed

Franklin search in 1853. Months of planning gave archaeologists a clear starting place in Mercy Bay, which was clear of ice a week before tents went up on the shoreline in late July. Then a gale drove ice floes into the search zone, where the divers planned to draw their towfish, the torpedo-shaped sonar device. Two days after divers arrived, Ryan Harris, a rangy, dry-witted scientist with an encyclopedic knowledge of his prey, set out with longtime field partner Jonathan Moore in their small boat. The towfish was only in the water three minutes before Harris saw something on his laptop computer screen that looked out of place. He spent the next two hours making passes over the unidentified feature some twenty-five feet down, checking the sonar data over and over, to be certain they had a shipwreck. When it was confirmed, Zagon e-mailed the archaeologists to suggest his ice study could help them locate the real deal, *Erebus* and *Terror*. Silence. The archaeologists got a lot of unsolicited tips from armchair experts, in various parts of the world, certain they know the right place to find Franklin's ships. Zagon took the nonreply as a hint. But after a few months, something told him to try again. This time, Harris set up a briefing.

After watching Zagon's PowerPoint slides, the team quickly brought him on board. It was well known that sea ice flows south through Victoria Strait, but Zagon's report showed it moves faster on the western side. Islands slow it down on the eastern side, which Zagon thinks blocked any early escape for *Erebus* and *Terror* and slowed their drift southward with the sea ice. That could explain why one of the ships abandoned in 1848 wasn't spotted well to the south until as much as two years later, according to various Inuit accounts. The ice analyst concluded from shear lines that if either of the ships remained afloat long enough, the natural flow would have flushed her southward with the ice floes into Alexandra Strait, which runs past the southwest corner of King William Island into eastern Queen Maud Gulf, where Inuit said they saw men and a dog living aboard a big ship. Using his study, the search team calculated "a most probable vector," from the area where Franklin's men abandoned their ships to eastern Queen Maud Gulf, where Inuit say one ended up.

Zagon continued to play with pieces of the puzzle, especially the map that In-nook-poo-zhee-jook drew for Charles Francis Hall in 1869. For generations, southerners who looked at the sketch assumed the line drawn around the land beneath King William Island was all coastline. Zagon was at work on a routine day when a fresh image of eastern Queen Maud Gulf rolled out of the machine. It was upside-down because of the satellite's orientation orbiting over the North Pole. Over the years of getting to know ice through images from space, Zagon had come to see the Arctic the way Inuit do on the ground. Staring at the fresh satellite image, it hit him: The Inuk had drawn an island edged with land-fast ice, which formed a similar shape each year. Zagon was seeing it now in a view from some five hundred miles above the planet. In-nook-poo-zhee-jook had marked the wreck site just north of land that he drew large, roughly like a left-handed thumbs-up. It appeared to be south of King William Island, but in a sketch so out of proportion that it was hard to judge distance or precise location. Unless you understood the peculiar habits of ice.

"Oh, my God!" Zagon gasped.

It was O'Reilly Island. In-nook-poo-zhee-jook had been trying to tell Hall he could find a Franklin shipwreck just northeast of it.

LINES OF FATE were converging fast. Martin Bergmann's Mansbridge plan had worked perfectly. Broadcasting live from the Northwest Passage got the news anchor so jazzed about the North again that he couldn't stop talking about it. Through Tim MacDonald, a friend who was doing well in the auto parts and electrical supply business, Mansbridge got in touch with Jim Balsillie, the billionaire cofounder of Research In Motion (RIM), the firm that invented the BlackBerry smartphone. The newscaster told the businessman he should get up to the Arctic, a challenge Balsillie couldn't resist.

Bergmann connected Balsillie to the Arctic and its people in three trips together. In 2010, when the government-led hunt for the Franklin wrecks was in its third year, Balsillie and MacDonald joined the Philosopher Cruise through the Northwest Passage aboard the icebreaker CCGS *Louis S. St-Laurent*. At Cape Felix, they choppered over with Steve MacLean, an astronaut who was then head of the Canadian Space Agency. At another stop, they paid their respects at the Franklin sailors' gravesites on Beechey Island. From the air, flying low over the Northwest Passage in the oscillating shadows of the thumping rotor blades, Balsillie spotted a Russian-flagged icebreaker. The helicopter pilot circled the ship, about five miles off Victory Point, in the same area where *Erebus* and *Terror* were sacrificed to the ice in 1848. A crewmember was standing at the bow, seemingly like an officer keeping watch.

"He's looking for Franklin," someone said.

"Why isn't Canada doing this?" Balsillie wondered. "These are Canada's waters. This is *our* Arctic."

Back on the icebreaker, he was still steaming.

"So what are those guys doing out there?" Balsillie asked Bergmann and others. "Why haven't they found it yet? What's the problem? That's really important. Why haven't they found it yet? Let's go look for it. Let's start a proper search."

The more he heard about Stephen Harper's search project, the more Balsillie realized: "There is no plan."

He got to work organizing one, and he committed to spend at least $10 million of his own money to find at least one Franklin wreck—at the same time that he was fighting to keep the multibillion-dollar company he helped build from falling apart. The partnerships Harper's government had boasted about were largely just on paper. Some internal resistance was just run-of-the-mill bureaucratic inertia. But there was also pushback from agencies squeezed by budget tightening.

If science and other projects were being shut down, and thousands of workers were losing their jobs in the civil service and industries hit by the recession, skeptics demanded to know why there was money to look for nineteenth-century British shipwrecks.

"All these departments didn't want to work together," Balsillie said. "We were trying to get them to cooperate because they were all playing games with each other."

Balsillie decided to knock heads, gently, at a wooded acreage in the southern Ontario countryside, then part of a think tank he funds, the Center for International Governance Innovation. David Woodman's phone rang. It was Bergmann.

"Listen, there's a big meeting going on and everyone I talk to says there's no reason to have it unless you're there. There's a bunch of specialists, but nobody has background. We need you to come and give us some."

Woodman gave the opening presentation at the meeting where Balsillie kicked the Franklin search into high gear. Nudged on by Bergmann, Balsillie and MacDonald cofounded the Arctic Research Foundation in early 2011 to support a more coordinated search. In the warm glow of chandeliers and old leather at Ottawa's Rideau Club, where the rich and powerful have been doing deals in wingback armchairs since 1865, Balsillie asked Parks Canada Vice President Andrew Campbell and other agency officials what was essential to success.

"We need a dedicated vessel," Campbell replied.

Balsillie decided then and there to buy one. He asked for guidance from Bergmann, who thought his friend was joking. If a boat is a hole in the water that sucks up money, an Arctic boat is one that gobbles gold. Voraciously. Without care for anyone who might get hurt. To improve the chances of getting a vessel that would survive long enough to find a Franklin wreck, Bergmann let his assistant, Oksana Schimnowski, take leave to run the new foundation and find it a seaworthy vessel. As

Balsillie waited to launch, friend and history buff Scott Burk suggested he brush up on Franklin history with first editions of the explorer's journals. Balsillie bought a thick volume bound in brown leather, with a richly aged luster, only slightly worn at the edges. It was Franklin's *Narrative of a Journey to the Shores of the Polar Sea, in the Years 1819, 20, 21, and 22*, published in London in 1823, when he was an up-and-coming Royal Navy captain who won fame as "the man who ate his boots."

Sitting at his dining-room table in Waterloo, with logs burning in the fireplace on a winter weekend, Balsillie read Franklin's low opinion of the local Cree, whose blood the billionaire shared. Balsillie has Métis ancestry, with indigenous and Scottish roots inherited from his father. Criticizing the indigenous men for swapping women with traders like chattel, Franklin also faulted French voyageurs and Scottish factors, the sales reps of their day. They tricked Cree trappers into giving up their winter's haul of fur pelts, mainly beaver, fox, lynx, and marten in imbalanced barter for imported goods such as butcher's knives, coarse blankets, and ammunition. Still in debt from the previous season, and hoping to leverage competition between the Hudson's Bay Company and the rival North West Company, the trappers were often reluctant to show all they had to offer before agreeing on a good price. The factors cracked open a barrel of rum, a cynical ploy to drown any Cree bargaining power in alcohol.

"However firm he may be in his denials at first," Franklin wrote, "his resolutions are enfeebled by the sight of a little rum, and when he has tasted the intoxicating beverage, they vanish like smoke, and he brings forth his store of furs, which he has carefully concealed from the scrutinizing eyes of his visitors."

The routine of getting Cree drunk, and keeping them in debt, was stoking violent resentment and "will, probably, ultimately prove destructive to the fur trade itself," Franklin predicted. "Indeed the evil has already, in part, recoiled upon the traders; for the Indians, long deceived, have become deceivers in their turn, and not unfrequently after having incurred a heavy debt at one post, move off to another, to play the same game."

A few pages later, Balsillie reached Franklin's account of preparing to leave Cumberland House. Opened in 1774, the trading post sat on a wild frontier in what is now the eastern border of central Saskatchewan. A network of rivers, lakes, and mountain passes created natural highways for furs and goods moving to and from Montreal and Hudson Bay in the east and the disputed Oregon Country to the west, by way of the Rocky Mountains. In January 1820, Franklin strapped on snowshoes and headed west with George Back and John Richardson. Their group followed dogsleds packed with fifteen days' provisions to the next shelter at Carlton House, on the South Saskatchewan River, en route to the Arctic coast. At 8 a.m., they set out from the fort. Two days later, a fur trader from Cumberland House caught up with them to deliver some pemmican that the expedition had left behind, an extraordinarily kind gesture for a party of men who would end up starving. The fur trader was on his way to look for native trappers who hadn't been heard from since the previous October. A few weeks earlier, he had gone four days without food for himself or his dogs, until he picked up the trappers' trail. Balsillie was stunned when his eyes fell on the selfless trader's name, which Franklin wrote as Isbester, a Scot from the Orkneys.

Balsillie recognized him as a blood relative, the same Isbister that his cousins had told him about some eight years earlier. Until that moment, Balsillie knew his roots ran back to the fur trade, but he had no idea there was a Franklin connection. The dots connecting, like electrons firing down a wire, sent a jolt to Balsillie's soul. Now he wasn't just another Franklin-mystery voyeur. This was personal.

"I was a dog on a scent at that point," he said.

By 2011, Schimnowski had reduced a shortlist of five used ships, checked out over as many months, to a sixty-two-foot trawler, built in 1979 to catch crab, shrimp, and groundfish on the Grand Banks, off Newfoundland. Balsillie bought the *Ocean Alliance*, which reached Cambridge Bay that summer, when he was back aboard the *Louis* for several days as she headed west for a another seabed mapping voyage with the US Coast Guard icebreaker USCGC *Healy*. When Balsillie got off at Cambridge Bay, and his BlackBerry locked onto a cell signal again, it rang with bad news. Turmoil roiling at RIM had taken another casualty in the boardroom. The $5 billion company, holder of at least 3,400 US patents, was crumbling. Just a month after Balsillie finished that third Arctic trip with Bergmann, the bureaucrat called and practically begged him to fly north again. The prime minister, Bergmann reported, was on his way to an annual Arctic photo op, this one a joint military exercise with the US and Danish navies to train for air and sea disasters.

"Really, I've got a lot of work to do," Balsillie told him. "I'm up to my gills."

This was one Arctic trip Bergmann wasn't looking forward to, and not just because he had failed to persuade his friend to go along. He chafed at Harper's tightening gag on scientists; he needed freedom to keep evangelizing for the Arctic. More often, he had to get permission from department flaks before he could speak to anyone outside the razor-wired walls of Harper's government. He would buck the restraints, talk to a journalist without permission, say what he thought needed to be said, and warn his wife, Sheila McRae: "Oh-oh, I'm going to get in trouble. He tried to be very diplomatic, but a lot of it was about climate change and sovereignty concerns." Bergmann traveled a lot to countries such as China and Russia, where competition in the warming Arctic was a growing concern. That made him even more suspect in the eyes of political operatives trying to enforce Harper's control over experts for whom he had visceral distrust. Tired of being told to toe the line by people who didn't know what they were talking about, Bergmann was looking forward to early retirement. He wanted to pick and choose his own projects, do only the things that mattered to him, the ones he knew were important to the cause.

The day before he left for Resolute, Bergmann spent time with his children. That night, under pressure to pack and to organize the Power-Point presentation for the prime minister and other dignitaries, he took an hour's break to keep a solemn promise. Bergmann had bought three mini horses for his family and their supply of hay came from a farm outside Winnipeg. Neil, the farmer who owned the place, enjoyed hearing Bergmann's Arctic stories. Just as he did with anyone who showed interest in the North, Bergmann happily obliged with more. Neil returned the favor by teaching Bergmann the Zen of horse training. The farmer thought people used too many words with horses. Be quiet, he counseled Bergmann, and just look in their eyes. Let them relax. Guide them gently to what you want them to do. Bergmann promised Neil a cap with the logo of the Polar Continental Shelf Program in return. That couldn't wait until he got back. He had to deliver them that night.

The next morning, August 20, 2011, Bergmann flew to Yellow-knife and caught First Air flight 6560, a chartered Boeing 737 carrying passengers and freight. The trip northeast to Resolute was scheduled to take just over two hours. Bergmann was one of fifteen people on board, including the flight crew. In midflight, the company dispatcher warned of deteriorating weather at Resolute, a common glitch in Arctic air travel. The flight crew and the dispatcher discussed landing somewhere else, but all agreed they would press on for Resolute. At 4:23 p.m., air traffic control gave the green light to begin the descent. At seven knots, the wind at ground level was a gentle breeze. The runway was wet. The aircraft made a left turn to prepare for the final approach to Runway 35T. Then things rapidly started to go wrong.

First Officer David Hare told Captain Blair Rutherford five times within twenty seconds that the plane wasn't lined up on the right course to the runway. They went back and forth over whether or not the navigation was accurate. Hare reminded Rutherford of a hill to the right of the runway. The first officer suggested that the pilot abort the landing and solve the navigation problem. The captain overruled him. Just over a second later, as the aircraft's pitch increased, the worry was stark in Hare's voice.

"Blair," the first officer said to Rutherford, "I don't like this."

"Go around," he added seconds later.

"Go around thrust," the captain called out.

An instant later, at 4:41:51 in the afternoon, as the flight crew aborted the landing, the plane crashed into a low hill about one nautical mile short of the runway. Eight passengers and all four crewmembers died. Three other passengers, including a seven-year-old girl, escaped the flaming wreckage despite serious injuries. Bergmann was not one of them. He was dead, age fifty-five. Troops stationed at the airport, waiting for the start of the military exercises, heard the blast and ran out to see a dense plume of oily black smoke billowing into the Arctic sky. Navy diver Larry Lyver, a corporal at the time, was expecting a mock operation to raise the wing of a downed plane from the sea. For a split second, he thought the exercise had started early. Just as quickly, he realized this was the real thing. He rushed to the crash site with other troops to look for survivors. In the following days, he had the grim task of searching for human remains. A garment bag caught his eye. He took a closer look and saw a name on it: Bergmann. His remains, along with those of other passengers and crew, were moved to the wet lab of the logistics center that he once ran. It was now a makeshift morgue.

On the way to Bergmann's funeral, Balsillie decided to ask his friend's widow for permission to rename the ship hunting for *Erebus* and *Terror* in his honor. The giant white polar bear logo emblazoned on the side of R/V *Martin Bergmann* was designed from one that the two men had seen together. The scientist woke up Balsillie one morning at 2 a.m. to watch the bear on an ice floe in the Northwest Passage. Balsillie, a deep sleeper, wanted to stay in bed, but Bergmann coaxed him out on the icebreaker's cold steel deck in his underwear. Together, they marveled at the polar bear, hungry because disappearing ice made it harder to catch seals. The animal reared up on its hind legs, sniffing for scraps of food, like a king reduced to a beggar in a vanishing kingdom. Bergmann's children flew up to Cambridge Bay to help paint the vessel. Oksana Schimnowski, her husband Adrian, and their kids worked on it with them. Under pressure to get the ship ready for the Arctic, her new name gave Schimnowski a new sense of purpose to honor her late mentor.

"It became really, really important, for so many reasons," she said. "It wasn't just to find shipwrecks anymore, but to continue to be brave and continue to take risks. And not let anything deter you from your goals. That was Marty."

15

"That's It!"

For all that had changed since the Arctic lured Sir John Franklin deeper, with a late season of clear sailing followed by a freeze-up that snatched hold of *Erebus* and *Terror* and refused to let them go, one quirk never changed. Just when the Arctic seemed to be giving way, she swung around and bit hard. After several summers of relatively open waters for searchers in the area where Franklin's men abandoned their ships, the sea ice was back with a vengeance in 2014. That was just the latest problem to plague a mission that was dragging on, at risk of becoming a political albatross for politicians long past the point where they predicted finding one of Franklin's missing ships.

Pressure was building for results, and not just because taxpayers were getting restless. Jim Balsillie's ship was recovering from an inauspicious start. On her first day out in 2011, rust damage in the sputtering engine forced the ship back to Cambridge Bay. Someone had forgotten to put an upturned bucket over the *Bergmann*'s engine exhaust, an essential last step to keep snow out of the engine before her first Arctic winter. It needed a complete rebuild, not an easy task in a good month that far north, and a major migraine when the federal search team was counting on five solid weeks of work from the vessel. Skeptics had a field day. Instead of wondering what Balsillie's angle was, now they figured he was just another southern blowhard who didn't have a clue how to make it in the Arctic.

"The Parks guys were really quite bothered," Balsillie told me, recalling how angry he was too at the time.

Fortunately, his foundation partner, Tim MacDonald, was big in the hardware business. He flew up a team of mechanics and had the ship in good shape in time to complete about ten days of wreck hunting. The skeptics turned. They praised "the little ship that could" for covering a lot of square miles after missing 80 percent of the season under repairs.

"It worked," a federal team member conceded to Balsillie. "We now believe."

But there seemed to be competition on the horizon. In the fall of 2012, software billionaire Paul Allen's $250 million yacht M/Y *Octopus* was at the top of Victoria Strait, where the crews had left *Erebus* and *Terror* locked solid in ice. With thirteen cabins for guests, another twenty-eight for the vessel's fifty-seven crew, this was not just any yacht. It was a 414-foot exploration platform, equipped with a submarine and a remotely operated vehicle perfect for scanning the deep seabed. A hangar had room for two helicopters.

Canadian naval surveillance picked up the *Octopus* running what appeared to be a zigzag navigation pattern. That suggested the ship might be interested in more than the scenery, perhaps even a historic sighting of a Franklin wreck. Allen never claimed publicly to be looking for *Erebus* or *Terror*. But the Microsoft cofounder's attraction to shipwreck hunting was confirmed three years later when he led a team aboard the *Octopus* that discovered the remains of the 863-foot Japanese battleship *Musashi*, a heavily armed warship that US forces sank in the Philippines on October 24, 1944.

Allen's "interest in exploration is driven by his belief in finding the undiscovered, especially historic marvels like the *Musashi*," a statement on the reclusive tycoon's website explained.

The *Octopus* sighting off King William Island, regardless of Allen's intentions, was an urgent reminder to frustrated members of Canada's federal mission that they weren't the only ones who might like to find Franklin's wrecks.

When the Arctic threw a wrench in the works again in 2014, talk of a curse was making more sense.

The first day of September 2014: Almost 168 years to the day that a storm likely caught *Erebus* and *Terror*, Arctic gales would be back to howl again any day now. But for a moment, the Arctic was still calm, allowing a cloistered quiet to settle on the icebreaker's bridge. For the shipwreck searchers aboard the CCGS *Sir Wilfrid Laurier*, in their sixth year of a high-pressure mission to find the wrecks of the lost Franklin Expedition, it was an auspicious sign. Maybe this day the Arctic would finally yield some of her secrets. There was no radio squawk. No crew banter. Not a tremble from the *Laurier*'s three huge diesel-electric engines, deep in the icebreaker's steamy belly. The deck crew had dropped anchor and lowered three boats into the frigid waters: the hydrographers' *Kinglet* and *Gannet*, and the marine archaeologists' *Investigator*. The hunt was on for another day. Perched above the broad, powerful bow, a captain could look out across the endless, mesmerizing wilderness and believe for the moment that he was in charge and everything was under control. But not Coast Guard Captain Bill Noon. His wise mariner's head is crammed with memories of hammering gales, pitching decks, and the endless watch for hidden shoals or ice traps. He never forgets that the Arctic always has the final word.

"Patience is the key up here," Noon wrote in his captain's log on September 1, 2014, "so we will go hard wherever the ice and weather let us work."

The 2014 Victoria Strait Expedition was off to a good start, but time was short. The first faint chills of winter were blowing on the pure Arctic air, and the brief search window was about to slam shut.

In a matter of weeks, the waters where the *Laurier* lay peacefully at anchor in eastern Queen Maud Gulf would be a vast block of ice, shifting and fracturing under immense pressure with cracks as loud as rifle shots.

This was set up to be the most sophisticated search ever for *Erebus* and *Terror*. More than a dozen government agencies and private partners had teamed up, and the Canadian Space Agency provided satellite support. Federal hydrographers, the experts at surveying the seabed, painstakingly scanned the ocean bottom, slowly filling in vast blanks in uncharted waters as they kept an eye out for shipwrecks. Some 90 percent of the Canadian Arctic waters still hadn't been charted to modern standards, and in stretches of the Northwest Passage where at least one of the Franklin wrecks might lie, navigators had to rely on soundings that dated back to the original nineteenth-century search expeditions.

Parks Canada's underwater archaeologists were still officially in the lead as the hunt entered its sixth year. The Royal Canadian Navy tasked HMCS *Kingston*, a lightly armed coastal defense vessel built for minesweeping, to help. The military's secretive research arm sent a robotic sub named *Arctic Explorer*. Some twenty-three feet long, and weighing more than two tons, the autonomous underwater vehicle was built to work at depths beyond sixteen thousand feet, even beneath a cover of thick ice, without any contact with the surface. Wired to an inertial navigation system with precise fiberoptic gyroscopes, the device's computer brain was programmed with limited intelligence, allowing it to make basic decisions. The robot could decide how to get around undersea obstacles, without any guidance from satellites or radio commands. Its mission complete, the robot could find its own way back to home base, even if that was a drifting ship or ice camp. *Arctic Explorer* bristled with cutting-edge technology, including high-frequency synthetic aperture sonar, which a team of handlers expected to provide a high-resolution look at the seabed hundreds of feet below the surface.

A partner under contract with the expedition, a Canadian firm specializing in high-end Arctic cruises, chartered a ship to deliver the military's smart submersible to the High Arctic. It turned to the Russians. If Moscow wanted to get a better understanding of the Canadian military's secret robotic marine technology, it could now take a front-row seat. *Arctic Explorer*'s handlers would spend days working with the state-of-the-art device, troubleshooting problems and discussing workarounds, aboard *Akademik Sergey Vavilov*. The 383-foot vessel was built in Finland for scientific research, but it was now pure luxury, with fine dining, a hotwater spa, sauna, massage room, theater-style presentation room, and other amenities for affluent cruisers. On this expedition, its passengers included well-heeled tourists and executives from large companies that came in as partners with the Royal Canadian Geographical society. They paid for the privilege of watching what, on paper at least, would be the front line in the hunt for Franklin's lost ships. The armada was led by the *Sir Wilfrid Laurier*, on which the core team of archaeologists, hydrographers, their two survey boats, and other critical components were based, and the *Bergmann*, which covered by far the most territory each year that it took part. For the third year in a row, searchers aimed to explore two zones in the same short season between the summer ice melt and the fall storm season. The northern block was at the top of Victoria and Alexandra Straits, where ghost ships might have drifted or sailed from the 1848 point of desertion. The southern hunt was to concentrate on Wilmot and Crampton Bay, northeast of O'Reilly Island, in the extreme eastern end of Queen Maud Gulf.

That was the plan. The Arctic, as she usually does, decided otherwise. For years, climate change had been warming up the Arctic, but she remained as unpredictable as ever. After several summers of rapidly shrinking ice cover and relatively clear sailing in the passage north of King William Island, sea ice had come roaring back. The Royal Navy's *Kingston* was tasked to come south into the northern search zone after acting as a stage for Stephen Harper's annual High Arctic photo opportunity. But the sea ice was so heavy that the *Kingston* never made it close to Victoria Strait. The *Vavilov*, renamed *One Ocean Voyager* for better media optics, steamed into position in the northern search area, crewed by Russians and proudly flying a large Russian flag. The military's engineers put the robotic sub in the water, but it never got beyond test runs. They kept the cruise-ship passengers entertained for a while, but they did nothing to help locate the shipwrecks. Handlers didn't want to let *Arctic Explorer* head down under the ice. Losing a multimillion-dollar robotic sub would make for more humiliating headlines than news that they were operating it off a Russian-flagged ship had already generated.

Not long after the thirty-nine-day expedition began on August 13, the Royal Canadian Geographical Society and its partners were bickering about being stranded in the northern search area while the experts worked the far more promising southern area. The plan called for the *Laurier* to bring the core team north to join up with the Russian cruise ship, but with so much ice still clogging the northern search area, Bill Noon stayed to the south. Just as sea ice streaming down through McClintock Channel, like cement down a trough, had trapped Franklin and his men, it now blocked the people trying to find his ships. They were particularly interested in the bottleneck that Tom Zagon's research had shown, where ice flowing south from Victoria Strait passes through the constricted entrance to Alexandra Strait. If *Erebus* or *Terror* had been drifting among ice floes that were crashing into each other, with heavy sea ice rafting one or both of the bomb vessels, they might well have gone down there.

John Geiger, a Harper ally and Conservative Party contributor who heads the Royal Canadian Geographical Society, was aboard the Russian cruise ship. If the mission failed, he would have to sell it as a success. And if a shipwreck were discovered, he would make sure Harper got credit for a historical breakthrough certain to make news around the world. But reporters weren't likely to care what Geiger had to say if they knew he was far out of the picture, surrounded by sea ice, cornered on a Russian cruise ship that the Arctic had reduced to a stymied bystander.

At the daily 7 a.m. briefing on Captain Noon's bridge, the search team heard that their icebreaker base would be staying in the area of Wilmot and Crampton Bay. Doug Stenton and Robert Park, the land archaeologists, were hoping the *Laurier* would steam north into Victoria Strait. They had used up half their allotted time on the icebreaker's helicopter, and Stenton was mildly concerned that he wouldn't get farther north for some planned survey work. The sea ice choked off that choice. No big deal. There was more work to be done in the southern bay. Stenton had his eye on some small islands that he wanted to reach at some point to complete a systematic check of places archaeologists had never visited.

Scott Youngblut, head of a team of six hydrographers on the expedition, turned to Stenton during the morning meeting and said he needed to set up a temporary GPS reference station in Wilmot and Crampton Bay to give his two survey boats an accurate fix as they continued to head up and down lanes in the sea, scanning the bottom with multibeam sonar mounted to their hulls. The icebreaker carried a pole-mounted multibeam sonar unit, which meant three vessels were producing high-resolution 3-D imagery of the seafloor's topography. They weren't just looking for shipwrecks. With each pass, the digital images filled in another bit of the vast hole in navigation charts for Canada's Arctic, slowly making it safer for the increasing number of ships expected to transit the Northwest Passage as the warming climate melts the ice cover. Youngblut told Stenton he wasn't picky about where in the bay he put the GPS station, and he offered him and Park seats on the helicopter when he flew out to do it later that day.

Archaeologists had never done a proper study of the islands in Wilmot and Crampton Bay, on the west coast of the Adelaide Peninsula. Stenton talked to Parks about the various options and narrowed them down to a shortlist of small islands. One, several miles northeast of O'Reilly Island, was Stenton's preferred target. It worked for Youngblut, too, so he got ready to fly aboard the *Laurier*'s red-and-white Messerschmitt-Bölkow-Blohm Bo 105 chopper, a light-duty German helicopter developed in the 1970s. The pilot was Captain Andrew Stirling, a quick-witted wisecracker with a gray goatee. In his bright orange survival suit, with a tasseled woolen toque drawn down tight to his ears, he could be mistaken for an unusually tall elf—except that on land in the Arctic he walks with a shotgun slung over his shoulder. On guard for wayward polar bears.

Stirling had his own personal connection to the Franklin search. Born a Scot in Dundee, he was from a Royal Navy family. His father, Harvey, was a sailor in the Royal Navy for more than two decades. In World War II, he survived two torpedo attacks. The pilot's grandfather, wounded by a German dum-dum bullet in World War I, joined the staff at the Royal Family's Balmoral Castle, where he specialized in buffing furniture to a mirror sheen in the art of French polish. He once scolded the future Queen Elizabeth II when the monarch was a child princess who thought she could boss around the hired help. Stirling had inherited something else important from his father, a fascination with archaeology. If anyone was specially suited to ending the long, exasperating hunt for a Royal Navy Franklin wreck, it was Captain Andrew Stirling.

He powered up the helicopter's twin engines, the rotors thumping like a jackhammer in the Arctic quiet, and within minutes was over the windswept island that Stenton had requested. In a quick flyover, he confirmed there were no bears, only caribou. So Stirling gently set the chopper's skids on the rocky permafrost and shut her down. Now the only sound was the Arctic breeze, and the odd voice when one of the team felt the need to speak. While the archaeologist went to work studying circles of stones that Inuit hunters used to anchor their animal-hide tents, Youngblut set up his GPS equipment. Stirling walked the shoreline. Following lessons he had learned from the experts, the pilot kept his eyes to the ground, glancing up from time to time to check again for any bears. He soon spotted something that didn't seem to belong, rust-brown against gray rock. Anyone else with an untrained eye might have walked right past, seeing nothing. But Stirling went closer.

He waved for Park to come take a look, and Stenton followed. He knelt down and picked up an iron object, which was lying against a lichen-covered rock, on the side facing away from the shore. The archaeologist looked for the telltale broad arrow.

"Shame," he thought. There wasn't one.

Until Stenton moved the heel of his hand and saw two broad arrows that marked the artifact as Royal Navy property. In between them was the number 12, stamped by a metalworker's hand generations earlier. A little farther along the shoreline, Stirling found two semicircular pieces of wood, grayed, covered in lichen and weathered by time and the elements. Once back on the icebreaker, Stenton took the artifacts to the forward lab for the marine archaeologists to check them against the ship plans for *Erebus* and *Terror*. Jonathan Moore quickly identified the iron piece—about the length of a man's forearm and shaped like a hairpin—as a davit pintle. Corroded from more than a century and a half in the Arctic, but still solid, it was part of the device sailors used to lower and raise boats along the side of the ship.

The wooden objects, which had square wrought-iron nails protruding, were two halves of a plug for a deck hawsehole, an iron pipe where the ship's anchor chain ran down into a locker below. The davit piece was too heavy to blow in the wind, even an Arctic gale. The archaeologists suspected that ice deposited the iron on shore when it severed the sunken ship's masts. Archaeologists later concluded that a tangle of shrouds, the rigging that once held up *Erebus*'s three masts, probably caught on the lee-side davits and ripped them off. The searchers had a good feeling they were about to find a Franklin wreck. Pumped on adrenaline, eager to show their finds to colleagues on the *Laurier*, Stirling thundered back to the icebreaker and set the helicopter down gently on its skids. As the rotor wash stirred up a windstorm on the ship's stern deck, Bill Noon waited on the small hangar's edge. He always came down from the bridge to wait when Stirling radioed that he was on his approach to land with Stenton and Park. The icebreaker's skipper, a fervent lover of old ships and seafaring lore, wanted first look at anything the archaeologists found. From the smirks on their faces, Noon knew something big was up.

"I've got something cool to show you," Stenton whispered to the captain as they headed inside, the Royal Navy relics still stashed, like a wary prospector's gold nuggets, in the chopper.

Within half an hour, Noon was on the bridge looking at the iron piece of a Royal Navy ship whose sailors had sacrificed their lives to open navigation through the Arctic Archipelago. The weight of the moment wasn't lost on the icebreaker commander who was living their legacy. He knew the importance of the broad arrows right away and rushed down a narrow stairwell to his cabin on the next deck to study ships' plans for *Erebus* and *Terror*. Within minutes of Moore's identification of the relic as a davit piece in the archaeologists' forward lab, Noon reached the same conclusion. The pace quickened as Harris and Youngblut planned the move into uncharted waters, agreeing on long search lanes in what was still a big, poorly known part of the Arctic seas. The archaeologist and the hydrographer always attempted to draw search patterns that followed the undersea geology in seas where shoals and submerged drumlins molded by ancient glaciers can easily tear a hole in the hull of the divers' boat, *Investigator*. The aim was to follow search lanes running parallel to likely hazards that could suddenly come out of nowhere in poorly charted areas like this. But after years of endless hunting for the Franklin wrecks, Harris also had a good feel for the nuances of the Arctic, how she moved things around, where she might likely hide a very important secret. If nothing else, the detailed planning improved efficiency.

"If you run against the grain, you're always having to stop and start, stop and start," Moore explained.

The icebreaker's crew lowered *Investigator* over the side the next morning, September 2, shortly after seven. The archaeologists had little reason to think this wasn't just another day. The latest artifacts were exciting, the most important Franklin Expedition relics discovered since US Army Lieutenant Frederick Schwatka searched in the late 1870s. But they weren't exactly arrows pointing to a wreck hidden somewhere underwater in a vast area full of possibilities. Inuit, ice, or some other force could have moved the objects a significant distance from the ship where they belonged. The ship in the Inuit accounts that told of several men living aboard, apparently with a dog, may have described a location long before the vessel actually sank, perhaps after drifting with the sea ice, or under the control of sailors. Her wreck could literally be anywhere.

First, the team finished off a search block left over from a previous day. Then the archaeologists moved closer to the small island where Stirling had found the artifacts on shore. They deployed their Klein 3000 side-scan sonar, housed in the towfish, small and light enough for a diver to hold in his arms, attached to two hundred meters of armored cable. Harris, eyes fixed on a laptop computer in front of the high chair next to the pilot's wheel, watched grainy live sonar images of the seabed slowly scroll down the screen. A thick black line ran up the middle, the shadow created by the towfish's electronic pings bouncing off the ocean floor to either side. After technologist Chriss Ludin finished the first planned line, he handed control of the boat over to technician Joe Boucher. *Investigator* did a tight turn and headed back down the second line, chugging along just fast enough to keep the towfish from hitting bottom, but slow enough to get a good look at anything important that might be sitting down there, without hitting it. Except for some ice scours, the seabed was the same monotonously featureless world that had eaten up more months of the team's lives than they cared to remember. Until suddenly the sonar pings began to reflect off something big and solid, standing tall on the ocean floor.

"That's it!" Harris shouted when a grainy image of the wreck scrolled down the laptop computer screen mounted across from the pilot's wheel.

The ship was firmly on her keel, proudly upright amid hard-packed flat cobblestone, gravel, and sand, in just thirty-six feet of water. With roughly nine feet of clear ocean separating the top of her deck from the surface, anyone looking down from a boat or a hole in the ice could see the wreck as clear as day. Camouflaged in a thick forest of kelp, it might have looked like a reef to anyone who may have passed over before now. The wreck was nestled in between shoals, open at the northern end and protected from heavy scraping by sea ice that could have torn her apart. Some shoals were hiding just six feet beneath the surface, waiting to rip a hole in a passing ship's hull. Yet, apart from a large bite out of the Franklin wreck's stern, she was in remarkably good shape. As the next step in officially confirming they had in fact found either *Erebus* or *Terror*, Harris showed sonar images to Marc-André Bernier, head of the underwater archaeology unit, on the icebreaker. They still weren't precisely sure which wreck they were looking at, but there was no doubt the long Franklin ship hunt was finally over.

Yet they couldn't tell anyone—the historic discovery had to stay secret. This was Stephen Harper's political gold, and he had to be the one to reveal it to the world. The delay would also make sure the British government could be informed through proper channels that the wreck of a Royal Navy vessel had been located. Every possible step was taken to make sure the news didn't leak. Even Bill Noon, a Coast Guard commander, couldn't be told that an expedition headed by his icebreaker had found one of Franklin's ships. Four days passed from the marine archaeologists' discovery to the call over the ship's intercom for the captain to go to his quarters on the evening of September 6. The marine archaeologists were waiting for Noon and closed the captain's door behind him, normally not a good sign on a Coast Guard icebreaker in the Arctic. He feared the worst. But as he sat next to his bookshelf lined with volumes on nautical history, Noon heard news that astonished him. He watched a digital recording of the sonar images on a laptop, but it took a few minutes for the reality to sink in. The men hugged and cried. Then the captain realized he had to immediately unplug his ship from the world.

Activating a strict government secrecy protocol worked out months in advance, Noon shut down all communications from the icebreaker to the outside world except the icebreaker's satellite phone, high-speed Internet link, and radio communications he and his officers controlled on the bridge. An announcement over the ship's PA system summoned Youngblut to his office on the *Laurier*, where Chief Officer Rich Marriott closed the door behind him and asked the hydrographer to turn in all his satellite comms gear. That was when Youngblut, who had seen the artifacts found on the island and knew they could mark a turning point, first realized that they had led to a Franklin wreck. Until senior officials had been informed, and a fitting announcement was organized, even Harper wouldn't know history had been made. That remained a carefully guarded secret, known only to a close circle of searchers and a few officials in Ottawa, for a week before Harper had a news conference in Ottawa to announce the discovery.

I went out on *Investigator* a few days after the find and spent a day bobbing on the ocean with Jonathan Moore and the team. I watched as they went through the motions of wreck hunting, listening to Van Morrison and Pink Floyd on a tablet speaker Boucher made out of a paper cup, never once getting a hint that they had already found a Franklin ship. I finally got confirmation from my bunkmate, Marc-André Bernier. Our cabin was at the icebreaker's stern, just off the crew's weight room, a couple of decks down from the helicopter pad. He kept the secret from me, under orders from the top, until he was frantically packing for a trip to Ottawa for Harper's news conference.

"You almost think this ship wanted us to find it," Bernier told me in our cabin. He teared up describing the moment the marine archaeologists knew they were looking at one of the most sought-after wrecks on the planet, one that had for so long eluded the biggest, most costly hunt in maritime history. As I watched Bernier stuff his things into a duffel bag, I could see the gates slowly starting to swing open on years of pent-up pressure to produce.

"I cried. We all did," he confided.

"You really have to trust in yourself and in your colleagues. There's constant pressure and scrutiny because we're government. And it's this quest: Some people love it, some people think we shouldn't be doing this. There are also people saying, 'You're not looking in the right place.' And the more you look, and the more you don't find, the more criticism you can have."

When the wreck was found, the *Vavilov* was still stranded in the northern search area, at times meandering through the minefield of ice floes at less than one knot. John Geiger, who wasn't told about the discovery of the crucial artifacts, was steaming. Just after 11 p.m. local time on September 1, hours before the next morning's discovery, he tried again to get Andrew Campbell, the Parks Canada vice president, to tell the *Laurier* to head north to escort the Russian cruise ship into prime search territory.

"We are in a very frustrating situation as you can imagine," Geiger wrote. "There is open water as you can see on the satellite image, but we have no way of getting there without [an icebreaker] escort."

Campbell wouldn't budge. The parks executive had already told Geiger he would leave deployment decisions up to the expedition's lead experts.

"As all logistics and planning for the operation has been managed effectively by the professional teams, I trust they are still doing so with the full knowledge of the situation," Campbell wrote on August 30.

Geiger insisted his vessel was in a good position to make a find and implied that the *Laurier* was wasting time running search patterns in the south, in lanes as monotonous as cutting grass.

"I still think we have a shot," Geiger pleaded, "but not if the *Laurier* is mowing the lawn down in the southern search area."

STILL WORKING UNDER a shroud of secrecy, the marine archaeologists prepared to explore the wreck before the looming winter entombed Wilmot and Crampton Bay in sea ice. They loaded scuba gear, underwater cameras, and a remotely operated vehicle, bright yellow and the size of a portable generator, aboard *Investigator*. The icebreaker's crew worked davit winches to gently lower the survey boat into rolling seas. Before the divers set off, unauthorized witnesses were ordered off the icebreaker's decks. Keeping the precise location of the shipwreck under wraps was essential for protecting her from treasure hunters. Bill Noon even alerted his sailors that he wanted to know if anyone spotted or heard aircraft flying over, in case someone was running surveillance. Only later, when the Canadian government declared an exclusion to the area around the wreck site, was it clear where she lay on the seabed. The final resting place of Sir John Franklin's flagship, HMS *Erebus*, is ten miles southeast of the tip of Grant Point. She was found, not far below the surface, right where Inuit had been saying for generations that a large ship sank after several men, and perhaps a dog, had been living aboard.

In the archaeologists' first dive, lasting just forty minutes, they were overwhelmed by the trove of artifacts littering the ship and the surrounding seabed. They quickly identified two brass cannon off the wreck's stern. The ship's cast-bronze bell, a powerful symbol of any vessel, was easier to raise. When the divers brought it up, and the bell was cleaned, it gave new life to the spirits of 129 courageous men who gave their lives to expand the horizons of human knowledge. Dated 1845, the year they said good-bye to home and country for the last time, it was embossed with the British government's broad arrow. The archaeologists later found the handle of a sword, a gilded hilt, minus the blade. It is easy to imagine someone like Sir John Franklin closing his hand on the sharkskin grip. The wreck was confirmed to be *Erebus*, Sir John Franklin's 104-foot-long flagship, where he lived and worked in the commander's cabin at the stern.

Over several dives, including some through triangular holes in thick sea ice the following winter, the archaeologists retrieved numerous other objects, including part of the ship's wood-and-metal wheel, a patent medicine bottle, and a round piece of frosted glass encircled by brass. It was one of Preston's patented illuminators that brought light down to the men crowded into the Franklin ships' dank lower decks. Even better, it could be switched out with a ventilation fan.

THE SUMMER AFTER *Erebus* was found, underwater archaeologists stationed themselves near the site on the *Martin Bergmann*, which gave them much more time to explore the wreck. They identified around seventy relics of interest, including a sextant. Then a gale struck, with winds pounding the sea at more than sixty miles an hour, forcing the wreck team to ride out the storm in Cambridge Bay for five days. While they were gone, waves more than a dozen feet high crashed over the wreck site. With just nine feet of water between her and the surface, the storm may have exposed *Erebus* to the hammering wind and waves. It was almost as though a dead ship were stirring back to life, riding out another polar storm with whatever strength she could muster, as *Erebus* had done so many times before the one that had trapped her.

"By the time conditions cleared, and the *Martin Bergmann* was able to set sail back to the site, the water went from crystal clear to zero visibility," said Adrian Schimnowski, who had taken over from his wife as the Arctic Research Foundation's operations chief.

"You couldn't even see your hand in front of you underwater. Almost every artifact that had been documented had moved. Even some of the timbers had moved. Some artifacts that were just lying on the deck had disappeared. They don't know where they went."

Like a flailing animal, the furious storm had shoved huge timbers around, tossed invaluable relics about, and caused untold damage to clues that might have solved the mystery of how the Franklin Expedition met its end. The sextant was buried under heavy timbers. Plates and other items were washed overboard.

The archaeologists could only plan for another expedition, in another year, to see what they might be able to salvage as the search for *Terror* continued.

16

Terror Bay

Conflict became so ingrained in the Franklin search over the decades that even a dramatic success like the discovery of *Erebus* unleashed an ugly squabble. Nunavut refused to issue archaeological permits to Parks Canada's divers working on the site unless Canada's government surrendered authority over any relics the archaeologists wanted to raise from the seabed. The feds relented, fearing the Mounties might arrest the archaeologists, and then reasserted authority by declaring the wreck and surrounding waters a national historic site. Invoking a land-claims agreement, Inuit pressed for negotiations to sort out ownership and control of more than fifty Franklin Expedition objects marine archaeologists had brought up from the ocean floor. Inuit argued the relics should be displayed in their communities to boost tourism.

In 2016, the Coast Guard icebreaker CCGS *Sir Wilfrid Laurier*, the Arctic Research Foundation's R/V *Martin Bergmann*, and the Royal Canadian Navy's HMCS *Shawinigan* went looking for the *Terror*'s wreck. But with only nine days set aside for the search, hopes weren't very high. No reporters were allowed on the expedition. Experts assumed sea ice had likely torn *Terror* apart and scattered the remains in deep ocean, not far south of where the ships were abandoned in 1848 at the northern end of Victoria Strait.

Before making its rendezvous with the rest of the expedition, the

Bergmann set off to do some science. Marine scientist Lina Rotermund, freshly graduated from Halifax's Dalhousie University, was on board to study Chantrey Inlet, at the mouth of the Back River. The *Bergmann* spent two days at the same place Franklin Expedition survivors had hoped to reach 168 years earlier, expecting to free themselves from the Arctic by following the river south. Rotermund was focused on the habitat of Arctic char, armed with an array of instruments to measure ocean currents, study the seabed and its sediments, measure the ocean's salinity, and gather other data aimed at improving the iconic fish's chances of surviving the rapid warming of the Far North's climate.

The first stage of a longer study was part of the Arctic Research Foundation's broader attempt to make sure Inuit enjoyed lasting benefits from *Erebus*'s discovery. In Gjoa Haven and Cambridge Bay, shipping containers were transformed into artists' studios and science labs, powered by solar panels and wind turbines. Young Inuit were recruited as trainees to offer hope of good jobs and a more promising future. A related project worked to build sustainable tourism. Parks Canada promised a new facility in Gjoa Haven, with a list of options under discussion with Inuit that included a visitor center and conservation labs for recovered Franklin artifacts.

From the inlet, the *Bergmann* set a course to reach Gjoa Haven early on September 2, 2016. Adrian Schimnowski had to pick up his tenth crew member, a forty-nine-year-old Inuk named Sammy Kogvik. A member of the Canadian Rangers, the military's largely Inuit northern reserve force, he was hired by Parks Canada to assist the latest search for the *Terror*. Schimnowski had trouble tracking down Kogvik and realized why when the two finally met. Kogvik, who speaks English softly and slowly, was wary of outsiders. The increasingly bitter dispute over the handling of the *Erebus* excavation was further fraying trust between Inuit and *qalunaaq*. After sizing up the *Bergmann* expedition's lead, Kogvik confided that he had been offered a choice of which ship to join. The Inuk asked around and local people told him he could be sure Schimnowski wouldn't betray him or the Inuit. So he wanted to sail on the *Bergmann*.

Like other *qalunaaq* who manage to thrive in the Arctic, Schimnowski traveled a winding road to get there. He is a trained paramedic and firefighter, once worked on TV as a music-channel video jock, was an interior designer, built custom furniture, and competed in a world dragon-boat championship. He is also an installation artist and a commercial scuba diver. And, like Kogvik, he loves to fish. Above all, Schimnowski has what seems a limitless patience to sit and listen respectfully when Inuit want to be heard. It is a trait all too rare for southerners in the North, where outsiders often come across as pushy, even manipulative, to the Inuit, whose stories recall the times when they were the Arctic's only humans.

As the *Bergmann* steamed east through Simpson Strait, her 450 hp Detroit Diesel engines humming on what was expected to be a thirty-hour voyage to Cambridge Bay, Schimnowski stood on the bridge, quietly listening to Kogvik point out familiar landmarks along the coast. A man of few words, who generally spoke only when spoken to, Kogvik chirped up when he saw a favorite spot, a family member's hunting cabin, an abandoned piece of equipment, or anything that sparked a pleasant memory. After another long silence, the Inuk suddenly started to talk about Terror Bay, far from sight to the north. About six years earlier—it could have been seven or eight, Kogvik said—he was on his snowmobile crossing the sea ice in Terror Bay to go fishing in the spring with his buddy, an Inuk from Baker Lake. Kogvik called him Uncle Jimmy. Spotting something strange to his left, sticking up from the ice as high as a tall man, the Inuk stopped his snowmobile.

"What is that?" he asked his friend.

"I don't know," Uncle Jimmy replied.

Once they got closer, Kogvik knew he was looking at a pole made of wood, roughly a foot and a half in diameter. It looked like part of a ship's mast. The two men walked up to it, Kogvik pulled his camera from his parka pocket, and he asked his friend to take a picture. Smiling, Kogvik posed for the first one, with his left arm around the object. Then he grabbed on with his right arm and both legs, in a big bear hug, for another snapshot. The sun was getting ready to set, so they hurried off to make camp. The next day, Kogvik's father-in-law, Ben Putuguq, caught up with them by following their trail in the snow. He had seen the mast too, and he told them stories of a sunken ship from the old days.

But when they got back to Gjoa Haven, Kogvik reached for his camera in his parka pocket and realized he hadn't zipped it up. The camera was gone. Without pictures, he had no proof that a mast rose from the ice of Terror Bay. Worse than that, though, losing his camera after the encounter seemed a bad omen. A serious warning. Kogvik and his father-in-law resolved to keep the story secret. Uncle Jimmy was silenced another way: The next year, he plunged through the ice and drowned in a lake not far from Gjoa Haven.

Others might have listened to the story, smiled dismissively, and changed the subject. But Schimnowski knows that the Arctic often reveals her secrets in strange ways.

"The Arctic presents a gift to you when you're ready," is the way he put it.

Besides, it wasn't the first time Schimnowski had heard odd stories about Terror Bay. Inuit spoke of seeing shimmers of a ship beneath the surface, sometimes when the sunlight cut just right across the sea, or when they were flying over in aircraft. Louie Kamookak told me that things that went on in and around the bay were a lot less mundane than that.

"Terror Bay is known for many spooky encounters in the past," Kamookak said. "Gives me the shivers."

Schimnowski asked his team if they wanted to make a detour and take a look. They were game. In a satellite phone call to Jim Balsillie, each man pausing to let his voice echo back from space, Balsillie greenlighted the *Bergmann* to change course for Terror Bay. The ship arrived at 4 a.m. Cocaptain David McIsaac eased back the throttle to creep into uncharted waters. Without modern charts to show seabed hazards, there is no way to know what is lurking beneath you in Terror Bay until it rears up on the sounder display or your vessel comes to a screeching halt on a hidden shoal. During the 2014 search, the sixty-four-foot vessel briefly ran aground on a sandy shoal in Simpson Strait, but the crew managed to free her without serious damage. It's not something you want to experience twice in the High Arctic. Especially in the darkness before dawn. McIsaac slowly brought the *Bergmann* north into the bay to a depth of just over forty-nine feet. At 6 a.m., the crew launched their Dolphin, a sixteen-foot aluminum-hulled skiff with two 20 hp outboard motors. With no ice cover or snow on the land, it was difficult for Kogvik to recall precisely where he had seen the mysterious mast.

Inuit stories described the silhouette of a masted ship that could be seen from an island in the bay at sunset in spring, so the searchers headed for a group of islands to the east. They had to skirt numerous shoals, often motoring in waters just three to nine feet deep. Yves Bernard, a diver and petty officer, first class, in the Royal Canadian Navy, watched the seafloor with a side-scan sonar device mounted on the skiff's transom. The fruitless search in the shallows jogged Kogvik's memory of his track across the bay years earlier, and the searchers shifted to deeper waters. Still nothing. They gave it about fifteen minutes and then headed back to the *Bergmann* to have some breakfast and discuss options.

By 8:20 on the morning of September 3, the crew had agreed to give up and continue on to Cambridge Bay. McIsaac set the auto-pilot to take the *Bergmann* out of the bay about 1,300 feet to the west of the route she took in, partly to get a wider field of depth soundings to make any return that much safer. He handed over the helm to his son Daniel and went below for a bathroom break while the others squeezed in around the galley table to eat omelettes, hash browns, and bacon with hot coffee. Fifteen minutes later, with the engines running at full RPMs to propel the ship at seven knots, the bay's very flat bottom suddenly started to peak. The *Bergmann* was roughly seven hundred feet north of open water. A large object appeared on the sounder's display, mounted to the right of the helm, as a reddish-orange silhouette. *Too big to be a school of fish*, Daniel McIsaac thought. *Too soft an image to be a large boulder.* McIsaac wondered if he had actually seen masts, but he was more focused on not running into something. Heart thumping, he throttled back immediately to stop the boat.

"What do you think that is there?" McIsaac said to Navy Master Seaman Matt Briggs, the only other person on the bridge. After a quick head-scratch and some raised eyebrows, McIsaac hollered: "Adrian! Can you come up here?"

No reply. McIsaac told the boatswain to get Schimnowski. Quick.

"You guys better get up here!" Briggs shouted down from the top of the wheelhouse ladder. Cocaptain Gerry Chidley, who grew up on the trawler that became the *Bergmann* and was the most seasoned mariner aboard, reached the bridge first. He leaned in to squint at the sounder screen. For the first time anyone could remember, Chidley was speechless.

"What's that?" he blurted.

"I have no idea," McIsaac replied, bug-eyed with his hands in the air. "I was hopin' you would tell me."

Seconds later, the whole crew was crowding around the sounder display, craning for a look. Awestruck. The bridge erupted in laughter when someone asked Captain David if he had flushed the toilet into the sea. A second pass over the object revealed it to be a ship with three masts sitting on the bottom, in just under seventy-nine feet of water. At the highest point, she stood about thirty feet above the seabed.

From the Dolphin, crewmembers confirmed with side-scan sonar and a high-end chirp sounder (more commonly used as a fish finder) that they were looking at a large shipwreck similar in size to *Erebus*. They returned to the *Bergmann* and deployed a camera array: Four GoPros, one of them sealed in a high-pressure underwater casing, were fastened to a stainless-steel cage some two feet high, a foot across, and a foot deep. Lights to illuminate the seabed and laser markers to measure objects were attached to the bottom. The whole thing weighed fifteen pounds and transmitted live video to the ship along an umbilical cord designed to detach if the array got snagged. With the *Bergmann* drifting at under two knots, the cameras picked up stunning images of an almost completely intact ship, with wooden pieces that had broken off the standing masts scattered about her deck, and what appeared to be an anchor on the starboard bow. The *Terror* had sailed with several anchors, of different sizes. A bowsprit, about twenty feet long, pointed like a giant lance from the ship's bow.

By the time the camera batteries were changed, and the array was deployed for a third time, the wind and currents had started to shift. The camera cage was getting too close to the bow, so Schimnowski ordered it drawn up on the hand spool. Then the array suddenly disconnected from the umbilical, close to the seafloor, either because it touched the wreck's bow or the umbilical itself brushed against a mast or the bowsprit, triggering a quick release mechanism that let the cameras go to avoid snagging on the wreck. Either way, the video was lost. The crew hadn't saved any of it as instructed. Like Kogvik before them, the discovery team had nothing to show for their find. No pictures, no proof. So the *Bergmann* set off for Cambridge Bay to pick up a remotely operated vehicle (ROV) with a high-definition video camera, refuel and resupply, and hurry back to Terror Bay. That's not easy in a vessel as small as the *Bergmann*. She often rolls and pitches when Arctic seas become heavy in late summer. When the ship is punching through large swells, any crewmembers trying to catch some sleep suffer the torture of levitating above their bunks as the bow dips, only to crash down as it rises. Again and again, through the night.

But the return to Terror Bay made the bruises and queasy stomachs worth it. Bernard maneuvered the green-and-black SeaBotix ROV, equipped with a robotic arm, spotlight, high-definition camera, and a GPS locator. Like an eye peeping into a frozen past, the camera spotted the ship's bell, lying on its side, on the deck. There was also a cannon. Glass panes were still firmly in three of four tall windows of the cabin where the *Terror*'s commander, Franklin's deputy, Captain Francis Crozier, slept and worked at the stern.

"This vessel looks like it was buttoned down tight for winter and it sank," Schimnowski told me. "Everything was shut. Even the windows are still intact. If you could lift this boat out of the water, and pump the water out, it would probably float."

The team first thought they were looking at a ship listing at about forty-five degrees to starboard on the seabed. But the third dive with the ROV led to a much different conclusion: "We noticed the wreck is sitting level on the seabed floor not at a list—which means the boat sank gently to the bottom," Schimnowski said in an update e-mailed from the High Arctic as news of the discovery spread around the world.

Bernard maneuvered the ROV through an open hatch to get a look at the *Terror*'s interior.

"We spotted two wine bottles, tables and empty shelving," Schimnowski e-mailed from the site. "Found a desk with open drawers with something in the back corner of the drawer."

At least one of the bottles was lying on its side on what appeared to be a shelf. Plates were neatly stacked in the mess hall. A pot was still sitting in the hole of a rack that once held several. But Schimnowski was struck that divers had found many more things scattered around *Erebus*. He speculated that *Terror*'s crewmen had taken off as much as they could before locking her up.

Even more intriguing, the ROV video showed a thick rope, some thirty feet long, running from a capstan through a hole in the deck. It was lilting in the ocean current alongside the *Terror*'s starboard side. To the eye of an experienced Arctic mariner like David McIsaac, it looked like a line that had broken free from an anchor. He thinks archaeologists will find the anchor dug into the seafloor. But it's also possible the ship was anchored to an ice floe that carried the vessel there on the currents.

"Sailors definitely took her there," McIsaac insisted. "It would be impossible for her to get to where she was by drifting."

If he's right, that would undercut the old lead-addled-sailors theory even more. To somehow return to their abandoned ships and navigate both of them south toward the continental mainland, crews who were decimated by sickness, hunger, and frostbite must have fought a gargantuan struggle to keep sailing. At least some of them had managed to complete their mission and find the missing link in the Northwest Passage. They just didn't live to claim the honor.

Finding the second Franklin wreck in Terror Bay was like slipping a long-missing piece of a jigsaw puzzle snugly into place. It fit perfectly with various elements of the mystery that seemed already solved. The next body of water to the southeast is Washington Bay. The distance is just twelve miles from one bay's coast to the next. The *Terror*'s proven proximity to the place where one of the most credible, and compelling, Inuit accounts of an encounter with starving *qalunaaq* sent expert minds racing. Washington Bay is where Inuit said a group of hunters came across white men at a crack in the sea ice. They called the leader of that group Aglooka. Historians suspect he was Crozier. If his ship were in fact anchored not far away when the *qalunaaq* demanded seal meat from the Inuit at Washington Bay, how could the explorers have run out of food? After all, ROV video shows a can of something sitting on a shelf in the mess hall. Did the crew just give up on their canned meat after comrades fell ill, and likely died, poisoned by *Clostridium botulinum* bacteria?

Inuit testimony offers evidence of mass death at Terror Bay. A Netsilingmiut woman named Ahlangyah, about fifty-five years old, told of seeing the *qalunaaq* at the ice fissure in Washington Bay and camping with other Inuit near them for five days, during which five white men lived in a tent and the same number stayed in the boat they had all been dragging over the ice. The Inuit family killed several seals and gave some to the outsiders, Ahlangyah said, and then the whole group, Inuit and *qalunaaq*, headed off together for the Adelaide Peninsula, hurrying across the melting sea ice before they were trapped for the summer on King William Island. Dragging their boat on a heavy sledge, the white men couldn't keep up. The Inuit waited for them at Gladman Point, fishing in nearby lakes, but the laggards never made it.

"Ahlangyah concluded her statement by saying that, in the following spring, when the ground was almost clear of snow, she saw a tent standing on the shore at the head of Terror Bay," wrote William Henry Gilder, Lieutenant Schwatka's second-in-command on the American expedition, in 1882. "There were dead bodies in the tent, and outside lay some covered over with sand. There was no flesh on them, nothing but the bones and clothes. She saw nothing to indicate that they had belonged to the party she met before. The bones had the cords or sinews still attached to them. Outside were one or two graves, which the natives did not at that time open. Numerous articles were lying around, such as knives, forks, spoons, watches, many books, clothing, and blankets."

Historians think the fallen may have been left in a large hospital tent, with two graves nearby. The *Terror*'s demise in the same bay, with *Erebus* lying on the seabed due south, raises another tantalizing possibility: Did both ships stop at what became known as Terror

Bay? If dozens of men did, in fact, die ashore, perhaps there was only a small group left, not enough to sail two Royal Navy bomb ships out of the bay. If the few remaining survivors were crewmembers with just the right skills, and bold leadership, it is possible that the four or five men whom Inuit recalled living aboard *Erebus* farther south sailed the hulking ship there on their own, David Woodman told me.

The wreck of *Erebus* is roughly forty miles south of the *Terror*, across Queen Maud Gulf. Looking at both sites on a map, it's easy to imagine them voyaging together, only to separate as more sailors died, and there were fewer hands on deck. Until archaeologists dive to come up with enough hard facts for a solid rewrite of history, Franklin theorists can enjoy a long field day. Armchair historians, even the braver pros, will be free to speculate, musing on the many possibilities, including mutiny or a valiant struggle to catch up to ships spotted drifting by and reboard them. David Woodman was reluctant to wade too early into what is certain to be a vigorous debate. The Franklin mystery has a way of burning even meticulous researchers like him. But while he awaited more conclusive evidence, Woodman leaned toward the theory that Crozier and 104 survivors started walking south and reached Erebus Bay—just north of Terror Bay—where the growing number of sick and lame men forced them to halt and establish a large encampment.

"Many, if not all of them, are sent back to the ships and re-man them," he suggested.

Tom Zagon, the federal ice expert, believes it is possible that both ships were locked in a floe of thick multiyear ice that would have protected them from intense pressure as they drifted with the current, surrounded by shifting ice floes, through Alexandra Strait. After studying years of satellite imagery, and knowing the damage moving sea ice can do, he finds it hard to believe that men fearing for their lives would try to sail through it.

"Once through Alexandra Strait, the ice conditions in Queen Maud Gulf to the south are fairly benign, and once any ice surrounding the ships broke up, at that point it would have been possible to regain control," he said.

SOON AFTER THE WORLD heard the *Terror* had been found, the tide of snide remarks struck social media: Why did it take so long for the geniuses to find the *Terror* when she was submerged in the very bay named after her? people asked. The connection can only be a coincidence, however telling it might be. Francis McClintock named Terror Bay, and numerous other spots along King William Island's coast, when he was searching for Sir John and his men on behalf of Lady Franklin in 1859.

"My plan for naming that previously unexplored coastline was to call the two principal Bays after the two ships & all the minor bays,—points, islands, etc. after officers of these ships; those of the Erebus being grouped about 'Erebus Bay', similarly those of the Terror about 'Terror Bay.' I regarded that coastline as sacred to their mummies, I attached no other names than theirs' to it," he wrote two decades later.

When Parks Canada officials heard of the discovery, they were livid that the *Bergmann* team had kept it secret for a week instead of notifying marine archaeologists aboard the *Wilfrid Laurier* so they could steam south and take control of the site. But Schimnowski and his crew, who were operating under a Nunavut scientific research license, wanted to be sure they had found the *Terror* first. When they were certain, Balsillie called Prime Minister Justin Trudeau's office. As word spread through the bureaucracy, an ugly turf battle broke out. In private discussions, the Parks Canada camp accused the foundation's discovery team of damaging the wreck with their lost camera array before divers had visited the wreck to check. After more than a century and a half, the Franklin Expedition hadn't lost its power to rile people. Like sailors priming their cannons, parties lawyered up.

I couldn't help but think Kamookak must be right, that peace for himself and his people, and an end to all the suffering, political manipulations, and recriminations that have followed the first Royal Navy explorers, can't come unless Franklin's body is found: freed from the permafrost, or wherever he may lie, to go home and be at eternal rest in the nation that he, and his courageous men, so proudly served.

17

An Offering to the Dead

Not long after the discovery of *Erebus* in 2014, Louie Kamookak fell ill again. He was rushed to the hospital for six more hours of heart surgery. Doctors saved his life once more by repairing the heart valve they had given him during his last brush with death, after the historian thought he was closing in on Franklin's grave.

"I believe it's a mystery within a mystery," he told me later.

Kamookak held on and recovered, and the wreck that had occupied a corner of his mind since he was a boy became real on a Saturday morning in the summer of 2015. Adrian Schimnowski asked him whether he wanted to visit *Erebus*'s ocean grave, and, after deliberating a bit, he opted to go. His wife, Josephine, who had been a partner in his research, wanted to go too, but there was no room.

"Why don't you bring something there?" she asked him the evening before the visit.

They talked about how their elders, when they were having trouble finding game to hunt or weather was frighteningly bad, would take hunks of meat, or anything useful they could give up, as an offering to the dead. They would toss it in the air and ask their ancestors for good luck. Many believed the ritual sacrifices worked.

"Why don't you take some sand from the elders' gravesites?" Josephine suggested.

Growing up, Kamookak had seen his dad do it quite a few times. His heart told him now was the time to do the same. He went to Gjoa Haven's graveyard with a small plastic bag and scraped in some sand. With the offering in his pocket the next morning, he went to the *Martin Bergmann* first to watch members of the wreck exploration team take samples of marine life that had made the shipwreck their home, such as sea cucumber, starfish, clams, anemones, worms, and kelp. Kamookak asked if he could sprinkle his sand into the water over the *Erebus*, and an archaeologist approved. The *Bergmann*'s cocaptain, Gerry Chidley, buzzed Kamookak and Jacob Keanik, who runs Gjoa Haven's Nattilik Heritage Centre, over the edge of the wreck site in an inflatable Zodiac. The pilot shut down the outboard engine, letting the boat drift with the current, with nothing but the Arctic wind and lapping water to disturb the silence. Kamookak was expecting to be excited. It had taken a long time for him to reach a Franklin ship. The sheer size of the ship was a bit startling. But oddly, the encounter felt almost ordinary, as if this weren't the first time.

"It seemed like it was not new," he told me, his voice subdued, choosing his words carefully. "I'd been thinking about it for a long time."

He took a deep breath and let out a long sigh.

"It was quite a feeling of my ancestors being there, and of my elders not being there to witness what they'd been passing on for a long time. The stories about it."

The boat made a slow pass over the Royal Navy behemoth, and, peering down through seawater as clear as the lens in his rectangular eyeglasses, Kamookak could see divers carefully moving about her. Marine archaeologists had spent days gently plucking thick kelp from *Erebus* to reveal more of her hull and deck and give the divers a better look at a treasure trove of artifacts. Using a plastic measuring tape as a datum line, they measured and recorded the objects' locations in relation to each other. An underwater laser mounted on a tripod fired fans of blue light through the sea to create 3-D images for further study.

After a complete pass over the wreck, Chidley fired up the outboard and headed back to the ship's stern, where Franklin once slept and worked at his chart table in the commander's cabin. There they came alongside a second Zodiac and waited for each dripping diver to climb back in. Everyone except Kamookak sat on the bobbing boats. Those wearing hats removed them as he began to speak in a quiet ceremony. He asked for calm weather and a safe research expedition. After a minute of silence, Kamookak spread the sand onto the ocean that had protected *Erebus* from the ravages of time and Arctic ice. A gentle puff of warm wind blew from the southeast. He felt that Hummahuk and his other ancestors were there with him. That they were part of him.

A wave of sadness rolled over Kamookak. He thought again of all the elders he had interviewed, especially the ones who had passed on, and of Sir John Franklin and his men, the suffering they shared with Inuit, and the peace he sought for all, the dead and the living. Then the Zodiac drifted for a second time along the length of *Erebus*. For some five minutes, Kamookak watched her broad wooden deck pass beneath him, no faster than if he were a sailor making his way up to the mighty bow that had tried to break free from a prison of ice. Remnants of the forest of kelp fronds that divers had been trimming from the wreck undulated on the current, like wings on the breeze.

"It was a relief," Kamookak told me, not because he wanted or needed any vindication for himself or his people. He was just glad no one could doubt anymore that "what my ancestors were saying about the ship being in that area was true and strong."

He had faithfully followed the path of his great-grandmother Hummahuk, who had taught him to revere the stories and the power they hold. Yet Kamookak's quest was not over. He still longed to see what she saw: the gravesite with the headstone that seemed it must hold the remains of a great man.

"A lot of elders I interviewed, I knew, had seen more than they could say. They kept it to themselves. Inuit believe that you stay away from dead people. You leave them alone. Elders told me, 'Stay away from them.' They worried about spirits.

"About three elders told me about word that was passed down through the years: 'If you are travelling on King William Island, you don't travel alone. Because there's bad spirits.' I think there is a lot of them because people have experienced many mysterious things happening there."

After visiting the wreck site, Kamookak cleared up the question of the place's name for me. In 1869, when In-nook-poo-zhee-jook marked the spot where the ship went down on his sketch map for Charles Francis Hall, he drew an islet nearby.

"*Kivevok*," the Inuk must have said, meaning: "Where it sank."

Hall named the islet that instead, Kamookak told me. Over time, that toponym must have stuck. Inuit guides working at that site where divers explored the wreck from an ice camp in 2015 told me, with broad smiles, that an island hidden by the thick sea ice not far from our feet was called Kivevok. They wondered why it took the *qalunaaq* so long to figure out that the ship they sought was sitting right there. *Where it sank.*

In-nook-poo-zhee-jook likely drew the map in the snow. That's what Inuit usually did for each other in those days, from the perspective of the hunting grounds where they camped, Kamookak said. From his research into Inuit family trees, the historian believes Hall's source was likely part of a group that lived on islands west of King William Island. The top of the map he drew wasn't north, as Hall and many other outsiders had assumed over the years.

"The Inuit never think of north, east, south, and west," he explained. "It's always where you're originally from, their own hunting grounds and areas, even though they were nomadic."

That basic cultural misunderstanding meant that Hall, and most of those over the generations who studied the map he brought home, couldn't see the precise location the Inuk had pointed out because they didn't see the Arctic as Inuit did.

THE STORMS stayed away after Kamookak's ceremony, allowing divers to look again for the numerous artifacts that had moved and disappeared from sight. The brief Arctic calm did not mean, however, that there was peace in Inuit hearts or those of others who had virtually given their lives over the Franklin mystery. Answers only breed new questions. The hauntings have not stopped. Kamookak's theory that Inuit encounters with white men suffering slow agonizing ends, the walking dead of Netsilingmiut territory, might explain some of the stories of spirits wandering the Arctic, made sense to me at first. But then, after we got to know each other better, he told me more about his recurring nightmare, and the night his parents said something was pulling him from their tent.

I thought I saw a tremble, maybe a faint shiver, in his large hands, weathered and worn by a long, hard life in the High Arctic. The fingertips on his left hand were bent and slightly twisted, as if years earlier, they had been caught in a machine and wrenched. Kamookak had told me why on a cold winter's day, after he took me to meet his eighty-three-year-old father, George, who was living in a neatly kept house overlooking the frozen, blinding white expanse of the Rasmussen Basin. The diesel furnace was blowing heat like a desert breeze. A picture of Jesus at the Last Supper hung on the wall behind him.

Later, as he was leaving me at my hotel, Kamookak shared an intimate secret. He held up his left hand to show me those gnarled fingertips. The fingernails had fallen off when he was a child. It never occurred to him that he was different until he got older, Kamookak told me, so he asked his parents what had happened. His mom said his hand changed when he was a boy, right after the night his parents stopped the dark being, whether spectral or real, from pulling him away into the Arctic night.

Saying nothing more, leaving me to find meaning in the gesture, Kamookak pulled on his down-filled mitt, drew the fur-lined hood of his heavy parka up over his head, and stepped out into the Arctic. A wispy, ethereal vapor cloud swirled around him, like a blast of steam.

Shivering in the doorway, watching through frosted glass as he left, I wondered whether a ghost had come off the ice to grab Louie that day, and whether it might still be restless, angry enough to come again.

AFTERWORD

From the start, the epic hunt for the lost Franklin Expedition was a tug-of-war between establishment experts sure of their knowledge and outsiders following an inexplicable compulsion, an inner voice, or an educated guess. Whalers working from generations of Arctic experience were pitted against revered Royal Navy men who looked down their noses at merchant mariners. Staid bureaucrats chafed at the distraction of clairvoyant visions. Lady Franklin had to fight the Admiralty tooth and nail before the private 1859 expedition that she organized discovered the first written proof of what happened to Sir John and his men. Too often, Inuit were dismissed as untrustworthy savages.

The establishment's endless politics, posturing and bickering condemned brave sailors to death in the mid-19th century. It threatens their legacy early in the 21st century.

In the end, laymen won the day. Helicopter pilot Andrew Stirling found the breakthrough clue, the rusting iron davit piece that led Parks Canada's underwater archeologists to HMS *Erebus* in 2014. Inuk Sammy Kogvik and his ghostly encounter with what seemed a ship's wooden mast poking through ice guided the *Martin Bergmann* crew to Terror Bay, and a propitious autopilot setting delivered the hunters to the wreck of HMS *Terror* in 2016. To the discovery team's leader Adrian Schimnowski, finding the *Terror* was not only surreal. It was another hint from the Arctic to search deeper.

"There's something else mysterious here," he told me through the oscillating whine of a satellite phone call from the *Bergmann*, "something else we're starting to touch beyond the Franklin story. Maybe it's about human nature. How people treat each other. How things can go wrong in a place that's so isolated. Our connection to the land is stronger in the Arctic because we're not distracted. Maybe we can sense things we can't normally sense in the south. There's something pretty powerful up here."

Like the Inuit whose knowledge was ignored for so long, the Arctic may be trying to tell the world something as the region that helps cool Earth warms roughly twice as fast as the rest of our planet.

"It's about respect for one another, and respect for the environment, and working within what's there already and not trying to fight against those elements," Schimnowski said.

Now that *Erebus* and *Terror* are no longer missing, experts can focus on solving the bigger mystery of how two of history's most storied ships ended up far south of where they were abandoned, standing upright at the bottom of Arctic seas. Inuit have always known that working together is essential to survival. That same spirit of cooperation will be the key to solving the complex Franklin mystery as the world watches archaeologists, historians and armchair theorists try to sort out the many clues that will come to light as the long excavation of *Erebus* and *Terror* unfolds.

The government of Great Britain ceded control of Franklin's Royal Navy ships and their contents to Canada in a 1997 agreement. Canada promised to conserve any relics brought up from the site and make them available for public display and research, including in Britain. Any gold recovered, apart from privately owned coins, would be shared between the two countries, after deducting any portion due by law to a third party. But the first priority was to ensure that the archaeological sites were properly handled once discovered.

That was enshrined in the Memorandum of Understanding's opening clause, which declared: "Research and disclosure shall prevail over interests of financial gain and media coverage." Critics of former Prime Minister Stephen Harper's handling of the *Erebus* discovery questioned whether his government upheld that agreement. He seemed determined to squeeze as much good publicity as possible from the historic find in the months leading up to the 2015 election, only to lose in a defeat that forced his retirement from politics.

Louie Kamookak made another search for Franklin clues in the summer of 2016. Traveling in late July with two young Inuit apprentices, Jamie Takkiruq and Michael Eleehetook, the historian and his team set out on all-terrain vehicles to visit sites in Hummahuk's stories. They had enough food and fuel for a week to ten days. The rapidly warming Arctic climate complicated things: July was the world's hottest month since records began in 1880, according to NASA. Sea ice, which so bedeviled explorers in the nineteenth century, is a lamented loss in the twenty-first. As the cooling ice cover disappears, the feedback loop of atmospheric warming speeds up, and weather patterns shift. Several days of heavy rain on King William Island turned the frozen tundra so muddy that the expedition couldn't reach the intended sites. But one vexing pattern remained the same.

Once again, Kamookak fell gravely ill after searching for clues to Sir John Franklin's demise. And once again, surgeons had to save his life, this time at a hospital in Yellowknife, capital of Canada's Northwest Territories. What Kamookak called "the mystery within a mystery" only deepened.

High in the stark Arctic, where there is less to interfere with human perception, Inuit do not need modern scientists to tell them of existence beyond what they can touch. Spirits are as real to them as the sea, snow, and ice. Those who still believe as their ancestors did are well aware that the souls of the dead are free to travel to the eternal hunting grounds only if they have peace. They fear Sir John Franklin's soul is among them.

A restless spirit trapped in the land of the living "does all it can to persecute those that are to blame for its life after death having been ruined," Knud Rasmussen wrote. "Only very great shamans are now and then fortunate enough to kill these evil spirits."

Kamookak would rather appease Sir John's spirit, by helping him get back where he belongs.

ACKNOWLEDGMENTS

Like the long search for the lost Franklin Expedition, telling the story of that epic hunt required the good fortune of serendipity. I am forever grateful to literary agent Joy Tutela for reaching out to me in the Arctic and suggesting I had a book to write. I owe an equal debt to W. W. Norton editor Matt Weiland, whose wise guidance and steady hand made an idea real. Finally, to all who trusted me to tell their part of a complex tale, I hope your faith and commitment to the memory of Sir John Franklin and his brave men is rewarded in these pages.

SOURCE NOTES

Writing a true story that spans centuries into the recent past melds history with journalism. While this is not a scholarly work, I have been faithful to facts and analyses as they were written by original sources and experts in their fields. More contemporary events were described to me in interviews with dozens of people who participated in the matters they recount. Anything in direct quotes comes either from primary sources, including letters, diaries, or journals, or from the mouths of those who spoke or heard the quoted words.

To ease the reader's passage on the epic search for Her Majesty's Ships *Erebus* and *Terror*, I have not cited sources in footnotes. Instead, I summarize the principal works here by section.

Finally, the current value of nineteenth-century British pounds was estimated using the Purchasing Power Calculator at MeasuringWorth.com and then converting pounds to US dollars at a 2015 value.

Introduction

Richard J. Cyriax is the dean of Franklinology, whose numerous works set the standard on the subject. I relied for background on *Sir John Franklin's Last Arctic Expedition: A Chapter in the History of the Royal Navy*. William Scoresby Jr., whose scientific mind was rooted in an early life as a whaler, was in many ways ahead of his time with analysis in *An Account of the Arctic Regions, with a History and Description of the Northern Whale-Fishery, Volume 1*, published in 1820. His letter to Sir Joseph Banks, as quoted by Robert Edmund Scoresby Jackson, *The Life of William Scoresby*, also shed light on his views. The debate between Scoresby and the Admiralty's Sir John Barrow over the existence of an Open Polar Sea, and the negative consequences of Barrow's snubbing the whaler and scientist, plays out in Constance Martin's "William Scoresby Jr. (1789–1857) and the Open Polar Sea—Myth and Reality," in *Arctic* 41 (1988). Captain James Fitzjames's descriptions are a vivid look at the last days of the Franklin Expedition's ships and the men who sailed them to their deaths, in "Captain James Fitzjames Journal," from the "Nautical Magazine and Leader," as reprinted in *Papers and Despatches Relating to the Arctic Searching Expeditions of 1850–51–52*.

William Battersby and Peter Carney give an excellent account of the Royal Navy's upgrades in "Equipping HM Ships *Erebus* and *Terror*, 1845," *International Journal for the History of Engineering and Technology* 81 (2011). Scoresby's account of the sudden Arctic warming comes from Sir John Leslie, Robert Jameson, and Hugh Murray, *Narrative of Discovery and Adventure in the Polar Seas and Regions: With Illustrations of Their Climate, Geology and Natural History; And an Account of the Whale Fishery*.

Barrow makes his case for renewed Arctic exploration in *A Chronological History of Voyages into the Arctic Regions*, published in 1818. Sir John Ross counterattacks in *Observations on a Work Entitled, "Voyages of Discovery and Research within the Arctic Regions," by Sir John Barrow, Being a Refutation of the Numerous Misrepresentations Contained in That Volume*, published in 1846.

Insight into Franklin Expedition clothing comes from Barbara F. Schweger in *Documentation and Analysis of the Clothing Worn by Non-Native Men in the Canadian Arctic Prior to 1920, with an Emphasis on Footwear* (PhD thesis, University of Alberta, 1983). William Scoresby Jr. revived his case for polar exploration by animal-drawn sled in 1828, in *The Edinburgh New Philosophical Journal, Exhibiting a View of the Progressive Discoveries and Improvements in the Sciences and the Arts*, vol. 5, April–September. The Arctic Council's *Arctic Marine Shipping Assessment* (2009), as excerpted by Arctis Knowledge Hub in *The Canadian Maritime Arctic and Northwest Passage*, provides a detailed look at the various routes that make up the modern Northwest Passage. W. Gillies Ross provides an excellent account of "The Type and Number of Expeditions in the Franklin Search 1847–1859," in *Arctic* 55 (March 2002) and quotes Alfred Friendly on the grandiosity of the epic hunt for *Erebus* and *Terror* in "The Admiralty and the Franklin Search," *Polar Record* 40 (2004).

PART I: THE EXPEDITION

~~~

Chapter 1: Franklin's Last Mission

Sir John Franklin's service at war and in the Arctic is chronicled in Henry Duff Traill's *The Life of Sir John Franklin R.N.*, published in 1896. W. F. Rawnsley's *The Life, Diaries and Correspondence of Jane Lady Franklin 1792–1875*, published in 1923, is a source for numerous quotes from Jane throughout this book and describes in detail the Franklins' political problems in the colony of Van Diemen's Land.

Ross recounts the fateful day of the mirage in Captain John Ross, *A Voyage of Discovery, Made Under the Orders of the Admiralty, in His Majesty's Ships Isabella and Alexander, for the Purpose of Exploring Baffin's Bay, and Inquiring into the Probability of a North-West Passage*, published in 1819. The science of how the Arctic plays with the senses is clearly explained by the US National Snow and Ice Data Center in its "Arctic Phenomena," available online at *All About Arctic Climatology and Meteorology*: https://nsidc.org/cryosphere/arctic-meteorology/phenomena.html.

William Parry's fulsome praise for Franklin is quoted in Augustus Henry Beesly's 1881 biography, *Sir John Franklin*. The diary entries describing the courtship of Franklin and his second wife, Jane, come from Frances J. Woodward, *Portrait of Jane: A Life of Lady Jane Franklin*, a superb source, published in 1951, that I rely on frequently for Lady Franklin's own words as well as Woodward's research into Jane's complex character. Thomas Allen reported the sheriff's responsibilities in 1839 in *The History and Antiquities of London, Westminster, Southwark, and Parts Adjacent, Volume Two*. The accomplishments of the expedition Sir Felix Booth funded are listed by Rear Admiral James Ross and James M. Savelle, "'Round Lord Mayor Bay with James Clark Ross: The Original Diary of 1830," in *Arctic* 43 (March 1990). David Woodman, whose extraordinary research into Inuit oral history is covered later in this book, points out that Inuit were not frequent visitors to northwest King William Island as late as 1879. A contemporary account of the insufficient clothing British sailors brought to the High Arctic is in Sir John Ross's 1835 journal, *Narrative of a Second Voyage in Search of a North-West Passage and of a Residence in the Arctic Regions During the Years 1829, 1830, 1831, 1832, 1833*.

Frances J. Woodward touches on Lady Franklin's prison-reform efforts in "Franklin, Lady Jane (1791–1875)," *Australian Dictionary of Biography* 1 (1966).

Shayne Breen examines the plight of Van Diemen Land's aboriginal people in "Extermination, Extinction, Genocide: British Colonialism and Tasmanian Aborigines," in René Lemarchand, ed., *Forgotten Genocides: Oblivion, Denial, and Memory* (2011).

The *Literary Gazette* reported detailed descriptions of HMS *Erebus* and HMS *Terror*, which were reprinted in *The Gentleman's Magazine*, October 1839. Sir James Clark Ross dramatically chronicled the ships' ordeal in his 1847 book, *A Voyage of Discovery and Research in the Southern and Antarctic Regions, During the Years 1839–43, Volume One*. Hamish Maxwell-Stewart describes the "Macquarie Harbour Penal Station," in the Centre for Tasmanian Studies' *The Companion to Tasmanian History*, online at http://www .utas.edu.au/library/companion_to_tasmanian_history/M/Macquarie%20 Harbour%20penal%20settlement.htm, and T. J. Lempriere's contemporary account of the brutality is in *The Penal Settlements of Van Diemen's Land, Macquarie Harbour, Maria Island and Tasman's Peninsula*. The Franklins' grueling trip comes to life in "Narrative of the Overland Journey of Sir John Franklin and Lady Franklin and Party from Hobart Town to Macquarie Harbour," *Colburn's United Service Magazine and Naval and Military Journal*, published in June, 1843.

Ward and Lock's Pictorial Guide to London is an 1879 travel guide that lists the Admiralty's semaphore tower as a Victorian London landmark. The original architectural drawing of the Admiralty Screen is online at Sir John Soane's Museum Drawings, http://collections.soane.org/ARC1031. D. Murray Smith gives an account of Franklin's meeting with Lord Haddington in the 1877 book *Arctic Expeditions from British and Foreign Shores from the Earliest Times to the Expedition of 1875–76*. The Admiralty's instructions to Franklin for his 1845 expedition are printed in full in *Accounts and Papers: Twenty-eight Volumes: Army, Navy and Ordnance* (Session 18 November 1847–5 September 1848, Vol. XLI, Arctic Expedition). The Parry Expedition's ordeal, which hints at what life may have been like for Franklin and his men decades later, is revealed in fascinating detail in the explorer's 1821 journal: William Edward Parry, *Journal of a Voyage for the Discovery of a North-West Passage from the Atlantic to the Pacific; Performed in the Years 1819–20 in His Majesty's Hecla and Griper*. S. R. C. Malin and D. R. Barraclough provide an excellent account of Alexander von Humboldt's extraordinary contribution to global science in "Humboldt and the Earth's Magnetic Field," *Quarterly Journal of the Royal Astronomical Society* 32 (1991).

Fitzjames's letter to his wife describing *Erebus*'s upgrade is quoted in James P. Delgado's excellent *Across the Top of the World: The Quest for the Northwest Passage*. Lieutenant Peter Halkett's adventurous trial run in his cloak boat is recalled in his book *Boat-Cloak or Cloak-Boat constructed of Macintosh India-rubber cloth with Paddle, Umbrella-sail, Bellows, Also an Inflated India-Rubber Cloth-Boat for Two Paddlers*, as quoted in "Footnotes to the Franklin Search," *The Beaver* (Spring 1955). George Back recounts his exciting journey aboard HMS *Terror* in his 1838 *Narrative of an Expedition in H.M.S. Terror, Undertaken with a View to Geographical Discovery on The Arctic Shores in the Years 1836–7*.

Chapter 2: HMS *Erebus* and *Terror*

Richardson's nearly fatal plunge, and the lesson learned, is described in riveting detail in Sir John Franklin, *Thirty Years in the Arctic Regions; Or, The Adventures of Sir John Franklin*, 1859. Richard J. Cyriax goes deep into the expedition's pharmaceuticals in "A Historic Medicine Chest," *Canadian Medical Association Journal* 57 (1947). To appreciate the rigors of daguerreotype photography, see George M. Hopkins, "Reminiscences of Daguerreotypy, *Scientific American* 56, no. 4 (January 1887), as quoted by The Daguerreian Society, http://daguerre.org/?page=DagFAQ.

Ross wrote of his solemn promise to Sir John Franklin a decade later in *Rear Admiral Sir John Franklin: A Narrative of the Circumstances and Causes Which Led to the Failure of the Searching Expeditions Sent by Government and Others for the Rescue of Sir John Franklin*. Franklin expressed his regret at not being able to see his Van Diemen's Land defense published before departing in the introduction to his *Narrative of Some Passages in the History of Van Diemen's Land During the Last Three Years of Sir John Franklin's Administration of Its Government*. Geraldine Rahmani reports Crozier's unrequited interest in Sophy in "Francis Crozier (1796–1848?)," *Arctic* 37 (1984).

Chapter 3: Frozen In

William Battersby probes the *Erebus* captain's clouded family history in *James Fitzjames: The Mystery Man of the Franklin Expedition*. James Fitzjames wrote colorful descriptions of the Franklin Expedition ships, crew, and their final days before entering Lancaster Sound in his final journal, reprinted by James

Mangles in 1852 in *Papers and Despatches Relating to the Arctic Searching Expeditions of 1850–51–52*. Ice master James Reid's letter to his wife, dated July 11, 1845, was reprinted in May 1920 by *The Register* newspaper in Adelaide, Australia. Thomas Blanky's optimistic prediction was quoted in "Search for Sir John Franklin," *Quarterly Review*, reprinted in *The Eclectic Magazine of Foreign Literature, Science and Art*, May to August 1853. Ralph Lloyd Jones quotes the report of the positive reaction to the Royal Marines in "The Royal Marines on Franklin's Last Expedition," *Polar Record* 40 (2004).

What caused the deaths of the sailors buried on Beechey Island is still a matter of debate among experts. Dr. Roger Amy, Rakesh Bhatnagar, et al., suspect a combination of factors in "The Last Franklin Expedition: Report of a Postmortem Examination of a Crew Member," *Canadian Medical Association Journal* 135 (July 15, 1986). William Battersby debunks the theory that lead from canned food poisoned Sir John and his men in "Identification of the Probable Source of the Lead Poisoning Observed in Members of the Franklin Expedition, *Journal of the Hakluyt Society* (September 2008).

B. Zane Horowitz, MD, investigates another possible lethal agent in "Polar Poisons: Did Botulism Doom the Franklin Expedition?" *Clinical Toxicology* 41 (2003). Exhumations carried out by forensic anthropologist Owen Beattie and his team in the mid-1980s revealed numerous details of their graves and corpses, including evidence of cannibalism described decades earlier by Inuit accounts. Beattie laid out his theory that lead poisoning might explain the Franklin Expedition's demise in *Frozen in Time: The Fate of the Franklin Expedition*, a book he cowrote with John Geiger. But more recent scientific studies have cast significant doubt on that hypothesis, including Keith Millar et al., in "A Re-Analysis of the Supposed Role of Lead Poisoning in Sir John Franklin's Last Expedition, 1845-1848," *Polar Record* 51 (May 2015). A 2013 study by University of Western Ontario chemists, including Professor Ron Martin, dismissing lead as the cause of death, is reported by the Canadian Press news agency in "Study Debunks Lead Poisoning Theory in Franklin Mystery," posted by CBC News online on April 8, 2013, http://www.cbc.ca/news/canada/north/study-debunks-lead-poisoning-theory-in-franklin-mystery-1.1396399. Clifford G. Hickey et al. analyze "The Route of Sir John Franklin's Third Arctic Expedition: An Evaluation and Test of an Alternate Hypothesis," in *Arctic* 46 (March 1993).

Various versions of the Washington Bay encounter, which Woodman analyzes as perhaps the most solid Inuit description of a meeting with Franklin Expedition survivors, are recounted by searchers who heard the story in *John Rae's Arctic Correspondence 1844–1845* and in *Narrative of the Second Arctic Expedition Made by Charles F. Hall: His Voyage to Repulse Bay, Sledge Journeys to the Straits of Fury and Hecla and to King William's Land, and Residence among the Eskimos During the Years 1864-69*, edited by J. E. Nourse USN, in 1879, and in *Schwatka's Search: Sledging in the Arctic in Quest of the Franklin Records*, by William H. Gilder, second in command, published in 1881.

PART II: THE HUNT

Chapter 4: The Hunt Begins

Nicolas Appert outlined his canning technique in 1811 in *The Art of Preserving All Kinds of Animal and Vegetable Substances for Several Years*, while Constantin Ardeleanu delves into the troubles of Stephen Goldner's factory in "A British Meat Cannery in Moldavia (1844–52), *Slavonic and East European Review* 90 (2012). W. Gillies Ross profiles "William Penny (1809–1892)" in *Arctic* 36 (1983), while the life of Eenoolooapik (Bobbie) is described in *Canadian Dictionary of Biography*, Volume VII (1836–1850), http://www.biographi.ca/en/bio/eenoolooapik_7E.html.

Alexander McDonald gave a contemporary account of Eenoolooapik's death in his 1841 book *A Narrative of Some Passages in the History of Eenoolooapik, a Young Eskimaux, Who Was Brought to Britain in 1839*. Clive A. Holland showed the Admiralty's paltry support for Penny and his Inuit guide in "William Penny, 1809–92: Arctic Whaling Master," *The Polar Record* 15 (1970).

The severely cold summer of 1846 was recalled a few years later in "The Arctic Expeditions," reprinted from *Fraser's Magazine* in *Littell's Living Age* 248 (February 17, 1849). William Penny's letter to John Barrow was reprinted in the same edition of *Littell's Living Age*. *The Athenaeum: Journal of English and Foreign Literature, Science and Fine Arts* gave its high praise to Lady Franklin's courage in "The Arctic Mystery" (July 1859). Charles Dickens's walking tour with Longfellow is colorfully recounted in Henry Wadsworth Longfellow Dana, "Longfellow and Dickens: The Story of a Transatlantic Friendship," *The Cambridge Historical Society* 28 (1943). The crewmen recall the horror of the *Cove*'s run-in with a vicious storm in M. J. Ross, *Polar Pioneers: John Ross and James Clark Ross*.

Sir John Ross's January 27, 1847, appeal to the Marquis of Northampton for support in the effort to go looking for Franklin and his men is reprinted in "Extracts of Letters Alluded to from Captain Sir John Ross," *Accounts and Papers: Twenty-eight Volumes: Army, Navy and Ordnance* (Session 18 November 1847–5 September 1848, Vol. XLI, Arctic Expedition). Ross's letter to the Marquis of Northampton is reprinted in Ross's *A Narrative of the Circumstances and Causes Which Led to the Failure of the Searching Expeditions Sent by Government and Others for the Rescue of Sir John Franklin.*

Lady Franklin's request to Moore is detailed in William James Mills's "Moore, Thomas (1819–1872)," *Exploring Polar Frontiers: A Historical Encyclopedia, vol. 1.* In 1850, William Scoresby turned his expert eye on failed search efforts, including the Rae–Richardson Expedition, in *The Franklin Expedition: or, Considerations on Measures for the Discovery and Relief of our Absent Adventurers in the Arctic Regions.* Eleanor's 1849 praise for her stepmother's perseverance is cited in Alison Alexander's *The Ambitions of Jane Franklin: Victorian Lady Adventurer* (2013). Captain Francis Leopold McClintock detailed numerous items that the Franklin Expedition abandoned in the gripping 1859 book *In the Arctic Seas: A Narrative of the Discovery of the Fate of Sir John Franklin and His Companions.*

Lawrence A. Palinkas and Peter Suedfeld discuss research into polar madness in their article "Psychological Effects of Polar Expeditions," published in *The Lancet* in January 2008.

Chapter 5: Lady Franklin's Mission

The layman can get a quick understanding of how Arctic ice moves at the US National Snow and Ice Data Center's "All About Sea Ice: Dynamics," online at https://nsidc.org/cryosphere/seaice/processes/dynamics.html.

Lady Franklin's respect for Scoresby is revealed in Constance Martin's valuable look at the pioneer of Arctic science: "William Scoresby Jr. (1789–1857) and the Open Polar Sea—Myth and Reality," *Arctic* 41 (March 1988). The *Athenaeum* reported that Lady Franklin's pitch to whalers appeared in "Our Weekly Gossip" on June 9, 1849. Lady Franklin's extraordinary letter to US President Zachary Taylor is reprinted in Erika Behrisch Elce's *As Affecting the Fate of My Absent Husband: Selected Letters of Lady Franklin Concerning the Search for the Lost Franklin Expedition, 1848–1860.*

W. Gillies Ross presents a lengthy and intriguing study in "Clairvoyants and Mediums Search for Franklin," *Polar Record* 39 (2003). The nineteenth-century debate between scientists and spiritualists plays out in Richard Noakes's "Spiritualism, Science and the Supernatural in Mid-Victorian Britain," *Cambridge Studies in Nineteenth-Century Literature and Culture* 42 (2004). *Natural and Mesmeric Clairvoyance with the Practical Application of Mesmerism in Surgery and Medicine*, by James Esdaile, MD, is an 1852 attempt to merge medicine with the paranormal. Frank Podmore reported details of how Mrs. M. contacted the clairvoyant Dawson in *Modern Spiritualism: A History and a Criticism, Vol. 1*, published in 1902. Mrs. M. wrote her account in a letter reprinted by *The Zoist: A Journal of Cerebral Physiology and Mesmerism, and Their Applications to Human Welfare* VII (March 1849–January 1850). Caroline Roberts makes the link between diagnoses of hysteria and rejection of male authority in *The Woman and the Hour: Harriet Martineau and Victorian Ideologies*, published in 2002.

Ralph Lloyd-Jones takes a modern, scholarly look at the mysterious ghost story in "The Paranormal Arctic: Lady Franklin, Sophia Cracroft, and Captain and 'Little Weesy' Coppin," *Polar Record* 37 (2001). A Victorian view of Weesy's ghost story comes from M. A. in "Fate of Sir John Franklin Discovered by a 'Revelation,'" which appeared in *Light: A Journal of Psychical, Occult, and Mystical Research* IX (April 27, 1889). The description of the words said to have appeared on the wall, along with skepticism about gaps in evidence from Lady Franklin's estate, comes from "How Sir John Franklin Was Not Found," *The Saturday Review of Politics, Literature, Science and Art*, LXVIII (May 4, 1889). W. Gillies Ross shows how well the Admiralty was apprised of paranormal tips in his extensive and entertaining "False Leads in the Franklin Search" *Polar Record* 39 (2003). John Rae's discovery of Victoria Strait, and the first chart showing a waterway through the archipelago with that name in the *Journal of the Royal Geographical Society* (1852), is noted in *John Rae's Arctic Correspondence, 1844–1855*, with a foreword by Ken McGoogan.

The numerous transformations of London's Spring Gardens neighborhood are detailed by *British History Online*, at http://www.british-history.ac .uk/survey-london/vol20/pt3/pp58-65. Ken McGoogan quotes Sophy's defense of her aunt in *Lady Franklin's Revenge: A True Story of Ambition, Obsession and the Remaking of Arctic History* (2005).

Chapter 6: The Arctic Committee

David Woodman provides the figure for the massive cost of the Franklin search, just in the period 1848 to 1854. William Parker Snow wrote a compelling account of the expedition in *Voyage of the Prince Albert in Search of Sir John Franklin: A Narrative of Every-day Life in the Arctic Seas*, published in 1851. A compelling nineteenth-century profile, which detailed Snow's troubled life and tormenting regret at not being allowed to follow up his clairvoyant vision in the Franklin search, appears in "Character Sketch—April: William Parker Snow," *The Review of Reviews* VII, January–June 1893. Roland Pietsch provides a fascinating look at the Royal Navy's child sailors in "Ships' Boys and Youth Culture in Eighteenth-Century Britain: The Navy Recruits of the London Marine Society," *The Northern Mariner* XIV, no. 4 (October 2004).

The Dane Carl Petersen's account appears in Samuel M. Smucker's 1858 book *Explorations and Discoveries During the Nineteenth Century, Being Detailed Accounts of the Several Expeditions to the North Seas, Both English and American*, which includes a letter from Captain Sir John Ross, sent from the discovery yacht *Felix*, off Admiralty Inlet, Lancaster Sound, to Admiralty Secretary W. A. B. Hamilton, dated August 22, 1850.

Secretary of the Navy William Ballard Preston's instructions to US Navy Lieutenant Edwin J. De Haven, dated May 15, 1850, are reprinted in Elisha Kent Kane, MD, *The United States Grinnell Expedition in Search of Sir John Franklin: A Personal Narrative* (1856). Captain William Penny detailed his discovery in a letter dated April 12, 1851, from HMS *Lady Franklin* to the Secretary of the Admiralty, reprinted in *Report of the Committee Appointed by the Lords Commissioners of the Admiralty to Inquire into and Report on the Recent Arctic Expeditions in Search of Sir John Franklin* XLVII (1852). Captain Horatio T. Austin expresses the conclusion that some of Franklin's men had camped at Bowden Point in a July 14, 1851, letter from HMS *Resolute* to Secretary of the Admiralty, reprinted in *Report of the Committee Appointed by the Lords Commissioners of the Admiralty to Inquire into and Report on the Recent Arctic Expeditions in Search of Sir John Franklin* XI (1852). Clive A. Holland writes about the enmity between Penny and Ross in "William Penny, 1809–92: Arctic Whaling Master," *Polar Record* 15 (1970). Holland's "The Arctic Committee of 1851: A Background Study," *Polar Record* (1980), gives an essential account of the Royal Navy's investigation and testimony to the tribunal.

The extreme cold in February 1851 was described the following year in

Peter C. Sutherland, MD, *Journey of a Voyage in Baffin's Bay and Barrow Straits in the Years 1850–51 Performed by H.M. Ships "Lady Franklin" and "Sophia," Under the Command of Mr. William Penny, Vol. 1*. Austin's remark urging Penny to go up Wellington Channel comes from testimony to the Arctic Committee, as quoted in Clive Holland, "The Arctic Committee of 1851: A Background Study (Part 2)," *Polar Record* 20 (1980). Penny's concerns about the fierce tide in Wellington Channel are expressed in the 1852 "Report of the Arctic Committee," *Report of the Committee Appointed by the Lords Commissioners of the Admiralty to Inquire into and Report on the Recent Arctic Expeditions in Search of Sir John Franklin*. Criticism of Austin's slight against Penny the whaler appeared in "The Arctic Expeditions," *Athenaeum*, January 3, 1852. A transcript of Rear-Admiral Sir John Ross's testimony to the Arctic Committee on October 31, 1851, was published in *Report of the Committee Appointed by the Lords Commissioners of the Admiralty to Inquire into and Report on the Recent Arctic Expeditions in Search of Sir John Franklin*.

Scoresby expressed his doubts that both of Franklin's ships could have been lost in a letter to Mr. Frederick James Fegen, secretary to the Arctic Committee, dated November 14, 1851, and reprinted in *Report of the Committee Appointed by the Lords Commissioners of the Admiralty to Inquire into and Report on the Recent Arctic Expeditions in Search of Sir John Franklin*. A good summary of McClintock's accomplishments, including the arduous sledge search in 1851, is online in "McClintock, Sir Francis Leopold," *Dictionary of Canadian Biography*, http://www.biographi.ca/en/bio/mcclintock_francis_leopold_13E .html. The surgeon Bradford's recommendations for improving Arctic clothing and equipment are in a letter to Mr. Fegen, secretary to the Arctic Committee, dated November 5, 1851, and reprinted, along with other experts' views, in *Report of the Committee Appointed by the Lords Commissioners of the Admiralty to Inquire into and Report on the Recent Arctic Expeditions in Search of Sir John Franklin*.

Chapter 7: Ghost Ships

George Calder tells of Franklin tutoring a young William Kennedy in *The William Kennedy Story*, published by the Bruce County Historical Society. Kennedy's grueling overland expedition by dogsled is summarized in Mark Nuttall, ed., *Encyclopedia of the Arctic*. Kennedy published his 1853 account, which includes such gripping details as snow blindness in the painful Arctic wind, in *A Short Narrative of the Second Voyage of the Prince Albert, in Search of Sir John Franklin*. Sir Edward Belcher's hard-nosed temperament comes through in his own words in the 1855 book *The Last of the Arctic Voyages*. The profile "Belcher, Sir Edward," in the *Dictionary of Canadian Biography*, provides more background online at http://www.biographi.ca/en/bio/belcher_edward_10E.html.

Jonathan M. Karpoff covers the tribulations of McClure and HMS *Investigator* in "Robert McClure: Essay Prepared for *The Encyclopedia of the Arctic*, available online at http://faculty.washington.edu/karpoff/research/McClure.pdf. Ship's surgeon Alexander Armstrong's regrets come from Andrew Cohen, *Lost Beneath the Ice: The Story of HMS* Investigator (2013). Pim is profiled in "Pim, Bedford Clapperton Trevelyan," *Dictionary of Canadian Biography*, http://www.biographi.ca/en/bio/pim_bedford_clapperton_trevelyan_11E.html. George F. McDougall chronicled Kellett's heroic efforts aboard HMS *Resolute* in the 1857 book *The Eventful Voyage of H.M. Discovery Ship "Resolute" to the Arctic Regions*.

Fawckner recounted *Breadalbane*'s demise in the *Illustrated London News*, October 22, 1853, which was reprinted in Doug Payne's "Technology Lights up an Arctic Shipwreck," *New Scientist*, January 15, 1981. Belcher defended his character in testimony quoted by Elizabeth Matthews in *From the Canadian Arctic to the President's Desk: HMS Resolute*. The remarkably good state of the abandoned *Resolute* when discovered by American whalers was described in the *Illustrated London News*, December 27, 1856. Lady Franklin's request was recorded in 1861 by Leone Levi, ed., *Annals of British Legislation*, Vol. VIII. A complete history of the Resolute Desk and the presidents who sat behind it is available online at http://www.whitehousemuseum.org/furnishings/resolute-desk.htm.

Chapter 8: Starvation Cove

John Rae's account of the discovery of wooden pieces in August 1851 was reprinted nine years later in *University Magazine: A Literary and Philosophic Review* 55 (January–June 1860).

Kenn Harper reported Ouligbuck's contribution, and paltry compensation, in "William Ouligbuck, John Rae's Interpreter," NunatsiaqOnline, November 27, 2008. He is profiled by Shirlee Anne Smith in "Ooligbuck," *Dictionary of Canadian Biography*.

John Rae's account of his fateful meeting with the Inuk hunter In-nook-poo-zhee-jook comes from rough notes written on April 21 and 22, 1854, in *John Rae's Arctic Correspondence, 1844–1855*. Rae described the officers' initials scratched on their abandoned silverware in a letter to the secretary of the Hudson's Bay Company, dated September 1, 1854, as reprinted in *John Rae's Arctic Correspondence 1844–1855*. In another letter from the same volume, he informs governors of the Hudson's Bay Company on December 20, 1854, of his disgust over the pay dispute. C. Stuart Mackinnon describes the Anderson–Green Expedition in "James Anderson (1812–1867), Arctic Profiles," *Arctic* 38 (1985). Lady Franklin expressed her extreme disappointment with the Admiralty's decision to send the poorly equipped Anderson–Green Expedition in *A Letter to Viscount Palmerston, K.G. from Lady Franklin*, published in 1857. In the same letter, she cited Kane's view that a search by dogsled was the best option, which he explained in a letter to his friend Henry Grinnell.

David Murphy provides details of Lady Franklin's purchase of the *Fox* in *The Arctic Fox: Francis Leopold McClintock, Discoverer of the Fate of Franklin*. McClintock wrote a riveting account of the turning point in the early Franklin search in his 1881 book *Fate of Sir John Franklin: The Voyage of the 'Fox' in the Arctic Seas in Search of Franklin and His Companions*. Snow's attempt to have Franklin Expedition artifacts placed in Lincoln's coffin is recalled in the New-York Historical Society's *Lincoln and New York*, edited by Harold Holzer. Lady Franklin's trip to Alaska with Sophy is detailed in *Lady Franklin Visits Sitka, Alaska 1870: The Journal of Sophia Cracroft, Sir John Franklin's Niece*, edited by R. N. DeArmond.

PART III: THE DISCOVERY

Chapter 9: An Inuk Detective

Louie Kamookak spoke with me, over a period of several months, about his great-grandmother Hummahuk. These lengthy interviews are also the basis for details of his research into oral history covered elsewhere in this book.

Jens Peder Hart Hansen, Jorgen Meldgaard, and Jorgen Nordqvist discuss ancient Inuit tattoos in *The Greenland Mummies*, which American explorer Charles Francis Hall also discussed in *Life with the Esquimaux: The Narrative of Captain Charles Francis Hall of the Whaling Barque "George Henry" from the 29th May, 1860, to the 13th September, 1862, vol. 2*. Danish explorer and anthropologist Knud Rasmussen reports Inuit accounts of their encounters with the Ross Expedition in *The Netsilik Eskimo: Report of the Fifth Thule Expedition, 1921–24: The Danish Expedition to Arctic North America, vol. VIII*, which also provides essential insight into traditional life and beliefs. Background on Rasmussen is from Terrence Cole's introduction to Rasmussen's *Across Arctic America: Narrative of the Fifth Thule Expedition*. In addition to quoting directly from Rasmussen's report, I relied on quotations in Asen Balikci's *The Netsilik Eskimo*. Erhard Treude, "The Work of Knud Rasmussen in the Canadian Arctic as Described by RCMP Inspector Stuart Wood," *Études/Inuit/Studies* 28 (2004), was also helpful.

The government of Manitoba's *Hudson's Bay Company Archives* provides a résumé of Louie Kamookak's grandfather, William "Paddy" Gibson. Gibson's colorful career is described online at https://www.gov.mb.ca/chc/archives/hbca/biographical/g/gibson_william-paddy.pdf. Gibson's obituary appeared in *The Globe and Mail*, March 20, 1942, in "William Gibson Rites Saturday: Well Known Arctic Trader Will Be Buried Here." Inuit elders' memories of Gibson are included in Kitikmeot Heritage Society, *Angulalik: Kitikmeot Fur Trader*, http://www.kitikmeotheritage.ca/Angulalk/hudsons/hudsons.htm.

To understand the Inuit tradition of conjugal swaps, I relied on scholars' research, mainly Michael J. Kral's PhD thesis, "Transforming Communities: Suicide, Relatedness, and Reclamation among Inuit of Nunavut," submitted to Department of Anthropology, McGill University, in January 2009, and anthropologist Arthur J. Rubel's "Partnership and Wife-Exchange among the Eskimo and Aleut of Northern North America," 1961.

Gibson wrote of seeing the cairn in "The Dease and Simpson Cairn," *The Beaver*, September 1933, while a contemporary account of the explorer's astounding efforts to map the Canadian Arctic is in Alexander Simpson, *The Life and Travels of Thomas Simpson, Arctic Traveler*, published in 1845, the same year the final Franklin Expedition departed for the Arctic. L. H. Neatby provides more details in "Arctic Profiles: Thomas Simpson (1808–1840)," *Arctic* 40 (December 1987).

The history of the aircraft Gibson died on is Norduyn Aviation Limited, *The Aircraft: A Brief History of Each Individual Norseman*, available online at http://www.norsemanhistory.ca/Aircraft.htm. The official crash details are online at Flight Safety Foundation, *Aviation Safety Network*, ASN Wikibase Occurrence #122253, http://aviation-safety.net/wikibase/wiki.php?id=122253. The Franklin link to the site of Gibson's death is established by background in the Northwest Territories Education, Culture and Employment's *Gazetteer of the Northwest Territories*.

Gibson's colleague Lorenz A. Learmonth wrote about "The Curse of Neovitcheak" in *The Beaver*, September 1946.

Chapter 10: He Who Takes Long Strides

Sarah Bonesteel gives an expert's assessment of "Canada's Relationship with Inuit: A History of Policy and Program Development," online at https://www.aadnc-aandc.gc.ca/DAM/DAM-INTER-HQ/STAGING/texte-text/inuit-book_1100100016901_eng.pdf. Peter Collings focuses on Matchbox Houses in "Housing Policy, Aging, and Life Course Construction in a Canadian Inuit Community," *Arctic Anthropology* 42 (2005). The complete report of Canada's Truth and Reconciliation Commission is online at http://www.trc.ca/websites/trcinstitution/index.php?p=890.

Cameron Treleaven recalled in an interview his trip with Ernest Coleman, his chance meeting with Louie Kamookak, and their friendship. Coleman's 1992 expedition is briefly described in Alan Day's *Historical Dictionary of the Discovery and Exploration of the Northwest Passage*. Coleman told the Lincolnshire, England, newspaper *Market Rasen Mail*, in a report published September 17, 2014, that he had told Canadian officials where to find a Franklin wreck, to no avail.

Sheila Nickerson quotes Queen Victoria's diary on Her Majesty's meeting with Tookoolito and Ebierbing in *Midnight to the North: The Untold Story of the Inuit Woman Who Saved the Polaris Expedition*.

Chapter 11: Operation Franklin

The Canadian military's Operation Franklin was reconstructed from documents in the file obtained under the Access to Information and Privacy Act, with additional details learned in an interview with former army diver Bob Shaw.

Chapter 12: The Hunt Goes Underwater

Peter Adams and Maxwell J. Dunbar provide an overview of the "Arctic Archipelago" in *The Canadian Encyclopedia*, online at http://www.thecanadian

encyclopedia.ca/en/m/article/arctic-archipelago/. Pioneer George F. Bass recalled the profession's founding years in his introduction to *The Oxford Handbook of Maritime Archaeology*, edited by Ben Ford, Donny L. Hamilton, and Alexis Catsambis.

Walter Zacharchuk described his life and role in founding marine archaeology in Canada in several interviews with the author. For the history of "Fort Lennox National Historic Site of Canada," Saint-Paul-de-l'Île-aux-Noix Nautical Capital, see http://www.ileauxnoix.com/eng/tourisme/lieu-historique.html. Gagnan's move to Canada is explained in Bradford Matsen's *Jacques Cousteau: The Sea King* (2009). Archaeologist James A. Tuck's excavation of the Basque whalers' graves is described in "Unearthing Red Bay's Whaling History," *National Geographic* 168 (July 1985). The international Convention on the Protection of the Underwater Cultural Heritage is outlined in Robert Grenier, David Nutley, and Ian Cochran, eds., *Underwater Cultural Heritage at Risk: Managing Natural and Cultural Impacts*.

Lydia Dotto profiled MacInnis in "Joe MacInnis, Pioneer in the Underwater World," *Canadian Geographic* 100 (June/July 1980). Bill Mason's thoughts on his friend, along with scenes and dialogue leading up to the discovery and exploration of the *Breadalbane*, come from the documentary film *The Land That Devours Ships*, directed by Bill Mason, 1984, National Film Board of Canada / Undersea Research. Other details come from MacInnis's 1982 book on the shipwreck hunt and discovery, *The Breadalbane Adventure*.

Douglas L. Hicks describes the development of *Sublimnos* in "'Bargain Basement' Habitat," *Popular Mechanics*, April 1971. MacInnis's full speech, "Diving Under the North Pole," an address to The Empire Club of Canada, Toronto, February 26, 1976, is available online at http://speeches.empireclub .org/61998/data. Dome Petroleum's interest in the "industrial applications" of MacInnis's work on *Breadalbane* was reported in *New Scientist* 98 (June 23, 1983).

Robert Grenier expressed his views about the effect of the binnacle crashing onto Breadalbane's deck on the parties' agreement about how the dive was supposed to proceed in an email exchange with me in February 2016.

Chapter 13: Skull Island

Kamookak expressed his disinterest in personally searching underwater to Ashleigh Gaul in "If Any Living Inuk Knew," *Up Here* magazine, December

2014. Rachel Ewing wrote about the discovery of the fish fossil, and the scientists' decision to honor Martin Bergmann, in "New Fossil from a Fish-Eat-Fish World Driving the Evolution of Limbed Animals," available online at http://drexel.edu/now/archive/2013/March/Fossil-Species-from-Fish-Eat-Fish -World/.

In interviews with me, David Woodman recalled life highlights and his relentless search for the Franklin wrecks. Woodman's seminal 1991 book, *Unravelling the Franklin Mystery: Inuit Testimony*, was also a guide. Further details on Woodman's search efforts, and those of other modern expeditions, come from Parks Canada's annual reports, "Erebus and Terror National Historic Site: Remote Sensing Search," for the years 2010 through 2014.

The 1999 report for Parks Canada by Kamookak and Darren Keith, "Franklin Oral History Project," was obtained under Canada's Access to Information and Privacy Act.

Chapter 14: Fast Ice

Events and conversations have been reconstructed through my extensive interviews with those involved, principally Peter Mansbridge, Douglas Stenton, Tom Zagon, Jim Balsillie, and Oksana and Adrian Schimnowski. I am especially grateful that Martin Bergmann's widow, Sheila McRae, shared memories, both joyful and painful.

The final report of the Transportation Safety Board of Canada's investigation into the crash of First Air flight 6560 is available online at http://www .tsb.gc.ca/eng/enquetes-investigations/aviation/2011/a11h0002/a11h0002.asp.

Chapter 15: "That's It!"

Paul Allen's visit to the Northwest Passage, with John Geiger aboard the superyacht *Octopus*, was reported by Jane George from Cambridge Bay in NunatsiaqOnline's "Private Yacht Visitors to Nunavut Create Mixed Impression in Cambridge Bay," October 1, 2012, available online at http://www.nunatsiaq online.ca/stories/article/65674private_yacht_visitors_to_nunavut_create_ mixed_impression_in_cambridge/. A senior source in the Royal Canadian Navy discussed privately the military's observations of the yacht's movements.

Chapter 16: Terror Bay

Details of the discovery of HMS *Terror* come from satellite-phone interviews and e-mail exchanges with Arctic Research Foundation Operations Director Adrian Schimnowski and other MV *Martin Bergmann* crewmembers, in the days before news of the historic find broke in my exclusive report for *The Guardian*. https://www.theguardian.com/world/2016/sep/12/hms-terror-wreck -found-arctic-nearly-170-years-northwest-passage-attempt.

CBC reported the Inuit dispute with the federal government over the wreck of HMS *Erebus* in "Parks Canada juggles competing claims to Franklin wrecks," published online March 8, 2016, at http://www.cbc.ca/news/politics/ parks-canada-franklin-wrecks-artifacts-1.3479595.

Parks Canada's effort to cooperate with Inuit on a Gjoa Haven facility is reported in "Feds announce money for Nunavut-based centre to house Franklin relics," Nunatsiaq Online, March 18, 2016, http://www.nunatsiaqonline.ca/ stories/article/65674feds_announce_money_for_nunavut-based_centre_to_ house_franklin_relics/.

In our interview, Sammy Kogvik attempted to spell his hunting buddy Uncle Jimmy's surname phonetically as Qingniacktok. In a report on the discovery for *MacLean*'s magazine, Chris Sorensen spells it Klungnatuk, http:// www.macleans.ca/news/canada/how-trust-led-to-hms-terror/.

William Henry Gilder reported Ahlangyah's account in *The Search for Franklin: A Narrative of the American Expedition Under Lieutenant Schwatka, 1878 to 1880*, published in London by T. Nelson and Sons in 1882.

Francis McClintock explained the naming of Terror Bay, and various other spots along King William Island during his search for the Franklin Expedition, in a letter to fellow searcher US Army Lieutenant Frederick Schwatka, dated October 2, 1880, and posted online at http://www.canadianmysteries .ca/sites/franklin/archive/text/McClintockSchwatka_en.htm.

Chapter 17: An Offering to the Dead

I obtained the private e-mail exchange between John Geiger and the Parks Canada vice president under Canada's Access to Information and Privacy Act.

The discovery of the submerged wreck of HMS *Erebus* was reconstructed through numerous interviews, over many months, with many participants, most notably Captains Andrew Stirling and Bill Noon; archaeologists Marc-

André Bernier, Ryan Harris, Jonathan Moore, Douglas Stenton, and Robert Park; and hydrologist Scott Youngblut.

Afterword

Louie Kamookak described his summer 2016 expedition in "Searching the Arctic for Traces of the Sir John Franklin Expedition," *Canadian Geographic*, http://www.canadiangeographic.ca/article/searching-arctic-traces-sir-john -franklin-expedition.

CREDITS

INDEX

Page numbers in *italics* refer to maps.